T0302127

WELFARE THEORY, PUBLIC ACTION, AND ETHICAL VALUES

This innovative history of welfare economics challenges the view that welfare economics can be discussed without taking ethical values into account. Whatever their theoretical commitments, when economists have considered practical problems relating to public policy, they have adopted a wider range of ethical values, whether equality, justice, freedom, or democracy. Even canonical authors in the history of welfare economics are shown to have adopted ethical positions different from those with which they are commonly associated. *Welfare Theory, Public Action, and Ethical Values* explores the reasons and implications of this, drawing on concepts of welfarism and non-welfarism developed in modern welfare economics. The authors exemplify how economic theory, public affairs, and political philosophy interact, challenging the status quo in order to push economists and historians to reconsider the nature and meaning of welfare economics.

Roger E. Backhouse is Professor of History and Philosophy of Economics at the University of Birmingham and endowed Professor of Methodology and History of Economics at Erasmus University Rotterdam.

Antoinette Baujard is Professor of Economics at the University of Lyon and Jean Monnet University at Saint-Etienne.

Tamotsu Nishizawa is Professor of Economics at Teikyo University, Japan.

Welfare Theory, Public Action, and Ethical Values

Revisiting the History of Welfare Economics

Edited by

ROGER E. BACKHOUSE
University of Birmingham and Erasmus University Rotterdam

ANTOINETTE BAUJARD
University of Lyon and Jean Monnet University at Saint-Etienne

TAMOTSU NISHIZAWA
Teikyo University

CAMBRIDGE
UNIVERSITY PRESS

CAMBRIDGE
UNIVERSITY PRESS

University Printing House, Cambridge CB2 8BS, United Kingdom

One Liberty Plaza, 20th Floor, New York, NY 10006, USA

477 Williamstown Road, Port Melbourne, VIC 3207, Australia

314–321, 3rd Floor, Plot 3, Splendor Forum, Jasola District Centre,
New Delhi – 110025, India

79 Anson Road, #06–04/06, Singapore 079906

Cambridge University Press is part of the University of Cambridge.

It furthers the University's mission by disseminating knowledge in the pursuit of
education, learning, and research at the highest international levels of excellence.

www.cambridge.org
Information on this title: www.cambridge.org/9781108841450
DOI: 10.1017/9781108882507

© Cambridge University Press 2021

First published 2021

A catalogue record for this publication is available from the British Library.

Library of Congress Cataloging-in-Publication Data
Names: Backhouse, Roger, 1951– editor. | Baujard, Antoinette, editor. | Nishizawa, Tamotsu,
1950– editor.
Title: Welfare theory, public action, and ethical values : revisiting the history of welfare
economics / edited by Roger E. Backhouse, University of Birmingham, Antoinette Baujard,
Universite Jean Monnet, Tamotsu Nishizawa, Teikyo University Japan.
Description: Cambridge, United Kingdom ; New York, NY : Cambridge University Press,
2021. | Includes bibliographical references and index.
Identifiers: LCCN 2020047388 (print) | LCCN 2020047389 (ebook) | ISBN 9781108841450
(hardback) | ISBN 9781108794848 (paperback) | ISBN 9781108882507 (ebook)
Subjects: LCSH: Welfare economics – History. | Economics – Sociological aspects – History. |
Public welfare – History.
Classification: LCC HB99.3 .W436 2021 (print) | LCC HB99.3 (ebook) | DDC 330.15/56–dc23
LC record available at https://lccn.loc.gov/2020047388
LC ebook record available at https://lccn.loc.gov/2020047389

ISBN 978-1-108-84145-0 Hardback

Contents

Figures and Tables

Figures

Table

Contributors

Richard Arena, University Côte d'Azur, GREDEG

Rogério Arthmar, Federal University of Espírito Santo

Roger E. Backhouse, University of Birmingham and Erasmus University Rotterdam

Antoinette Baujard, University of Lyon and Jean Monnet University, GATE Lyon Saint-Etienne

Constanze Binder, Erasmus University Rotterdam

Peter Cain, Sheffield Hallam University

Maxime Desmarais-Tremblay, Goldsmiths, University of London

Muriel Gilardone, Normandy University, CREM

Michael McLure, University of Western Australia

Steven G. Medema, Duke University

Tamotsu Nishizawa, Teikyo University

Nao Saito, Hokkaido University

Yuichi Shionoya (deceased), Hitotsubashi University

Kotaro Suzumura (deceased), Japan Academy

Satoshi Yamazaki, Kochi University

Acknowledgements

Most of the chapters in this volume were presented at a series of workshops at Hitotsubashi University (in Tokyo) from 2013 to 2016, and a workshop in Nice in March 2017. These formed part of an ongoing project on 'Welfare Economics and the Welfare State in Historical Perspective' out of which an earlier volume, *No Wealth but Life: Welfare Economics and the Welfare State in Britain, 1880–1945* (2010) also emerged. These were generously funded by the Japan Society for the Promotion of Science, Grants-in-Aid for Scientific Research, number 25245032. We also benefitted from the grant of the Excellence Chair 'Welfare Economics' funded by CNRS and Jean Monnet University at Saint-Etienne. We are indebted to Muriel Dal Pont for her kind assistance in organising the Nice workshop and to Michie Kano for her work over many years on workshops at Hitotsubashi University, including one disrupted by the 2011 earthquake and tsunami. We are also grateful to Mrs Nobuko Matsuzawa for permission to reproduce the chapter by her father, Yuichi Shionoya, previously published in *History of Economic Ideas*, Anno XXII, 2014(1), pp. 16–49, and to Mrs Akiko Suzumura for permission to include the chapter by Kotaro Suzumura. We also wish to thank Prasanta Pattanaik, three anonymous referees, and several contributors to the volume, for their helpful comments on the Introduction and Conclusion. Of course, none of them should be held responsible for any errors that remain.

Introduction: Revisiting the History of Welfare Economics

Roger E. Backhouse, Antoinette Baujard and Tamotsu Nishizawa

1 Welfare Economics

Welfare economics is the part of economics that deals with evaluating states of the world and formulating recommendations for policies that would improve the well-being of society as a whole. It covers not only a body of policy advice but, arguably more important, a body of principles on which such evaluations and recommendations should be based. Economists frequently make the claim that how well-off society is, which we refer to as social welfare, depends solely on the well-being of the individuals making up that society. In other words, if a change does not make any individual better off, then social welfare cannot have increased. The claim made in this book is that whether we are talking about old, new or contemporary welfare economics, when economists have tackled practical problems, they have adopted a much broader range of ethical judgements beyond welfarism. For example, they have seen greater equality in the distribution as desirable in itself; they have argued that we should respect the rights of individuals to do certain things; and they have attached importance to the way economic outcomes are achieved.

The notion that social welfare depends solely on the well-being, or welfare, of individuals has come to be known as 'welfarism'. The term 'welfarism' appears to have first been used by John Hicks (1959), when he defined it as meaning a concern with 'economic welfare', a term used by A. C. Pigou (1920: 11) to denote 'that part of welfare that can be brought directly or indirectly into relation with the measuring-rod of money'. This excluded considerations such as justice, freedom and rights to which money values could not be assigned. However, the term was not widely used until it was independently invented by Amartya Sen in the late 1970s,

who defined it as: 'The general approach of making no use of any information about the social states other than that of personal welfares generated in
them may be called "welfarism"' (Sen 1977a: 1559). In elaborating on this
statement, Sen (1979a, 1979b: 464) described welfarism as taking social
welfare to depend on nothing other than individual utility information.
Welfarism in this sense therefore requires making a distinction between
the information needed to establish the welfare of individuals (which
might, of course, depend on the welfare of others if people are altruistic),
on which social welfare is assumed to depend, from other information,
which should be ignored on the ground that it does not affect any one, or at
least does not affect them in any relevant way. To give a simple example, if
the only thing that mattered to individuals was their own income, then
provided the political regime did not affect anyone's income, the welfare
economist would not be justified in taking into account whether people
lived in a democracy or under a dictatorship. Although this may make it
seem simple, welfarism is a more complicated concept, for there are many
ways in which the restriction of information can be specified, and the latter
may have many unintended consequences.

Economists, in so far as they have reflected on the history of welfare
economics, have typically focused on the transition from the 'old' to the
'new' welfare economics that took place in the 1930s and 1940s (e.g.
Samuelson 1947: 249; Little 1950; Boulding 1952; Graaff 1957; Dobb
1969).[1] A key element in this transition was the rejection of interpersonal
utility comparisons, and therefore of utilitarianism, in favour of a Paretian
welfare economics that required as inputs no more than ordinal utilities or
preferences. Some questions have been asked about this transition, for
example, questioning whether standard accounts leave out economists
who were important at the time (Backhouse and Nishizawa 2010).
However, none of this historical literature has challenged the assumption
that economists adopted a welfarist approach to welfare economics, at least
until Sen and other modern welfare economists had developed other
conceptions of welfare.

The essays in this book argue that this was not the case and that, even
though their statements about welfare theory rarely acknowledged this,
economists repeatedly invoked non-welfarist criteria in their work. Our
conclusion is that, despite the focus on welfarism found in most histories of

---

[1] There are few histories of modern welfare economics, but these also focus on this
transition. The classic example is Blaug (1996), but see also Backhouse (1985); Mongin
(2006); Baujard (2017).

welfare economics, arguments that cannot be accommodated within welfarism have been widespread, the following chapters providing many examples of non-welfarist thinking by economists who were central to the evolution of welfare economics in the twentieth century.

If non-welfarist arguments have been pervasive, it is natural to ask whether there is a common underlying reason for why economists have repeatedly violated welfarism, which might be thought of as their 'official' methodology. Our answer is that even if economists have focused on welfarist criteria when theorising about welfare, when they become involved in practical problems they more or less have to step outside the welfarist framework (one explanation for this is that many economists hold values that, when examined closely, turn out to be inconsistent with welfarism). For example, Sen (1970a, 1970b) argued that liberalism, a value held by many economists, is inconsistent with Paretianism. However, as we will explain, this is one of several different reasons for moving away from welfarism.

The remainder of this introduction provides a fuller definition of welfarism, which is then used to identify and distinguish the various ways in which economists depart from welfarism. What unites these departures from welfarism is the demands imposed by practice.

2 The Meaning of Welfarism and Non-welfarism

Sen introduced the term welfarism as follows: 'welfarism is essentially an informational constraint for moral judgments about states of affairs' (Sen 1979b: 472). He did this in order to reorientate debates over welfare economics. In his paper, 'On weights and measures: Information constraints in social welfare analysis' (Sen 1977a), Sen studied the informational properties of individual utility functions and used this way of thinking about utility functions to clarify the problems of intrapersonal and interpersonal comparisons involved in aggregation. The outcome was a major advance in the ability to analyse and criticise the framework of welfare economics, going beyond the former exclusive focus on aggregative issues. Questions of welfare economics were reframed in terms of information: what information is relevant for measuring social welfare and deriving policy recommendations? Is there a problem when we deliberately exclude certain information from our analysis?

This approach is the basis for Sen's key point:

The general approach of making no use of any information about the social states other than that of personal welfares generated in them may be called 'welfarism'. I would like to argue that (i) welfarism as an approach to social decisions is very restrictive, and (ii) when the information on personal welfare is itself limited, it can be positively obnoxious. (Sen 1977a: 1559)

This leads to two distinct definitions of welfarism. The first, possibly less well known, defines welfarism as the claim that social welfare depends only on the welfare of the individuals in the society being considered, but does not need to consider how individual welfare is defined. This implies a bias towards individualism and consequentialism. Other sources of information, for example, relating to other moral values or deontological approaches, are not allowable. Sen's second definition of welfarism involves restricting information about what 'individual welfare' could mean and how it could be captured. Welfarism is often associated with a focus on subjective, ordinal, individual utilities, such as have become standard in microeconomic theory.

This focus on ordinal utilities and the consequent refusal to make interpersonal utility comparisons very significantly limits the capacity of welfare economics to provide policy recommendations (see Coyle 2019). Welfarism, in this sense, is problematic for many reasons, including that people may adapt to unfair conditions, and because there are operational difficulties in gathering reliable information on utility. Coyle (2019: 8), citing Tony Atkinson, argues that, in order to respond to contemporary economic challenges, it is vital to 'consider explicitly the moral consequences of particular models'. There already exists a substantial literature on axiomatic approaches to problems of social choice and welfare, in which ethical judgements are made explicit, much of which contributes explicitly to non-welfarist approaches. For example, there has been extensive debate over what is commonly known as the informational basis for justice. However, this literature, much of which is technical, involving philosophy as much as economics, has remained substantially separate from much of economic writing, which remains dominated by welfarist thinking.

If we take the first definition of welfarism, the restriction to utility information can be challenged from a normative perspective, turning to values other than utility. Non-welfarism can therefore involve acknowledging issues such as fairness, equity, solidarity and distributional concerns (Kolm 1971; Varian 1974; Fleurbaey and Maniquet 2011). Equality, for instance, may be the main value at stake (Atkinson 1970), or priority to the worst-off can be expressed by attaching a higher weight to worse-off individuals (Rawls 1971; Parfit 1995). Non-welfarism might also involve taking into account the fact that skills are unequally distributed, that handicaps should be compensated or that responsibility needs to be re-warded (Pazner and Schmeidler 1974, 1978; Bossert and Fleurbaey 1996; Roemer 1998; Fleurbaey 2008). Going beyond welfarism might also involve seeing both utility and freedom as intrinsically important. Such a move might mean defending pluralism in general (Sen 1985b, 2009), or consideration of equity as well as utility (Dworkin 1981a, 1981b; Fleurbaey and Maniquet 2011). Non-welfarism might also involve taking account of information about communities that would be neglected in a welfarist approach. For instance, Taylor's communitarianism is clearly non-welfarist (see also Walzer 1983; McIntyre 1988). Some have also claimed that history matters (Nozick 1974), or raised other non-consequentialist concerns (Suzumura and Xu 2001; Suzumura 2016).

Considering Sen's second definition of welfarism relative to the informational basis for justice, some welfare economists began to elaborate broader, non-welfarist approaches.[2] For example, considerations of justice have been used to focus on the provision of primary goods (Rawls 1971), resources (Dworkin 1981a, 1981b), capabilities (Sen 1985a; Nussbaum and Sen 1993), opportunities (Arneson 1990), advantages (Cohen 1989), rights (Gaertner, Pattanaik and Suzumura 1992), freedom of choice (Pattanaik and Xu 1990).

Restricting attention to utility rather than accepting a wider notion of welfare also implies that utility is unidimensional. Non-welfarism allows treating individual welfare as multidimensional (d'Aspremont and Gevers 2002). In this sense, synthetic indexes, such as the Human Development Index, belong to this family of non-welfarist evaluations.

The allowable information set is closely linked to the possibility of interpersonal comparisons of utility. For instance, if utilities are rationalised using revealed preference theory then it does not make sense to make interpersonal, or even intrapersonal, utility comparisons. More generally, the ability to make comparisons, and to derive fairness recommendations, depends on one's chosen interpretation of utility. However, in order to overcome Arrow's impossibility theorem, it was often thought necessary to allow for a certain element of interpersonal comparability of utility. That would mean that the restrictions on information associated with welfarism create a risk of making social choice impossible, suggesting that the need to

---

[2] Note that we use the term 'non-welfarism' (as do Kaplow and Shavell 2001, 2004) but other terms have also been used including 'post-welfarism' (Maguain 2002) and 'extra-welfarism' (Brouwer et al. 2008; Tessier 2009). For reviews of post-welfarist approaches, see Pattanaik (1994); Pattanaik and Xu (2003); Clément, Le Clainche and Serra (2008).

make policy decisions might make it essential to move towards non-welfarism (see Sen 1977b, 1999).

Rehabilitating interpersonal comparisons of utility for such reasons is a major development, for it rests on normative grounds, going against the idea that economics should be an ethically neutral, positive science. On the other hand, the acceptance of interpersonal comparisons of utility does not imply a commitment to non-welfarism. For example, some utilitarians (e.g. Harsanyi 1953, 1955; Ng 1999) accept interpersonal comparisons of utility. Conversely, non-welfarism does not imply acceptance for interpersonal comparisons, for some non-welfarist economics reject them (e.g. Fleurbaey, Tungodden and Chang 2003). It is even possible to justify a non-welfarist framework on the basis of ordinal utility only and no interpersonal comparisons, and still go beyond the Arrovian impossibility by introducing strong equity criteria (Mongin and Fleurbaey 2005).[3]

Almost all of these non-welfarist approaches take for granted that value judgements should be taken seriously and transparently explicated. This is usually done by capturing an axiomatic approach (see Thomson 2001; Mongin 2003). Normative principles, based on precisely specified value judgements, are expressed in a formal language, before studying the compatibility and their implications. This approach is clearly attractive but, at least so far, it has not led systematically to usable policy recommendations (Fleurbaey 2007).

3 Welfare Economics in Practice

When economists try to rule out value judgements, their ability to tackle practical matters is endangered; when they introduce into their welfare theories explicit value judgements that go beyond valuing individual

---

[3] There is a continuum of distinct definitions of welfarism. At a technical level, these restrictions of information on utility can be analysed through informational analyses (Sen 1977a; d'Aspremont and Gevers 1977, 2002) of utility with invariance conditions. Informational analyses make it possible to capture, formally and rigorously, a range of versions of ordinalism from strict ordinalism to complete cardinalism, and a range of positions on comparability of utility from complete comparability to complete incomparability. A possible definition of welfarism is a restriction to only strict ordinal preferences. Another one, linked to the Arrovian framework, is a restriction to only binary information on preferences. In the Arrovian framework, you can compare social state x to y, and y to z, but you have no information whatsoever on the intensity of your preference from x to y as compared to y and z. This notably rules out any ordinal information such as information conveyed in the standard marginal rate of substitution. Going from binary to ordinal information is already a departure from a stricter welfarist framework to a less limited set of information, allowing possibilities.

utilities, those theories become non-welfarist. But this book supports the view that there is more than this sharp well-known alternative. As we will argue, when (seemingly welfarist) economists engage with practice, they frequently step outside the welfarist framework. This is no accident because, in order to offer advice it is necessary to make value judgements and once value judgements are made, there is no reason to remain within the confines of welfarism. As the essays in this volume show, many economists have introduced non-welfarist elements into theoretical work if only implicitly or unconsciously.

As we have explained, non-welfarism is about being open to information and values that go beyond individual welfare. A helpful way to think about this is through considering the restrictions on information relevant to social welfare implied by different approaches to welfare economics.

(1) The old welfare economics of Marshall and Pigou has been said to restrict welfare-relevant information to utility or economic welfare, believed to be measurable in terms of money. In this context, non-welfarism means going beyond a focus on material wealth and aggregates of utilities measured in such terms. In the new welfare economics, welfarism involves a focus on a narrow set of acceptable notions of utility, either for operational reasons, or for the sake of scientific rigour, or by a deep belief that ordinal subjective well-being is all that counts for social welfare. In both cases, non-welfarism, therefore, can involve value pluralism: taking into consideration moral values other than utility, such as freedom, civil rights, equity and distributive concerns.

(2) The main feature of welfarism is that, for any concept of welfare, what is important for social welfare is individual welfare. As welfarism involves a focus on individual welfare, however that is defined, any information about groups or societies which is not reducible to information about individuals should be considered irrelevant. But such individualism sometimes fails to capture social welfare. Non-welfarism can therefore mean taking account of information about societies that cannot be reduced to information about individuals.

(3) The history of welfare economics has known periods when welfarism has been defended on the basis of consumer's sovereignty on the one hand and scientific rigour on the other. As a corollary, non-welfarism has been often criticised for presenting measurement problems, including the technical difficulties in capturing non-consequentialist ethics, and for its possible drift into paternalism,

notably due to the choice by external experts of relevant objective information. Those welfare economists who have supported a non-welfarist framework have faced these issues and posed solutions when they have engaged with practice.

One way to organise the book would, therefore, be to structure it according to these three different ways in which welfarism has been challenged: taking account of a wider range of information and values, overcoming individualism, tackling the problems posed by non-welfarism. The issue with such an approach is that, perhaps not surprisingly, most of the economists who challenged welfarism did so in multiple ways. For instance, Peter Cain's reading of Hobson reveals an economist who argued both against restricting attention to economic welfare and against individualism. Kotaro Suzumura's reading of Hicks and of the more recent evolution of normative economics concerns an argument against both monism of values and also the restriction of information on utility. The value of a less unequal distribution, as displayed in Backhouse's argument on Bergson and Samuelson, or in Yamazaki's chapter on Pigou, concerns both value monism and individualism. And so on.

We have, therefore, chosen to arrange the chapters chronologically. It is, however, useful to review the chapters in relation to the different ways in which the economists studied have departed from welfarism when they have engaged with practice.

4 Taking Other Values into Account

A major feature of economic welfarism is that welfare economics should be restricted to economic welfare – to welfare that can be measured in terms of money. One interpretation was that this had to be done through the market, and that this implied that material wealth should be all that counts. However, the examples of Ruskin and J. A. Hobson show that, even in Marshall's time, this view was controversial. Alternatively, welfarism can be interpreted as doing no more than imposing a single value in that it says that utility is what matters (without any presumption that this depends only on material goods) and anything else matters only in so far as it affects utility. On either interpretation, in such a framework, should other ethical values such as freedom or distributive issues count, they could have no more than instrumental value – valued because they contribute to raising utility. Close examination of major figures commonly taken to be welfarist, including Marshall, Pigou, Samuelson and Coase, shows that this view was never completely accepted.

The history of political economy in Britain during the nineteenth century can be told as an ongoing conflict between economists and their Romantic critics (Winch 1996, 2009). The economists, who include many well-known utilitarians, including the Philosophic Radicals, intellectual descendants of Jeremy Bentham, generally focused on the production and consumption of material goods and services, whereas their Romantic critics argued that they neglected higher values and overlooked the human costs of increased production. Among these Romantic critics, the most prominent was the art critic, John Ruskin, who drew on the ideas of the Romantic poet, William Wordsworth, and the social critic, Thomas Carlyle. He may not have been considered an economist himself, but his ideas inspired many who were clearly economists, notably Hobson. Ruskin's economics and his treatment of art have both been studied extensively, but Yuichi Shionoya (Chapter 1) brings the two sides of his thought together. He argues that, in line with the Romantics, Ruskin focused on human nature as a whole, life involving the pleasures and sensations derived from art as much as wealth. There was, therefore, much more to life than mere wealth, for beauty mattered too. Shionoya argues that Ruskin sees life in terms not of the flow of pleasure, but as a stock of capabilities. Ruskin argued that we should focus not merely on self-interest, but on social affection, self-sacrifice and on justice as a criterion for distributing wealth.

It was not just the self-proclaimed heretic, Hobson, who challenged the focus on economic welfare. So too did Alfred Marshall and A. C. Pigou – at different times embodiments of what was seen as economic orthodoxy. Tamotsu Nishizawa (Chapter 3) makes it clear that Marshall worked with a broader concept of well-being and a conception of 'organic life-growth', seeing 'the vigorous life of the whole' as a more appropriate welfare criterion than utilitarianism. The reason is that he saw economic progress and organic growth as bound up with improvement in human character and capabilities. Yamazaki (Chapter 4) points out that, between the first and second editions of *The Economics of Welfare* (1924) Pigou extended his definition of welfare to include not only states of consciousness but also 'their relations'. This change made it possible to include equity as an ethical value, entering social welfare independently of the utilities of individuals. Pigou also considered that having a variety of individuals was better than having individuals who were all the same. Such judgements concerning equity and variety are inconsistent with restricting attention to the values and information involved in welfarism. Pigou also parted from simple subjective welfarism when he wrote about the satisfaction of needs – objective, spiritual and urgent – that people might not themselves recognise.

The new welfare economics, the most visible outcome of which was a stress on Pareto efficiency, is commonly perceived as welfarist. The requirement to be scientific was widely taken to mean that the only information available was utility, now understood purely ordinal and subjective. However, one of its main proponents, Paul Samuelson, was willing to depart from welfarism. He used the social welfare function proposed by Abram Bergson (Burk) (1938) to show how ethical values could be used to derive welfare criteria. When confining himself to values that he believed were generally accepted he reached conclusions consistent with welfarism, accepting individuals' judgements of their own welfare. However, as Roger Backhouse (Chapter 8) argues, Samuelson consistently claimed that in order to draw conclusions for policy it was essential to go beyond such judgements. One reason for this was that be believed that policy had to take account of income distribution, an issue on which the Pareto criterion was silent. Another reason was that he attached importance to the process through which outcomes were achieved.

When, in the 1960s, what was taken to be the Pigovian approach was challenged by the Coase theorem, the argument that negotiation could achieve an efficient outcome was exclusively about efficiency. This was consistent with the new welfare economics and its focus on Pareto efficiency. However, when the Coase theorem was applied to environmental issues, economists did not remain within this framework but, as Steven Medema (Chapter 9) shows, brought in non-welfarist criteria. The argument that the social optimum involved weighing up the benefit of pollution to the polluter against the harm done to other people was widely challenged using moral arguments that went beyond welfarism, such as the argument that it was immoral to ask victims of pollution to bribe polluters not to pollute. It was argued that societies had value systems that went beyond efficiency and were reflected in social norms and embodied in common law.

Kenneth Arrow, one of the authors of the so-called fundamental theorems of welfare economics, might appear to rely on the normative criterion of Pareto optimality, but Nao Saito (Chapter 11) argues that between the 1950s and the 1990s, Arrow's thinking evolved towards clearly supporting non-welfarist theories of justice. He attached importance to the public utility of private goods, and to the redistribution of goods or incomes in order to maximise social welfare. He came to consider that majority decision should sometimes be rejected on ethical grounds: decisions favouring discrimination conflicted with his strong belief that discrimination is evil and, because individuals' preferences are blatantly not all that matter, Pareto-efficient judgements should be rejected on ethical grounds when they conflict with certain legal rights, as in the case of child trafficking.

5 Challenging Individualism

If welfare economics is essentially welfarist, with only individual utility counting in assessments of social welfare, collective arrangements or collective values can have no intrinsic significance for welfare economics. This explains why the standard view of welfare economics retains an individualist approach. However, looking back at Hobson, or at the standard authors in welfare economics, such as Marshall, Walras and Musgrave, and possibly Pigou, Pareto, Samuelson, we find that the individualist bias is less dominant than it is often taken to be.

Hobson, though he positioned himself as a heretic and an outsider – and he was an outsider to Marshall's Cambridge – was taken more seriously by other economists, especially in the United States. His affection for Ruskin presents a puzzle, for Hobson stood in a British liberal, radical tradition that can be traced back to Thomas Paine, whereas Ruskin was a conservative, harking back to an almost medieval way of thinking. Peter Cain (Chapter 2) asks what it was that Hobson found in Ruskin that he did not inherit from the liberal tradition out of which his work emanates. He argues that, from the 1880s, as socialism took hold with Labour representatives entering Parliament, Ruskin's denunciations of the modern, market economy began to look more revolutionary than Hobson's liberalism, leading Hobson to reassess what in Ruskin's work was consistent with the New Liberalism. He could accept Ruskin's ideas about the good life involving more than satisfying given preferences because he saw society as an evolving organism.

Richard Arena (Chapter 5) argues that, despite being the originator of modern general equilibrium theory, Léon Walras believed that society did exist and influenced individuals and that it could not be analysed simply as an aggregate of individuals. If the state can exist independently of individuals, it can make sense to speak of a public interest, for the state has its own ends – its own rationality. These ends include the implementation of justice.

Even the economist whose ideas were central to the creation of a welfare economics centred on individual preferences, Vilfredo Pareto, entertained ideas that departed from pure individualism. Rogério Arthmar and Michael McLure (Chapter 6) show that, when he turned to sociology, Pareto's views were not welfarist, for he saw people as social beings, acting in response to subjective assessments of the well-being of others. Individual utilities evolved in response to the prevailing social equilibrium. In addition, Pareto distinguished between two types of maximum: the maximum *for* a community, in which the Pareto-criterion is satisfied, and the maximum *of* a community in which the maximisation is not constrained by the requirement that no one is made worse off, and in which the utilities of different individuals are weighted.

Another important example of an economist who created a space for the social was Richard Musgrave, author of what was at one time the standard text on public finance. As Maxime Desmarais-Tremblay (Chapter 10) explains, Musgrave saw great technical and political merits in individualism but he consistently argued implicitly for a more collective approach to the provision of 'merit' goods. Early on, he argued that socially important needs could be identified through taking account of the 'cultural, political and social forces' operating in a society, while later, he made arguments for redistribution that made sense only in relation to a community, defending notions such as the equal-sacrifice criterion for taxation. In the 1980s, working together with Peggy Musgrave, he argued even more strongly for the existence of community interests, criticising theories based on self-interest as too narrow.

6 Questioning Non-welfarism

Economists have often assumed that, if it is to achieve its scientific objectives, welfare economics should either be free of any value judgements, attributing such a view to Lionel Robbins (1932), or it should be based only on generally accepted value judgements. Considering only utility information so that the only judgements involved are those that come from individuals whose welfare is being analysed was, therefore, a way to defend the consumer's sovereignty, generally considered more acceptable in a free society than paternalism. However, even the economists most closely associated with the welfarist approach, when considering operational issues and practical matters, came to support a non-welfarist framework. Conversely, when some welfare economists who support a non-welfarist framework have engaged with practice, they have faced issues of measurement and paternalism, being forced to provide solutions.

Kotaro Suzumura (Chapter 7) examines the work of John Hicks whose 'Manifesto' (1959) used the term 'Economic Welfarism' as a label for the view that he did *not* hold. He asks how far Hicks was prepared to go from welfarism, concluding that he was prepared to abandon consequentialism: not only may a wide set of consequentialist information besides utility be relevant, but some non-consequentialist information could also be invoked, examples including opportunity sets, procedure and rights. It is significant that this departure from welfarism came in a book titled *Essays in World Economics*, for this makes clear that the context was dealing with practical problems. Suzumura responds to Hicks's challenge to welfarism by drawing on the past fifty years of normative economics to explore the possibilities for integrating non-welfarist and non-consequentialist information into the analysis of welfare.

Because it was Sen who stimulated modern discussions of welfarism and non-welfarism, the case that he challenged welfarism does not need to be made. One well-known aspect of Sen's contribution to justice issues is the capability approach, presented as an alternative to both 'utility fetishism' and 'resource fetishism' (Sen 1985a, 1985b). However, describing Sen's capability approach as *the* alternative to standard welfare economics would fail to capture the major turning point represented by the capability approach, and would involve a misunderstanding of Sen's much more drastic criticism of welfarism.

Constanze Binder (Chapter 12) presents the wide diversity of capability approaches after Sen and Martha Nussbaum introduced the notion. All capability approaches seek to justify normative theories of justice and to provide operational tools for the evaluation of decision-making which overcome the issues raised by welfarism. Some attach intrinsic importance to freedom, some tackle the issues of preference adaptation and some avoid the neglect of diversity which can arise in the context of paternalism. However, Binder argues that none of them succeeds in providing a satisfactory response to all three challenges. In other words, some problems occurring with welfarism may reappear with non-welfarism. Binder explains why this is so, and argues that a way out of this problem requires more attention to democratic values, such as human agency.

Given that Sen is generally considered one of the pre-eminent contemporary welfare theorists and social choice theorists, it is not obvious that his movement beyond welfarism came in the context of addressing practical problems. That this was the case is argued by Muriel Gilardone (Chapter

13), who links Sen's development of the capability approach to his extensive work on theories of justice and to his applied work on poverty, inequality and entitlements. His theoretical welfare economics is part of a novel approach in which, with a particular consideration of avoiding paternalism, agency and public reasoning are the core elements.

7 Concluding Remarks

The technical limitations of welfarism come with consequences on a restriction of possible value judgements. The individualist framework itself, focusing on individual welfare only, excludes relevant values and obscures certain relevant information and solutions at the collective level. The restriction of information on utility is an impediment to expressing certain desirable ethical views. We have shown that welfare economists did not respect these limitations when they faced the problems this causes in a practical context. In particular, Sen has shown that welfare economics may raise problems with democratic values because it restricts information and denies agents the right to decide for themselves what information should or should not be relevant.

The essays in this volume show that, at least since the nineteenth century, when economists have faced practical problems such as public decision-making, concrete environmental or social concerns, they have abandoned one or more of the features of welfarism, adopting a non-welfarist approach. They have taken account of dimensions of welfare that cannot be measured, such as distributive justice and freedom of choice, paying attention to more than the satisfaction of preferences, and more information on utility that what the framework of welfare economics imposed. They have viewed welfare from a social point of view and they have introduced value judgements going beyond the very narrow range of values generally considered uncontroversial. The essays included here are clearly not comprehensive in their coverage; that would be impossible. But they cover many of the major figures in twentieth-century welfare economics – Marshall, Pigou, Pareto, Hicks, Samuelson, Coase, Musgrave, Arrow and Sen. Even though we also consider some self-consciously heterodox economists, notably Ruskin and Hobson, the instances of non-welfarist thinking that are presented here should not be dismissed as the views of minor, marginal figures for they were very influential in their own day. In view of this, there is a strong case that the history of welfare economics needs to be rewritten, and we regard this book as a first step in that process.

References

Adler, M. D. 2012. *Well-Being and Fair Distribution: Beyond Cost-Benefit Analysis*. New York: Oxford University Press.

Arneson, R. J. 1990. Liberalism, distributive subjectivism, and equal opportunity for welfare. *Philosophy & Public Affairs* 19, 158–94.

Arrow, K. J. 1951. *Social Choice and Individual Values*. New York: Wiley. 2nd ed., New Haven, CT and London: Yale University Press, 1963.

Arrow, K. J. and Debreu, G. 1954. Existence of an equilibrium for a competitive economy. *Econometrica* 22(3), 265–90.

Arrow, K. J. and T. Scitovsky (eds.) 1969. *Readings in Welfare Economics*. London: George Allen and Unwin.

Atkinson, A. B. 1970. On the measurement of inequality. *Journal of Economic Theory* 2 (3), 244–63.

Backhouse, R. E. 1985. *A History of Modern Economic Analysis*. Oxford: Basil Blackwell.

Backhouse, R. E. and Nishizawa, T. 2010. *No Wealth but Life: Welfare Economics and the Welfare State in Britain, 1880–1945*. Cambridge: Cambridge University Press.

Bator, F. M. 1958. The anatomy of market failure. *The Quarterly Journal of Economics* 72(3), 351–79.

Baujard, A. 2014. *A Utility Reading for the History of Welfare Economics*. Mimeo Gate Lyon Saint-Etienne.

Baujard, A. 2016. Utilitarianism and anti-utilitarianism. In G. Faccarello and H. D. Kurz (eds.), *Handbook of the History of Economic Analysis*, Vol. 3, Cheltenham: Edward Elgar, 577–88.

Baujard, A. 2017. L'économie du bien-être est morte. Vive l'économie du bien-être! In G. Campagnolo and J. S. Gharbi (eds.), *Philosophie économique*, Paris: Editions Matériologiques, 77–128.

Baujard, A. and Gilardone, M. 2017. Sen is not a capability theorist. *Journal of Economic Methodology* 24(1), 1–19.

Baujard, A., Gilardone, M. and Salles, M. A conversation with Amartya Sen, to be published in *Social Choice and Welfare* (video overview available at www.unicaen .fr/recherche/mrsh/forge/262).

Baumol, W. J. 1946. Community indifference. *Review of Economic Studies* 14(1), 44–8.

Bergson (Burk), A. 1938. A reformulation of certain aspects of welfare economics. *The Quarterly Journal of Economics* 52(2), 310–34.

Blaug, M. 1996. *Economic Theory in Retrospect*, 5th ed. Cambridge: Cambridge University Press.

Bossert, W. and Fleurbaey, M. 1996. Redistribution and compensation. *Social Choice and Welfare* 13(3), 343–55.

Boulding, K. E. 1952. Welfare economics. In B. F. Haley (ed.), *A Survey of Contemporary Economics*, Vol. II, Homewood, IL: R. D. Irwin for the American Economic Association, 1–34.

Brouwer, W. B. F., Culyer, A. J., van Exel, N. J. A. and Rutten, F. F. H. 2008. Welfarism vs. extra-welfarism. *Journal of Health Economics* 27(2), 325–38.

Chipman, J. S., and Moore, J. C. 1978. The new welfare economics, 1939–1974. *International Economic Review* 19, 547–84.

Clément, V., Le Clainche, C. and Serra, D. 2008. *Economie de la justice et de l'équité*. Paris: Economica.

Coase, R. H. 1960. The problem of social cost. *Journal of Law & Economics* 3 (Oct.), 1–44.

Cohen, G. A. 1989. On the currency of egalitarian justice. *Ethics* 99(4), 906–44.

Coyle, D. 2019. Homo Economicus, AIs, humans and rats: Decision-making and economic welfare. *Journal of Economic Methodology* 26(1), 2–12.

d'Aspremont, C. and Gevers, L. 1977. Equity and the informational basis of collective choice. *Review of Economic Studies* 44(2), 199–209.

d'Aspremont, C. and Gevers, L. 2002. Social welfare functionals and interpersonal comparability. In K. J. Arrow, A. K. Sen and K. Suzumura (eds.), *Handbook of Social Choice and Welfare*, Vol. 1, Amsterdam: Elsevier, 459–541.

Dobb, M. 1969. *Welfare Economics and the Economics of Socialism*. Cambridge: Cambridge University Press.

Dworkin, R. 1981a. What is equality? Part 1: Equality of welfare. *Philosophy & Public Affairs* 10(3), 185–246.

Dworkin, R. 1981b. What is equality? Part 2: Equality of resources. *Philosophy & Public Affairs* 1(4), 283–345.

Fleurbaey, M. 2007. Social choice and just institutions: New perspectives. *Economics and Philosophy* 23, 15–43.

Fleurbaey, M. 2008. *Fairness, Responsibility, and Welfare*. Oxford: Oxford University Press.

Fleurbaey, M. and Maniquet, F. 2011. *A Theory of Fairness and Social Welfare*. Cambridge: Cambridge University Press.

Fleurbaey, M., Tungodden, B. and Chang, H. F. 2003. Any non-welfarist method of policy assessment violates the Pareto principle: A comment. *Journal of Political Economy* 111(6), 1382–5.

Gaertner, W., Pattanaik, P. and Suzumura, K. 1992. Individual rights revisited. *Economica* 59S, 161–77.

Galbraith, J. K. 1958. *The Affluent Society*. London: Penguin Books.

Graaff, J. de V. 1957. *Theoretical Welfare Economics*. Cambridge: Cambridge University Press.

Harsanyi, J. 1953. Cardinal utility in welfare economics and in the theory of risk-taking. *Journal of Political Economy* 61(5), 434–5.

Harsanyi, J. C. 1955. Cardinal welfare, individualistic ethics, and interpersonal comparisons of utility. *Journal of Political Economy* 63(4), 309–21.

Hicks, J. R. 1939. The foundations of welfare economics. *Economic Journal* 49(196), 696–712.

Hicks, J. R. 1941. The rehabilitation of consumers' surplus. *Review of Economic Studies* 9, 108–16.

Hicks, J. R. (no date; c. 1955): 'Another Shot at Welfare Economics, Lecture I and Lecture II', unpublished typescript, 19 pages folio + 21 pages, diagrams in the text.

Hicks, 1959. A preface and a manifesto. In *Essays in World Economics*, Oxford: Clarendon Press, viii–xiv. Reprinted in Arrow and Scitovsky, 1969.

Igersheim, H. 2017. The death of welfare economics: History of a controversy. *CHOPE Working Paper* 2017-03, 1–37.

Kaldor, N. 1939. Welfare propositions of economics and interpersonal comparisons of utility. *The Economic Journal* 49(195), 549–52.

Kaplow, L. and Shavell, S. 2001. Any non-welfarist method of policy assessment violates the Pareto principle. *Journal of Political Economy* 109(2), 281–6.

Kaplow, L. and Shavell, S. 2004. Any non-welfarist method of policy assessment violates the Pareto principle: Reply. *Journal of Political Economy* 112(1), 249–51.

Kolm, S.-C. 1971. *Justice et équité.* Paris: CEPREMAP. New ed., Paris: CNRS, 1972; English version, *Justice and Equity*, Cambridge, MA: MIT Press, 2002.

Lipsey, R. G., and Lancaster, K. 1956. The general theory of second best. *Review of Economic Studies* 24(1), 11–32.

Little, I. M. D. 1949. Economic behaviour and welfare. *Mind* 58(230), 195–209.

Little, I. M. D. 1950. *A Critique of Welfare Economics.* Oxford: Oxford University Press.

Maguain, D. 2002. Les théories de la justice distributive post-rawlsiennes. Une revue de la littérature. *Revue Economique* 53(2), 165–99.

Marshall, A. 1890–1920. *Principles of Economics.* London: Macmillan.

McIntyre, A. 1988. *Whose Justice? Which Rationality?* Notre Dame, IN: University of Notre Dame Press.

Mill, J. S. 1848. *Principles of Political Economy and Some of Their Applications to Social Philosophy.* Reprinted as *Collected Works of John Stuart Mill*, Vols. II–III, edited by J. M. Robson, Toronto, University of Toronto Press, 1963.

Mongin, P. 2003. L'axiomatisation et les théories économiques. *Revue Economique* 54 (1), 99–138.

Mongin, P. 2006. Is there progress in normative economics? *Economics and Philosophy* 22, 19–54.

Mongin, P. and Fleurbaey, M. 2005. The news of the death of welfare economics is greatly exaggerated. *Social Choice and Welfare* 25(2), 381–418.

Musgrave, R. 1959. *The Theory of Public Finance: A Study in Public Economy.* New York: McGraw Hill.

Ng, Y.-K. 1999. Utility, informed preferences, or happiness: Following Harsanyi's argument to its logical conclusion. *Social Choice and Welfare* 16(2), 197–21.

Nozick, R. 1974. *Anarchy, State and Utopia.* New York: Basic Books.

Nussbaum, M. C. and Sen, A. K. 1993. *The Quality of Life.* Oxford: Clarendon Press.

Parfit, D. 1995. Equality or priority. Lindley Lecture, University of Kansas Press. Reprinted in M. Clayton and A. Williams (eds.), *The Ideal of Equality*, New York: St Martin's Press and London: Macmillan, ch. 5, 81–125.

Pattanaik, P. K. 1994. Some non-welfaristic issues in welfare economics. In B. Dutta (ed.), *Welfare Economics*, Oxford: Oxford University Press, 197–248.

Pattanaik, P. K. and Xu, Y. 1990. On ranking opportunity sets in terms of freedom of choice. *Recherches Economiques de Louvain* 56(3/4), 383–90.

Pattanaik, P. K. and Xu, Y. 2003. Non-welfaristic policy assessment and the Pareto principle. Public Choice Conference, Nashville.

Pazner, E. A. and Schmeidler, D. 1974. A difficulty in the concept of fairness. *Review of Economic Studies* 41(3), 441–3.

Pazner, E. A. and Schmeidler, D. 1978. Egalitarian equivalent allocations: A new concept of economic equity. *Quarterly Journal of Economics* 92(4), 671–87.

Pigou, A. C. 1912. *Wealth and Welfare.* London: Macmillan.

Pigou, A. C. 1920. *The Economics of Welfare.* London: Macmillan. 4th ed. 1932.

Rawls, J. 1971. *A Theory of Justice.* Cambridge, MA: Harvard University Press.

Robbins, L. C. 1932. *Essay on the Nature and Significance of Economic Science.* London: Macmillan. 2nd ed. 1935.

Roemer, J. 1998. *Equality of Opportunity.* Cambridge: Cambridge University Press.

Samuelson, P. A. 1947. *Foundations of Economic Analysis*. Cambridge, MA: Harvard University Press.

Samuelson, P. A. 1950. Evaluation of real national income. *Oxford Economic Papers* 2 (1), 1–29.

Scitovsky, T. 1941. A note on welfare propositions in economics. *Review of Economic Studies* 9, 77–88. Reprinted in Arrow and Scitovsky 1969.

Sen, A. K. 1970a. *Collective Choice and Social Welfare*. San Francisco, CA: Holden Day.

Sen, A. K. 1970b. The impossibility of a Paretian liberal. *Journal of Political Economy* 78 (1), 152–7.

Sen, A. K. 1977a. On weights and measures: Informational constraints in social welfare analysis. *Econometrica* 45(7), 1539–72.

Sen, A. K. 1977b. Social choice theory: A re-examination. *Econometrica* 45(1), 53–89.

Sen, A. K. 1979a. Personal utilities and public judgements: Or what's wrong with welfare economics. *The Economic Journal* 89(355), 537–58.

Sen, A. K. 1979b. Utilitarianism and welfarism. *The Journal of Philosophy* 76(9), 463–89.

Sen, A. K. 1979c. Equality of what? In S. McMurrin (ed.), *The Tanner Lectures on Human Values*, Vol. 1, Cambridge University Press, 197–220. New ed. in A. K. Sen, *Choice, Welfare and Measurement*, Cambridge, MA: MIT Press, 1982.

Sen, A. K. 1985a. *Commodities and Capabilities*. Oxford: Oxford University Press.

Sen, A. K. 1985b. Well-being, agency and freedom: The Dewey Lectures 1984. *The Journal of Philosophy* 72(4), 169–221.

Sen, A. K. 1999. The possibility of social choice. *American Economic Review* 89(3), 349–78.

Sen, A. K. 2009. *The Idea of Justice*. Cambridge, MA: The Belknap Press of Harvard University Press.

Stigler, G. J. 1966. *The Theory of Price*, 3rd ed. New York: Macmillan.

Suppes, P. 2005. The pre-history of Kenneth Arrow's social choice and individual values. *Social Choice and Welfare* 25(2/3), 319–26.

Suzumura, K. 2016. *Choice, Preferences, and Procedures: A Rational Choice Theoretic Approach*. Cambridge, MA: Harvard University Press.

Suzumura, K. and Xu, Y. 2001. Characterizations of consequentialism and non-consequentialism. *Journal of Economic Theory* 101, 423–36.

Tessier, P. 2009. Harsanyi, Sen ou Bentham. Quelle perspective adopter pour l'évaluation du bien-être en santé? *Revue Economique* 60(6), 1309–33.

Thomson, W. 2001. On the axiomatic method and its recent applications to game theory and resource allocation. *Social Choice and Welfare* 18, 327–86.

Varian, H. R. 1974. Equity, envy, and efficiency. *Journal of Economic Theory* 9, 63–91.

Walzer, M. 1983. *Spheres of Justice*. New York: Basic Books.

Winch, D. 1996. *Riches and Poverty: An Intellectual History of Political Economy in Britain, 1750–1834*. Cambridge: Cambridge University Press.

Winch, D. 2009. *Wealth and Life: Essays on the Intellectual History of Political Economy in Britain, 1848–1914*. Cambridge: Cambridge University Press.

PART I

PLURALITY OF WELFARE IN THE MAKING
OF WELFARE ECONOMICS

1

Ruskin's Romantic Triangle

Neither Wealth Nor Beauty but Life*

Yuichi Shionoya

1.1 Ruskin the Romantic

John Ruskin's (1819–1900) vast amount of work roughly consists of two groups on art and economy.[1] We may locate a watershed dividing his life and career at about 1860. He was engaged in the aesthetics of painting and architecture in his early years through the celebrated publication of *Modern Painters* (five vols., 1843–60), *The Seven Lamps of Architecture* (1849), and *The Stones of Venice* (three vols., 1851–3), and then he turned to the controversial criticism of economy and society in his later years through the publication of *The Political Economy of Art* (1857), *Unto This Last* (1862), and *Munera Pulveris* (1872). In addition to these major publications, there are a variety of discourses on art and economy in the forms of university and public lectures, and also the series of open letters on public affairs addressed to the British labour class.

Let me clarify my approach to reading Ruskin. First, in past studies of Ruskin, his thoughts on art and economy were treated separately by the specialists in each field, so that they were never discussed as an integral whole in any satisfactory way. By and large, the ways in which specialists in art discussed economy and society were less convincing, while specialists in economy and society paid the least attention to Ruskin's thoughts on art. The object of this paper is to present a way in which Ruskin's thoughts on art and economy can be interpreted in a unified manner. My

---

* This chapter was previously published in *History of Economic Ideas*, Anno XXII, 2014(1), pp. 16–49.
[1] Quotations from Ruskin are cited in the text by volume and page number in Cook and Wedderburn (1903–12).

framework for interpretation is a reference to romanticism, or the romantic world view.

Second, Ruskin's thoughts on art and economy are historically given, allowing us to apply two different approaches: rational reconstruction (i.e., logical, theoretical, and methodological interpretation) and historical reconstruction (i.e., biographical, psychological, and historical interpretation). My approach is an attempt at a rational reconstruction of Ruskin by means of the conceptual framework of romanticism, in which I emphasize the key notions of the 'entire human nature', covering 'reason, feeling, and will', on the one hand, and of the 'organism' of 'nature, mind, and society', on the other. In other words, romanticism is construed from both sides of multiple humanity and organic objects.

Third, I construct this framework by the image of 'Ruskin's triangle', integrating 'Wealth, Life, and Beauty' by reformulating the central concept of Life in terms of 'capability, composition, and labour'. This framework should enable Ruskin to be revived in the present world, transcending the historical circumstances of Victorian Britain. In other words, the purpose of the present paper is not only to discover Ruskin's link between art and economy but also to explore the possibility of economic thought, which will be an alternative to the mainstream economic doctrines.

Regarding Ruskin's work on art (but not his work on economics), the following appraisal seems to have been accepted among art scholars: '*Modern Painters* is the last great statement of the English romantic renovation of sensibility as the *Lyrical Ballads* is the first. Nature is the central term in both, Wordsworth equating it with "simplicity" in his attack on Augustan poetry, Ruskin with the "truth" in his attack on the Grand Style in art' (Rosenberg 1986, 7). *Lyrical Ballads* (1798), co-authored by Wordsworth and Coleridge, is regarded as an epoch-making monumental work in the birth of British romanticism. In 1798 in Germany too, the *Athenäum*, the core organ of the early German romantic movement, was published by the Schlegel brothers. The limitation of space in this paper does not allow me to discuss the philosophical and aesthetical dimensions of German romanticism. The picture of Ruskin as a romantic will be drawn in the course of my argument without imposing a rigid conceptual frame of German romanticism.

Romanticism, in the sense of the philosophical world view as well as the style of art, is the overall criticism of the Enlightenment and classicism. The fundamental thesis of classicism claims that the grasp of truth by reason provides invariable ideals even in art and morality. In Britain, aesthetics underwent a shift from classicism to romanticism concerning the criteria of taste or beauty. In Britain, however, there was no radical change from the classical thesis to the romantic notion that art is the product of the human soul, feelings, and imaginations and that the judgements of tastes are intuitive and relative. Under the influence of the British empirical philosophy the shift was mediated by the idea of 'association' (Bate 1946).

In psychology, 'association' is the process of forming mental connections between sensations, perceptions, or memories. Hume argued that association of ideas was derived by imaginations, and he attributed to imaginations the primary status in mental activity, comparable to the law of gravity. Although in aesthetical judgements the subjectivity or relativity of tastes is often emphasized on empirical grounds, the theory of association was applied to the coordination of various ideas emerging from individual experiences. Thus, the combination of empiricism and intuition yielded a particular type of aesthetics in British romanticism, in which although imaginations, intuitions, and feelings were emphasized as the source of life, they were incorporated into the mould of ideas, or intellect, so that ideas might become the conceptualization of experience. British romanticism under the influence of the empiricist tradition is sometimes characterized as 'intuitive empiricism' or 'poetic realism' and was able to avoid the extreme positions of idealism, subjectivism, and transcendentalism of German romanticism that stemmed from the philosophical climate of German idealism. It is possible to mention two names among the British romantics who directly affected Ruskin: William Wordsworth (1771–1855) and Thomas Carlyle (1795–1881).

1.2 Wordsworth, Carlyle, and Ruskin

Ruskin started writing *Modern Painters* in defence of the work of J. M. W. Turner, who was criticized by the Establishment in the artistic circle. On the title pages of its five serial volumes published over seventeen years, Ruskin quoted lines from poems on nature and truth in Wordsworth's *Excursion*. This indicates his sympathy for and devotion to Wordsworth. Moreover, when Ruskin designed an extensive treatise on art and beauty in general apart from the analysis of Turner's painting, he often quoted Wordsworth's poems and statements on poetry to support his points of argument. This is because Ruskin found common intention with Wordsworth with regard to his core approach to the truth of nature. The truth is pursued not by mere realism or imitations of

nature but speculations or imaginations of subjects. Creative imaginations, the romantic emphasizes, are best displayed by extracting symbolic images from experiences and observations of reality. The British
romantics approach the internal, the illusory, and the infinite through
the external, the visible, and the finite, with the infinite being religious or
moral. The characteristic of British romanticism consists of realism and
the dailiness of moments in artistic activities. Ruskin was most directly
affected by Wordsworth among the British romantics.

Wordsworth defines the purpose of poetry to be:

[T]o illustrate the manner in which our feelings and ideas are associated in a state
of excitement. But speaking in less general language, it is to follow the fluxes and
refluxes of the mind when agitated by the great and simple affections of our
nature . . . . [I]ts object is truth, not individual and local, but general, and operative;
not standing upon external testimony, but carried alive into the heart by passion;
truth which is its own testimony, which gives strength and divinity to the tribunal
to which it appeals, and receives them from the same tribunal. Poetry is the image
of man and nature. (Wordsworth and Coleridge 2006 [1798], 231, 247)

For Wordsworth, poetry must be written in 'the real language of men'
about 'the incidents of common life'. In terms of 'association of ideas'
referred to here, feelings of sensations from the outside world are coordinated and directed by ideas of the inner perceptions of the poet in order to
get to the truth of man and nature. Wordsworth asks: 'What then does the
Poet?' His answer is:

[The Poet] is the rock of defence of human nature; an upholder and preserver,
carrying every where with him relationship and love. . . . The Poet binds
together by passion and knowledge the vast empire of human society, as it is
spread over the whole earth, and over all time. (Wordsworth and Coleridge
2006 [1798], 249)

Ruskin's key notion of 'the entire human nature' accepts Wordsworth's
idea of 'the complex scene of ideas and sensations' as the source of pleasure
and sympathy caused by art.

Ruskin was generally admitted to be Carlyle's disciple. Carlyle had no
interest in art, and their intellectual friendship emerged solely from
Ruskin's awakening to social issues during the course of his writing on
art and his sympathy with Carlyle's scathing social criticism. Ruskin had
gained a reputation as an art critic, but faced almost uniform hostility from
the conservative circle of society after he converted to social criticism. As
an honourable exception, Carlyle praised and encouraged him. Ruskin felt
that Carlyle was the only sympathetic reader in the world; his loyalty to
Carlyle was unquestioning.

Unlike Wordsworth and Ruskin, Carlyle had a clear contact with German thought through his study of Kant, Fichte, Goethe, and Schiller. His central theme was how to acquire the belief in the transcendental order which forms the basis for approaching the phenomenal world. The best work that represents his philosophical position is *Sartor Resartus*, in which, he argues, social rules and customs are, as it were, visible emblems or clothes that represent invisible spiritual ideas, so that it is necessary to get at the transcendental basis for perceiving the phenomenal world, including nature, man, and society. His grand propositions are: 'Society is founded upon Clothes' (Carlyle 1987 [1833], 41); 'Matter exists only spiritually, and to represent some Idea' (56); and 'The philosophy of Clothes attains to Transcendentalism' (193). His idea of 'natural supernaturalism' (the title of bk. 3, ch. 8) is the philosophical core of German romanticism.

Sartor Resartus contains many characteristic claims of Carlyle in the subsequent years, the essence of which is the insight that 'Liberals, Economists, and Utilitarians' (177) tear down and destroy the society. His prophetic concerns include: hatred towards free competition and utilitarianism, the maximization of capability instead of happiness, the moral values of labour, the religious foundation of society, misgivings about class disintegration, advocacy of cooperation instead of competition, and the need for heroes. For Carlyle, a hero is a leader who discerns the spiritual reality of the age hidden behind material appearances and poses it as the problem which now confronts us. He is regarded as belonging to a wide range of 'anti-rationalism, anti-empiricism, and anti-Enlightenment' (Le Quesne 1998).

In view of the general periodization of British romanticism as 1785–1825, the romantic movement had already been started by Wordsworth and Coleridge a few decades before Carlyle's writing activity. However, there is no evidence that Carlyle inherited some elements of the British romantic literary movement. He essentially depended on German philosophy. Ruskin comprehended romantic artistic thought from Wordsworth's poetry and literary theory, on the one hand, and grasped romantic social thought from Carlyle's social criticism, on the other. Ruskin himself evaded a reference to German philosophy. The skeleton of his romantic thought was constructed by the combination of Wordsworth and Carlyle, though he needed Turner to develop Wordsworth's theory of poetry into the art of painting.

Ruskin wrote a short article, 'German Philosophy' (appendix to *Modern Painters*, vol. 3), in which he ridiculed statements such as 'a finite realization of the infinite' in German metaphysics as pure nonsense and not suited to the British people. He mentioned that those who want philosophy not for show but for practical use are advised simply to read Plato, Bacon, Wordsworth, Carlyle, etc. (vol. 5, 424–6). This happens to reveal Ruskin's intellectual source and propensity.

1.3 Ideas of Truth, Beauty, and Relation

The unique characteristics of Ruskin's thoughts on art include, among others, devotion to Wordsworth, praise of Turner, defence of pre-Raphaelitism, and admiration of Gothic architecture. In *Modern Painters*, Ruskin regards Turner as 'the father of modern art' and aims to establish the principles of landscape painting to demonstrate the modernity of Turner's art. For Ruskin, Turner's landscape was a major innovation in the nineteenth century. The following exaggerated passage almost deifies Turner:

> Turner – glorious in conception – unfathomable in knowledge – solitary in power – with the elements waiting upon his will, and the night and the morning obedient to his call, sent as a prophet of God to reveal to men the mysteries of His universe, standing, like the great angel of the Apocalypse, clothed with a cloud, and with a rainbow upon his head, and with the sun and stars given into his hand. (vol. 3, 254)

At the outset of the first volume, he raises a serious question about what is greatness in art, and replies without hesitation:

> It is not by the mode of representing and saying, but by what is represented and said, that the respective greatness either of the painter or the writer is to be finally determined. . . . I say that the art is greatest which conveys to the mind of the spectator, by any means whatsoever, the greatest number of the greatest ideas. (vol. 3, 88, and 92)

Ruskin calls the mental and psychic faculty of artists that produces the great works of art 'excellent', whilst the terms 'beautiful', 'useful', or 'good' are applied to the great works as such.

He defines the subject matter of *Modern Painters* as the investigation of three grand ideas: truth, beauty, and relation. They represent the methods, criteria, and aims of great art respectively. The essentials of each idea may be summarized as follows:

1.3.1 Ideas of Truth

The first volume of *Modern Painters* discusses ideas of truth by dealing with Turner. Ruskin challenges the classical view of art, then dominant, that the task of art is to imitate and represent natural objects faithfully. For him, the end of art is not merely 'representation of fact' but rather 'expression of ideas' shaped by imaginations; art must pursue the 'truth' of nature by combining fact and ideas. 'Ideas of truth are the foundation, and ideas of imitation, the destruction, of all art' (vol. 3, 108).

Ruskin's praise of Turner is based on an appraisal of his excellence in presenting the truth of nature. The inspiration or revelation he got from Turner's work is that it is the task of art to discover the divine attributes hidden in nature through a display of the whole human nature. His view that art is a tool that represents and contributes to life follows Wordsworth's theory of poetry. Ruskin analyses Turner's landscape in terms of techniques of 'tone, colour, chiaroscuro, and space', on the one hand, and in terms of objects of 'sky, earth, water, and vegetation', on the other. He concludes that Turner is the only painter who has ever drawn the changing skies with various forms of clouds; that he is the only painter who has ever drawn a mountain or a stone on the earth; that he is the only painter who has ever drawn the stem of a tree; that he is the only painter who has ever represented the surface of calm, or the force of agitated, water; and that he is the only painter who has represented the effects of space on distant objects or who has rendered the abstract beauty of natural colour (vol. 3, 252).

Turner restrained the use of various colours and made the contrast between light and shade predominant over colour, keeping tones of blue, brown, and grey. It is due to this treatment of light that Turner is often regarded as the pioneer of the Impressionists. According to Ruskin, the highest attainment of Turner's technique is 'light without colour' (vol. 3, 234). Abstraction of light from colour is based on the painter's power of imagination aimed at 'expression of ideas'.

In a pamphlet entitled *Pre-Raphaelitism* (1851), Ruskin defended, along with Turner, the movement of the young painters who were then called the Pre-Raphaelites. They rebelled against the art education of classicism in the Royal Academy of Arts and urged a return to the Medieval Italian painters before Raphael who was a representative of Renaissance art. The pamphlet of the defence, though titled *Pre-Raphaelitism*, is largely devoted to the admiration of Turner and the disparagement of Raphael. In 'Pre-Raphaelitism' (1853b), one of his public lectures in Edinburgh, he says: 'Pre-Raphaelitism has but one principle, that of absolute, uncompromising truth in all that it does, obtained by working everything, down to the most minute detail, from nature, and from nature only' (vol. 12, 157).

Turner is 'the first and greatest of the Pre-Raphaelites'. Pre-Raphaelitism is nothing but Turnerism.

1.3.2 Ideas of Beauty

In the second volume of *Modern Painters* Ruskin turned to the second subject of art, in other words ideas of beauty. Already in the first volume he made explicit an aspect of his fundamental position of art, that is, beauty as morality:

> Any material object which can give us pleasure in the simple contemplation of its outward qualities without any direct and definite exertion of the intellect, I call in some way, or in some degree, beautiful. . . . Perfect taste is the faculty of receiving the greatest possible pleasure from those material sources which are attractive to our moral nature in its purity and perfection. . . . Ideas of beauty, then, be it remembered, are the subjects of moral, but not of intellectual perception. By the investigation of them we shall be led to the knowledge of ideal subject of art. (vol. 3, 109–11)

He asks about the relation between beauty and pleasure, that is, whether the end of art is practical for life or spiritual as it is related to the end of life itself. He distinguishes between 'practical' and 'theoretic' art in accordance with Aristotle's distinction between *praxis* and *theoria*. The two kinds of art are compared with the distinction between carpenter and architect, or between plumber and artist.

> I wholly deny that the impressions of beauty are in any way sensual; they are neither sensual nor intellectual, but moral: and for the faculty receiving them, whose difference from mere perception I shall immediately endeavour to explain, no term can be more accurate or convenient than that employed by the Greeks, 'Theoretic', which I pray permission, therefore, always to use, and to call the operation of the faculty itself, Theoria . . . . The mere animal consciousness of the pleasantness I call Aesthesis; but the exulting, reverent, and grateful perception of it I call Theoria. For this, and this only, is the full comprehension and contemplation of the Beautiful as a gift of God. (vol. 4, 42, and 47)

We should remember that from 'Theoria' arise 'Joy, Admiration, and Gratitude', Ruskin's key words for art and economics (vol. 4, 47). In using these words, he explains how the idea of beauty is essentially moral:

> It is necessary to the existence of an idea of beauty, that the sensual pleasure which may be its basis should be accompanied first with joy, then with love of the object, then with the perception of kindness in a superior intelligence, finally, with thankfulness and veneration towards that intelligence itself; and no idea can be at all considered as in any way an idea of beauty, until it be made up of these emotions. (vol. 4, 48)

Ruskin uses the term 'Theoria' (or theoretic) in place of the term 'aesthetic', commonly employed in art theory, in order to challenge the traditional conception of beauty, which denies intellectual pleasure and is biased towards sensual pleasure. For him, the perfect conception of beauty is neither mere intellectual faculty nor mere sensual faculty but the faculty of Theoria that consists in moral will. The meaning of art as morality is that by the pursuit of true beauty one should raise human capacity and character so as to approach from an animal-like aesthetic towards divine Theoria. Morality for evaluating human capacity and character is the ethics of virtue. Ruskin's beauty is inseparable from virtue.

Supposing the concept of beauty requires the perceptions of 'Joy, Admiration, and Gratitude', how are they produced? Ruskin distinguishes between the two kinds of theoretic beauty which Theoria may yield, in other words Typical Beauty and Vital Beauty:

By the term Beauty, then, properly are signified two things. First, that external quality of bodies already so often spoken of, and which, whether it occur in a stone, flower, beast, or in man, is absolutely identical, which, as I have already asserted, may be shown to be in some sort typical of the Divine attributes, and which therefore I shall, for distinction's sake, call Typical Beauty: and, secondarily, the appearance of felicitous fulfilment of function in living things, more especially of the joyful and right exertion of perfect life in man; and this kind of beauty I shall call Vital Beauty. (vol. 4, 64)

Typical Beauty is the divine attributes inherent in God's creatures, while Vital Beauty is excellence of functions in living creatures. Typical Beauty represents the static and eternal order of an object, while Vital Beauty represents dynamic and disturbing innovation caused by imaginations of an artist. Typical Beauty indicates the objective criteria of great art, while Vital Beauty indicates its subjective criteria such as morality in the choice of subject, love of beauty, sincerity to truth, and imaginative creativity of an artist, all of which involve the whole powers of the human soul. Balancing the two kinds of beauty is the task of the Theoria of an artist.

Ruskin specifies six types of Typical Beauty: Infinity, Unity, Repose, Symmetry, Purity, and Moderation. Characteristic of his argument is that each type presupposes antinomy or paradox caused by the existence of an opposite type of beauty which is mostly classified as Vital Beauty, such as the finite versus infinite, unity versus diversity, statics versus dynamics, symmetry versus irregularity, purity versus impurity, and restraint versus freedom. Ruskin's polygon or *Romantische Ironie* has a secure foothold in the definition of Beauty.

1.3.3 Ideas of Relation

The third subject of Ruskin's project in *Modern Painters*, ideas of relation, was not taken up until the fifth and last volume, published seventeen years after the first one. Under this subject everything relating to the
conception of art is arranged and all sources of pleasure are investigated
as the synthesis of art theory by the ideas of relation or 'association':

> In this last division we have to consider the relations of art to God and man:
> its work in the help of human beings, and service of their Creator. We have to
> inquire into the various Powers, Conditions, and Aims of mind involved in the
> conception or creation of pictures; in the choice of subject, and the mode and
> order of its history. (vol. 7, 203)

Ruskin formulates the ideas of relation in a general form as the interdependence among parts or elements in the composition of the picture and
extends it metaphorically from the picture to mineralogy and social relations by the 'law of help', as will be discussed in Subsection 1.5.2. The
concept of 'composition' will become the link between art and economy,
both contributing to life. Ruskin's aesthetics has a far-reaching range of
application. He provides the definition of the greatest art as producing 'the
greatest number of the greatest ideas' (vol. 3, 92), which proves the substitute for the utilitarian definition of 'the greatest number of the greatest
happiness'.

1.4 'Air, Water, and Earth' and 'Admiration, Hope, and Love':
Nature and Mind

The most famous passage in Ruskin's critical book of economics, *Unto
This Last*, reads as follows:

> THERE IS NO WEALTH BUT LIFE. Life, including all its powers of love, of
> joy, and of admiration. That country is the richest which nourishes the
> greatest number of noble and happy human beings; that man is richest who,
> having perfected the functions of his own life to the utmost, has also the
> widest helpful influence, both personal, and by means of his possessions, over
> the lives of others. . . . The maximum of life can be reached by the maximum
> of virtue. (vol. 17, 105)

In this passage relating to economic and social issues there is no explicit
reference to the concept of beauty, but the words of 'love, of joy, and of
admiration', defined here as the 'powers of life', are similar to 'joy, admiration, and gratitude', defined above in Ruskin's ideas of art as the perceptions of Theoretic (*Theoria*) beauty. As mentioned above, this conception

of beauty is distinguished from sensual pleasure and is classified into Typical Beauty and Vital Beauty. In vol. 2 of *Modern Painters*, Ruskin explains the source of the usage 'love, joy, and admiration' by adding a footnote on the word 'admiration' (vol. 4, 29). The words are taken from Wordsworth's following poem:

> We live by Admiration, Hope and Love;
> And, even as these are well and wisely fixed,
> In dignity of being we ascend.
> (Wordsworth, *The Excursion*, bk. 4, lines 763–5)

It is important to recognize the intrusion of the notions of art and beauty into the critical discourse of economics as essential to his argument. It follows that Ruskin's thesis of 'No Wealth but Life' cannot be discussed without regard to his thoughts on art and beauty. The mind of 'love, joy, and admiration' as the condition of true beauty is allegorically applied to economics as the condition of true wealth.

However, the thesis of 'No Wealth but Life' is one-sided because it relates only to the subjective conditions of Life (Mind), not to the objective conditions (Nature). For Ruskin, the concept of Nature contributing to Life is also the basis of his thoughts on art and economy. Later Ruskin gives a bird's-eye view of the integration of art and economy by the identification of six elements as useful and essential to Life. The following passage in one of his open letters addressed to the labour class, *Fors Clavigera*, is an important key to understanding the entire structure of his thought:

There are three Material things, not only useful, but essential to Life. No one 'knows how to live' till he has got them. These are, Pure Air, Water, and Earth. There are three Immaterial things, not only useful, but essential to Life. No one knows how to live till he has got them. These are, Admiration, Hope, and Love. . . . These are the six chiefly useful things to be got by Political Economy, when it has become a science. (Letter 5, 1871, vol. 27, 90–1)

Here the immaterial things 'Admiration, Hope, and Love', which Ruskin inherited from Wordsworth, appear again together with the material things 'Air, Water, and Earth', both as contributing elements to Life.

In his early art discourse, first, 'Air, Water, and Earth' are major components of landscape painting, as exemplified in the analysis of Turner, and we call them in a lump 'Nature' as the objects of artistic Beauty. Second, 'Admiration, Hope, and Love' are major components of 'Mind' as the source of artistic Beauty. This pair of concepts (i.e. Nature and Mind) makes up the world of Beauty in Ruskin's early years.

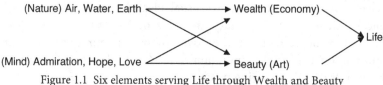

Figure 1.1 Six elements serving Life through Wealth and Beauty

In his later years, the same pair of concepts is applied to economic discourse on the world of Wealth. First, 'Air, Water, and Earth' are Nature to be protected either by or despite economic activity; second, 'Admiration, Hope, and Love' are nothing but Mind to be accepted as the moral source of honourable Wealth. The parallelism of Nature and Mind between art (Beauty) and economy (Wealth) is noteworthy.

Figure 1.1 illustrates the interactions between Wealth (economy) and Beauty (art), on the one hand, and Nature and Mind, on the other. Two human values, Wealth and Beauty, contribute to human Life through the engagement of Mind with Nature. Balance between Wealth and Beauty should be sought through social mechanism in order that Life might be best served.

In the same open letter Ruskin elaborates on each concept of 'Admiration, Hope, and Love':

Admiration – the power of discerning and taking delight in what is beautiful in visible Form, and lovely in human Character; and necessarily, striving to produce what is beautiful in form, and to become what is lovely in character.

Hope – the recognition, by true Foresight, of better things to be reached hereafter, whether by ourselves or others; necessarily in the straightforward and undisappointable effort to advance, according to our proper power, the gaining of them.

Love – love both of family and neighbour, faithful, and satisfied. (vol. 27, 91)

The concepts of 'Admiration, Hope, and Love', defined as the 'powers of life' in the thesis of 'No Wealth but Life', are expounded here as the powers of perceiving as well as creating what is valuable. Six elements in Nature and Mind are to be taken seriously in both art and economy for the betterment of life. Ruskin argues that economics, which should be a 'science of life', is in fact concerned with the distorted world of self-interest and market transaction, entailing the destruction of 'Pure Air, Water, and Earth', on the one hand, and leaving and even accelerating the extinction of 'Admiration, Hope, and Love', on the other. Economics has become a 'science of death' rather than a 'science of life'. As a result, art itself suffers from corruption.

1.5 'Ruskin's Triangle': Wealth, Life, and Beauty

'Beauty' is a term of aesthetics. In his early years, Ruskin challenged the current notion of beauty (imitation of nature for the purpose of sensual pleasure) and claimed that 'Beauty is Life'. 'Wealth' is a term of economics. In his later years, Ruskin challenged the current usage of wealth (accumulation of useful commodities for the purpose of self-interest) and insisted that 'Wealth is Life'. Thus, the trinity of Wealth = Life = Beauty is established. Ruskin's link between economics and aesthetics is the romantic notion of Life.

Referring to Figure 1.2, the equilateral triangle is called 'Ruskin's triangle' apex and with Wealth and Beauty at the other two angles. This corresponds to the right half of Figure 1.1. Although Ruskin explicitly claims in the aphoristic form only the economic thesis 'No Wealth but Life', he consistently holds the comparable aesthetic thesis 'No Beauty but Life', which is just what he means by Vital Beauty. He means that beauty exists only in life and that art for the sake of art without relevance to life does not produce beauty. Thus, 'Ruskin's triangle' integrates his aesthetic and economic theses and represents the integrated thesis that 'There is neither Wealth nor Beauty but Life.'

Before we deal with Ruskin's economic discussions, it is necessary to clarify the meanings of Life from his perspective of art because they are imposed upon his economic discourse. Three points are important: Life as a stock of capability, Life as a composition, and labour as the Life's agent as well as the aim of Life.

1.5.1 Life as a Stock of Capability

The concept of Life is interpreted as a 'stock' of the being. Unlike the utilitarian doctrine, Ruskin's conception of Life is not a series of

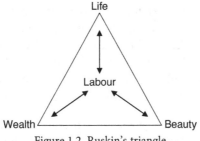

Figure 1.2 Ruskin's triangle

behaviours producing a 'flow' of pleasure, but a 'stock' of capability, functions, and character of human beings. His statement in the famous thesis that 'Life includes all its power of love, of joy, and of admiration' proves Life to be a stock of powers, especially moral powers.

Moreover, for Ruskin, the concept of Life is a normative one. The desirable life is prescribed as the maximum degree of virtue or excellence of 'being', not as the maximum net sum of pleasures and pains produced by 'doing', as the utilitarian ethics claims. The pleasure of art is produced by the exertion of the overall capability of artists and transmitted from artists to observers. Underneath art lies an ethical value for evaluating the 'stock' of human beings, which is the ethics of virtue as distinct from the utilitarian ethics of good.

1.5.2 Life as a Composition

An aspect of his concept of Life depends on the metaphor of 'composition' in painting. In vol. 5 of *Modern Painters*, Ruskin takes up the third subject matter of art, that is, 'ideas of relation', by interpreting it as 'composition' or association between various parts of the whole of the object in question: 'Composition may be best defined as the help of everything in the picture by everything else' (vol. 7, 205). True 'composition' must be the mutual 'help' conducted with the highest energy of each component. Originally 'composition' was a concept in art, but his interpretation of it in the context of 'ideas of relation' in the fifth volume published in 1860 is largely affected by his growing concern with social issues.

In the case of inanimate things, the removal of one part may not injure the rest. But in the case of animate objects such as plants, animals, human beings, and a society conceived as an organism, each portion in the structure is functionally interdependent upon other portions and insufficiency or absence of some portions injures the rest. The full exertion of functions and capabilities in organisms is defined as a condition of Vital Beauty. The notion of 'composition' also aims at the value of Unity, which is one of the types of Typical Beauty as the latent divine attributes in creatures.

The powers which cause the several parts of creatures to help each other Ruskin calls 'Life'. Intensity of Life depends on intensity of helpfulness. The absence of help means corruption and ultimately leads to death. He submits the 'law of help':

A pure or holy state of anything, therefore, is that in which all its parts are helpful or consistent. They may or may not be homogeneous. The highest or organic purities are composed of many elements in an entirely helpful state. The highest and first law of the universe – and the other name of life is, therefore, 'help'. The other name of death is 'separation'. Government and co-operation are in all things and eternally the law of life. Anarchy and competition, eternally, and in all things, the laws of death. (vol. 7, 207)

Although the notion of 'composition' is primarily related to painting, generally it means the 'relations' among multifarious elements in an object of art. A work of art is an expression of ideas concerning how to design the composition for various objects. Ruskin's hostility to anarchistic market competition was metaphorically derived from the idea of 'help' in the composition of living organisms. Competition severs the social bonds of mutual 'help' which should be the basic condition of Life.

1.5.3 Labour as Life's Agent as well as the Aim of Life

Ruskin substantiates the vague notion of Life by the concept of 'labour'. He writes in *Unto This Last:*

Labour is the contest of the life of man with an opposite; – the term 'life' including his intellect, soul, and physical power, contending with question, difficulty, trial, or material force. Labour is of a higher or lower order, as it includes more or fewer of the elements of life: and labour of good quality, in any kind, includes always as much intellect and feeling as will fully and harmoniously regulate the physical force. In speaking of the value and price of labour, it is necessary always to understand labour of a given rank and quality, as we should speak of gold or silver of a given standard. (vol. 17, 94–5)

Life as a durable stock fights against the external or internal obstacles by the use of labour based on human powers as a whole, including 'reason', 'feeling', and 'will'. The relationship between Life and labour is bilateral. On the one hand, labour (or work) is an agent of Life. For Ruskin, labour is not only a negative factor causing pains, but also a positive factor realizing a desirable Life. Hence, the concept of labour sometimes takes the place of the vague notion of Life and opens the way to the production of Beauty and Wealth through the use of Mind and Nature. These activities of labour explain what is happening in the left half of Figure 1.1. On the other hand, the concept of labour serves as the standard that evaluates the contribution to Life. Therefore, it is convenient to locate labour at the centre of the 'Ruskin's triangle' in Figure 1.2 and to explain Ruskin's ideas in terms of the interactions (shown by several arrows) between labour, on the one hand, and Wealth, Beauty, and Life, on the other.

In economic activity, Wealth is a means of contest for labour. Labour is not only toil and trouble that must be tolerated in producing Wealth, but a major force for creating Wealth for Life through both production and consumption. Labour must contribute to Life by selectively disposing of and producing Wealth to promote Life. In artistic activity, on the other hand, labour is a producer as well as consumer of Beauty, both causing the quantitative and qualitative improvement of Life.

In both economic and artistic activities, labour must be directed to the production of the pleasures of Life which are the source of Beauty. The desirable allocation of labour for life-promoting Beauty in artistic activity is a metaphorical model for the desirable allocation of resources for life-promoting Wealth in economic activity. Ruskin's underlying idea of labour in both activities is that labour must be pleasant and creative. He writes on work and pleasure in 'Pre-Raphaelitism': 'It may be proved, with much certainty, that God intends no man to live in this world without working: but it seems to me no less evident that He intends every man to be happy in his work' (vol. 12, 341). Ruskin insists that activities of art and economy must represent the pleasures of labour in contributing to Life. This is what labour as the aim of Life really means.

To summarize: The pair of Nature and Mind with their six components is essential to Ruskin's ideas of Life. All elements or components contribute to Life through the enjoyment of the values of Beauty (art) and Wealth (economy). The contribution to Life is always carried out by the medium of labour located in a social framework. A society conceived as an organic whole consists in the institutions for organizing and managing labour as the agent of Life. More exactly, labour is located in the social framework of mutual 'help' and 'cooperation', as suggested by the 'composition' in painting. In this sense, moralistic labour is at the centre of gravity in 'Ruskin's triangle' and the target of life-availing reform.

1.6 Architecture, Political Economy of Art, and Art Education: Mind and Society

Following the studies of painting, Ruskin started to work in new fields – art of architecture, political economy of art, and art education. As explained above, Ruskin's aesthetics of painting are enough to construct 'Ruskin's triangle' that integrates his views on art (Beauty) and economy (Wealth). Our next discussion of his work on the new fields can be shortened to a minimum that may supplement the foregoing account by its extension and implementation.

1.6.1 Art of Architecture

During the ten years after Ruskin published the second volume (1846) of *Modern Painters* and before he resumed publishing the third and the fourth volumes (1856), he extended his perspective on art from painting to architecture and published *The Seven Lamps of Architecture* (1849) and *The Stone of Venice* (1851–3). For him, architecture is a synthetic art comprising sculpture and painting. The reason for his shift of interest was that the public as producer and consumer of art is more accessible to architecture than painting and that ugly modern buildings tend to expel the great old styles of architecture in the current materialistic age. The study of architecture made him recognize the moral connection between art and society more firmly than the study of painting; it encouraged the transition from the aesthetics of landscape to the ethics of social relations. Thus architecture became a stepping stone from art to society.

In *The Seven Lamps*, Ruskin formulates seven normative principles for the art of architecture: Sacrifice, Truth, Power, Beauty, Life, Memory, and Obedience. The book concerns not only the technicalities of architectural styles, but also the spirit or morality of architecture. Lamp is a metaphor for indicating a right direction. His presumption that art is based on morality is much confirmed in his study of architecture. Among the seven principles, the lamp of Life unifies all the others; it means that architecture must represent the pulse of Life, not technical regularity or balance. 'They [all objects] become noble or ignoble in proportion to the amount of the energy of that mind which has visibly been employed upon them' (vol. 8, 190). This is in accord with the definition of Vital Beauty proposed in *Modern Painters*.

What characterizes Ruskin's study of architecture is the admiration of Gothic buildings and this is accomplished by the three magnificent volumes of *The Stones of Venice*. The work describes the historical changes of architectural styles (Byzantine, Gothic, and Renaissance) in Venice on the basis of the theoretical analysis in *The Seven Lamps* and the vision that architecture is a record of the spiritual activities of ages. It is not merely value-neutral historical research but also sophisticated social criticism of modernity.

Ruskin admires the Medieval Gothic style but, at the same time, he criticizes the subsequent Renaissance style for arrogance, gaudiness, and impiousness, which he regards as representing the degradation and fall of society. He superimposes a decay of morality in Venice upon the danger of culture in a modern society and warns against the modern life relating to art, morality, and society.

In Western Europe after the Romanesque style of the Medieval age (from the tenth to the twelfth centuries), Gothic architecture flourished from the latter half of the twelfth century to the fifteenth century, with Christianity as the internal motivation. Afterwards, the Gothic style was replaced by the Renaissance style in the fifteenth and the sixteenth centuries. From the modern viewpoint, which regards the Renaissance as the awakening of the human mind from medieval oppression, the culture of art represented by the Gothic was deemed as rough, barbaric, and inhuman. As a result, Christian morality, courage, and intellect, and the Gothic art nurtured by them, were doomed to collapse. What Ruskin attacks is the spirit of Renaissance architecture based on the modern point of view. As the forerunner of the Enlightenment, the rationalists in the Renaissance period attempted the rationalization of art and humanities. Ruskin remarks: 'This rationalistic art is the art commonly called Renaissance' (vol. 9, 45).

At the end of the third volume of *The Stones of Venice* Ruskin summarizes what he calls the 'theorem' of all of the volumes:

All the architects who have built in that [Renaissance] style have built what was worthless; and therefore the greater part of the architecture which has been built for the last three hundred years, and which we are now building, is worthless. We must give up this style totally, despise it and forget it, and build henceforward only in that perfect and Christian style hitherto called Gothic, which is everlastingly the best. (vol. 11, 357)

In the famous chapter 6 on 'The Nature of Gothic' in the second volume, the characteristic or moral elements of Gothic are presented as follows: Savageness, Changefulness, Naturalism, Grotesqueness, Rigidity, and Redundancy (vol. 10, 184).

The approval for crudeness, imperfection, diversity, and abundance of architectural work and the tolerance for variety of imagination and tenacity of will in the Gothic style are the expression of humility and sincerity of the human soul. Ruskin's view of architecture as a social phenomenon combines the 'cooperation' of all workers on the producer's side of architecture with the 'sympathy' of all people on the consumer's side. It accords with the view of 'composition' and 'help' in his idea of painting art. Life is an act of 'social cooperation' and all the components of Life must help each other. He finds in Gothic architecture the best style of art for representing 'cooperation'.

In the concluding chapter of *The Stones of Venice*, Ruskin expounds 'the great principle' as the core of his theory of art:

All art is great, good, and true, only so far as it is distinctively the work of *manhood* in its entire and highest sense; that is to say, not the work of limbs and fingers, but of the soul, aided, according to her necessities, by the inferior powers; and therefore distinguished in essence from all products of those inferior powers unhelped by the soul. (vol. 11, 201)

In his public lecture on 'The Unity of Art' (1859b), contained in *The Two Paths* (1859a), Ruskin defines Fine Art as the cooperative product of 'hand, head and heart of man' (vol. 16, 294). Fine Art, unlike technique and manufacture, must represent the 'whole humanity'; even if certain aspects of faculties are defective for a building's architecture, it is important that all the components help each other to attain unity within the scheme of 'composition'. How the ideas of 'composition' are designed by imagination determines a nature of art that consists in the expression of ideas. Therefore, a further analysis of 'composition' will clarify the framework of Ruskin's ideas of art and their further implications for economic discussion.

It is worthwhile to notice two aspects of 'composition': social and mental. First, for Ruskin, a great work of art must exert and exploit the whole powers of Life rather than obeying the techniques, rules, and customs of art, addressed to the privileged rank of a society. This enables the 'social cooperation' between the members of a society, including artists and workers; this is the reason why Ruskin was much concerned with art education for labour. Second, among the different kinds of faculties, in other words 'intellect', 'feeling', and 'will', there is the 'pre-eminence of the soul' compared with intellect (vol. 11, 204). 'Admiration, Hope, and Love' indicate the noble and moral aspects of the soul.

The 'social cooperation' and the 'pre-eminence of the soul' are the two principles for locating labour within the 'composition' in question. They are also the principles for substantiating both the dynamic Vital Beauty and the static Typical Beauty within the 'composition' of an artistic work. When the idea of the 'composition' in art is applied as a metaphor of economic society, the design of an economy should be interpreted in terms of these principles.

1.6.2 Political Economy of Art

The shift of Ruskin's interest from art to economics was marked by his two public lectures at Manchester, held as part of an art treasures exhibition in

1857. The lectures were published as *The Political Economy of Art* (later re-entitled *A Joy for Ever*). The audience was shocked by the unexpected event that the celebrated art critic, instead of arguing on art, delivered vehement criticism of industry at the growing industrial center of Manchester. These lectures, unlike his later works on economics proper, are explicitly concerned with the relation between art and economy and cannot be neglected if we are to understand the early view of the art critic heavily oriented to social criticism.

Although a full-scale presentation of Ruskin's system of economic thought equipped with necessary numbers of concepts must wait for his later works, *The Political Economy of Art* succeeds to describe the skeleton of an economic model. Since it directly purports to encourage art activity within the capitalist economic system, it presents a unique attempt to locate problems of art within a framework of economic model. It may be called an art-oriented model of normative economics with paternalistic control. Some characteristic views can be mentioned.

First, Ruskin argued that after a century of industrialization, economic goods necessary for survival were already sufficiently secured. It is now possible to allocate resources not only for physical being but also for well-being. This is the postulate of 'abundance' underlying his economic view (vol. 16, 18).

Second, he distinguished between economic and cultural values of cultural goods (art and science) and proposed a theme of resource allocation for cultural goods. Cultural goods, which are public goods in the modern terminology, contribute to Life in an affluent society through their production, distribution, and accumulation. He suggested that a principle of required resource allocation is not 'Utility' based on scarcity but 'Splendour' based on abundance (vol. 16, 20).

Third, he derived a paternalistic social system founded on superior knowledge and wise will from the organic conception of community. Ruskin's idea of social justice, that of 'fraternity or brotherhood', is not merely *noblesse oblige* or humanism but that of 'paternity or fatherhood' required for the ideal leader of community (vol. 16, 24).

Ruskin combines paternalism with what he calls the truth that 'the notion of Discipline and Interference lies at the very root of all human progress or power; that the "Let-alone" principle is, in all things which man has to do with, the principle of death' (vol. 16, 26). Apart from moral paternalism as the ground for encouraging art, some of the topics discussed in *The Political Economy of Art* are considered as a precursor of cultural economics.

1.6.3 Art Education

There is a group of articles and speeches by Ruskin that can be termed art education, which took place rapidly after his Manchester speech. It deals with the practical questions of how we should approach art to promote it on a national level, and its central point is the account of the influences of art on people's minds. His efforts in this field, mainly in the form of public lectures, summarize in popular terms the theory of art that he has worked out in larger treatises. It is crucial for him to diffuse the knowledge and implications of art and to appeal to the public mind all the more because the success of both art and economy are equally based on morality. I argue that his concerns for art education consist of asking how art relates to three key concepts: 'morality', 'nature', and 'society'.

First, art and morality. In his inaugural address at the Cambridge School of Art (1858b), Ruskin suggests that the great enigma of art history is that the development of art is desirable as well as undesirable; on the one hand, it is found that great art is developed only by people who delight in art; on the other hand, it is also found that the pursuit of art only for delight causes the decline of a nation. He proposes the solution:

The solution of that enigma is simply this fact; that wherever Art has been followed *only* for the sake of luxury or delight, it has contributed, and largely contributed, to bring about the destruction of the nation practicing it: but wherever Art has been used *also* to teach any truth, or supposed truth – religious, moral, or natural – there it has elevated the nation practicing it, and itself with the nation. (vol. 16, 197)

The essence of his belief is that only if art expresses the truth of Nature and Mind can it create Beauty for Life. In his public lecture on 'Education in Art' (1858a), he declares: 'Perhaps we should find in process of time that Italian connexion of art with *diletto*, or delight, was both consistent with, and even mainly consequent upon, a pure Greek connexion of art with *arête*, or virtue' (vol. 16, 145). In other words, art should not be left to the dilettantism of the rich but be combined with virtue. It is his first thesis of art education that the production and consumption of art should be based on morality.

After he moved to the study of economics, Ruskin was elected the first Slade Professor of Fine Art at Oxford University. In his inaugural lecture (1870), he proceeded from the previous stage in which he linked art with morality in abstract terms to a new stage in which he connected art with economy, politics, and social life by formulating the following tenet:

The art of any country *is the exponent of its social and political virtues.* . . .The art, or general productive and formative energy, of any country, is an exact exponent of its ethical life. ... The most perfect mental culture possible to men is founded on their useful energies, and their best arts and brightest happiness are consistent, and consistent only, with their virtue. (vol. 20, 39–40)

Ruskin asks the audience to take the thesis that art depends on morality as the most important, because it implies that we find in the laws which regulate art activities the clue to the laws which regulate all industries in economic activities. He maintains that an allegory holds between art and society, which applies the theme of art education to the theme of social reform through the medium of morality.

Second, art and Nature. The second theme of art education concerns the observation and interpretation of Nature as the essential link between art and morality. In his public lecture on 'The Deteriorative Power of Conventional Art over Nations' (1858c), Ruskin argues on the relationship between art and Nature:

You will find enough to justify you in concluding that art, followed as such, and for its own sake, irrespective of the interpretation of nature by it, is destructive of whatever is best and noblest in humanity; but that nature, however simply observed, or imperfectly known, is, in the degree of affection felt for it, protective and helpful to all that is noblest in humanity. You might then conclude further, that art, so far as it was devoted to the record or interpretation of nature, would be helpful and ennobling also. (vol. 16, 268)

This thesis relates to the effects of art through the observation of Nature ('Pure Air, Water, and Earth') on morality. Through the involvement of art with the truth of Nature, man becomes conscious of his own existence in the natural universe and develops his character of humility and devotion. It is because God stamped His figures of Beauty on the universe of Nature and made love for them the nature of human Mind. Through the artistic expression and interpretation of Nature as the determinant of Life, artistic energy and its development bring about national energy and its development. Love of Nature is the supreme condition of art, which Ruskin shares with Wordsworth and Turner.

Third, art and society. Ruskin focuses on social relations as the intervention between art and morality in addition to Nature. For him, social relations play the role of representing 'social cooperation' as the embodiment of the 'composition' of art. This constitutes the third theme of art education. He argues for the place of art in society in his public lecture on 'Modern Manufacture and Design' (1859c):

The great lesson of history is, that all the fine arts hitherto – having been supported by the selfish power of the noblesse, and never having extended their range to the comfort or the relief of the mass of the people – the arts, I say, thus practiced, and thus matured, have only accelerated the ruin of the States they adorned. . . . For us there can be no more the throne of marble – for us no more the vault of gold – but for us there is the loftier and lovelier privilege of bringing the power and charm of art within the reach of the humble and the poor; and as the magnificence of past ages failed by its narrowness and its pride, ours may prevail and continue, by its universality and its lowliness. (vol. 16, 341–2)

By changing the direction of artistic activity, Ruskin argues, we can view the peaceful and vigorous society which leans neither to the oppression of labour nor to the extravagance of vanity. Changes in the direction of both art and society are derived from the principle of 'social cooperation' which is the allegory of the 'composition' in art.

Thus, the three themes of art education, which consist of 'morality, nature, and society', maintain that 'labour', as the social agent of Life, must interact with Mind and Nature to contribute the best to Life. They in all give us a kind of summary of ideas on the 'compositions' of the six determinants of Life in Figure 1.1 and 'Ruskin's triangle' in Figure 1.2.

1.7 *Unto This Last* and Criticism of Economics

The essence of Ruskin's view on art is to relate Beauty to Life. I have argued that his conception of Life consists of the three key concepts of 'capability', 'composition', and 'labour'. Their combination entails the two fundamental theses of art: 'There is no Beauty but Life' and 'Art is based on Mind and Nature'. The reputation of Ruskin as the art critic by around 1860 was established through the invocation of these theses. However, he soon realized that the pursuit of art alone neither prevents the destruction of Life and the corruption of Beauty nor encourages the enhancement of Life and Beauty, because he found by the investigation of the history of the rise and fall of Venice that one could not solve the enigma that the development of art only causes the decline of morality. He proceeded from the recognition that art cannot be independent of economic society to the resolution that the economic system which has bought about the destruction of natural beauty and the decline of the artistic mind should be changed. He applies the structure of aesthetics to economy by developing the ethics of labour as demonstrated by using Gothic architecture as a metaphor. By the reform of the economic system, he intends to achieve the enhancement of Life at which his art theory aimed.

His economic idea is a kind of transformation of his aesthetics. Corresponding to the two fundamental theses of art, we find two fundamental theses of economics: 'There is no Wealth but Life' and 'Economy is based on Mind and Nature'. These ideas were first presented in a queer form of aphorism in *Unto This Last*, but it was in *Munera Pulveris*, a sequel to the former book, that he tried to systematize these ideas by reformulating the specific concepts of economics rather than twiddling aphorisms.

Unto This Last was published as four serial articles in *Cornhill Magazine* in 1860 and as a book with the subtitle *Four Essays on the First Principles of Political Economy* in 1862. In the preface he writes about the two objects of the book: first, to give an accurate and stable definition of Wealth, and second, to show that the acquisition of Wealth is possible only under certain moral conditions of society (vol. 17, 19). He not only challenges the fundamental assumptions of classical economics, but also severely criticizes the inhumane social institutions of capitalism justified by it.

The first essay ('The Roots of Honour') discusses the assumption of self-interest in economics. According to Ruskin, the failure of economics is its argument that the principles of social action may be determined by greedy self-interest independently of the influence of social affection. He does not deny abstract theory itself but its applicability as a solution to problems in the real world. However, classical economics pretends its theory is natural law and justifies the ideology of *laissez-faire*. He calls it the 'bastard science' different from 'real science'. With regard to social issues such as poverty, inequality, depression, unemployment, labour dispute, and environmental destruction, it is impossible to deduce rules of conduct from the balance of profit and loss based on self-interest. The solutions should be found in the judgments of justice based on social affection and self-sacrifice of people. In the real world everyone has a moral sense of justice and injustice. The engine of economic action should not be a mechanical motive of self-interest but a whole range of the human mind.

For this purpose, it is necessary to recognize the social and public importance of economic activities. Producers and merchants have the vocation of employing workers and providing goods and services to society. Their work is no less important than that of lawyers, physicians, soldiers, and clergymen who are socially respected for their unselfish contributions to society.

The second essay ('The Veins of Wealth') compares 'mercantile economy' with 'political economy'. While the first essay deals with the preferences and motives of economic actors, the second essay discusses the nature of economic systems. 'Mercantile economy' is the institution of the free market, in which entrepreneurs pursue profits primarily with the motive of self-interest, and which is the research subject of traditional economics. Instead, 'political economy, the economy of a State, or of citizens' is a desirable institution which aims at increasing the happiness of all members under the Greek tradition of government control, and which is the object of normative economics proposed by Ruskin.

To develop the idea of 'political economy', first, Ruskin denies the assumption of self-interest and starts with the assumption of the whole man consisting of 'reason', 'feeling', and 'will'; second, he refuses to be absorbed in the themes of mercantile wealth and takes life-promoting activities seriously; and third, he discards the monetary criterion and proposes the conception of Life as the standard of value. Paternalistic guidance is required for this system.

The third essay ('Qui Judicatis Terram') is concerned with the idea of justice. Whereas market competition in pursuit of wealth and richness causes inequality of distribution, Ruskin insists that distribution should be determined not by demand and supply of labour but by the idea of justice. Because the basic needs of labour are the same, the wage of labour should be a fixed amount. 'The market price of labour is the momentary price of the kind of labour required, but the just price is its equivalent of the productive labour of mankind' (vol. 17, 64). This is what the parable of the title *Unto This Last* means.

The fourth essay ('Ad Valorem') examines the basic concepts of economics, such as value, wealth, price, capital, and product, from the consistent viewpoint of the contribution to Life, and integrates all of his relevant discussions. Ruskin takes issue with the definition of Wealth (the central theme of classical economics) as useful and agreeable objects which possess exchange value, and proposes what he calls true definitions of Wealth and value. Challenging the traditional definition of Wealth, he urges the conversion from the mere possession of useful material to the possession of useful goods which can be used. For him, a focus on the accumulation of capacity is required for an alternative definition of Wealth. The reason for the change is explained by the basic idea he posits between value and Life:

To be 'valuable' is to 'avail towards life'. A truly valuable or availing thing is that which leads to life with its whole strength. In proportion as it does not lead to life, or as its strength is broken, it is less valuable; in proportion as it leads away from life, it is unvaluable or malignant. (vol. 17, 84)

Thus, on the one hand, Wealth is a stock of something valuable, but not a stock of useful materials with exchange value. On the other hand, value is

a power to contribute to Life. Therefore, as a result of syllogism, one is led
to the idea that Wealth consists of a stock of all powers and capacities to
contribute to Life and his famous thesis of economics that 'There is no
Wealth but Life'. The synthesis of the economic thesis with the art thesis
that 'There is no Beauty but Life' leads to the synthetic thesis 'There is
neither Wealth nor Beauty but Life'.

1.8 *Munera Pulveris* and Normative Economics

In 1862 and 1863, Ruskin wrote four economic articles in *Fraser's
Magazine* as a sequel to *Unto This Last* and published a book *Munera
Pulveris – Six Essays on the Elements of Political Economy* in 1872 after ten
years of intellectual struggle. In the preface, he again denies the view that
the determination of prices including wages by demand and supply is the
unchangeable law, and insists that a wise economy should consist in
a different scheme from market competition (vol. 17, 136–7). He does
not criticize classical economics for the account of how a market economy
works. *Munera Pulveris* is not descriptive, positive economics which purports to compete with J. S. Mill's *Principles of Political Economy*. Ruskin
intends a treatise on 'political economy' as normative economics. Its chief
purpose is 'to examine the moral results and possible rectifications of the
laws of distribution of wealth' (vol. 17, 144).

Ruskin tries to construct the framework of argument by focusing on the
concept of Life. 'The object of political economy is the continuance not
only of life, but of healthy and happy life. But all true happiness is both
a consequence and cause of life.' Life is defined again as 'the happiness and
power of the entire human nature, body and soul' (vol. 17, 149). For
Ruskin, Life is a normative concept in which perfection or excellence of
body, feeling, and intellect is to be pursued by all members of a society.

For all the efforts he made to formulate his vision, *Munera Pulveris*
remains the preface to a larger treatise on political economy that was never
written. Given the overall relationship between art and economics, it is
nevertheless worthwhile to examine Ruskin's economic thought by interpreting how the three key concepts of Life ('capability', 'composition', and
'labour') were elaborated and developed in the field of economics.

1.8.1 Commodity and Capability

In his discussion of Wealth and richness in *Munera Pulveris*, Ruskin
newly introduces the distinction between 'intrinsic value' and 'effectual

value'. 'Intrinsic value is the absolute power of anything to support life' (vol. 17, 153). In order that this value may become effectual, a certain power is necessary in the recipient of it. 'Where the intrinsic value and acceptant capacity come together, there is Effectual value, or wealth' (vol. 17, 154). Wealth in the true meaning involves two requirements: the production of a thing essentially useful to Life and the production of the capacity to use it.

Ruskin's shift of attention from a stock of commodity to a stock of capacity in the definition of Wealth, the view anticipated by Xenophon, is the ground for criticizing classical economics under the perspective of Life. From Ruskin's standpoint of aesthetics, Life is regarded as a stock of overall human capacity to create the pleasure of Beauty in opposition to the utilitarian flow of pleasure or happiness. Traditionally, the well-being of a nation has been represented by either the aggregate of commodities as an index of Wealth or the aggregate of utilities as an index of happiness. Ruskin's notion of capacity or capability lies between commodity and utility. In a sense, his approaches to aesthetics and economics are synthesized by the idea of the double needs of Wealth.

As shown in the interpretation of the trinity thesis (Wealth = Life = Beauty), the focus on capacity is based on the conception of Life as a stock of powers to produce excellence of human nature in economic as well as artistic activities. Art is not only a representation of Life but also a means to Life. Similarly, economy is not only a representation of Life but also a means to Life. In both cases, the trinity is established by the development of capacity. What does not contribute to the enhancement and development of Life should be excluded from 'Wealth' and be regarded as 'Illth' (vol. 17, 89).

The recognition that Wealth depends upon the capacity of human beings is heterodox in economics, whose mainstream approach is a commodity approach or a utility approach. Ruskin's idea of locating intrinsic and effectual values between both approaches is succeeded by Amartya Sen's capability approach a hundred years later (Sen 1985).

1.8.2 Composition and Cooperation

Ruskin's view of the richness or happiness of a nation is that it cannot be argued independently of distributive justice. The institution of competition motivated by the self-interest of individuals should be replaced by the scheme of cooperation based on social affection. For him, the 'composition' of the economic system is provided by imagination. This is the

metaphorical application of aesthetics to economics. The idea of 'composition' in painting is that Beauty is produced by the structural balance of the
whole consisting of interdependence between parts on the canvas, and is
now transformed into the theory of 'cooperation' and 'help' among the
members of society as an organism. As was argued in his study of the
Gothic architecture, the 'cooperation' between workers in producing art is
essential to increasing the powers of Life, and is called 'social cooperation'.

Time and Tide (1867) is a collection of Ruskin's open letters to the
labour class. Its first letter is important for it deals with the two kinds of
'cooperation' (vol. 17, 315–18). Whereas he treated 'cooperation' as
opposed to 'competition' when he first applied the idea of 'cooperation'
to the economic world, he now interprets 'cooperation' as opposed to
'mastership' in the mercantile system. 'Mastership', used also as the title
of chapter 6 of *Munera Pulveris*, denotes hideous labour-management
relations and distributive relations based on the egoistic profit motives of
employers. The principle for the scheme of 'cooperation' is social justice
based on paternalism. Thus, the idea of 'composition' inspired by aesthetics is expanded as grounds for construing Life as the countermeasure
against 'competition' and 'mastership' in Ruskin's economic thought.

1.8.3 Labour as the Agent and Aim of Life

It is the role of labour as the agent of Life that combines Beauty and
Wealth and contributes to Life in Ruskin. In this sense it is located at the
centre of gravity in 'Ruskin's triangle'. Like other key concepts, in other
words 'capability' and 'composition', the concept of 'labour' also plays
a critical role against classical economics. When Adam Smith characterized capitalist economic development, the division of labour was regarded as the institutional framework for increasing industrial efficiency.
Ruskin argues that it is not labour that is divided, but men; men are
divided into mere segments (vol. 10, 196). While workers of the Gothic
architecture enjoyed happiness of Life that consisted of the whole human
nature, the pursuit of mechanical efficiency in the dangerous, painful,
and monotonous work of factory production means a denial of human
Life. Workers cannot enjoy pleasures from factory labour and are liable
to find pleasures solely from the satisfaction of material desires.

By the latter half of the nineteenth century, the criticism of capitalism for
the alienation of labour was by no means novel. Ruskin was directly
influenced by Carlyle's religious view on the gospel of work, his originality
was his critique on the grounds of aesthetic Life: his standpoint was

a normative theory of virtue based on the idea of 'cooperation' that enables the full exertion of 'capability' at the site of 'labour'. It is Thomas Hill Green who fully developed Ruskin's artistic idea of 'composition' into the perfectionist ethics of 'common good' in a community.

In chapter 2 ('Store-Keeping') of *Munera Pulveris*, Ruskin argues about how to manage the Wealth of a nation. While Mill's wage fund doctrine that labour is limited by the size of capital may hold in the 'mercantile economy' consisting of competition, the true limiting factor in the 'political economy' with which Ruskin is concerned is moral imagination of employers.

Out of a given quantity of funds for wages, more or less labour is to be had, according to the quantity of will with which we can inspire the workman; and the true limit of labour is only in the limit of this moral stimulus of the will, and of the bodily power. ... Labour is limited only by the great original capital of head, heart, and hand. (vol. 17, 177)

In his study of art Ruskin postulated that the cooperation of 'head, heart, and hand', which constitutes the entire human nature, is the condition of great art. He now talks about 'the great original capital of head, heart, and hand', because he regards that what constitutes Life is power as a stock of the whole of human nature.

Following the definitions of Wealth and richness, cost and price are defined. In classical economics, labour means the pains and sacrifices of life and the wage is a price for the cost of toil and trouble. In contrast, Ruskin thinks that labour is an effort to create Life and wage is paid as a reward for the exertion of capabilities. 'All labour may be shortly divided into positive and negative labour: positive, that which produces life; negative, that which produces death' (vol. 17, 97). For him, the ideal economic management is to minimize negative labour and to maximize positive labour.

The theory of value he wishes to establish is neither an embodied-labour theory nor a commanded-labour theory, nor subjective utility theory, all of which are based on the assumption of 'mercantile economy'. His goal is a normative theory of 'political economy' with the criteria of contributions to Life. He offers a critical examination of various aspects of 'mercantile economy' in which monetary values prevail. He is furiously offended with the economic doctrine that wage is determined by competition, and offers his style of invective: 'I have no terms of English, and can find none in Greek nor Latin, nor in any other strong language known to me, contemptuous enough to attack the bestial idiotism of the modern theory that wages are to be measured by competition' (vol. 17, 263). In chapter 6 on mastership concerning the relations between employers and workers and between the rich and the poor, it is argued that wages must depend on moral conditions. At the heart of Ruskin's endeavours is the belief that a series of moral virtues should be respected to support the scheme of 'cooperation' in place of *laissez-faire.*

1.9 The Structure of Values

Finally, the characteristics of Ruskin's conception of morality, which lies beneath the ideas of Beauty and Wealth, should be identified. Although he tried to define his own concepts of Beauty and Wealth with much effort, he took the ideas of morality for granted without further elaboration. Although in his critical economic discourse he discusses Mill's economics, he does not refer to the utilitarianism of Mill and Sidgwick as the object of his underlying anti-utilitarian attack in aesthetics and economics. His sporadic and casual writings on morality and ethics are the sources of this inquiry.

1. In his 1882 preface to *Sesame and Lilies* (1865), he writes that the book depends on the conviction that 'there is such a thing as essential good, and as essential evil, in books, in art, and in character; – that this essential goodness and badness are independent of epochs, fashions, opinions, or revolutions' (vol. 18, 50). A belief in the universal moral values is Ruskin's fundamental attitude towards values long nourished by his religious parents at home.

2. Perhaps for the purpose of confirming the self-evident moral basis, Ruskin attaches an appendix to the end of *Munera Pulveris* and explains the 'fortifying virtues' that should counter the doctrine of *laissez-faire.* This appendix reveals the entirety of the values of Life which he implicitly acknowledges. First, referring to the four cardinal virtues since the antiquity, 'Prudence, Justice, Fortitude, and Temperance', he remarks: 'These cardinal and sentinel virtues are not only the means of protecting and prolonging life itself, but they are the chief guards, or sources, of the material means of life, and the governing powers and princes of economy' (vol. 17, 285). But he warns against neglecting the Christian virtues such as 'Faith, Hope and Charity'. When he inherited the idea of 'Admiration, Hope, and Love' from Wordsworth and defined Life as 'its powers of love, of joy, and of admiration', he had these inner virtues in mind. He refers to 'industry, frugality, and discretion' as the moral foundations of economy in the preface to *Munera Pulveris* (vol. 17, 138). They are the minimum

essentials of economic morality at the level of efficiency, which belongs to the cardinal virtues and is lower than the Christian virtues. The ethics he takes for granted is neither theory of good nor of justice, but of virtue.

3. In one of his lectures, *The Political Economy of Art* (1857), Ruskin talks about the fresco of the *Allegory of Good Government* drawn by Ambrogio Lorenzetti for the town hall of Siena (vol. 16, 54–6). This painting represents the state of the good civic government by personification of various virtues, where a monarch is surrounded by the symbolic figures of six virtues (the four cardinal virtues plus Magnanimity and Peace), and three figures of virtues (Faith, Hope, and Charity) with wings right above the monarch. Ruskin consents to the status of the three virtues as the primary values in the artistic 'composition' of the political and economic system.

4. Ruskin's work that deals exclusively with morality is *The Ethics of the Dust* (1866), a dialogue with schoolgirls. It is a peculiar parable of ethics against the background of mineralogy. By the ethics of dust he means a metaphor, in which particles of dust gather round to crystallize into various minerals. He teaches the formation of order in human society on the basis of what might be called the ethics of crystallization. The content of what he regards as morality is 'virtue'. 'The very word "virtue"' means, not "conduct", but "strength", vital energy in the heart' (vol. 18, 288). 'The essential idea of real virtue is that of a vital human strength, which instinctively, constantly, and without motive, does what is right' (vol. 18, 301). Referring to the view of a linguist, Ruskin argues that words beginning with 'V', for example, vital, virtuous, and vigorous, are interrelated. Thus, we arrive at the relationship between Life as a stock of capabilities and virtue as its evaluating value. The moral values of efficiency and justice are superseded by virtues, while justice is much more important than efficiency.

5. Three volumes of *Fors Clavigera* (1871–84), a collection of his open letters addressed to workers, are miscellanies of the ideas of his ideal society. Of all others, letter 67, a summary of his social ideas in the form of sixteen aphorisms, is noteworthy as it shows the place of morality in his entire plan of reform. For him, the most important measure for social reform is education. The gist of his view on education is as follows:

All education must be moral first; intellectual secondarily. Intellectual, before – (much more without) – moral education, is, in completeness, impossible; and in incompleteness, a calamity. (No. 12)

Moral education begins in making the creature to be educated, clean, and obedient. (No. 13)

Moral education consists next in making the creature practically serviceable to other creatures, according to the nature and extent of its own capacities. . . . Moral education is summed when the creature has been made to do its work with delight, and thoroughly; but this cannot be until some degree of intellectual education has been given also. (No. 14)

Intellectual education consists in giving the creature the faculties of admiration, hope, and love. These are to be taught by the study of beautiful Nature; the sight and history of noble persons; and the setting forth of noble object of action. (No. 15)

The words 'admiration, hope, and love', the key concepts of the 'Wealth = Life = Beauty' thesis, reappear here in aphorism no. 15 as the central task of education.

6. The essence of Ruskin's view of education is not better described than by the following passage in *Munera Pulveris*: 'True education has, indeed, no other function than the development of these faculties, and of the relative will. It has been the great error of modern intelligence to mistake science for education. You do not educate a man by telling him what he knew not, but by making him what he was not' (vol. 17, 232). Ruskin's precept of education is a corollary of his conception of Life as a stock of capabilities. Moral and intellectual education should raise capabilities and contribute to higher Life through economic and artistic activities.

1.10 Concluding Remarks

We have tried to understand Ruskin's work of aesthetics and economics as a whole by the image of 'Ruskin's triangle', or the trinity of Wealth = Life = Beauty. Our last questions are how we evaluate his economic thought and its relation to romanticism.

1.10.1 Economics of Ruskin

If we concentrate on the aspect of economics, his economics may be safely called 'Economics of Artistic Life'. This image model has two aspects. First, formally speaking, his economics largely depends on the use of a metaphor of aesthetics, at which the structure of aesthetics in terms of 'Life', 'Beauty', 'Mind', and 'Nature' is applied to the exploration of economic systems in terms of 'Life', 'Wealth', 'Mind', and 'Nature', as observed in Figure 1.1. In this enterprise, the integration of art and economy relies on the common conception of Life. Second, substantially speaking, his economics urges the organization of economy dominated by the conception of Beauty with an emphasis on the functions of 'labour', as observed in Figure 1.2. Formally as well as substantially, Ruskin's normative economics is, as it were, romanticization of economy (or *Romantisierung der Welt* à la Novalis). This approach is exactly what Isaiah Berlin termed the essence of romanticism as 'a kind of tyranny of art over life' (Berlin 1999, xi).

In view of the relationship between economics and ethics, I would prefer to call Ruskin's economic thought the 'Economics of Virtuous Utilization of Resources' in order to identify it with a distinctive status in normative economics, which is different from 'Economics of Efficient Allocation of Resources' and 'Economics of Just Distribution of Resources'. The three grand systems of ethics, Right (Justice), Good (Efficiency), and Virtue (Excellence) should have their counterparts in economics (Shionoya 2005).

I have argued elsewhere that the rise of the idea of the welfare state (new liberalism) in Britain, or the departure from nineteenth-century liberalism at the end of the nineteenth century and the early twentieth century, was not based on the ideas of utilitarian philosophy and neoclassical economics of the Cambridge School, but rather on the ideas of idealist philosophy and historical economics at Oxford, and proposed the 'Oxford approach to the welfare state' (Shionoya 2010).

In the 'Oxford approach' Ruskin and Green played the leading role and were followed by A. Toynbee, J. A. Hobson, L. T. Hobhouse, and other new liberals. While Ruskin's normative economics was founded on the conception of the artistic life, it was Green who delved into a philosophy of ethical life by developing the perfectionist ethics of British idealism. Linking Green with Ruskin is essential for the 'Oxford approach' to welfare thought. Their normative thoughts share in common the values of virtue as self-realization. The 'Oxford approach' enables us to conceptualize the economics of virtue. Although Ruskin's paternalism did not allow all workers the ability to work freely, his basic idea of reforming society on the basis of capability and cooperation can be accepted in the form of liberal perfectionism instead of elitist perfectionism.

1.10.2 Romanticism of Ruskin

The question of why art (Beauty) can play a dominant role over economy (Wealth) in Ruskin has much bearing on the interpretation of romanticism. Why does this role of art belong to the core attribute of romanticism? The 'tyranny of art over life' in itself is not the essence of romanticism; it is simply an appearance of something more fundamental. The fundamental premises of romanticism are twofold: first, what Ruskin calls Life as the 'entire human nature', which includes 'reason', 'feeling', and 'will', or 'head, heart, and hand', and second, what might be called the organic conception of 'nature', 'man', and 'society'. Art is the most easily available practical candidate for expressing the working of the 'whole human nature' through observations of nature. Hence, art, literature, and music among others became the symbolic carriers of the romantic movements. In Britain and Germany poetry (*Romantische Poesie*) played the role of the pioneer. The same role for implementing romanticism is carried out also by ethics and history because they are essentially concerned with the life of the 'whole human nature'.

Over the past two hundred years there has been a controversy around the definition of romanticism. Referring to the criteria of romanticism which were proposed by the representative authors in the debate during the past century, we have the following list: 'originality, creativity, imagination, and genius' (Smith 1925); 'organicism, dynamism, and diversitarianism' (Lovejoy 1941); 'imagination, organic nature, symbol and myth' (Wellek 1974 [1949]); 'individualism, imagination, and feeling' (Furst 1979); and 'dynamic organicism (i.e. change, imperfection, growth, diversity, creative imagination, and unconscious' (Peckham 1974 [1951]). It is not difficult to find these elements in Ruskin's writings, but it is not convincing to identify his thought with romanticism by such fragmentary features. Moreover, most of these criteria emphasize critical aspects against the world view of the Enlightenment, but romanticism as anti-Enlightenment does not consist of critical elements alone; rather it endeavours to grasp the world as a whole on the basis of entire human capability and to take a moderate course in the midst of the extremes. Therefore, romanticism is always confronted with various contradictions within itself: that is, dynamics versus statics, change versus order, progressive versus conservative, growth versus stability, imagination versus reason, creativity versus routine, fragment versus system, creation versus imitation, eternity versus perfection, etc. The German romantics called these contradictions '*Romantische Ironie*' ("romantic irony").

Although Ruskin does not talk about the term romanticism, he states that 'the real and proper use of the word romantic is simply to characterise an improbable or unaccustomed degree of beauty, sublimity, or virtue' (vol. 12, 54) in one of his Edinburgh lectures (1853a): these feelings are regarded as the holiest and truest part of our being. We now see that his favourite words 'Admiration, Hope, and Love' are identified by himself

with 'romantic', and are concerned with the aggressive aspect of romanticism urging the roles of the irrational, the imaginative, the spontaneous,
and the visionary. However, he never forgets to add the other conservative
and orderly aspects of the world in order to approach the totality of reality
with the entire human soul: 'All that you have to do is to add to the
enthusiastic sentiment, the majestic judgment – to mingle prudence and
foresight with imagination and admiration, and you have the perfect
human soul. But the great evil of these days is that we try to destroy the
romantic feeling, instead of bridling and directing it' (vol. 12, 55). At
the end of the 1850s when the final stage of Ruskin's inquiry into art and
the initial stage of his social inquiry were overlapping, he argues about the
entire human nature in the fifth volume of *Modern Painters*, paying equal
attention to art and economy:

Man being thus the crowning and ruling work of God, it will follow that all his
best art must have something to tell about himself, as the soul of things, and
ruler of creatures. It must also make this reference to himself under a true
conception of his own nature. Therefore all art which involves no reference to
man is inferior or nugatory. . . . Now the basest thought possible concerning him
is, that he has no spiritual nature; and the foolishest misunderstanding of him
possible is, that he has or should have, no animal nature. For his nature is nobly
animal, nobly spiritual – coherently and irrevocably so; neither part of it may,
but at its peril, expel, despise, or defy the other. All great art confesses and
worships both. (vol. 7, 264)

In *Unto This Last*, Ruskin uses the word 'romantic' for economic discourse:

Three-fourths of the demands existing in the world are romantic; founded on
visions, idealisms, hopes, and affections; and the regulation of the purse is, in its
essence, regulation of the imagination and the heart. Hence, the right discussion of
the nature of price is a very high metaphysical and psychical problem; sometimes
to be solved only in a passionate manner. (vol. 17, 94)

Relating to romantic irony, too, he mentions the paradoxical inconsistency
of his polymathic statements owing to his pursuit of the totality of objects,
although he does not use the German concept, but a jest, in his Cambridge
inaugural address (1858b):

Perhaps some of my hearers this evening may occasionally have heard it stated of
me that I am rather apt to contradict myself. I hope I am exceedingly apt to do
so. . . . Mostly, matters of any consequence are three-sided, or four-sided, or
polygonal; and the trotting round a polygon is severe work for people any way
stiff in their opinions. For myself, I am never satisfied that I have handled a subject
properly till I have contradicted myself at least three times; but once must do for
this evening. (vol. 16, 187)

The notion of 'polygon' is central to Ruskin's approach. He was convinced of the so-called theory of polygonal truth that the truth should be pursued in various ways from different angles because objects are many-sided, and that as a result, the consequences of such pursuit are liable to contradict each other. Ruskin attempted the romantic synthesis of knowledge, starting from the overall human soul and pursuing the total organic system of thought with regard to nature, man, and society. The result is the 'polygon' of his thought. 'Ruskin's triangle' is the simplest example of his 'polygon'. In 'Ruskin's triangle' Life integrates two other angles, that is, Beauty and Wealth. Whatever angles there may be in Ruskin's 'polygon', Life integrates all other angles.

References

Bate W. J. 1946, *From Classic to Romantic: Premises of Taste in Eighteenth-Century England*, Cambridge, MA, Harvard University Press.

Berlin I. 1999, *The Roots of Romanticism*, Princeton, NJ, Princeton University Press.

Carlyle T. 1987 [1833], *Sartor Resartus*, ed. K. McSweeney and P. Sabor, Oxford, Oxford University Press (*Oxford World's Classics*).

Cook E. T. and Wedderburn A. (eds.) 1903–12, *The Works of John Ruskin*, 39 vols., London, George Allen.

Furst, L. R. 1979, *Romanticism in Perspective: A Comparative Study of Aspects of the Romantic Movements in England, France and Germany*, 2nd ed., London, Macmillan.

Le Quesne A. L. 1998, 'Thomas Carlyle', in E. Craig (ed.), *Routledge Encyclopedia of Philosophy*, London, Routledge, Vol. 2, 205–6.

Lovejoy A. O. 1941, 'The Meaning of Romanticism for the Historian of Ideas', *Journal of the History of Ideas*, 2, 3, 257–78.

Peckham M. 1974 [1951], 'Toward a Theory of Romanticism', in R. F. Gleckner and G. E. Enscoe (eds.), *Romanticism: Points of View*, 2nd ed., Detroit, Wayne State University Press, 231–57.

Rosenberg J. D. 1986, *The Darkening Glass: A Portrait of Ruskin's Genius*, New York, Columbia University Press.

Ruskin J. 1843, 1846, 1856, 1856, 1860, *Modern Painters*, 5 vols. (Cook and Wedderburn, vols. 3–7).

Ruskin J. 1849, *The Seven Lamps of Architecture* (Cook and Wedderburn, vol. 8).

Ruskin J. 1851, *Pre-Raphaelitism* (Cook and Wedderburn, vol. 12), 338–93.

Ruskin J. 1851, 1853, 1853, *The Stones of Venice*, 3 vols. (Cook and Wedderburn, vols. 9–11).

Ruskin J. 1853a, 'Architecture', in *Lectures on Architecture and Painting* (Cook and Wedderburn, vol. 12), 53–80.

Ruskin J. 1853b, 'Pre-Raphaelitism', in *Lectures on Architecture and Painting* (Cook and Wedderburn, vol. 12), 134–64.

Ruskin J. 1854, *Lectures on Architecture and Painting* (Cook and Wedderburn, vol. 12), 5–164.

Ruskin J. 1857, *The Political Economy of Art* [included as *A Joy for Ever* (Cook and Wedderburn, vol. 16)], 5–169.

Ruskin J. 1858a, 'Education in Art' [supplementary additional papers to *A Joy for Ever* (Cook and Wedderburn, vol. 16)], 143–52.

Ruskin J. 1858b, 'Inaugural Address at the Cambridge School of Art' (Cook and Wedderburn, vol. 16), 175–201.

Ruskin J. 1858c, 'The Deteriorative Power of Conventional Art over Nations', in *The Two Paths* (Cook and Wedderburn, vol. 16), 259–92.

Ruskin J. 1859a, *The Two Paths* (Cook and Wedderburn, vol. 16), 245–424.

Ruskin J. 1859b, 'The Unity of Art', in *The Two Paths* (Cook and Wedderburn, vol. 16), 293–318.

Ruskin J. 1859c, 'Modern Manufacture and Design', in *The Two Paths* (Cook and Wedderburn, vol. 16), 319–45.

Ruskin J. 1862, *Unto This Last* (Cook and Wedderburn, vol. 17), 5–114.

Ruskin J. 1865, *Sesame and Lilies* (Cook and Wedderburn, vol. 18), 5–187.

Ruskin J. 1866, *The Ethics of the Dust: Ten Lectures to Little Housewives on the Elements of Crystallisation* (Cook and Wedderburn, vol. 18), 193–368.

Ruskin J. 1867, *Time and Tide* (Cook and Wedderburn, vol. 17), 299–482.

Ruskin J. 1870, 'Inaugural', in *Lectures on Art* (Cook and Wedderburn, vol. 20), 17–44.

Ruskin J. 1871-3, 1874-6, 1877-84, *Fors Clavigera*, 3 vols. (Cook and Wedderburn, vols. 27-9).

Ruskin J. 1872, *Munera Pulveris* (Cook and Wedderburn, vol. 17), 119–298.

Sen, A. 1985, *Commodities and Capabilities*, Amsterdam, North-Holland.

Shionoya, Y. 2005, *Economy and Morality: The Philosophy of the Welfare State*, Cheltenham, Edward Elgar.

Shionoya, Y. 2010, 'The Oxford Approach to the Philosophical Foundations of the Welfare State', in R. E. Backhouse and T. Nishizawa (eds.), *No Wealth but Life: Welfare Economics and the Welfare State in Britain, 1880-1947*, Cambridge, Cambridge University Press, 91–113.

Smith L. P. 1925, 'Four Romantic Words', in *Words and Idioms: Studies in the English Language*, London, Constable, 66–134.

Wellek R. 1974 [1949], 'The Concept of Romanticism in Literary History', in R. F. Gleckner and G. E. Enscoe (eds.), *Romanticism: Points of View*, 2nd ed., Detroit, Wayne State University Press, 181–205.

Wordsworth W. and Coleridge S. T. 2006 [1798], *Lyrical Ballads*, ed. C. De Piro, Oxford, Oxford University Press (*Oxford Student Texts*).

2

Radicalism versus Ruskin

Quality and Quantity in Hobson's Welfare Economics

Peter Cain

It has been argued that Hobson and Ruskin, who is discussed by Shionoya in the previous chapter, can be bracketed together as 'Oxford' economists (Shionoya 2010). That label is rather misleading in Hobson's case since, as the first part of this paper shows, the original basis of his thinking was a radical tradition stretching back to Thomas Paine; and the concept of an 'unproductive surplus' which grew out of that remained central in Hobson's mature thought (Cain 2002, ch. 2). As he developed his ideas, however, Hobson did put far greater stress on the qualitative side in the welfare debate. Spencer was his chief liberal guide here; but, as will be seen, Spencer's influence was far outweighed by that of the illiberal Ruskin whose own inspiration was pre-capitalist in origin. The latter half of this chapter is concerned with how Hobson managed to reconcile what he learned from Ruskin with his liberal-radical origins and, in the process, produce an approach to welfare that was quite distinct from the liberal orthodoxy that began to establish itself in his lifetime.

2.1 Painite Radicalism, Spencerian Liberalism and the Origins of Hobson's Thought

Hobson's earliest critique of capitalism, and his first step on the way to becoming a welfare economist, involved an extension of the argument of the later Mill that rent of land was the 'unearned increment' and that land should be taxed as such, and open to purchase by public bodies. Like the Fabians, Hobson claimed that monopoly power accruing to any factor of production produced rents which the state had the right and the duty, in an emergent democratic society, to appropriate and distribute (Hobson 1891). Rents could be earned by any factor of production but were now more likely to arise from the ownership of capital than from land. The whole of

Hobson's purely economic analysis of maldistribution of wealth, under-consumption, over-saving and imperialism can be derived from this early analysis of rent, as can the remedies he proposed for them. In Hobson's most complex piece of economic reasoning (Hobson 1910a) he divided costs of production into (a) costs of maintenance, which were those payments needed to keep existing factors of production in a state of stable equilibrium; (b) costs of growth, payments that would bring new factors into play or enhance the productivity of existing ones; and (c) the 'unproductive surplus' which was the result of privilege and monopoly power and was not only unnecessary to evoke growth but was also taken from other factors – principally labour – whose growth was thereby inhibited. The unproductive surplus could be redistributed by governments through progressive taxation without impairing economic growth (Hobson 1911). This was a radical, rather than a purely liberal, programme; and in assessing Hobson's thought it is worth taking a look at the history of radicalism to put his ideas in a broader context than is provided by labelling him as an 'Oxford' welfare economist (Shionoya 2010).

Although his crusade for free trade made Richard Cobden one of Hobson's enduring heroes (Hobson 1918), from a purely economic standpoint, the radical voice closest to Hobson's own was Thomas Paine, though Hobson did not appear to be aware of it. In the first half of the nineteenth century, the Painite radical movement developed against the backdrop of the vast government expenditures of the Napoleonic wars, which prompted radical attacks on the 'Old Corruption' of the aristocratic elites who ran the British state and inspired a movement for a small state and low taxation (Cain 1985; Thompson 1998). Cobden and Spencer both espoused that cause. Paine, who admired Adam Smith, had, like them, attacked aristocratic privilege and monopoly and had championed the cause of capitalism and free international commerce as emancipating the common man. What, however, marked him out as different from them were his proposals for a welfare state, in part II of the *Rights of Man* (1791) and, especially, in *Agrarian Justice* (1797) (Paine 1987).

In the latter work, Paine, who like Hobson believed in universal suffrage, based his claim for a redistribution of income on two main intellectual props. First, he argued that monopoly of land had taken away the 'natural' right that every man had to a share in it. He admitted that ownership by the few had increased productivity on the land so he did not propose to disturb that directly; rather he wanted to tax land and then compensate the masses for what they had lost through state payments which would include child benefits to promote education, old age pensions and support for the sick.

Second, and of particular interest in the context of Hobson and the New Liberalism, Paine went on to consider all accumulations of wealth, not just those arising from land, and argued that modern capitalist society produced very marked inequalities in wealth. A new hereditary poor was being created which was dangerous to social stability. So there was a case to be made for redistribution on prudential grounds. Beyond that, Paine clearly believed that much wealth was gained without effort while the poor were often exploited, so that the distribution of wealth was unjust. So, again, he argued for progressive taxation to bring about equality of opportunity through government as the representative of democracy (Philp 1989, 84–93).

Hobson, like the other New Liberals including the members of the progressive think tank, the Rainbow Circle, were well aware of Paine as a revolutionary political force but none of them seem to have been familiar with the way that he had approached the question of economic welfare (Rainbow Circle 1989, 96–8; Hobson 1910b). In fact, Paine had anticipated Hobson's crucial idea of an unproductive surplus, and he also thought, as did Hobson, that part of what was produced was always a social rather than a purely individual product. So even had there ever existed a society so perfectly competitive that no unproductive surplus was generated, a part of what was produced would always be a social product, and the state, as the representative of democratic society, would have the right to take it and use it for public purposes (Hobson 1910a, 81; Allett 1981, ch. 3). In looking back at radical predecessors such as Cobden and Spencer, whose focus was mainly on eradicating aristocratic privilege, Hobson would have seen himself as making a mighty shift from 'negative' to 'positive' liberty (Berlin 1969) whereas, in fact, he was unwittingly reviving a long-forgotten radical programme.

However, it is also important to note that, by the time his economic thought had matured, the core economic argument was interwoven with different strands of thought which shifted its emphasis away from the simple notion that a redistribution of income and wealth in favour of the poor was all that was needed to create a better society, and towards a more qualitative assessment of welfare. However, despite his Oxford education, T. H. Green and his followers probably had less influence on Hobson in this regard than the self-educated Herbert Spencer (Taylor 1992). Hobson agreed that he took something from the 'atmosphere' of Green's Oxford though it had no immediate impact on him, whereas he claimed reading Spencer's *Study of Sociology* as a teenager had a 'profound influence' on him (Hobson 1976, 23, 25; Freeden 1988, 60–4). It is also the case that much of Hobson's analysis of the social problem was set within a framework of Spencerian biologism in which the social organism was declared to be healthy or unhealthy depending on the degree to which its members were parasitic, and consumed too much for their own good, or were underfed and therefore undeveloped (Freeden 1976). Admittedly, some of Hobson's increasing stress on the importance of qualitative forms of welfare was also a product of a liberal-evolutionary train of thought that ran through Green and L. T. Hobhouse. He argued, against Benjamin Kidd and other Social Darwinists, that the competitive struggle amongst humans would in future take place more on the non-material plane than the physical; it was becoming a battle between ideas rather than one of crude economic and military strength, and was reaching the point where men could exercise a conscious control over their environment rather than blunder blindly down a Darwinian evolutionary path (Hobson 1895). Again, however, he was probably as much influenced in this direction by Spencer as by his Oxford connections since the former looked forward to a time far ahead in which work would be for life rather than life for work, and when the current individualist striving would give way to the pursuit of the common good (Spencer 1972, 260–3; Taylor 1992). Hobson's debt to Spencer is evident, too, in the fact that the latter's distinction between traditional 'militant' societies – which were warlike and enforced 'compulsory co-operation' through the state and high taxation – and the new 'industrial' societies – based on 'voluntary co-operation' through the market system and naturally peaceful and prosperous – became a key part of Hobson's own mature thinking (Spencer 1972, 149–66).

However, the argument here is that the biggest single influence moving Hobson in the direction of a qualitative assessment of wealth and welfare was not Spencer but the illiberal John Ruskin. Even if judged from a purely quantitative perspective, Hobson's concept of surplus, and the rejection of marginal analysis that it implied, would have distanced him from Pigou and the Cambridge school discussed in this book. But Hobson was also determined to put his reasoning in an ethical, qualitative frame; and Ruskin was the key figure in guiding him in that direction from the early 1890s onwards, as will be seen (Hobson 1894; Hobson 1976, 41–2).

2.2 The Pre-capitalist Origins of Ruskin's Thought

It might also be useful to peer a little more behind Ruskin's own 'Oxford' label, for what is decisively different about Ruskin was that he was looking back beyond current market society for his inspiration (Cockram 2007; Winch 2009; Hewison 2018). What he valued was what has been called 'customary' society (Macpherson 1962), one where the vast majority of people were allocated work, there was a very restricted free market in factors of production and where rewards were dispensed mainly according to status. Markets of course existed especially in urban centres, but they were carefully regulated by the authorities: production was controlled and limited, and prices and wages often fixed. This is the world of the ancient civilisations of Greece and Rome which Ruskin revered, and of their direct successor, Christianity. In his most famous piece of economic writing, *Unto This Last* (1862), Ruskin justified his own approach to the subject thus: 'The real gist of these papers, their central meaning and aim, is to give, as I believe for the first time in plain English – it has often been incidentally given in good Greek by Plato and Xenophon, and in good Latin by Cicero and Horace – a logical definition of WEALTH' (Ruskin XVII, 18).

In setting out how he would organise his ideal society in the present, he quite deliberately followed the lead of Plato's *Laws*; and he went to the trouble, late in life, to pay for a translation into English of Xenophon's book on the management of the Greek household economy, Oeconomicus, because he believed it had much to teach his contemporaries (Xenophon 1994). Religion also played a big role in his writings. Although his belief in God wavered as he grew older, Ruskin nonetheless remained convinced throughout his life that the Bible, the foundation document of the Christian religion, had been the key element in forming the British people's moral and cultural values, and that it should remain so. In this context, he professed himself perplexed by businessmen whose formal adherence to Christianity never impacted on their business decisions (Ruskin XVIII, 392–6). However, despite his artistic, literary and religious background, it needs emphasising that as the son of a successful wine merchant, who as a young man often accompanied his father on business, Ruskin knew rather more about everyday economic life than did many of the economists he attacked (O'Gorman 2001, ch. 1).

The market society into which Ruskin was born was based on the assumption that the production of wealth was an end in itself, an automatic bringer of utility in whatever form it was produced. The traditional societies he admired and wished to emulate did not despise wealth production but they thought it should be created and distributed to support non-economic ends, whether that be the Greek city-state and the Roman Empire, or a Christian commonwealth whose chief aim was to save as many souls as possible for happiness in the afterlife. Because all these societies imposed a vision of the common good on their citizens, they thought of goods and services in terms of use values, their capacity to further the ends of society, rather than the exchange values assumed in capitalist societies.

In the ancient and Christian universes, pursuing wealth for its own sake was usually seen as a dishonourable activity. Competition was often frowned on as creating division and instability, luxury condemned as diverting men from the 'good life' of serving the community. If the pursuit of honour was the driving force in ancient societies, in the Christian world, an ascetic ideal was frequently promoted as a means of bringing people nearer to God and to salvation – the monastic movement and priestly vows of poverty were outcomes of that approach to life. At the same time, although vast disparities in wealth between elites and the bulk of the population were regarded as inevitable in mediaeval times, something to be accepted as ordained by God, all professed Christians of whatever status were seen as children of God and therefore capable of salvation; and the rich were enjoined to help to save their own souls by supporting their poor brethren to live a life of basic sufficiency and to receive aid in sickness and old age (Backhouse 2002, chs. 1 and 2). A rudimentary welfare system was thus part of the Christian commonwealth.

Starting from this traditional approach to economic life, Ruskin developed a new perspective on what the good life should be which reflected his own vision of the world as an artist and art critic. Although he professed Christian values, including asceticism of a kind, he did not stress salvation in the afterlife but the creation of what he called 'happy souls' in this world. Happy souls were to be made by the leaders of society, both the traditional aristocracy and the new class of the industrial rich, embracing the creation of a community infused with the artistic ideals and practices that Ruskin had learned from Wordsworth and Turner. In Ruskin's vision, these Romantic ideals would help transform the nature of work and of production; infuse both public and private architecture with a new Grecian grandeur in order to elevate the people; and distribute what was produced in a manner that would change the stunted and starved masses of Victorian Britain into healthy and even beautiful human beings whose own capabilities could be exercised to the full. This ideal underlies his most famous statement '*THERE IS NO WEALTH BUT LIFE*', where 'Life' is based on 'Love and Joy and Admiration' and devoted 'to the creation of the greatest number of noble and happy beings'. In that world, a man was 'rich' not because he had a huge command over commodities or money but because he had led a good life and had done his best to help others to live the same way (Ruskin XVII, 105; see previous chapter).

True to this art-based vision of community, Ruskin denied Mill's claim that wealth was whatever had exchangeable value and claimed that it was an intrinsic quality of things, including non-tradeables such as fresh air and clean water, and natural beauty. He argued with passion that very few people understood what real wealth was and that the pursuit of profit in modern society often led them to produce its opposite, 'illth' (Ruskin XVII, 89, 168). In *The Crown of Wild Olive* (1875) Ruskin offered a striking illustration of the above. He vividly recalled the former beauty of the rivers and streams of a part of Surrey he knew well, and condemned 'the insolent defiling of these springs' and the 'festering scum' left on the waters now by their capitalist exploiters. He then shifted his reader's attention to a set of ugly iron railings around a public house in nearby Croydon, which had cost far more than cleaning the river would have done and served no useful purpose, and asked: 'How does it come to pass that this work was done instead of the other; that the strength and life of the English operative were spent in defiling ground, instead of redeeming it; and in producing an entirely (in that place) valueless, piece of metal . . . instead of fresh air and pure water?'

The answer he gave was that there was no profit to be gained by cleaning rivers because there was no understanding of their importance as wealth; and so some of that wealth was being extinguished. However, there was plenty to be gained by persuading Croydon publicans to buy iron railings which were 'illth' intended to make their hostelries 'more conspicuous to drunkards'. For such reasons, men were put to work in hard and dangerous conditions, dangers Ruskin underlined by reprinting a newspaper account of a horrific accident in an iron foundry. So, by inciting ignorant people to indulge their follies, capitalists robbed society of its real wealth and re-placed it with illth. The river was silently polluted; and the seller of useless iron was 'thanked as a public benefactor, and promoter of commercial prosperity'. Having offered this riveting contrast, Ruskin then concluded that 'the real good of all work, and of all commerce, depends on the final intrinsic worth of the thing you make, or get by it'. Yet the public, supported by economic orthodoxy, believed that 'business is always good, whether it be busy in mischief or benefit; and that buying and selling are always salutary, whatever the intrinsic worth of what you buy or sell' (Ruskin XVIII, 383–91).

Ruskin's central concerns are all here: that wealth was about life as a whole and not just what was produced by business; that much of what was produced was illth and destructive of existing wealth as well; that producing illth sometimes involved horrific and dangerous work practices for the employees; and that such work encouraged consumption patterns that were harmful not only to individuals but to the wider community. Generalised, vivid examples like this summed up to Ruskin's picture of industrial capitalism creating an ugly, polluted world filled with workers being exploited to produce cheap commodities in nasty conditions and consumed in harmful ways. Worst of all, their employers treated the human beings they employed as just another commodity, labour, accepted no other responsibility for their welfare than to pay their wages and could dismiss them at will. Ruskin saw this as an abdication of responsibility on the part of elites whose main aim should be to produce more wealth and less illth, helping as much as possible the poor to do work of real value in decent conditions and to realise as much of their potential as they could. To do that, elites would have to economise drastically on the use of machinery. Ruskin was not entirely opposed to machine technology, but he argued that it had increased inequality, created awful working conditions for the poor and had taken the creativity out of work (Ruskin X, 189–96: XVIII, 509–12). Rather than *multiplying* wants, as capitalism encouraged them to do, Ruskin's elite was exhorted to *extinguish* them where possible and, in so doing, remove a large part of the demand for machinery and lessen the demand for servile labour (Ruskin XVII, 423–5). It was the elite's duty not only to create good work for the poor but to cut down on the production of anything that created degrading forms of labour and encouraged harmful consumption.

Besides that, as controllers of the state, elites were to be generous in the patronage of creative work and in the provision of public goods, from parks to great architectural monuments, spending on the community before they spent on themselves. As a part of that commitment to public service, Ruskin expected his elite to provide opportunities for the poor to learn skills through setting up workshops on the lines of mediaeval guilds, run by the state if necessary. They should also do for their workforces what was done for those in the army and navy, and pay them fixed wages; and he even argued, at one point, that men should receive an income for seven years after marriage, a payment designed specifically to help them set up a home – a recommendation Paine would have approved (Ruskin XVII, 421–2). Ruskin summed up his attitudes to elites when, in a striking phrase, he asked them to combine 'a Spartan simplicity of manners with Athenian sensibility and imagination' (Ruskin XVI, 134). But he added to that a religious dimension; for a noble life, lived by Christian principles, was not just an ascetic one but the one which, because it saw the poor as children of God, allowed for the full stimulus of artistic creation to be felt at every level of society.

So Ruskin envisioned a world where far more work would be creative and cost less in terms of painful effort. Rather than discuss production in the context of a world of individuals, he was also suggesting an organic economic analysis of society, in which the lives of rich and poor were intimately related, one that paid as much attention to consumption as production, and where work was recognised as a key element in shaping lives. Judged in terms of the prevailing capitalist accountancy in which anything produced and exchanged was called wealth, and where the appalling social costs of the system were often ignored, Ruskin's elite-led economy would undoubtedly have had a lower GDP than did the industrial Britain of his day. But he was implicitly arguing that in terms of welfare – in quality of life for the mass of the population – it would be a far better society than the existing one. Indeed, Ruskin claimed that, if his regime was applied, 'in a few generations a beautiful type of face and form and a high intelligence would become all but universal, in a climate like that of England' (Ruskin XVII, 405–6) though at the expense of heavy cuts in the incomes of the privileged.

Consistent with the pre-modern origins of his thought, Ruskin had no sympathy with democracy and little with liberty. In his opinion, society should be run by the 'wise and the kind' with the 'unwise and unkind' rigorously controlled. Inequality should be reduced but through the beneficent actions of those in authority. The social costs of labour should also be reduced and its utility increased where possible: but in Ruskin's universe, there would always be many poor people and much of the work they had to do would be unskilled, hard and lacking in dignity. The rich could mitigate that by regulating their demands for goods and services that required degrading labour but they could not remove it. Social mobility was not encouraged: the lower orders should be helped to live in a more fulfilling manner but advised not to move out of the station in life in which they were born (Ruskin XVII, 248, 321, 406–7).

In sum, Ruskin's world was aristocratic at its economic base, backward-looking in terms of leadership and anti-libertarian: his notion of intrinsic value was ancient in origin and had authoritarian implications, since only those who accepted his version of what true value was would be allowed to organise the economy. Ruskin's world would have been equally backward-looking in economic structure since agriculture – which he saw as the foundation of a good life, and reflective of the natural beauty which was not only God's work but the font of artistic creation – would remain at its centre. As he grew older, Ruskin's conservatism hardened: he changed his mind about the taking of interest on loans, which he had originally thought fair, reverting to the classical and mediaeval idea that it was usury and therefore unjust.

However, though scorned when first written, Ruskin's ideas were proving very influential by the late 1890s when Hobson wrote his intellectual biography (Eagles 2011). Given the origins of his own thinking there is a deep irony in the fact that Ruskin's popularity was strongest amongst skilled workers and trades unionists: when a survey was taken of the thirty-seven Labour MPs elected to the 1906 Parliament Ruskin proved to be their leading intellectual inspiration, with William Morris, who translated Ruskin's ideas into an anarchic form of socialism, also prominent in the list. Ruskin's condemnation of a system that treated workers as 'labour' and his support for well-paid employment provided by the state could easily be translated into a vision of socialism and the backward-looking elements in his thinking put aside or forgotten. In that context, Ruskin's ideas appeared no longer archaic, as they had in the 1860s, but revolutionary. In fact, despite his revival of a Painite style of radicalism, Hobson's position looked quite conservative in comparison because of its acceptance of the market system as the basis of economic life (Matthew 1990, 16). In writing to support Ruskin's economic ideas, Hobson was trying to show that the former's critique of political economy was compatible with New Liberal welfare policies: and in doing so he was also trying to destroy the dangerously socialist Ruskin that Morris had helped to create.

2.3 Ruskin and the Emergence of Hobson's New Liberalism

It was Ruskin who convinced Hobson that society was an organism rather than simply the sum of the individuals it contained. Although the latter resisted the idea that economics was no more than a branch of ethics (which Ruskin's critique of the market often implied) he did argue strongly that economic activities had to be seen as part of a complex 'life', modifying that life and being modified by it. Ruskin was also more influential than Green or Spencer in encouraging Hobson to believe that welfare provision should be about aiming for the 'good life' rather than simply accepting consumer preferences as a given. In the 1920s, that meant Hobson sided with Hawtrey against Pigou and Robbins (Hobson 1930, 125–30) but the Ruskinian bias of his own argument then came across clearly in his refusal to accept the current 'errors and depravities of taste and appetites' and his use of the word 'illth' to describe much of what was produced in his time (Hobson 1930, 130). Moreover, his idea of how to bring the good life into being was basically the same as Ruskin's: an endeavour to give the broad mass of the population the means and the opportunities to express themselves as creatively as possible in work and in leisure.

As Roger Backhouse has shown (Backhouse 2010), within that qualitative framework Hobson was a utilitarian; and the latter also saw Ruskin in the same light (Hobson 1904, 85–6). Indeed, Hobson thought his main task as an economist was to translate Ruskin's insights, which were scattered throughout his works, into a thorough study of 'costs' and 'utility', where the main aim of policy was to reduce the first and raise the second as much as possible (Hobson 1904, 97–100). Following Ruskin, he recognised, for example, that cost as measured by money failed to account for the non-monetary costs of brutal, back-breaking, monotonous labour which made the lives of so many unfulfilling in the extreme. On the other hand, the orthodox economists' notion of utility as confined to consumption completely missed the creative aspect of work and the way in which it could transform the lives of those lucky enough to practice it (Cockram 2007, ch. 6).

Hobson had to reject some of Ruskin's most basic ideas. He had no truck with leadership by elites, whether aristocratic or otherwise, frankly embraced democracy and championed the idea of social mobility through education. At the same time, as a supporter of a reformed capitalism rather than a socialist, he was not, like his fellow Ruskinian William Morris, an egalitarian but, as we shall see, a believer in equality of opportunity, a stance that involved accepting that factors of production could receive differential payments depending on circumstance (Hobson 1904, 176–209). True to that approach, Hobson also argued that the payment of interest was legitimate in so far as it aided growth (Hobson 1904, 144–8). And, despite his belief that the good life would be enhanced if more people worked on the land, Hobson knew that Britain could never again become an agricultural society nor was it desirable that it should do so.

Since he was a Darwinian and liberal in the Spencer–Green evolutionary mould, he could not accept wholesale Ruskin's ideas about intrinsic value. He agreed with Ruskin that much of what was produced and consumed was illth, but he accepted Mill's – and later Pigou's – point about exchange determining value in the market and also believed that what was deemed valuable would change over time (Hobson 1904, 101–6). But the differences between them on this issue were not so great as they seemed on the surface. Ruskin accepted that, in a world ignorant of what wealth really was, exchange value ruled in practice. Hobson thought that, once the people were free of poverty and sufficiently educated, they would develop a common view on what the good life was. That would lead them to produce and consume only those goods and services which they had learned to appreciate had the value that would sustain that common life. Exchange value ruled in the present; but, in the future, use value would take a bigger place.

Mixing together Ruskin with Spencer, Green and Hobhouse, Hobson believed that society was evolving in a direction which allowed for greater creative freedom, a greater use of the powers of mind and imagination. The role of the social reformer was to hasten on this transformation by urging the adoption of policies which would reduce the unproductive surplus and transfer it to those members of society who needed it for growth both in material, and in mental and moral, terms. For, like Ruskin, Hobson was convinced that the expenditure of the owners of the unproductive surplus was a key factor in maintaining the degrading conditions of work and life endured by the working majority (Hobson 1914, 158). Unnecessary or excessive consumption inexorably begat degrading production and the reverse was also true. There was 'a necessary relation between getting and spending' (Hobson 1914, 294).

Hobson's attitude to machinery and its place in life was much more cautious than Ruskin's since he recognised its importance in enhancing productivity and its role in abridging wearisome labour. He knew that machinery had come to dominate in the production of many of the necessaries of life but, since these businesses often had monopolistic tendencies, it was right that the state should intervene to regulate prices and ensure decent minimum wages for the workforce (Hobson 1902, 141–54, 174–86). In the longer term, however, as excessive incomes were eliminated by taxation, average living standards rose and leisure time increased, Hobson expected that the bulk of people would spend relatively less of their income on the standardised products of the machine process and more upon individually produced commodities which would reflect the emancipation of the imaginative and moral powers he was convinced had hitherto been squeezed out of people's lives by the pressures of poverty and excessive physical toil. As he put the essence of the matter in 1901:

If social progress be interpreted in purely quantitative terms and taken to consist in the multiplication of human life at a low level of character, using an increased control over natural resources ... to supply larger quantities of common routine goods for the fuller satisfaction of the lower grades of animal wants, under these conditions an increased quantity of work will be void of intrinsic worth, the rights of individual property will continually grow, and the instincts of personal greed hold unabated sway. But if social progress implies higher individuation of tastes and a growing demand for qualitative satisfaction, measuring the greatness of a man or a nation by refinement of wants and growing complexity of character, such life will react as a demand for finer and more 'artistic' qualities of work, restructuring the rights of individual property in products and continually educating worthier motives of work (Hobson 1902, 110–11).

It is worth noting that this picture of the good life melded together Ruskin's stress on the importance of art and artistic expression with the small-scale capitalist economy that radicals since Paine had hoped to see. It is a reminder, too, that Hobson was always a believer in a mixed economy rather than the thoroughly socialised one that the Fabians proposed (Thompson 1994).

Hobson's vision of the gradual unfolding of the good life in a purified market system modified by government was alien to Ruskin's static and elite-led society and also far removed from Morris's anarchic world of plenty brought to fruition by proletarian revolution. But there is no denying the affinities between Hobson's utopian vision and theirs, or their mutual conviction that the uninhibited pursuit of profit under capitalism was incompatible with the welfare of society. Like them, Hobson was convinced that the role of machinery and of division of labour – in which, as Ruskin said in *The Nature of Gothic*, the man was often divided as well as the labour – had to be limited and far more time devoted to creative occupations, reducing the costs of work in terms of painful human effort and enhancing its utility. Like both Ruskin and Morris, Hobson had a very strong sense of the inhibiting effects of overspecialisation, both mental and physical, and his work betrays a deep longing for a society in which all would participate in the production of its routine commodities (Hobson 1914, 314) and where everyone would be able to express themselves in craft or similar kinds of work where the division of labour and its alienating effects were not experienced (Hobson 1902, 181–3, 224–37). He readily accepted that this could mean that there could be a smaller output in the new moral world compared with the old, but felt that this was an acceptable price to pay for an increase in human welfare measured by Ruskinian standards (Hobson 1914, 288, 301).

Nonetheless, as seen above, he was worried, as were both Ruskin and Morris, by the possibility that progress would actually take a quantitative path and that could spell disaster. 'We have', he claimed in 1914, 'grown so accustomed to regard business as the absorbing occupation of man . . . that a society based on any other scale of values seems inconceivable'. Previous high civilizations which had valued the good life above material possession had rested on a basis of unfree labour, but civilisation had now reached the point when, 'for the first time in history two conditions are substantially attained which make it technically possible for a whole people to throw off the dominion of toil. Machinery and Democracy are these two conditions' (Hobson 1914, 241).

Together, these forces could make industry 'the servant of all men' but only if, 'after the wholesome organic needs are satisfied, the stimulation of new material wants should be kept in check' and he continued: 'for if every class continues constantly to develop new complicated demands, which strain the sinews of industry even under a socially-ordered machine economy, taking the whole of its increased control of Nature in new demands upon Nature for economic satisfaction, the total burden of Industry on Man is nowise lightened. If we are to secure adequate leisure for all men, and so displace the tyranny of the business life by the due assertion of other higher and more varied types of life, we must manage to check the lust for competitive materialism which Industrialism has implanted in our hearts' (Hobson 1914, 242). Or, as he put it elsewhere, 'Absorbed in earning a livelihood, we have no time or energy to live.' So it was important 'to keep life simple in regard to material consumption' (Hobson 1914, 290, 315–16). One casualty of an unchecked desire for material progress would, he thought, inevitably be democracy itself. 'More leisure is a prime essential of democratic government. There can be no really operative system of popular self-government as long as the bulk of the people do not possess the spare time and energy to equip themselves for effective participation in politics.' Other forms of voluntary social interaction would also be hindered and the growth of social consciousness retarded (Hobson 1914, 248–9).

2.4 Hobson, 'Society' and Ruskin

Hobson had to accept that there were problems in meshing the needs of the individual and of society in what would remain in large measure a capitalist system. Machinery might lighten toil, and the conditions of work and pay in socialised industries would be much improved in the New Liberal welfare state, but it would still be the case that large numbers of people would be condemned to work which could offer little direct satisfaction. Also, since Hobson admitted that human beings varied greatly in natural abilities, equality was impossible. Equality of opportunity, encouraged by better education, would make it easier for many more people to attain qualifications for skilled and professional work. This would reduce differentials in pay dramatically and Hobson once claimed that, given equal opportunities, there was no reason why the pay of a bricklayer should be less than a doctor's. But usually he admitted the need for differential pay and also confessed that if people with rare skills in high demand insisted on demanding what the Fabians called 'rents of ability' then society would have to pay them. It was also the case, Hobson believed, that 'brainworkers' had greater consumption needs than mere manual workers and had to be paid more (Hobson 1914, 167–70). Shavian equality was not acceptable in a New Liberal world (Collini 1979, 134–6).

So, given that the lust for material things was so strong, how would people become reconciled to participating in this new society in which inequalities were reduced but not removed and much work was still unpleasant? Ruskin had assumed a return to a more hierarchical and deferential society in which status differences and unequal life chances were naturally accepted; but this was clearly hopelessly out of date and conflicted with the liberal tradition Hobson inherited. Morris – as Hobson rather sharply observed (Hobson 1904, 306–7) – had wished the problem away, rather than solved it, by assuming an anarchic equality and a community from which machinery was largely removed.

The problems of inequality and the class divisions and conflicts to which it gave rise had, of course, exercised liberal thinkers long before Hobson. What Green, Mill and Spencer had hoped to see was the spontaneous growth of what was called 'altruism', an increasing consciousness of the interdependence of society which, it was assumed, would induce people to behave with greater awareness of the social benefits and consequences of their actions and modify their behaviour accordingly (Collini 1991, esp. ch. 2). Hobson took this line of thinking much further by postulating that society was an organism with a life of its own, independent of the individuals who composed it, and that the individuals within society would lead fulfilling lives the more they could recognise that. At this juncture, Hobson developed the notion that society was an organism to a point where few of his liberal colleagues could follow him (Hobhouse 1964, 68). There is also a strong possibility that, in moving so far in this direction, he was, whether consciously or not, still under Ruskin's influence.

Hobson admitted that the 'growing recognition on the part of individual workers, that the structure of society establishes a strong community of interests, will no doubt supply some incentive to each to do his fair share to the necessary work'. But that might not be sufficient to rouse 'the selfishness or sluggishness of feebler personalities'. Then in a passage which shows the influence of both Ruskin's argument that the prestige of different occupations should be measured by the extent to which they served a social cause rather than pursue gain and of Hobson's own brand of evolutionary

Idealism, he claimed that 'the social will means more than the addition of separately stimulated individual wills' and went on to claim that it would in future inspire an '*esprit de corps*, a corporate spirit of service capable ... of evoking an enormous volume of united effort' and 'stimulating those that are weaker and raising them to a decent level of effort, reducing dissension, and importing conscious unity of action into the complex processes of co-operation' (Hobson 1914, 302–3).

Hobson applied this reasoning directly to the mechanised industries which would be socialised in the new commonwealth. Here he was thinking along the same lines as Ruskin when the latter argued that, to be regarded as honourable men, capitalists would have to show the same devotion to the public good as the military and other professions were capable of (Ruskin XVII, 36–9). Hobson went further, claiming that what was merely routine or dull or distasteful from the standpoint of the mere individual might be full of 'interest and variety' to Society conceived as an entity in itself. 'Once we accept the view of Society not as a mere set of social institutions, or a network of relations, but as a collective personality, the great routine industrial processes become the vital functions of this collective being, interesting to that being alike in their performance and their product' (Hobson 1914, 306).

Individuals were to Society as individual cells were to the human body. The whole was greater than the parts: but, Hobson pointed out, it was only at this stage of evolution, when mind was becoming conscious of itself, that it was possible to grasp the significance of that. He believed that it was because people now had an inkling of this wider social will that they were willing to accept limitations on their own activities when they recognised that they were motivated by selfishness. Once it was realised that Society 'has a unity and a life of its own ... the so-called sacrifices we are called upon to make for the larger life will be considered no longer encroachments on but enlargements of our personality'. And it was vital that people should come to recognise Society in this way because this is 'the spirit of social reform'. Reform would be an impossibility if Society were thought of as merely an abstraction. 'For an abstraction is incapable of calling forth our reverence, regard and love. And until we attribute to Society such a form and degree of "personality" as can evoke in us those interests and emotions which personality alone can win, the social will not be able to perform great works' (Hobson 1914, 309).

How does this square with Hobson's repeated insistence, derived from both Ruskin and his liberal predecessors, on the need for individuality of imaginative and artistic expression in the unfolding social drama? There is no doubt that Hobson thought that free expression was a necessary part of social progress and he frequently worried, for example, that the municipal provision of libraries and other amenities, however generally desirable, might inhibit individual effort. He was also concerned to argue that, as social reform took place, the share of publicly directed enterprise in total output would not increase. However, there can be no doubt that Hobson promoted the idea of individuality of expression and enterprise not for its own sake but because it was conducive to the healthy growth of his ideal society. He remained adamant that the 'rights and interests of society are paramount: they override all claims of individuals to liberties which contravene them' (Hobson 1914, 303–4).

Hobson's liberal Hegelianism may seem very remote from Ruskin's own view of organic society, but the kind of super-entity that Hobson described here may actually have been influenced by Ruskin's vision of the elite-run state. For that, ultimately, owed its moral authority to the fact that its source of power and inspiration was a Christian God who, while granting mankind a high degree of creative freedom, also demanded worship, obedience and humility as the price of that freedom. It is in that context that Ruskin considered how society might view the low-grade, even humiliating, tasks that had to be done even in his new moral world. For, if undertaken in a certain spirit, 'such work might be the holiest of all'. And he called on men and women to live by the Christianity they professed and to 'adopt some disagreeable and despised, but thoroughly useful, trade' for the sake of the community (Ruskin XVII, 407). From that perspective, Hobson's 'Society' was the secular and evolutionary equivalent of Ruskin's Christian commonwealth.

2.5 Conclusion

As is so often the case in reading Hobson, it is difficult to be sure whether the good society would simply emerge inexorably, with Hobson acting as a humble intellectual midwife, or to what extent its development would depend upon the accidents of politics. But it is reasonably certain that Hobson believed that, although the vested propertied interests could stave off reform, especially through imperialism for a while, in the long run progress of the kind he had outlined was inevitable. He was frank and unapologetic about the teleological bent of his work (Hobson 1902, 66, 282–3) and was convinced that he was marching in step with the evolving common sense of the common man (Hobson 1914, 319–22).

As suggested at the beginning of this paper, a good understanding of the basis of Hobson's welfare economics can be derived simply from looking at what he took from his liberal and radical predecessors. But, as I have tried to show, Hobson thought it vital to add to that a Ruskinian dimension, a qualitative element, one that painted a picture of the good life for the community inspired by art and creativity rather than simply worried itself about how to increase incomes or to encourage equality of opportunity. In doing this, Hobson distanced himself very clearly from the emerging liberal orthodoxy discussed in other chapters of this book. It is arguable, however, that in doing so, he veered towards a view of 'Society' as an organism which, partly under Ruskin's influence, took him from a truly liberal path (Allett 1990).

References

Allett, John. 1981. *New Liberalism: The Political Economy of J. A. Hobson*. Toronto: Toronto University Press.

Allett, John. 1990. 'The Conservative Aspect of Hobson's New Liberalism', in Michael Freeden, ed. *Reappraising J. A. Hobson: Humanism and Welfare*. London: Unwin Hyman, 74–99.

Backhouse, Roger E. 2002. *The Penguin History of Economics*. London: Penguin Press.

Backhouse, Roger E. 2010. 'J. A. Hobson as a Welfare Economist', in Roger E. Backhouse and Tamotsu Nishizawa, eds. *No Wealth but Life: Welfare Economics and the Welfare State in Britain, 1880–1945*. Cambridge: Cambridge University Press, 114–35.

Berlin, Isaiah. 1969; 1958. 'Two Concepts of Liberty', in *Four Essays on Liberty*. Oxford: Oxford University Press, 118–72.

Cain, Peter J. 1985. 'Hobson, Wilshire and the Capitalist Theory of Capitalist Imperialism', *History of Political Economy* 17, 455–60.

Cain, Peter. 2002. *Hobson and Imperialism: Radicalism, New Liberalism and Finance, 1887–1938*. Oxford: Oxford University Press.

Cockram, Gill G. 2007. *Ruskin and Social Reform: Ethics and Economics in the Victorian Age*. London: I. B. Taurus.

Collini, Stefan. 1979. *Liberalism and Sociology: L. T. Hobhouse and Political Argument in England, 1880–1914*. Cambridge: Cambridge University Press.

Collini, Stefan. 1991. *Public Moralists: Political Thought and Intellectual Life in Modern Britain, 1850–1930*. Oxford: Oxford University Press.

Eagles, Stuart. 2011. *After Ruskin: The Social and Political Legacies of a Victorian Prophet, 1870–1920*. Oxford: Oxford University Press.

Freeden, Michael. 1976. 'Biological and Evolutionary Roots of the New Liberalism in England'. *Political Theory* 4, 471–90.

Freeden, Michael, ed. 1988. *J. A. Hobson: A Reader*. London: Unwin Hyman.

Hewison, Robert. 2018. *Ruskin and His Contemporaries*. London: Pallas Athene.

Hobhouse, L. T. 1964; 1911. *Liberalism*. Oxford: Oxford University Press.

Hobson, J. A. 1891. 'The Law of the Three Rents', *Quarterly Journal of Economics* 5, 263–88.

Hobson, J. A. 1894. 'The Subjective and the Objective View of Distribution', *Annals of the American Academy of Political and Social Science* 4, 378–403.

Hobson., J. A. 1895. 'Mr. Kidd's "Social Evolution"', *American Journal of Sociology* 2, 299–312.

Hobson, J. A. 1902; 1901. *The Social Problem: Life and Work.* London: James Nisbet.

Hobson, J. A. 1904; 1898. *John Ruskin: Social Reformer.* London: James Nisbet.

Hobson, J. A. 1910a; 1909. *The Industrial System: An Inquiry into Earned and Unearned Income.* London: Longman, Green.

Hobson, J. A. 1910b. *The Modern Outlook: Studies of English and American Tendencies.* London: Herbert and Daniel.

Hobson, J. A. 1911. *The Science of Wealth.* London: Williams and Norgate.

Hobson, J. A. 1914. *Work and Wealth: A Human Valuation.* London: Macmillan.

Hobson, J. A. 1918. *Richard Cobden: The International Man.* New York: Henry Holt.

Hobson, J. A. 1930. *Wealth and Life: A Human Valuation.* London: Macmillan.

Hobson, J. A. 1976; 1938. *Confessions of an Economic Heretic.* Brighton: Harvester Press.

Macpherson, C. B. 1962. *The Political Theory of Possessive Individualism.* Oxford: Oxford University Press.

Matthew, H. G. C. 1990. 'Hobson, Ruskin and Cobden', in Michael Freeden, ed. *Reappraising J. A. Hobson: Humanism and Welfare.* London: Unwin Hyman, 11–30.

O'Gorman, Francis. 2001. *Late Ruskin: New Contexts.* Aldershot: Ashgate.

Paine, Thomas. 1987. *The Thomas Paine Reader.* M. Foot and I. Kramnick, eds. London: Penguin Books.

Philp, Mark. 1989. *Paine.* Oxford: Oxford University Press.

Rainbow Circle. 1989. *Minutes of the Rainbow Circle, 1894–1924.* M. Freeden, ed. London: Royal Historical Society.

Ruskin, John. 1903–12. *The Works of John Ruskin.* E. T. Cook and A. Wedderburn, eds. 39 vols. London: George Allen.

Shionoya, Yiuchi. 2010. 'The Oxford Approach to the Philosophical Foundations of the Welfare State', in Roger E. Backhouse and Tamotsu Nishizawa, eds. *No Wealth but Life: Welfare Economics and the Welfare State in Britain, 1880–1945.* Cambridge: Cambridge University Press, 91–113.

Spencer, Herbert. 1972. *On Social Evolution.* J. Y. D. Peel, ed. Chicago: Chicago University Press.

Taylor, Michael W. 1992. *Men versus the State: Herbert Spencer and Late Victorian Individualism.* Oxford: Clarendon Press.

Thompson, Noel. 1994. 'Hobson and the Fabians: Two Roads to Socialism in the 1920s', *History of Political Economy* 26, 203–20.

Thompson, Noel. 1998. *The Real Rights of Man: Political Economies for the Working Class, 1775–1850.* London: Pluto Press.

Winch, Donald. 2009. *Wealth and Life: Essays on the Intellectual History of Political Economy in Britain, 1848–1914.* Cambridge: Cambridge University Press.

Xenophon. 1994. *Oeconomicus: A Social and Historical Commentary.* Sarah Pomeroy, ed. Oxford: Clarendon Press.

3

Alfred Marshall on Progress and Human Wellbeing*

Tamotsu Nishizawa

3.1 Introduction: Wealth and Wellbeing

Welfare economics is typically described as 'Pigovian' and 'Paretian' rather than 'Marshallian', but its roots can plainly be traced back to Alfred Marshall and Henry Sidgwick (Backhouse 2006; Medema 2006). It is also common to restrict attention to economic welfare (not welfare in general), to what John Hicks later called 'economic welfarism', thus making 'the Welfarist fence' (Hicks 1959, viii–ix) as will be seen in the later chapters. This chapter, however, aims to show what 'welfare' and 'wellbeing' were in fact taken to mean in Marshall's economic writings including his unpublished notes on 'Progress': it argues that Marshall was more concerned with welfare in general, in other words, with 'general wellbeing' or 'human wellbeing', which is far more commonly used in his economic thought. He wrote, in *Principles of Economics*, 'the spirit of the age' induces a closer attention to 'the question whether our increasing wealth may not be made to go further ... in promoting the general wellbeing' (Marshall 1961a, 85).

Marshall further explained in *Industry and Trade* that most Western countries 'can now afford to make increased sacrifices of material wealth for the purpose of raising the quality of life throughout their whole population' (Marshall 1919, 5). This seems to be a basis of his thought about economic wealth and human wellbeing. Marshall preferred the word 'wellbeing' to 'welfare' for true human happiness, partly because it fitted with his organic thinking, and because it more includes non-economic

* This work has been supported by the Japan Society for the Promotion of Science, Kakenhi (18K01533).

welfare.[1] The chapter will show how Marshall thought of 'welfare' and 'wellbeing' in relation to the 'quality of life' and 'standards of life', which cannot be estimated and measured by only economic and material wealth.[2]

As is well known, when Marshall had to decide whether to devote his life to psychology or economics in about 1871–2, 'economics grew and grew in practical urgency, *not so much in relation to the growth of wealth as to the quality of life*' (Whitaker 1996, II, 285, emphasis added). For him, 'wealth exists only for the benefit of mankind . . . its true measure lies only in the contribution it makes to human well-being' (quoted in Pigou 1925, 366).

Rather than limiting general welfare to economic welfare as Pigou did in the opening chapter of *The Economics of Welfare*, Marshall's ideas on wealth and welfare in general seem closer to what Hicks tried to do after his 'Non-welfarist Manifesto', that is, 'transition from Utility to the more general good, Welfare itself'.[3] Marshall's ideas about wellbeing are quite different from those of Pigou, who argued that the economist's concern lies not with welfare in general but with that part of general welfare which he calls economic welfare (utilities). As will be seen in the next section, for him, 'the term "economic progress" is narrow'; the economic aspect could be separated only temporarily and provisionally.[4] As has been shown elsewhere (Caldari and Nishizawa 2014, 2020b), Marshall's ideas on wellbeing cannot be reduced to his welfare economic analysis (based on the consumer's surplus), or the welfare arguments on taxes and bounties developed mainly in Book V of *Principles of Economics* (see also Groenewegen 2010). As Dardi has put it, Marshall's welfare economic

---

[1] See footnote 5 for what Marshall originally meant by 'wellbeing'.

[2] This point has been made more recently in *The Quality of Life* (Nussbaum and Sen 1993).

[3] Pigou, in the first chapter on 'Welfare and Economic Welfare' (*The Economics of Welfare*), attempted to limit the subject matter to 'that part of social welfare that can be brought . . . into relation with the measuring-rod of money', that is, 'economic welfare' (Pigou 1920, 10–11). As Hicks underlines, 'economic welfarism' has taken its origin from here. However, in his 'Non-welfarist Manifesto', Hicks wrote: '*the line between Economic Welfarism and its opposite . . . is concerned with transition from Utility to the more general good, Welfare itself*' (Hicks 1959, ix, emphasis added). Hicks seemed to prefer Pigou's earlier title *Wealth and Welfare*, which was 'much better' than the later and more celebrated title *The Economics of Welfare*, which could be interpreted as 'the Welfare (or Utility) Approach to the Theory of Wealth' (quoted in Suzumura 2013, 349–50). For Hicks's 'Non-welfarism Manifesto' or 'Hicks's farewell to economic welfarism', see Suzumura's chapter in this volume.

[4] Marshall wrote: 'the progressive nature of man is one whole. It is only temporarily and provisionally that we can with profit isolate for study the economic side of his life; and we ought to be careful to take together in one view the whole of that side' (1961a, 85). 'In economics we deal with the whole of man's nature . . . it must be history as a whole. We need more than economic history . . . we want a history of man himself, and economic history as contributing to that' (1897, 299).

theory constitutes 'only one chapter, and not even a very important one' in his evolutionary economics (Dardi 2010, 409).

For Marshall 'the Mecca of the economist lies in economic biology': his approach was biological and organic, not mechanical. 'The main concern of economics is with human beings who are impelled . . . to change and progress' (1961a, xv). This chapter aims to show a broader perspective of a more comprehensive reasoning of welfare and wellbeing, in other words the raising of quality of life, standards of life, and how 'the economic, as well as the moral, wellbeing of the masses of the people' could be attained in Marshall's ideas on 'Progress' and the 'organic life-growth' (1961b, 63; 1961a, 48).[5]

3.2 'Progress in Relation to Standards of Life'

'Progress' is at the core of Marshall's economics and economic thought, for he believed that economic problems are not mechanical, but concerned with 'organic life and growth' ('organic life-growth') (1961b, 63), from which human welfare and 'economic and moral wellbeing' cannot be separated. While *Principles of Economics* remains as 'a general introduction to the study of economic science', similar to Roscher's *Foundations* (*Grundlagen*) (1961a, xii), the volume concluded with a chapter titled 'General Influences of Economic Progress (on Value)'. In the fifth edition he further added a chapter on 'Progress in Relation to Standards of Life'. These give the *Principles* a historical and ethical colouration (economic ethology, economic sociology), increasing the emphasis on 'organic life and growth', which cannot be estimated only by economic or material wealth.[6]

---

[5] As to 'wellbeing', Marshall wrote in the chapter on 'Organization of Industry' (*The Economics of Industry*): 'A body is said to be highly *organized* when each part has its own work to perform, when by performing this work it contributes to the wellbeing of the whole, so that any stopping of this work injures the whole; while, on the other hand, each part depends for its own wellbeing on the efficient working of the other parts' (Marshall and Marshall 1879, 45–6). Again in the chapter on 'Industrial Organization' (*Principles*): 'the development of the organism, whether social or physical, involves an increasing subdivision of functions between its separate parts . . . Each part gets . . . to depend for its wellbeing, more and more on other parts, so that any disorder in any part of a highly-developed organism will affect other parts also' (1961a, 241).

[6] Referring to the chapters on the growth of free industry and of economic science (fourth edition), Marshall wrote that the main aim is to emphasize the notion that 'economics is a science of life', and is akin to biology rather than mechanics (1898, 8–9), offering a view continuous with that of classical tradition, but differing in the stress laid on 'organic life-growth' (1961b, 63). See, e.g., Schumpeter (1951); some chapters in Shionoya and Nishizawa (2008).

Marshall conceived that 'the progress of man's nature' (character) was 'the centre of the ultimate aim of economic studies' (1961b, 75).[7] Central to this was the interaction between 'organic life-growth', involving circumstances (economic wellbeing) and character formation (moral wellbeing). These two sides of organic growth cannot be separated.

Partly through the suggestions of biological study, the influence of circumstances in fashioning character is generally recognized as the dominant fact in social science. Economists have now learnt to take a larger and more hopeful view of the possibilities of human progress. *The human will, guided by careful thought, can so modify circumstances as largely to modify character; and thus to bring about new conditions of life still more favourable to character; and therefore to the economic, as well as the moral, wellbeing of the masses of the people.* (1961a, 48, emphasis added)

These ideas lie at the heart of the economic system Marshall tried to establish, for 'Progress' would eliminate poverty and provide material means for all the people to develop their faculties and activities. His message was repeated when he wrote of 'the distant goal where the opportunities of a noble life may be accessible to all' (e.g. 1897, 311).[8]

Elected as Professor of Political Economy in the University of Cambridge in December 1884, Marshall was asked to address the Industrial Remuneration Conference towards the end of January 1885; the Conference discussed the best means for a more equal distribution in the poverty midst plenty of the 1880s. He concluded his speech as follows, referring to 'the first aim of every social endeavour':

However great may be our distrust of forcible socialism, . . . no one can lay his head on his pillow at peace with himself, who is not giving of his time and his substance to diminish the number of the outcasts of society, and to increase the number of those who can earn a reasonable income and have the opportunity of living, if they will it, a noble life. (1885a, 66)

Marshall devoted his life to the problems of poverty, that is, practical affairs. This long message (of a few pages) in the Remuneration Conference is repeated in the same words, used for the last concluding paragraphs of his final published book, *Money, Credit and Commerce*. It means that his

---

[7] For the attention given to 'human character', see the chapter by Raffaelli on 'Character and Capabilities' in Raffaelli et al. (2006).

[8] E.g., the concluding part of 'The Old Generation of Economists and the New'; the final part of *Industry and Trade*, 'Possibilities of the Future'. And the final phrase of Marshall's inaugural address, 'The Present Position of Economics': 'how far it is possible to open up to all the material means of a refined and noble life' (Pigou 1925, 174).

basic ideas for the aims of social endeavour stayed throughout his life, to be further developed in his final volume on 'Progress'.[9]

As stated in the beginning of the *Principles*, the hope that poverty may gradually be extinguished derives much support from 'the steady progress of the working classes' during the nineteenth century. Wages had risen and education had been improved and, more generally, many artisans had ceased to belong to the 'lower classes'. This progress caused the question 'whether it is really impossible that all should start in the world with a fair chance of leading a cultured life, free from the pains of poverty' (1961a, 3–4); which was being pressed to the front by the growing earnestness of the age, and it was called 'the spirit of the age' by Edgeworth in his review of the *Principles* (in Groenewegen 1998, 12). This was a background of the welfare economics in the making, as exemplified in the Preface of Pigou's *Economics of Welfare*.

Marshall expressed his opinions on the progress of man's economic conditions in chapter xii, 'General Influences of Economic Progress' (Book VI): progress was fast improving the condition of the great body of the working classes. The statistics and records all indicated that middle-class incomes were increasing faster than those of the rich; the earnings of artisans were increasing faster than those of the professional classes, and the wages of healthy and vigorous unskilled labourers were increasing faster even than those of the average artisan (1961a, 687). From the time of Political Arithmetic in the seventeenth century onwards 'a constant and nearly steady increase' was found in the amount of accumulated wealth per head of the population: 'Man . . . has acquired a greater "telescopic" faculty' (1961a, 680).

In Marshall's view, though the inequalities of wealth were often exaggerated, this did not imply acquiescence to the present inequalities of wealth, which were a serious flaw in economic organization. While it was impossible to raise all earnings beyond the level of well-to-do artisan families, it was certainly desirable that those whose earnings were below that level should have their earnings raised, even if this meant reducing the earnings of those who were above it (1961a, 713–14).

Another thing is that prompt action was needed in regard to the large 'Residuum' of persons who were physically, mentally, or morally incapable of doing a good day's work with which to earn a good day's wage. The system of economic freedom is the best for those in good health of mind and body, but the Residuum cannot turn it to good account (1961a, 714).

---

[9] See Caldari and Nishizawa (2016) and (2020a).

Thus Marshall insisted that the most urgent steps in relation to the Residuum were regular school attendance in decent clothing, and with clean and fairly well-fed bodies. In case of failure 'the parents should be warned and advised: as a last resource the homes might be closed or regulated with some limitation of the freedom of the parents'. The expense would be great but there was 'no other so urgent need for bold expenditure. It would remove the great canker that infects the whole body of the nation' (1961a, 714–15).[10]

Then, discussing unskilled labour, he argued that machinery and mechanical progress, through the growth of national dividend, brought wages of unskilled labour that had risen faster than those of any other (1961a, 716). The poorer classes had derived a greater real benefit from economic progress on its mechanical and other sides.

In this context Marshall argues that the happiness of life, so far as it depends on material conditions, may be said to begin when income is sufficient to yield the *barest* necessaries of life; and then, an increase by a given percentage of the income will increase that happiness by about the same amount. This hypothesis leads to the conclusion that an increase by (say) a quarter of the wages of the poorer class of *bona fide* workers adds more to 'the sum total happiness' – which corresponds to what Pigou later called economic welfare – than an increase by a quarter of incomes of an equal number of any other class. It arrests positive suffering, and active causes of degradation, and it opens the way to hope. It is 'the duty of society to endeavor to carry yet further an increase of wellbeing which is to be obtained at so low a cost' (1961a, 717).[11]

Striving for mechanical progress would diminish the supply of unskilled work in order that the average income and the share of unskilled labourer might rise faster. So as to fit more of the children of the unskilled for higher work, 'education must be more thorough'. It is to educate 'character,

---

[10] Marshall wrote to Wescott (24 January 1900; Whitaker 1996, II, 263), summarizing the sources of industrial weakness and 'only one effective remedy': it is 'to improve the education of home life, and the opportunities for fresh-air joyous play of the young'. Then 'the Residuum should be attacked in its strongholds. We ought to expend more money, and with it more force, moral and physical, in cutting off the supply of the people unable to do good work, and therefore unable to earn good wages.'

[11] Marshall aimed at increasing the 'sum total happiness' ('Three Lectures on Progress and Poverty', 1883: 'If this class is too poorly paid, the redistribution increases the sum total of human happiness without violence' (192)); he held that the 'hurt' caused by raising 1,000 pounds by levies of 20 pounds from each of 50 incomes of 200 pounds is 'unquestionably greater' than that caused by taking it from a single income of 10,000 ('National Taxation after the War', 1917). See 'The Equitable Distribution of Taxation' (1917) in Pigou 1925, 348. (See Edgeworth in Pigou 1925, 71.)

faculties and activities'; so that the children even of those parents who are not thoughtful themselves, may have a better chance of being trained up to become thoughtful parents of the next generation. 'To this end public money must flow freely. And it must flow freely to provide fresh air and space for wholesome play for the children in all working-class quarters.' Thus 'the State seems to be required to contribute generously and even lavishly to that side of the wellbeing of the poorer working class which they cannot easily provide for themselves' (1961a, 717–18).

The main reason why Marshall, as an economist, wanted to eliminate poverty was because it caused degradation: 'the destruction of the poor is their poverty' (1961a, 3). In the world's history, he remarked, there has been 'one waste product, so much more important than all others', that is called 'THE WASTE PRODUCT'. It was the higher abilities of many of the working classes: 'the latent, the undeveloped, the choked-up and wasted faculties for higher work, that for lack of opportunity have come to nothing' (1889, 229). In the early 'Lectures to Women' (1873b), he wrote that man is 'the finest instrument of production in the world', 'the most important productive machine'; therefore, 'promote education at the expense of capital. Educate first; attend to its effects on capital afterwards.' 'We must regard a man as intelligent capital' and 'mental and moral capital' (Raffaelli et al. 1995, 98, 117–19). In the *Principles* Marshall also stressed the importance of education, using a subheading of 'Education National Investment' (1961a, 216).[12]

Economic conditions affect human life and its influence on character improves the people's qualities and elicits 'latent faculties' (i.e. it raises efficiency and wellbeing). In the *Principles*, studying the agents of production, Marshall says: 'If the character and powers of nature and of man be given, the growth of wealth and knowledge and organization follow from them.' From every point of view 'man is the centre' of the problem of production, consumption as well as distribution and exchange. 'The growth of mankind in numbers, in health and strength, in knowledge, ability, and in richness of character is the end of all our studies' (1961a, 139). As mentioned above, 'the progress of man's nature' or character was 'the centre of the ultimate aim of economic studies'. The 'study of man' was more important than a 'study of wealth' (1961a, 1).

Marshall's passage to economics from psychology (ethics, philosophy) is well known. In a letter to James Ward (23 September 1900), explaining how

---

[12] Given that these lectures were addressed to women, it is natural to wonder whether he used 'man' to mean 'mankind' or whether he did mean men and not women.

he left his home of mental science for economics, he wrote: 'the increasing urgency of economic studies as a means toward human wellbeing grew upon me' (Whitaker 1996, II, 285). The new vocation as reluctant economist answered Marshall's pressing need to know 'how far . . . the conditions of life of the British (and other) working classes generally suffice for fullness of life', for the realization of 'the possibilities of the higher and more rapid development of human faculties' disclosed by the 'fascinating inquiries' of psychology. Near the end of his life, he said again: 'If I had to live my life over again I should have devoted it to psychology. Economics has too little to do with ideals' (Keynes 1924, 171, 200).[13]

In his enthusiasm for moral progress, Marshall believed that the progress of man and society would eventually obliterate the distinction between the working man and the gentleman, matching with his views on the prospectiveness and 'telescopic' faculty of the working classes. The decisive factor was the influence of occupation on character: since 'work, in its best sense, the healthy energetic exercise of faculties, is the aim of life, is life itself'; ideally no man 'should have any occupation which tends to make him anything else than gentleman' (1873a, 114–15). Man's character is moulded by his everyday work. Man's 'character is being formed by the way in which he uses his faculties in his work', by the thoughts and feelings which it suggests. Work gave 'back bone' to the character of man. Marshall underlined 'the effect that his work produces on him rather than of the effect that he produces on his work' (1961a, 1–2; Caldari and Nishizawa 2020a, 346–7). In 'Progress', Marshall wrote of 'Life, Work and Art'; emphasizing a crucial sentence, '*Our true aim is the elevation of human life, the making it full & strong* (Life all round, individual and social, moral and religious, physical and intellectual, emotional and artistic)' (Caldari and Nishizawa 2020a, 344).[14]

Towards the end of the chapter on 'Value and Utility' (referring to 'broader aspects of the utility of wealth'), just after writing of the value of leisure and rest, Marshall introduced the notion of 'true happiness' – which he contrasted with 'sum total happiness'. It encompassed what Pigou called

[13] Marshall's earlier career was outlined by Whitaker: plunging into philosophy, Marshall came to ethics, psychology, and – rather reluctantly – political economy. 'I am a philosopher straying in a foreign land: I will go home soon' (Whitaker 1975, I, 5–7).

[14] It seems even to accord with Schumpeter's 'philosophy of life' and Ruskin's 'no wealth but life'. Schumpeter wrote of his 'unusual philosophy of life' and had an 'idea of rich and full life to include economics, politics, science, art, and love'; and called his long-standing research programme 'a comprehensive sociology' (*Harvard Crimson*, 4 November 1944, quoted in Shionoya 2012, 267). For Ruskin, see Shionoya's chapter in this volume.

'non-economic welfare'.[15] 'Fullness of life' lies in the 'development and activity of as many and high faculties as possible'. For ordinary people, 'a moderate income earned by moderate and fairly steady work offers the best opportunity for the growth of those habits of body, mind, and spirit in which alone there is true happiness' (1961a, 136).

Marshall questioned Edgeworth, asking 'whether the Utilitarians are right in assuming that the end of action is the sum of the happiness of individuals rather than the vigorous life of the whole' (28 March 1880; Whitaker 1996, I, 125). He thought of happiness as 'a process rather than a statical condition' (Whitaker 1996, I, 124). 'Social good lies mainly in that healthful exercise and development of faculties which yield happiness without pall' (Marshall 1897, 310). Ethical values involving virtue and moral character were more significant than utility. Human wellbeing was served by a matrix of such values and not by a scalar value of utility.[16] Marshall would not separate economic welfare (material wellbeing) from general welfare (moral and human wellbeing) in this context, as Utilitarians such as Jevons and Edgeworth did. The solution of economic problems was for Marshall 'not an application of the hedonistic calculus, but a prior condition of the exercise of man's higher faculties' (Keynes 1924, 170).

The chapter on 'Progress in Relation to Standards of Life' and his ideas on 'work and life' are in the line of thought on 'Wants in Relation to Activities'. 'Standards of life', distinct from 'standards of comfort', meant the standard of activities adjusted to wants. Thus

a rise in the standard of life implies an increase of intelligence and energy and self-respect; leading to more care and judgement in expenditure, and to an avoidance of food and drink that gratify the appetite but afford no strength, and of ways of living that are unwholesome physically and morally . . . . A rise in the standard of life for the whole population will much increase the national dividend, and the share of it which accrues to each grade and to each trade. (1961a, 689)[17]

---

[15] Pigou wrote of 'non-economic welfare': 'Human beings are both "ends in themselves" and instruments of production. On the one hand, a man who is attuned to the beautiful in nature or in art, . . . is in himself an important element in the ethical value of the world; the way in which he feels and thinks actually constitutes a part of welfare'; 'Non-economic welfare is liable to be moulded by the manner in which income is earned. For the surroundings of work react upon the quality of life' (Pigou 1920, 12–13, 14). For Pigou, see also Yamazaki's chapter in this volume.

[16] See, e.g., Shionoya's 'system of ethics' in Shionoya (2005).

[17] In short, if summarized in a chart it is as follows: rise of standards of life → increase of intelligence, morality, and energy; health and strength (physical, mental, and moral) ⟺ vigour (work and full life, happiness, wellbeing) → efficiency → productivity, national income, wages → wisely used → health and strength (physical, mental, and moral) = organic life and growth.

Marshall stated in the revision of the second edition, 'A general increase in the efficiency of all workers would increase the National Dividend, and raise earnings nearly in proportion.' He indicated that the cost of production of labour cannot be determined as definitely as can that of a commodity; for the 'conventional necessaries' of labour, as well as all superfluous comforts and luxuries are not a fixed sum, but depend on the efficiency of labour. The right means to raise wages is to raise, not merely the Standard of Comfort or of wants, but the Standard of Life which includes activities as well as wants (1961b, 40). He distinguished 'conventional necessaries, i.e. the Standard of Comfort' from 'the influence of modes and amounts of consumption over efficiency, and the Standard of Life' (1961b, 73). 'Standard of Life' was the keynote of progress or organic life-growth. This significance of the chapter 'Progress in Relation to Standards of Life' (and the previous chapter 'General Influences of Economic Progress') is emphasized by its being closely related to those parts of the final book on 'Progress' in which he discusses the complexity of wages, efficiency, and wellbeing.[18]

'The Health and Strength of the Population' (*Principles*, Book IV, ch. v) is very crucial because it is one of the fundamental conditions for progress. 'Health and strength, physical, mental and moral' is 'the basis of industrial efficiency, on which the production of material wealth depends'; while conversely the importance of material wealth lies in the fact that, when wisely used, it increases the health and strength of the human race. Although the power of sustaining muscular exertion seems to rest on constitutional strength, even it depends on force of will, and strength of character. 'This strength of the man himself, this resolution, energy and self-masterly, or in short this "vigour" is the source of all progress' (1961a, 193–4).

In 'Progress', working on 'Economic Ideals', he wrote: 'The ideal is not comfort but life, vigour. The comfort of the masses is to be thought for: they ought not to [be] robbed of their sugar, or their tobacco. But it is their *life*, the physical mental & moral vigour for which we ought to care' (Caldari and Nishizawa 2020a, 346). He wrote, '*Use public money freely in order to increase vigour rather than to diminish suffering*' (Caldari and Nishizawa 2020a, 221). Marshall's intentions are more on the science of activities

---

[18] This was discussed and further developed together with 'Sectional Interests' and 'Trade Unions' in Marshall's Book on Economic Progress. See Caldari and Nishizawa (2020a). Its Book I, chapter III is called 'Wages, Efficiency and Wellbeing' and it has very interesting sections on 'wages and efficiency' and 'efficiency and wellbeing'.

rather than on wants, or the standard of life (activities) rather than the standard of comfort (wants).[19]

In the very first part of his final book on 'Progress' (see Caldari and Nishizawa 2016), discussing 'the nature of economic progress', Marshall says that 'the term "economic progress" is narrow'. 'Progress', the core and aim of his economic studies, 'has many sides', because 'the progressive nature of man is one whole'. It 'includes developments of mental and moral faculties, even when their exercise yields no material gain'. This is why he concluded that 'the term "economic progress" is narrow'. It was wrong to see progress as 'merely an increase in man's command over the material requisites of physical mental and moral wellbeing; no special reference being made to the extent to which this command is turned to account in developing the higher life of mankind' (Caldari and Nishizawa 2020a, 30–1).

An implication was that 'great advance in material wellbeing is attainable only by those nations, whose industries are progressive, and whose men are strong in character and in action'. 'True human progress' involved 'an advance in capacity for feeling and for thought' that 'cannot be sustained without vigorous enterprise and energy' (Caldari and Nishizawa 2020a, 31), which implied a view of welfare much broader than Pigou's economic welfare. As we showed (Caldari and Nishizawa 2016), 'Progress' is, for Marshall, a very complex idea. 'A certain minimum of means is necessary for material wellbeing', but wellbeing is a far more inclusive concept and involves more than material wellbeing.

3.3 'Wants' and 'Activities' in 'Organic Growth'

Marshall discussed the connection between progress and standards of life as part of his discussion on wants and activities. As mentioned in Section 3.2, 'Progress in Relation to Standards of Life' was in the line of thought on 'Wants in Relation to Activities' in *Principles*' Book III on 'Wants and Their Satisfaction'. The chapter on 'Wants in Relation to Activities' was a response to the increased prominence given to the study of consumption and demand by Jevons. There was a special need to insist on this, because the reaction against the comparative neglect of the study of wants by Ricardo and his followers showed signs of being carried to the opposite

---

[19] In a letter to Helen Bosanquet (28 September 1902) Marshall wrote, saying thanks for her *Strength of the People*, 'I have always held that poverty & pain, disease & death are evils of much less importance . . ., except in so far as they lead to weakness of life & character; & that true philanthropy aims at increasing strength more than at diminishing poverty' (Whitaker 1996, II, 399).

extreme. Marshall asserted 'the great truth', that is, 'while wants are the rulers of life among the lower animals, it is to changes in the forms of efforts and activities that we must turn when in search for the keynote of the history of mankind' (1961a, 85).

Following an argument made by Talcott Parsons on 'wants' and 'activities', Stefan Collini emphasized that by confining itself to the study of the satisfaction of given wants, 'the material requisites of well-being', a Utilitarian conception of economics would cut the subject off from 'the high theme of economic progress'. By making activities and their dominant influence on the formation of character and ideals the central concern of economics, it could become the guiding discipline in any 'study of man' (Collini et al. 1983, 321). Marshall indeed thought his vision of social science as 'the reasoned history of man' (1897, 299; see ch. 4 and ch. 7 in Shionoya and Nishizawa 2008).

For 'the high theme of economic progress', in a concluding paragraph of Book V (ch. 12), introducing Book VI, Marshall wrote:

> We are here verging on the high theme of economic progress; and here therefore it is especially needful to remember that economic problems are imperfectly presented when they are treated as problems of statical equilibrium, and not of organic growth. For though the statical treatment alone can give us definiteness and precision of thought, and is therefore a necessary introduction to a more philosophic treatment of society as an organism; it is yet only an introduction. (1961a, 461)

Despite devoting Book III to 'Wants and Their Satisfaction', in its second chapter on 'Wants in Relation to Activities', Marshall played down the importance of consumption and demand by stressing 'human efforts and activities'. The new marginal utility theory provided a way of showing that the earnings of any agent of production depended on the value of the products they produce. Yet once more it was on the supply side of the market for factors that Marshall was keen to place his emphasis (Winch 2009, 273). Marshall separated the new generation of economists from their predecessors, but in making human efforts and activities so much a part of the agenda and method of economics, he also separated himself from those contemporaries, chiefly Jevons, Sidgwick, and Edgeworth, who preserved a closer relationship between economics and Utilitarianism (Collini et al. 1983, 318).

According to Marshall, the theory of wants can claim no supremacy over the theory of efforts. It is not true that 'the Theory of Consumption is the scientific basis of economics'. For much that is of chief interest in the science of wants, is borrowed from the science of efforts and activities. These two supplement one another; either is incomplete without the other.

But if either, more than the other, may claim to be the interpreter of the history of man, whether on the economic side or any other, it is the science of activities and not that of wants. J. R. McCulloch indicated their true relations when, discussing 'the progressive nature of man', said: 'The gratification of a want or a desire is merely a step to some new pursuit. In every stage of his progress he is destined to contrive and invent, to engage in new undertakings; and when these are accomplished to enter with fresh energy upon others' (quoted in 1961a, 90).[20]

Donald Winch summed up the argument that the adjustment of wants to activities and the creation of new wants as a result of new activities was the foundation on which Marshall wished to build his own scientific edifice rather than on any theory of consumption alone. Character formation then 'lay at the centre of Marshall's contribution to a subject'. Marshall was more ambitious in the inclusiveness of his conception of what he called the 'economic organon': his preference was to be regarded as someone who had redrawn the boundaries of economics sufficiently generously to make these larger 'organic' ('biological' as opposed to 'mechanical') themes part of the most advanced of the social sciences (Winch 2009, 273).

Given that wants and activities were so important, why had there been such a focus on consumers' demand? Marshall believed that it could be attributed to 'mathematical habits of thought' and to the making use of statistical evidence on consumption to throw light on questions of public wellbeing. Marshall wrote in Book III about 'Gradations of Consumers' Demand' (total utility, marginal utility, demand price) and 'the elasticity of wants (demand)'. Then in chapter vi 'Value and Utility', he discussed 'consumers' surplus' – a concept that would enable the academic economist to estimate the size of the gap between welfare and wealth produced by a wide range of policy choices. If consumers' surplus could be measured, it could be used to gauge how much welfare could be increased by policies such as taxes or bounties that shifted the demand and supply schedules in a direction that increased the amount of surplus available (Winch 2009, 272).

Marshall wrote of the 'high practical interest of consumer's surplus': if the money measures of the happiness caused by two events are equal, there is not any very great difference between the amounts of the happiness in the two cases. It is on account of this fact that 'the exact measurement of the

---

[20] For 'Rehabilitation of Ricardo', Marshall had 'an excursus of eight pages' on 'Ricardo's Theory of Cost of Production in Relation to Value' at the end of Book V, that is 'Note on Ricardo's Theory of Value', in the second to the fourth editions of the *Principles*, which became Appendix I in the fifth edition (Ashley 1891, 476; Marshall 1961b, 545).

consumers' surplus in a market has already much theoretical interest, and may become of high practical interest'. However, he noted here: 'the task of adding together the total utilities of all commodities, so as to obtain the aggregate of the total utility of all wealth, is beyond the range of any but the most elaborate mathematical formulae'. An attempt to treat it convinced Marshall that 'even if the task be theoretically feasible, the result would be encumbered by so many hypotheses as to be practically useless' (1961a, 131). Marshall indicated the limitation of doctrine of consumer's surplus: 'Our list of demand prices is highly conjectural except in the neighbourhood of the customary price; and the best estimates we can form of the whole amount of the utility of anything are liable to large error' (1961a, 133).

Guillebaud recalled Marshall's recollection that a major disappointment in his life had been the recognition, which gradually forced itself on him, that his concept of consumer's surplus was devoid of important practical application, because it was not capable of being quantified in a meaningful way. At the outset he had high hopes that it could have practical applications, and for many years he had wrestled with it, but had finally reached the conclusion that 'it was a theoretical and not a practical tool in the economist's workbox' (Guillebaud 1971, 96: Groenewegen 2010).

As Marco Dardi indicated, Marshall was aware of the very rough character of a social welfare index based on consumer surplus, and realized that its shortcomings rendered the scope of welfare policies rather narrow. He was also aware that all utilitarian social indexes had the defect of being unresponsive to the potential evolutionary impact of changes in the quality and distribution of welfare (Dardi 2010, 409). Marshall's welfare economics had little to do beyond waiting for evolution or progress to do its job. Marshall's conviction was progress and evolution rather than welfare policies. Welfare policies should refrain from making a substantial impact on the present social conditions until natural development of industrial and social structure has brought about a major change also in mental habits and moral attitudes (Dardi 2010 406, 409).

3.4 'Chivalry in Using Wealth': Moral Standard and Social Wellbeing

In Book III's final chapter on 'Value and Utility', writing about the dependence of wellbeing on material wealth, Marshall referred to the flow or stream of wellbeing as measured by the flow or stream of incoming wealth and the consequent power of using and consuming it (1961a, 134), and discussed the power of using wealth in relation to moral progress (or the improvement of standards of life including the forms of expenditure). Criticizing the misuse of wealth and the desire to display it, phenomena Thornstein Veblen had denounced, this line of reasoning led him to write about raising moral sentiments, and 'chivalry in using wealth', which seems to have something in common with the 'virtuous utilization of resources' (based on virtue ethics, not on utility ethics) (see Shionoya's chapter in this volume and Shionoya 2018).[21] Marshall stressed 'the power of rightly using such income and opportunities' was 'wealth of the highest order' by itself (1961a, 720).

Marshall concluded the chapter on 'Value and Utility', in which he discussed how the virtuous use of wealth could lead to higher activities, by arguing that the influence on general wellbeing of the way people spend their income is one of the more important of those 'applications of economic science to the art of living' (1961a, 137). His argument was that when the necessaries of life are provided, everyone should seek to increase the beauty of things rather than their number. Improvement in the artistic character of furniture and clothing trains the higher faculties of those who make them, a point also important for Ruskin and Hobson (see Peter Cain's chapter in this volume). The world would go much better if everyone would take the trouble to select for real beauty, buying fewer things made well by highly paid labour rather than many things made badly by low-paid labour (1961a, 136–7; cf. also 1961a, Book V, ch. xiii, §7).[22]

It was easier to work well than to use wealth well, and much easier than to use leisure well. In the final part of 'Progress in Relation to Standard of Life' as well as in 'Social Possibilities of Economic Chivalry', Marshall stressed the importance of the use of wealth, saying:

> The inequalities of wealth and the very low earnings of the poorer classes, have been discussed referring to their effects in dwarfing activities as well as in curtailing the satisfaction of wants. But here, the economist is brought up against the fact that the power of rightly using such income and opportunities, as a family has, is in itself wealth of the highest order, and of a kind that is rare in all classes. (1961a, 720)

Marshall went on to say that raising the standard of life would raise the moral standards and social wellbeing, arguing that, although a reduction in

---

[21] 'Virtuous utilization of resources' is distinguished from 'efficient allocation of resources' and 'just distribution of resources'; these three systems correspond to the three grand systems of ethics, virtue (excellence, capability, character), good (efficiency), and right (justice) (see Shionoya's chapter in this volume).

[22] Cf. Caldari and Nishizawa (2020a, 342–4), on 'Life, Work and Art'.

working hours would reduce the national dividend and lower wages, it would be good for most people to work less, provided that the consequent loss of material income could be met by the abandoning of the least worthy methods of consumption. His emphasis on rightly using income, or the 'virtuous utilization of resources', resonates with arguments in Keynes's 'Economic Possibilities for Our Grandchildren' (Keynes 1930). Leisure would be used less and less for just doing nothing as there would be a growing desire for athletic games and travelling which would develop activities (1961a, 89). Unfortunately, human nature improves slowly, and in nothing more slowly than in learning to use leisure well. In human history, far more have known how to work well than have known how to use leisure well. It is only through freedom to use leisure that people can learn to use leisure well. This meant that manual workers, devoid of leisure, could neither have much self-respect nor become full citizens, or 'gentlemen'.[23]

Marshall often referred to 'social ideals and the ultimate aims of economic effort' (1907, 324). He attached great importance to the power of using wealth because he took the view that even the working classes spent vast sums that added little to their happiness and higher wellbeing. Much expenditure conferred no solid benefits on the spenders beyond honour and influence. There was a general agreement among economists 'that if society could award this honour by less wasteful methods, then resources set free would open out to the mass of the people 'new possibilities of a higher life, and of larger and more varied intellectual and artistic activities' (1907, 325). In Marshall's age it was not so wasteful as sometimes represented, for much more than half of the total income of the nation was devoted to uses which made for happiness and a higher standard of life. Even so, there was a large margin for improvement; surely, then, 'it is worth while to make a great effort to enlist wealth in the service of the true glory of the world' (1907, 330).[24] Marshall contended that 'chivalry in work would run into chivalry in using wealth', arguing for 'social possibilities of economic chivalry', which is well illustrated by his own words:

---

[23] Free from the fatigue of work that tires without educating, is a necessary condition of a high standard of life (1961a, 720). See also 1961a, 249, referring to '*natura non facit saltum*'.

[24] Marshall wrote, 'Perhaps 100,000,000 pounds annually are spent by the working classes, and 400,000,000 pounds by the rest of the population, in ways that do little or nothing towards making life nobler or truly happier' (1961a, 720). He also noted, some years ago, that the annual income of some 49,000,000 people in the United Kingdom appeared to amount to more than 2,000,000,000 pounds (1961a, 713 footnote 1).

Economic chivalry on the part of the individual would stimulate and be stimulated by a similar chivalry on the part of the community as a whole. The two together might soon provide the one or two hundred million a year that appear to be available, without great pressure on the well-to-do, towards bringing the chief benefits which can be derived from our new command over nature within the reach of all.

Equipped with such funds, the State could so care for the amenities of life outside of the house that fresh air and variety of colour and of scene might await the citizen and his children very soon after they start on a holiday walk. Everyone in health and strength can order his house well; the State alone can bring the beauties of nature and art within the reach of the ordinary citizen. (1907, 344–5)

3.5 Concluding Remarks

This chapter places Marshall's views on welfare (or rather wellbeing) in a broader perspective of his economic thought, or in his 'high theme of economic progress'. Marshall's economic thinking has been aimed to bring about 'economic, as well as the moral, wellbeing', and to make coexist and develop both the material growth and the moral progress. Progress and 'organic growth' are 'the high theme' and more central and 'philosophic' for him rather than statical welfare analysis. Marshall stressed that the term 'economic progress' was narrow, for material wealth was 'but a means to the sustenance of man' and 'to the development of his activities, physical, mental, and moral'. This was why Marshall did not think of happiness only in terms of utility. His aim was that 'the opportunities of a noble life may be accessible to all'. In the context of progress and poverty elimination, Marshall referred to 'sum total happiness'; but he also wrote about 'true happiness' in life and work, or the healthy exercise and development of faculties and activities. This notion of 'true happiness' stemmed from his early work on psychology of 'the higher development of human faculties', which is based on ethics of virtue (character, capability), not on utility.

The progress of man's nature (or character) was 'the ultimate aim of economic studies'. Character formation (activities) lay at the centre of Marshall's contribution to the subject. The rise of 'standards of life' (distinct from 'standards of comfort'), meant efficiency in production, as well as the power of rightly using wealth; economic chivalry (moral standards) both in work (activities) and using wealth (wants). Marshall indicated 'the power of rightly using income and opportunities' was 'wealth of the highest order', could be described as 'virtuous utilization of resources', and was a crucial part of what he meant by 'organic growth'.

References

Ashley, W. J. 1891. 'The Rehabilitation of Ricardo', *Economic Journal*, 1–3, 474–89.

Backhouse, R. E. 2006. 'Sidgwick, Marshall and the Cambridge School of Economics', *History of Political Economy*, 38–1, 15–44.

Backhouse, R. E. and Nishizawa, T., eds. 2010. *No Wealth but Life: Welfare Economics and the Welfare State in Britain, 1880–1945*, Cambridge: Cambridge University Press.

Bateman, B. W. 2006. 'Wants and Activities', in T. Raffaelli, G. Becattini, M. Dardi, eds., *The Elgar Companion of Alfred Marshall*, Cheltenham: Edward Elgar, 288–92.

Caldari, K. and Nishizawa, T. 2011. 'Marshall's Ideas on Progress: Roots and Diffusion', in H. Kurz, T. Nishizawa, K. Tribe, eds., *The Dissemination of Economic Ideas*, Cheltenham: Edward Elgar, 125–57.

Caldari, K. and Nishizawa, T. 2014. 'Marshall's "Welfare Economics" and "Welfare": A Reappraisal Based on His Unpublished Manuscript on Progress', *History of Economic Ideas*, XXII–1, 51–67.

Caldari, K. and Nishizawa, T. 2016. 'Progress beyond Growth: Some Insights from Marshall's Final Book', *European Journal of the History of Economic Thought*, 23–1, 226–43.

Caldari, K. and Nishizawa, T. 2020a. *Alfred Marshall's Last Challenge: His Book on Economic Progress*, Newcastle: Cambridge Scholars Publishing.

Caldari, K. and Nishizawa, T. 2020b. 'Economic and Moral Wellbeing and Efficiency: Some Marshallian Insights from His Book on "Progress"', M. Dardi, S. Medema, K. Caldari, eds., *Marshall and the Marshallian Heritage: Essays in Honour of Tiziano Raffaelli*, London: Palgrave Macmillan.

Collini, S., Winch, D., Burrow, J. 1983. *That Noble Science of Politics: A Study in Nineteenth-Century Intellectual History*, Cambridge: Cambridge University Press.

Cook, S. J. 2009. *The Intellectual Foundations of Alfred Marshall's Economic Science*, Cambridge: Cambridge University Press.

Dardi, M. 2010. 'Marshall on Welfare, or: the "Utilitarian" Meets the "Evolver"', *European Journal of the History of Economic Thought*, 17–3, 405–37.

Dardi, M. 2011. 'Ideal Social Orders', in T. Raffaelli, T. Nishizawa, S. Cook, eds., *Marshall, Marshallians and Industrial Economics*, London: Routledge, 100–32.

Groenewegen, P. D., ed. 1998. *Alfred Marshall: Critical Responses*, Vol. II, London: Routledge.

Groenewegen, P. D. 2005. 'A Book That Never Was: Marshall's Final Volume on Progress', *History of Economic Review*, 42, 29–44.

Groenewegen, P. D. 2010. 'Marshall on Welfare Economics and the Welfare State', in Backhouse and Nishizawa, eds., 2010, 25–41.

Guillebaud, C. M. 1971. 'Some Personal Reminiscences of Alfred Marshall', reprinted in *Alfred Marshall Critical Assessments*, Vol. 1, London: Croom Helm, 1982, 91–7.

Hicks, J. R. 1959. 'Preface – and a Manifesto', *Essays in World Economics*, Oxford: Clarendon Press, v–xv.

Hobson, J. A. 1914. *Work and Wealth: A Human Valuation*, with a new introduction by P. Cain, London: Routledge/Thoemmes Press, 1992.

Hobson, J. A. 1929. *Wealth and Life: A Study in Values*, London: Macmillan.

Hutchison, T. W. 1964. *'Positive' Economics and Policy Objectives*, London: George Allen & Unwin.

Jones, G. S. 1971. *Outcast London: A Study in Relationship between Classes in Victorian Society*, Oxford: Clarendon Press.

Keynes, J. M. 1924. 'Alfred Marshall', in the *Collected Writings, X: Essays in Biography*, London: Macmillan, 1972.

Keynes, J. M. 1930. 'Economic Possibilities for Our Grandchildren', in the *Collected Writings, IX: Essays in Persuasion*, London: Macmillan, 1972.

Marshall, A. 1873a. 'The Future of the Working Classes', in Pigou, ed., 1925.

Marshall, A. 1873b. 'Lectures to Women', in T. Raffaelli, E. Biagini, R. M. Tullberg, eds., *Alfred Marshall's Lectures to Women*, Aldershot: Edward Elgar, 1995, 85–155.

Marshall, A. 1883. 'Three Lectures on Progress and Poverty', *Collected Essays*, Vol. 1, Bristol: Overstone Press, 1997.

Marshall, A. 1885a. 'How Far Do Remediable Causes Influence Prejudicially (a) the Continuity of Employment, (b) the Rates of Wages?' in Industrial Remuneration Conference (1885), reprinted in *Alfred Marshall: Critical Responses*, ed. P. Groenewegen, Vol. 1, London: Routledge, 1998, 59–66.

Marshall, A. 1885b. *The Present Position of Economics*, London: Macmillan, in Pigou, ed., 1925.

Marshall, A. 1889. 'Co-operation', in Pigou, ed., 1925.

Marshall, A. 1897. 'The Old Generation of Economists and the New', in Pigou, ed., 1925.

Marshall, A. 1898. *Principles of Economics*, 4th ed., London: Macmillan.

Marshall, A. 1907. 'Social Possibilities of Economic Chivalry', in Pigou, ed., 1925.

Marshall, A. 1917. 'National Taxation after the War', in W. H. Dawson, ed., *After-War Problems*, New York: Macmillan, 313–45.

Marshall, A. 1919. *Industry and Trade: A Study of Industrial Technique and Business Organization; and of Their Influences on the Conditions of Various Classes and Nations*, London: Macmillan, 4th ed., 1923.

Marshall, A. 1923. *Money, Credit & Commerce*, London: Macmillan.

Marshall, A. 1961a. *Principles of Economics* (1890); 9th (variorum) ed. with annotations, by C. W. Guillebaud, Vol. I Text, London: Macmillan.

Marshall, A. 1961b. *Principles of Economics* (1890); 9th (variorum) ed. with annotations, by C. W. Guillebaud, Vol. II Notes, London: Macmillan.

Marshall, A. and Marshall, M. 1879. *The Economics of Industry*, with a new introduction by D. O'Brien, Bristol: Thoemmes Press, 1994.

Medema, S. 2006. 'Welfare Economics: Marshallian Welfare Economics and the Economic Welfare of Marshall', in T. Raffaelli, G. Becattini, M. Dardi, eds., *The Elgar Companion of Alfred Marshall*, Cheltenham: Edward Elgar, 634–47.

Nussbaum, M. C. and Sen, A., eds. 1993. *The Quality of Life*, Oxford: Clarendon Press.

Parsons, T. 1932. 'Wants and Activities in Marshall', *Quarterly Journal of Economics*, 46–1, 101–40.

Pigou, A. C. 1920. *The Economics of Welfare*, London: Macmillan; 4th ed., 1932.

Pigou, A. C., ed. 1925. *Memorials of Alfred Marshall*, London: Macmillan.

Raffaelli, T. 2003. *Marshall's Evolutionary Economics*, London: Routledge.

Raffaelli, T., Becattini, G., Dardi, M., eds. 2006. *The Elgar Companion of Alfred Marshall*, Cheltenham: Edward Elgar.

Raffaelli, T., Biagini, E., Tullberg, R. M., eds. 1995. *Alfred Marshall's Lectures to Women: Some Economic Questions Directly Connected to the Welfare of the Labourer,* Aldershot: Edward Elgar.

Schumpeter, J. A. 1951. *Ten Great Economists from Marx to Keynes,* New York: Oxford University Press.

Schumpeter, J. A. 1954. *History of Economic Analysis,* London: George Allen & Unwin.

Shionoya, Y. 2005. *Economy and Morality: The Philosophy of the Welfare State,* Cheltenham: Edward Elgar.

Shionoya, Y. 2012. *Economic Thought of Romanticism: Arts, Ethics, and History* (in Japanese), Tokyo: Tokyo University Press.

Shionoya, Y. 2018. 'Philosophy, Arts, Economics of Keynes – in the Light of Enlightenment versus Romanticism', in T. Nishizawa and T. Hirai, eds., *Cambridge, Pursuit of Wisdom: Economics, Philosophy, and Literature* (in Japanese), Kyoto: Minerva-shobo, 261–80.

Shionoya, Y. and Nishizawa, T., eds. 2008. *Marshall and Schumpeter on Evolution: Economic Sociology of Capitalist Development,* Cheltenham: Edward Elgar.

Suzumura, K. 2013. 'Foundations of "Non-welfaristic" and "Non-consequential" Normative Economics: What Are the Connecting Links between Pigou, Hicks, and Sen', in T. Nishizawa and A. Komine, eds., *Welfare Economics and the Welfare State in the Formative Age* (in Japanese), Kyoto: Minerva-shobo, 339–64.

Whitaker, J. K., ed. 1975. *The Early Economic Writings of Alfred Marshall, 1867–1890,* 2 vols., London: Macmillan.

Whitaker, J. K., ed. 1996. *The Correspondence of Alfred Marshall, Economist,* 3 vols., Cambridge: Cambridge University Press.

Winch, D. 2009. *Wealth and Life: Essays on the Intellectual History of Political Economy in Britain, 1848–1914,* Cambridge: Cambridge University Press.

4

Pigou's Welfare Economics Revisited

A Non-welfarist and Non-utilitarian Interpretation*

Satoshi Yamazaki

4.1 Introduction

Arthur Cecil Pigou has generally been counted as a traditional hedonistic utilitarian in the tradition of Bentham and Sidgwick. For example, Edgeworth observed that he 'appears to have drawn inspiration from two high authorities on wealth and welfare. The good which philanthropy and statesmanship should seek to realise is defined by him in accordance with Sidgwick's utilitarian philosophy' (Edgeworth 1913, 62), and O'Donnell (1979) takes a similar view. However, recent studies have challenged this interpretation.[1]

In this chapter, we re-examine Pigou's concept of welfare, which constitutes the core of his welfare economics. We examine several studies that interpret the ethical basis of his welfare economics from different perspectives, asking whether it should be seen as welfarist or non-welfarist (more broadly, utilitarian or non-utilitarian). We would like to show that the non-welfarist aspects in Pigou, if they are detected, are considered to be a result of practical requirements. That is, practical issues made him,

* This chapter partially contains the English version of some parts of my works originally written in Japanese (Yamazaki (2011) and Yamazaki and Takami (2018); although the latter is a joint work with Takami, those parts featured this time are only my writing). Specifically, subsections '4.2.2 Incommensurability among Utilities', '4.2.3 Presupposed Egalitarianism: Incommensurability among People', '4.2.4 Non-welfarist Information: Needs', and '4.2.6 Methodological Individualism' are revisions of my Japanese work in Yamazaki and Takami (2018). This study is supported by the Japan Society for the Promotion of Science (KAKENHI: 15K03383). I would like to thank Steven Medema and Michael McLure for their helpful comments on the previous draft.
[1] For example, Shionoya (1984; 1993), Suzumura (2000; 2002; 2007), Hongo (2007), and Backhouse and Nishizawa (2010).

though implicitly, acknowledge the limitation of welfarism and forced him
to rely upon non-welfarist information (needs, justice, etc., as we will see).
This means that he took a substantial account of a wide range of non-
welfarist values.

According to the most standard accounts (e.g. Sen and Williams (1982)),
utilitarianism is comprised of three principles, which are (1) welfarism (all
the value and criteria of policies should be reduced to pleasure or utility),
(2) consequentialism (the rightness or wrongness of every policy is judged
by consequences), and (3) sum-ranking (every individual's good is to be
summed up for comparison). Therefore, in order for Pigou to be regarded
as non-utilitarian, it is enough to show that he denied at least one of those
principles (note that, although non-welfarism implies non-utilitarianism,
one can be a welfarist without being a utilitarian). Accordingly, our
examination of Pigou focuses on the first principle, bringing in the others
as necessary. We start, in Section 4.2, by considering previous studies of
Pigou's welfare economics, before providing a new interpretation, based on
modern theory, in Section 4.3.

4.2 Preceding Studies

4.2.1 A Historically Contextual View

The conventional view is that hedonism and utilitarianism are two sides of
the same coin, so that negation of one logically means negation of the
other. On this basis, even G. E. Moore could be regarded as non-utilitarian.
In fact, Moore (1903) himself fiercely attacked *hedonistic* utilitarianism as
espoused by Bentham, Mill, and Sidgwick. This historical fact has created
a complicated issue regarding interpretation of Moore's ethical position.
Focusing on his negation of hedonism will lead to a non-utilitarian interpretation of Moore. In contrast, to focus on his moral principle (as
contemporary ethical philosophers do) leads to a refined, ideal-utilitarian
interpretation of him. Like Moore, Pigou denied hedonism (i.e. he denied
that good was synonymous with pleasure) and espoused the plurality of
intrinsic good (welfare had many ingredients) including certain virtuous
factors (such as an 'ethical personality'). In addition, due to his retention of
a consequentialist framework, Pigou's position was similar to Moore's, and
therefore he may also be regarded as an ideal utilitarian. Thus, in the
same way that Moore can be interpreted as a non-utilitarian, Pigou
may be understood as non-utilitarian because of his denial of
hedonism in the utilitarianism of his day. However, whether he was

welfarist or non-welfarist becomes ambiguous, at least with respect to his axiology (multiple account of the good) which could be interpreted as welfarist.

4.2.2 Incommensurability among Utilities

It may have been Shionoya who first argued the non-utilitarian interpretation of Pigou's welfare economics. His argument can be summarized as 'two kinds of incommensurability' (Shionoya 1984; 1993). There is incommensurability among different kinds of utility and there is also incommensurability between different individuals. Based on these, Shionoya presented his own interpretation of Pigou as non-utilitarian.

According to Shionoya, the first correction made by Pigou to utilitarian welfare economics was his distinction between economic and non-economic welfare (general welfare), which essentially meant that Pigou focused not on welfare as a whole but only on one part, that of economic welfare. Traditional hedonistic utilitarianism is thought to have judged the rightness or wrongness of actions or arrangements in light of the sum of the resulting utility (pleasure or satisfaction). However, Pigou did not deal with the whole process of causes and effects, and instead focused on a partial process by devising the notion of economic welfare. This is because he assumed that economic welfare could be measured by the scale of money (reflecting the strength of our desire and thereby providing an approximation of the resulting satisfaction). Economic welfare was 'that part of social welfare that can be brought directly or indirectly into relation with the measuring-rod of money' (Pigou 1932, 11). At first glance, this definition of economic welfare based on money appears to embrace all the resulting utilities generated by goods and services in economic activities, but that is not what Pigou intended. Although introducing the measuring rod of money can define economic factors as the causes of resulting utilities, thereby excluding non-economic factors, Pigou's economic welfare is not supposed to include all utility consequences brought about by economic factors. The notion of making a distinction between consequences can be made possible by the introduction of a money measure (Shionoya 1984, 364–5).

Pigou distinguishes two ways in which economics factors can affect non-economic welfare: through earning income, and through using it. Non-economic welfare was thought to relate mainly to spiritual, athletic, and ethical aspects of human life (consciousness). Although Pigou did notice that there might be conflicts between the effects of economic causes on economic welfare and on non-economic welfare, he concluded that we should focus on economic welfare alone. He claimed that these two effects would generally work in the same direction, unless there were specific evidences to the contrary ('unverified probability') (Shionoya 1984, 365).

Shionoya unfolded his argument concerning the possibility of dishar-mony or conflicts between the effects of economic causes on economic and non-economic welfare as follows. There are two ways of thinking about welfare: satisfaction and desire. According to Pigou, economic welfare does not represent the amount of satisfaction yielded by certain causes (e.g. the consumption of goods), but the intensity of the desire for them. The money measure applied to the definition of economic welfare in essence means the demand-price for goods (i.e. the amount of money people are willing to pay for the expected benefit from gaining of certain goods is assumed to indicate the intensity of desire). With regard to this, Shionoya states that, even though economic welfare as consciousness means satisfaction, it is difficult to measure; accordingly, Pigou assumes that demand price (the intensity of desire) represents the amount of satisfaction (Shionoya 1984, 366).[2]

Accordingly, with respect to the money measure as an index of econom-ic welfare, the following cases naturally occur. Suppose there are two consumption goods, and one has an effect only on the consumer's personal pleasure while the other has the effect of benefiting not only the consumer but also other people. If, in this case, the intensity of consumer desire for the two goods is equal (i.e. demand prices are identical) there will be no difference in consequential economic welfare measured by the money scale. It follows that no qualitative difference in utility is reflected in such economic welfare, as measured by demand price. Does the same degree in intensity of desire necessarily mean the same degree in ethical good? On this matter, Shionoya observes the following. Pigou's account conceives of homogeneous economic welfare, which should negate any qualitative difference. This can have a crucial implication for utilitarianism. To be certain, Pigou's standpoint can be regarded as utilitarian as long as he has clarified the concept of homogeneous economic welfare using the money measure, and in doing so has made unitary assessment of welfare possible. Nevertheless, the homogeneity and unitary assessment of welfare can be valid only to the extent that the money measure can be applicable. On the other hand, he also admits the qualitative difference in utility by distin-guishing between economic and non-economic welfare. Thus, unless the

---

[2] On the other hand, though, we should not dismiss the fact that in 1903 Pigou was cautious about the limitation of such equivalence in his utility theory.

evaluation of the two categories is possible, an overall assessment of the consequences on the entire welfare cannot be completed, and we are not allowed to advocate any prescription. Accordingly, Pigou is thought to leave the question unsolved (Shionoya 1984, 366–7). After all, the applicability of the money measure indicates Pigou's admission of qualitative difference in utilities and incommensurability among them, which means deviation from typical utilitarianism. On these grounds, Shionoya asserts that Pigou's position is not simply utilitarian, but rather it is a relativistic treatment of utilitarianism (Shionoya 1984, 367).

For example, Edgeworth, who claimed that pleasure was measurable, advocated two kinds of commensurability (replaceability). One is commensuration of different kinds of utilities in the same person. The other is commensuration of different utilities owned by different people, as in the case of social utility summation (Edgeworth 1881, 59). As is well known, Pigou admitted that amelioration in economic welfare could possibly be counterbalanced by deterioration in non-economic welfare. Shionoya suspected that this counterbalance could not be subject to arithmetic calculation, because economic and non-economic welfare are different in quality, and it is not the latter but only the former to which the money measure can be applied. Pigou's division of total utility consequences made by economic factors into economic and non-economic welfare, Shionoya noted, means that Pigou recognized that both are incommensurable with each other (Shionoya 1984, 367).

4.2.3 Presupposed Egalitarianism: Incommensurability among People

Next, let us move to the second point Shionoya used to argue that Pigou was non-utilitarian. Pigou's welfare economics is constructed on the basis of a positive connection between national income and economic welfare, which is represented by the following two propositions. The first proposition is that an increase in the size of national income is conducive to increment in economic welfare and the second is that an increase in equality of income distribution is conducive to increment in economic welfare (Pigou 1932, 82, 89). Additionally, we should not fail to notice that each is subjected to the condition of 'other things being unchanged'. The accompanying condition in the first proposition is 'as long as distribution to the poor is not impaired', whereas in the second it is 'as long as national income is not hindered'.

Pigou demonstrated that, as long as an increase and equalization of income do not contradict each other, both tend to increase economic welfare. Regarding this proposition, Shionoya asserted that '[t]his idea deviates from the utilitarian thought' (Shionoya 1993, 15). Let us examine the grounds of his assertion, which appears to be exceedingly important, below, though it requires a somewhat large quotation.

Although ... his analysis in welfare economics is limited to economic welfare, the maximization of production in the first proposition means utility maximization ... . But the first proposition is subject to the condition that other things are equal, indicating that the distribution of income to the poor should not be injured. Utility maximization as is prescribed by the utilitarian principle concerns the aggregation of utility for all individuals and does not admit any independent criterion with regard to the distribution of utility among individuals. In utilitarianism the distribution pattern obtained under the state of production or utility maximization is approved without doubt as desirable. On the contrary, Pigou's second proposition provides an independent criterion of increasing economic welfare, again subject to the condition that production of income should not be hindered.

The second proposition is alien to utilitarianism. However, it is liable to be misunderstood as a utilitarian principle because the second proposition states that a transfer of income from the rich to the poor increases economic welfare. ... The basis of the second proposition is the assumption of decreasing marginal utility and the assumption of equality of utility functions for the rich and the poor. The latter assumption, as well as the assumption of equal marginal utility of money for all individuals, involves interpersonal comparisons of utility and is not a descriptive statement but a normative one. A factual statement may be rather that there are difference of temperament and taste between the rich and the poor ... . If these actual differences are assumed, a transfer of income from the rich to the poor will decrease total utility. (Shionoya 1993, 15–16)

In other words, Pigou introduced the normative assumption of equal utility functions for the rich and the poor (Shionoya 1984, 370). If utility calculation involves people whose capacity for enjoyment is low (e.g. the poor), the prescription for utility maximization must be less distribution because those people are less effective at generating utility for society. However, because Pigou implicitly embraced an orientation towards equalizing the distribution of income, he normatively presupposed that everyone had the same utility function so that utility would be maximized by an equal distribution of income.

Further, Shionoya advocates that the ground for Pigou's second proposition lies in natural right-based thought stipulating that all persons are equal and that both kinds of incommensurability may support a right-based moral theory, interpreting Pigou's position as non-utilitarian (Shionoya 1984, 370–1; 1993, 16–17). For example, Edgeworth noted the claim that more distribution to the more able in capacity will achieve more aggregation of social utility (Edgeworth 1879, 398). On the other hand, note that Pigou did intend to enhance the character and capacity of the less able through the arrangement of education or discipline (Pigou 1912, 26).

4.2.4 Non-welfarist Information: Needs

It was A. K. Sen who first presented a non-welfarist aspect in Pigou, and Suzumura has expanded it. In fact, Sen has said:

In fact, the notion of individual rights had been used earlier by Pigou in discussing people's claims to 'national minimum standard of real income' in his *Economics of Welfare*. He had characterized them in rather similar ways to what are now called 'basic needs'. Underlying all this was, of course, Pigou's firm belief that such rights could be justified on utilitarian grounds (in this respect Pigou was in the Benthamite tradition of seeing rights as intrinsically non-important but instrumentally crucial), but much of the discussion in *Economics of Welfare* on this takes place without going much into the *basis* or *justification* of these rights. Indeed, it is not even clear how consistent these Pigovian claims are with his general use of utility criteria to which he was totally loyal – in other sections of his book. (Gaertner and Pattanaik 1988, 74; italics in the original)

Suzumura takes this argument further.[3] While he does not go so far as to claim that Pigou was non-utilitarian, he questions whether Pigou himself viewed his *Economics of Welfare* as a welfarist approach to social well-being. Evidence for this is found in the fourth edition of *The Economics of Welfare*, in which there is an argument on the minimum standard of real income, which clearly shows that Pigou used non-welfare information in making judgements about social well-being (Suzumura 2007, 102). Pigou's minimum standard at issue is given below:

[I]t is desirable to obtain a clear notion of what precisely the minimum standard should be taken to signify. It must be conceived, not as a subjective minimum of satisfaction, but as an objective minimum of conditions. The conditions, too, must be conditions, not in respect of one aspect of life only, but in general. Thus the minimum includes some defined quantity and quality of house accommodation, of medical care, of education, of food, of leisure, of the apparatus of sanitary convenience and safety where work is carried on, and so on. Furthermore, the minimum is absolute. (Pigou 1932, 759)

Suzumura notes that Pigou's idea of a minimum standard of real income resembles the idea that is referred to as 'basic needs' in modern

---

[3] Suzumura (2000, 11n12) states that he has obtained the observation from Sen's interview conducted by Gaertner and Pattanaik (1988).

development economics. The issue of how much consistency and affinity such a non-welfarist notion could bear with Benthamite tradition-based welfare economics deserves comprehensive examination, as part of the problems of consistency and affinity between the Benthamite notion of public good and ideas about individual rights (Suzumura 2007, 102–3). This is because 'Pigou might have thought that such rights could be justified on utilitarian grounds in the Benthamite tradition of regarding rights as intrinsically unimportant, but instrumentally crucial, but *The Economics of Welfare* is completely reticent concerning the utilitarian justification of these rights' (Suzumura 2002, 6n11).

Suzumura also observes that 'Pigou ... made an early use of the non-welfarist notion of individual rights when he discussed people's claim to "minimum standard of real income", which "must be conceived, not as a subjective minimum of satisfaction, but as an objective minimum of conditions"' (Suzumura 2002, 6n11). Suzumura's conclusion is given as follows. There was a difficulty confronting Pigou. The problem, which he neither explicitly raised nor solved, was how to consistently incorporate the non-welfarist notion of basic needs that he admitted into the old welfare economics framework based on the utilitarian principle. However, we cannot find any trace of his efforts to squarely tackle this issue. Presumably, there seemed to be little time left for the scholar of old welfare economics to explore a way to systematically affiliate with the non-welfarist notion of basic needs and whose utilitarian foundation had already been demolished by the attack of Lionel Robbins in the beginning of the 1930s (Suzumura 2010, 108–9).

Even though they focused on different issues, like Shionoya, Suzumura similarly identifies a non-welfarist aspect in Pigou's welfare economics and implies a need to reread Pigou's work without starting from the assumption that it is utilitarian.

It is helpful to start by considering the context in which Pigou employed the need criterion discussed earlier. This is a formidable task but there are several significant hints. First, Pigou himself did not give any indication of where his need criterion came from. Second, Sidgwick, from whose texts (including *The Methods of Ethics*) Pigou confessed he obtained basic knowledge of ethics, indicates very little about the need criterion. Therefore, it is unlikely that Pigou's need principle (specifically, his contrast between desire and need in welfare economics (Pigou 1912)) is based on the writings of Sidgwick. Lastly, there is an interesting remark made by D. Collard (Collard 1981, 112; emphasis added):

The intellectual basis for favouring more equality (*cet. par*) was, of course, diminishing marginal utility. When it came to policy measures, however, Pigou's egalitarianism all but vanished. Following Marshall, he recognised that inequalities could be justified on grounds of differing *needs* as well as tastes: 'people bearing high responsibility and using their brains much, *need*, to keep them efficient, more house room, more quiet, more easily digested food, more change of scene, than unskilled workers'. (Pigou 1953, 51)

We may observe provisionally that Pigou has basically procured an idea of need principle from Marshall (otherwise, perhaps from a kind of common sense). Nevertheless, what does Pigou's invocation of the need criterion mean? We may reasonably claim that when he engaged in practice (with reference to policy measure, such as the minimum), he virtually admitted the informational limitation of welfarism and had to step into the non-welfarist realm.

4.2.5 Non-welfarist and Non-utilitarian Justification of the Validity of the National Minimum[4]

Next, we show another case of need as non-welfarism in Pigou's welfare economics: justification of the national minimum. He makes a demonstration as follows: 'The policy of practical philanthropists is justified by analysis, in the sense that it can be shown to be conducive to economic welfare on the whole, if we believe the misery that results to individuals from extreme want to be *indefinitely large*' (Pigou 1932, 760–1; emphasis added). In short, Pigou is somehow attempting to justify the enforcement of the minimum on the basis of the aggregation of economic welfare (utility), to which Sen and Suzumura did not seem to pay attention. By securing the minimum for the destitute, we are supposed to obtain a substantial increment of economic welfare. As such, the policy of securing the minimum is justified on the basis of the calculation of utility, representing roughly the same logic seen in his second proposition.

However, what if it is *not* the case that 'the misery that results to individuals from extreme want [is] to be indefinitely large'? To begin with, economic welfare can be obtained through the satisfaction of desire (preference) as measured by money. This refers to the satisfaction and pleasure we usually get under free transactions in the market (Pigou 1906, 379–80). Hence, satisfaction as economic welfare must be subjective in its

---

[4] This subsection includes some points of my previous examination (Yamazaki 2011; 2012) where I used to examine this topic from an exclusively utilitarian perspective, which is quite in contrast with the current argument.

character and it is necessary to investigate the following statement concerning the minimum:

[T]he minimum is *absolute*. If a citizen can afford to attain to it in all departments, *the State cares nothing that he would prefer to fail in one*. It will not allow him, for example, to save money for a carouse at the cost of living in a room unfit for human habitation. There is, indeed, some danger in this policy. It is a very delicate matter for the State to determine authoritatively in what way poor people shall distribute scanty resources among various competing needs. *The temperaments . . . of different individuals differ so greatly that rigid rules are bound to be unsatisfactory.* Thus Dr. Bowley writes: 'The opinion is quite tenable that the poor are forced (by the effect of the law to enforce a minimum quality and quantity of housing accommodation) to pay for a standard of housing higher than they obtain in food, and that they would make *more* of their income if they were worse housed and better fed.' This danger must be recognised; but *the public spirit of the time demands also that it shall be faced. A man must not be permitted to fall below the minimum in one department in order that he may rise above it in others.* (Pigou 1932, 759–60; emphasis added)

Here it is certain that the welfare of one who prefers to make merry at the expense of living in an unfit house is not desirable. However, is it true that their misery is so indefinitely huge as to overcome, in utility calculation, any other consideration? Pigou himself implicitly admits that those who prefer drinking to sanitation would gain more satisfaction (economic welfare) if their choice was left free (accordingly, 'the misery that results to individuals' is *not* 'indefinitely large'). In terms of rigorous utility calculation, the loss of economic welfare of the one who fails in just one or a few areas of the minimum standard could be socially compensated by substitutional increment in the utility of others, so that the enforcement of the minimum cannot be supported. Thus, the implication here seems that Pigou substantially admits that the obligation of securing minimum conditions for citizens must be valid regardless of the aggregation of social utility. Therefore, it must be impossible to fully justify the minimum on the ground of welfarism. However, the substantial basis for the minimum is the satisfaction of (non-welfarist) objective needs, as Sen and Suzumura argue above. If one's condition is below the minimum, it is not one's subjective satisfaction (economic welfare) that matters but the satisfaction of objective needs.

From what we have learned above, two more controversial points remain to be investigated: (a) even though the minimum's criterion is not utility but objective needs, how much weight is it supposed to have in comparison to any other consideration?; and (b) how is the prescription of the minimum validated? Regarding (a), we can obtain a clue from the following remark:

[N]ot enough of these things [social resources] can be available both to meet the minimum needs of all and *also* to provide as much as better-to-do persons would like to buy. In that case it is in the national interest that better-to-do persons shall be directly prevented from buying as much of these scarce goods as they would like to buy. (Pigou 1952, 210–11; italics in the original)

In short, satisfaction of the (minimum) needs of all members of society takes social priority over satisfaction of the desires of the well-to-do. This indicates the following: even when the 'satisfaction of primary needs' competes with other things such as 'satisfying of the whims of the rich' (Pigou 1937, 21), 'the satisfaction of some of the desires of the rich, such as gambling excitement or luxurious sensual enjoyment' (Pigou 1912, 10), 'the satisfaction of the poor which is derived from excessive indulgence in stimulants', 'satisfactions purchased by the rich – those, for example, connected with literature and art' (Pigou 1912, 11), it is evident from the related propositions in Pigou's argument that the satisfaction of the primary needs of people are to be socially prioritized, no matter what the need may be or for whom. Thus, satisfaction of needs is given priority despite the amount of economic welfare otherwise gained. Namely, satisfaction of 'more urgent needs' (Pigou 1937, 21), 'reasonable needs' (Pigou 1914, 55), and 'primary needs' (Pigou 1912, 11) take priority over any other consideration. And further,

I hold, *some* system of standards should be set up, and the lapse below any one of them should be made the occasion of intervention by the public authorities. For this position a good defence can, in many instances, be made upon grounds of economy; for expenditure of State moneys, so arranged as to maintain the efficiency of the poor, may often be profitable expenditure. But, even where this ground fails, the policy that I have sketched is amply maintained: for it is no more than the acceptance in fact of the compelling obligation of humanity. (Pigou 1914, 37; italics in the original)

Now, with respect to (b) validation of the minimum, it follows from this passage that Pigou recognized that the policy of the minimum standards can be justified by considerations of both economy and of the (compelling) obligation of *humanity*. It is to be noted that the former is supposed to correspond to welfarist justification, whereas the latter is supposed to correspond to non-welfarist justification. Even though Pigou did not dwell on the latter factor, it is barely conceivable that he based it on the aggregation of subjective satisfaction, namely economic welfare. It can be regarded as a non-welfarist and non-utilitarian approach.

In 'The Principle of the Minimum Wage' (Pigou 1913), Pigou observes that the doctrine of the minimum standard can be defended by various methods of reasoning. He mainly points out the three foundations for this doctrine as follows: the first is the absolute sacredness of human life, the second is the intrinsically crucial equality principle (related to distribution), and the last is teleological or consequential justification of the prescription of minimum standards (Pigou 1913, 645–6). Apart from the first reason which he regards as somewhat intuitive and less sophisticated, the second and the third can be viewed as being of ethical importance. Since Pigou does not commit himself to either of them there, he, from the beginning, seems to have embraced both the reasonings for the validity of the minimum arrangement, although he relied on exclusively the third (teleological and welfarist) justification in *Wealth and Welfare* and *The Economics of Welfare*.

4.2.6 Methodological Individualism

Another critical aspect of welfarism (or utilitarianism) is 'methodological individualism' in ethical axiology. Methodological individualism stipulates that everything that is valuable to society, and every aspect of public morality can be reduced to individuals' interests. To put it another way, individual interest is the ultimate foundation for all moral judgements, and public goods such as equality or justice that cannot belong to any individual are assumed to have no intrinsic value (cf. Singer 2011).[5] We can surely say that if one deviates from methodological individualism in ethics, one should be regarded as neither welfarist nor utilitarian. The following argument takes this perspective as a criterion to judge whether Pigou is welfarist or non-welfarist, or utilitarian or non-utilitarian, concluding that Pigou has, in principle, shown the possibility of deviation from welfarism or utilitarianism.

It is widely believed that Pigou espoused welfarism, whose ingredients are various states of conscious life. Under the banner of welfarism, however, the difference between monistic hedonism and (possibly) multiple non-hedonistic value accounts should be dismissed. Different from either the Benthamite or Sidgwickian comprehensive but simple account of hedonistic value, Pigou's welfare comprises multiple ingredients such as

---

[5] If this argument is related to or more directly meant to be what is called 'prudential value', then the critical point is a question of whether something is reducible to prudential value or not. If it is, it retains the methodological individualism in value account.

character, virtue, ethical personality, and of course happiness. His plural-istic account of value can be regarded as very close to that of Rashdall[6] and Moore. In spite of being multiple, all elements still come under the category of conscious states, therefore, his account of good may be regarded as 'refined hedonism' (cf. Baldwin 1990).

Although Pigou's concept of welfare is formally presented in *Wealth and Welfare* in 1912, he made a puzzling remark in the second edition of *The Economics of Welfare*, which differs in a very subtle way from what he had said in the first edition. In the first edition, it is stated that '[w]elfare ... is a thing of very wide range. There is no need to enter upon a general discussion of its content ... welfare includes *states of consciousness only*, and not material things' (1920, 10; emphasis added). This statement is precisely the same as in *Wealth and Welfare*. However, in the correspond-ing passage in the second edition, we find the statement 'that the elements of welfare are states of consciousness *and, perhaps, their relations*' (1924, 10; emphasis added). There were no further changes in later editions. But what did Pigou mean by this remark? We can find a clue in *A Study of Public Finance* (1928) where he mentions the relation between states of consciousness again. In the beginning part of this work he wrote: '[I]t is held by certain ethical philosophers that the only elements of good are states of consciousness. If this is so, *equity, which is a relation between states of consciousness*, clearly cannot be an element of good, or, apart from its effects, have any ethical value. The issue thus raised is an important one' (Pigou 1928, 8; emphasis added).

Incidentally, as Hongo (2007, 71) first noted, the element of 'the direct social and other relations of people with one another' is regarded as an intrinsic good (i.e. an element of welfare) in 'Memorandum' (Pigou 1907). Later, however, in 1928, Pigou refers not to 'people' but 'states of con-sciousness (good)', and we should regard 'the relation' there as the rela-tionship between good things (i.e. equity as one of patterns of distribution). Therefore, it follows from what we have already seen that Pigou, in the second edition of *The Economics of Welfare*, indicates the possibility of including certain norms of justice or equality in welfare as intrinsic goods.[7] At any rate, no matter what it may mean, the 'relation' is to be regarded as a kind of public good not capable of being reduced to

---

[6] H. Rashdall (1858–1924) was an English philosopher who expounded an ethical theory known as ideal utilitarianism, likewise Moore.

[7] As Shionoya observed, Pigou has introduced 'the normative assumption of equal utility functions' (Shionoya 1993, 16) for the rich and the poor. His remark that 'Pigou's second proposition in favor of the poor is based on the egalitarian idea' (Shionoya 1993, 16) can be

individuals' consciousness (prudential values). At this point, Pigou deviated from methodological individualism in axiology. To be certain, justice or equality cannot be individual goods, and if Pigou asserts that they are intrinsically good, he is seen to renounce welfarism (an individualistic axiology) in the strict sense of the term. Although the issue of why this change occurs remains to be further investigated, let us summarize the above with his own descriptions: 'Others hold that equality in the distribution of good is *itself an element in good*, and that a serious lapse from equality is in itself an evil so great as to outweigh any indirect loss of good that is likely to result from arrangements designed to prevent the occurrence of such a lapse' (Pigou 1913, 645–6; emphasis added). In addition, '[t]his view, it will be noted, is incompatible with the view – widely held among students of ethics – that good resides solely in states of consciousness' (Pigou 1913, 646n1). In regard to that, the following statement will come to be of significance: 'Inequality of income . . . is thus . . . an *evil in itself*' (Pigou 1937, 21; emphasis added). After all, Pigou appears to have come to hold both mutually incompatible views regarding whether equality is intrinsic good or not.

Additionally, we can detect one more pieces of evidence: 'it may well be held that *variety is in itself a good*, and that a group of varied persons, each a little less than perfect, will be better than a grope of persons all perfect and all exactly alike' (Pigou 1923, 81; emphasis added). Surely, 'variety' is to be considered not a private but a public good; accordingly, as long as he contends that it is intrinsically important, here, he, just as in the previous case in the second edition of *The Economics of Welfare*, can be thought of as deviating from methodological individualism in the theory of good, which may lead to a non-welfarist (or non-utilitarian) interpretation of his thought. Whether it may be methodological individualism or welfarism, however, these are notions formed afterwards, because he did not actually bear them in mind at that time. Although the issue of what we should think of this matter can be viewed as an academic problem, here we would like to present only the points at issue.

consistent with our finding and interpretation of 'relations' (certain equality as the intrinsic good) in the second edition of *The Economics of Welfare*. According to Shionoya, if we are to observe the genuine command of utility maximization, Pigou might assume the poor could not be considered. Then, in order for equal distribution to be secured (even in a utilitarian criterion), he must presuppose equal utility function among all. Thus, as long as whatever equality is presupposed without justification by utilitarian reasoning, Pigou's dependence on the equality, whether explicitly or implicitly, leads to non-utilitarian understanding of him as observed by Shionoya.

4.3 A Hybrid Strategy for Well-Being

Now, let us leave the dichotomy between welfarism and non-welfarism, and try to assess Pigou's overall welfare idea in the light of another modern viewpoint in the theory of well-being. To anticipate the argument, we are invoking a 'hybrid' aspect of Pigou's account of welfare.

Suzumura (1999) has argued that subjective satisfaction is not a pertinent index for people's well-being; however, the state of affairs seems more complicated. As Pigou stated, maximum satisfaction is not necessarily associated with maximum good, because some kinds of satisfaction, even though we *prefer* another kind, may do more good. However, Pigou mentions that there remains some ambiguity regarding that view (Pigou 1922, 7). Suppose we have two options: a classical concert or a drinking spree, then it is objectively considered more desirable to prefer the enjoyment of the former to that of the latter. However, if a certain person dislikes the former and loves the latter, is it still better for them to go to the concert, rather than on a drinking spree? Are we to contend that certain preferences or actions, regardless of actual preference, are judged as categorically good or right?

Pigou (1922, 7) gives the following answer: As long as the person does not recognize beforehand that the concert is good and the drinking spree is bad, to prefer the latter is good. However, if he recognizes this and still prefers the latter, his choice should be judged as wrong (still, this reasoning presumes that the consequence of his choice will not affect others. Essentially, Pigou assumes that if a choice affects others, the choice should be somehow regulated). Unsubstantiated as it may seem, Pigou's argument makes some important and interesting points regarding the modern account of well-being.[8] In the theory of well-being, what is generally identified with well-being should matter. Broadly speaking, identifying well-being with welfare (utility, in the wider sense) signifies welfarism, while non-identification means non-welfarism. The concept of well-being in ethics or welfare economics is generally classified into the subjective and objective theories (Griffin 1986; Sumner 1996).

According to Griffin and Sumner's classification, the former comprises hedonism, desire, or preference satisfaction, while the latter includes needs, function, capability, and perfectionism (there are more concepts

---

[8] For related studies, see Griffin (1986) and Sumner (1996). In particular, modern welfare economics seems to rank well-being above welfare; however, since welfare has been linked to (mere) utility or pleasure, modern welfare economics tries to refine the concept of and detach it from this soiled notion of welfare, almost identifying well-being with (intrinsic) goodness.

besides these that can be classified into either category). Viewed in terms of this classification, Pigou's position regarding well-being will prove to be interesting. His account of well-being can be placed in both categories, since his concept includes mental states, desire satisfaction, and need satisfaction approaches.

4.3.1 Mental States Approach

Pigou's early writings state that intrinsic good is limited only to 'states of conscious life'. However, Pigou's concept of good should be separated from the classical utilitarian concept (Bentham or Sidgwick), since he admits that his notion of good includes multiple elements, such as pleasure, happiness, character, virtue, ethical personality, etc., which is evidently contrary to the classical view that the only good thing is pleasure. Still, both concepts can be placed in the same category in the sense that intrinsic good is only a mental state and every other thing can merely be instrumentally valuable.

4.3.2 Desire Satisfaction Approach

As demonstrated by his concept of economic welfare, Pigou sometimes takes a desire-satisfaction approach to well-being (interestingly, Sumner (1996, 114–16) features Pigou in the context of desire satisfaction). To be certain, he evidently recognizes that satisfaction of a certain degree of desire does not necessarily assume any corresponding degree of goodness. However, to put it the other way around, with a certain qualification, the correspondence between desire and good can be admitted.

4.3.3 Need Satisfaction Approach

As has been already argued, Pigou stresses the importance of the need satisfaction criterion, in various forms. For instance, 'more urgent needs', 'needed even more than ... wanted' (Pigou 1937, 21, 23), 'satisfaction of primary needs', 'individual's needs', 'a normal working man's need' (Pigou 1912, 11, 401), 'for urgent needs' (Pigou 1935, 120–1), 'to meet the minimum needs of all' (Pigou 1952, 210), 'objective needs' (Pigou 1955, 80), 'various competing needs' (Pigou 1932, 759), 'spiritual needs' (Pigou 1951, 287), and 'reasonable needs' (Pigou 1914, 55). We can regard the following statement as summarizing this point.

Moreover, while there is a *presumption* that people, if their choice is left free, will spend their money more effectively than if they are interfered with, this presumption is sometimes wrong. What they *want* most is not always what they *need* most. They may not, for example, be inclined to spend as much money on hygienic housing or on education as in their own interest they 'ought' to do. (Pigou 1952, 158; italics in the original)

Thus, although his basic principle is welfarism, Pigou has adopted the three different approaches to augmenting people's well-being: the mental states, desire satisfaction, and need satisfaction approaches.

Next, relying on Griffin's exposition (1986), let us reconstruct Pigou's strategy for well-being enhancement as follows.[9] First, since his argument employs both desire and need criteria, and the latter is given priority over the former, Pigou's theory appears as 'quite attractive'.[10] Additionally, from his contention that '[i]f a citizen can afford to attain to it in all departments, the State cares nothing that he would *prefer* to fail in one' (Pigou 1932, 759; emphasis added), it is understandable that he does not admit mere desire or preference satisfaction, but pursues the enforcement of the minimum (need satisfaction) somewhat paternalistically from an objective perspective. In this context, Pigou seems to have placed the objective need criterion above the subjective desire one. Therefore, his welfare strategy is expected to remove prima facie unsound items, such as 'violence', 'luxurious', and 'tamed' preferences.

However, following the earlier argument, although preference for the classical concert is generally regarded as better than that of a drinking spree, to prefer the latter may admittedly be right depending on certain individuals' particular preference (e.g. drinking lovers). The former case is objective in the sense of being generally recognized, while the latter is subjective based on a particular individual's predisposition. In general, the need-satisfaction approach regards the essence of well-being as endowing people with objectively valuable things regardless of their subjective preferences. Still, Pigou admits the ultimate superiority of the subjective approach over the objective one but with certain qualifications. These qualifications are probably being well-educated, healthy, well-fed, and well-situated, that is, independently mature,

---

[9] The following part is a further development of my observation (Yamazaki 2011, 87–90) to present a new interpretation of Pigou (a hybrid strategy as is demonstrated) by referring to Griffin and Sumner.

[10] It is because Griffin observes '[o]ne quite attractive position, for instance, is that "well-being" includes both basic needs and mere desires, but that needs have priority over mere desires' (Griffin 1986, 41).

Table 4.1 *A hybrid strategy for well-being*

Trait/Phase	The first stage	The second stage	The final stage
Subjective	Raw preferences		Educated preferences
Objective		(basic) Needs	

which can be summarized into his notion of 'the capacity for enjoyment'. This capacity, he claims, largely depends on circumstantial and educational conditions, and hence, can be trained and enhanced for one to be considered mature.

To summarize this, suppose there are two characters: a person and the omnipotent observer (or, what we call the ethical observer). At first, the person satisfies their preference (say, for example, drinking) and obtains a certain happiness. However, from the perspective of the omnipotent observer, the person has not been educated nor well enough conditioned. Therefore, to modify their preference, the omnipotent helps the person detach themselves from such a seemingly degrading practice, and undertake some educational training. After this operation, the omnipotent asks the person what they want to do, and if they answer that their preference has not changed and that they still prefer drinking, the omnipotent observer should finally allow them to do so (in other words, the satisfaction of preference should be included when considering their welfare). This is essentially what Pigou argues, and the scenario is summarized in Table 4.1.

Coincidentally, the structure based on the reinterpretation of Pigou's work seems to correspond to Griffin's theory of prudential good for individuals. Griffin (1986, ch. 3) also shows the process: from bare desire to objective needs and finally to informed desire. Thus, it is reasonable to conclude that Pigou's well-being concept traverses both the subjective and objective spheres, and moreover, that it encourages the cultivation of people's internal capacities and tastes (we may call it a three-layered welfare strategy). In terms of modern well-being theory, Pigou's theory may be interpreted as one of the preceding examples of 'hybrid' theories regarding subjectivism and objectivism in welfare account (cf. Sumner 1996, 54).

If this reinterpretation of Pigou's welfare theory is valid, what evaluation can be conferred on his welfare theory? For instance, a modern philosopher, Sumner (1996, ch. 2) asserts that one of the most essential aspects of sound welfare theory is that of being subjective; hence, any objective theories would be ultimately refused because, based on the notion of 'life satisfaction' (i.e. the entire assessment of one's total life), any value should be reducible to each subjective satisfaction or recognition of one's life faring well. Mill also admits that happiness is ultimately subjective. Alternatively, with a critical remark, such as 'utility is simply the subjective vindication of individual advantages' (Suzumura 1999, 121), we can take another approach (non-welfarism). Although we are somehow capable of understanding each other's condition *objectively*, if the condition is ultimately found to be unsatisfactory and we thereby feel our lives are not faring well, what assessment should we confer to the objective approach? How can we demonstrate its validity? This is the point that Pigou's discussion makes – whatever non-welfarist approach we employ, if the final and overall outcomes were unsatisfying according to people's perception, the significance of the approach would be considerably diminished, although not completely.

4.4 Concluding Remarks

We have explored the possibility of a non-welfarist or non-utilitarian interpretation of Pigou. As has been shown, it is evident that Pigou invoked non-welfarist information and values. His recourse to need criteria and identification of equity (a distribution pattern) as the intrinsic values are thought to be a result of his practical concern rather than a theoretical one. Although he was a rigorous theorist, Pigou certainly retained a passion for social reform as a practitioner of welfare economics. The passion for practical concerns, as we have argued, made him drift from strict welfarism and turn to a non-welfarist approach. This may make us think that if welfare economics is to be truly worthy, its foundation must be beyond the narrow cage of welfarism.

Furthermore, we have pursued some new understanding of his entire welfare notion, the hybrid strategy for enhancement of people's well-being. Some critics have typically stressed utility, satisfaction, and welfare (i.e. the exceedingly subjective account of good) in Pigou's welfare economics. However, we should notice that he presupposed socially independent individuals (more or less mature) in his general argument. For instance, as his theory of charity (e.g. Pigou 1901b) evidently claimed, he never suggests that it is appropriate to just give the poor or the immature subjective satisfaction alone. Enhancement of character through education or intimate care must be prioritized for all (concretely, he stresses character and capacity for enjoyment, as well as a spirit of cooperation). Subjective desire, satisfaction, and pleasure are supposed to be meaningful if and only if they are freely pursued by those educated, independent, and mature individuals, which is essentially subsumed in the hybrid strategy.

References

Backhouse, R. E. and T. Nishizawa, eds. 2010. *No Wealth but Life: Welfare Economics and the Welfare State in Britain, 1880–1945*. Cambridge: Cambridge University Press.

Baldwin, T. 1990. *G.E. Moore*. London: Routledge.

Collard, D. 1981. A. C. Pigou, 1877–1959, in O'Brien, D. P. and John R. Presley, eds., *Pioneers of Modern Economics in Britain*. London: Macmillan, 105–39.

Edgeworth, F. Y. 1879. The Hedonical Calculus, *Mind*, 4 (15), 394–408.

1881. *Mathematical Psychics: An Essay on the Application of Mathematics to the Moral Sciences*. London: Kegan Paul.

1913. *Wealth and Welfare* by A. C. Pigou, *Economic Journal*, 23 (89), 62–70.

Gaertner, W. and P. K. Pattanaik. 1988. An Interview with Amartya Sen, *Social Choice and Welfare*, 5, 69–79.

Griffin, J. 1986. *Well-Being*. Oxford: Clarendon Press.

Hongo, R. 2007. *The Philosophy and Economics of A. C. Pigou: In the Intellectual Milieu of Cambridge* [in Japanese]. Nagoya: The University of Nagoya Press.

McLure, M. 2013. Assessments of A. C. Pigou's Fellowship Theses, *History of Political Economy*, 45 (2), 255–85.

Moore, G. E. 1903. *Principia Ethica*. Cambridge: Cambridge University Press.

O'Donnell, M. G. 1979. Pigou: An Extension of Sidgwickian Thought, *History of Political Economy*, 11 (4), 588–605.

Pigou, A. C. 1901a. *Robert Browning as a Religious Teacher*. London: C.J. Clay and Sons.

1901b. Some Aspects of the Problem of Charity, Masterman, C. F. G. *et al.*, eds., *The Heart of the Empire: Discussions of Problems of Modern City Life in England, with an Essay on Imperialism*. London: T. Fisher Unwin, 236–61.

1903. Some Remarks on Utility, *Economic Journal*, 13 (49), 58–68.

1906. The Unity of Political and Economic Science, *Economic Journal*, 16 (63), 372–80.

1907 (1910). Memorandum on Some Economic Aspects and Effects of Poor Law Relief in *Appendix* Vol. 9. Minutes of Evidence, Royal Commission on the Poor Laws and Relief of Distress, Cd.5068. London: His Majesty's Stationery Office and Wyman and Sons Ltd, 981–1000.

1912. *Wealth and Welfare*. London: Macmillan.

1913. The Principle of the Minimum Wage, *The Nineteenth Century*, 73, 644–58.

1914. Some Aspects of the Housing Problems, in Rowntree, B. and A. C. Pigou, *Lectures on Housing*. Manchester: Manchester University Press, 35–66.

1920, *The Economics of Welfare*, 1st ed. London: Macmillan.

1922. The Private Use of Money, *The Contemporary Review*, 121, 452–60.

1923. *Essays in Applied Economics*. London: P. S. King.

1924. *The Economics of Welfare*, 2nd ed. London: Macmillan.

1928. *A Study in Public Finance*, 1st ed. London: Macmillan.

1929a. *The Economics of Welfare*, 3rd ed. London: Macmillan.

1929b. *A Study in Public Finance*, 2nd ed. London: Macmillan.

1932. *The Economics of Welfare*, 4th ed. London: Macmillan.

1935. *Economics in Practice*. London: Macmillan.

1937. *Socialism versus Capitalism*. London: Macmillan.

1944. *The Road to Serfdom* by F. A. Hayek, *Economic Journal*, 54, 217–19.

1947. *A Study in Public Finance*, 3rd ed. London: Macmillan.

1951. Some Aspects of Welfare Economics, *American Economic Review*, 41 (3), 287–302.

1952. *Essays in Economics*. London: Macmillan.

1953. *Alfred Marshall and Current Thought*. London: Macmillan.

1955. *Income Revisited: Being a Sequel to Income*. London: Macmillan.

Sen, A. K. 1997. *On Economic Inequality*, expanded ed., with a substantial annexe by J. E. Foster and A. K. Sen. Oxford: Clarendon Press.

Sen, A. K. and B. Williams, eds. 1982. *Utilitarianism and Beyond*. Cambridge: Cambridge University Press.

Shionoya, Y. 1984. *The Structure of the Value Idea* [in Japanese]. Tokyo: Toyo Keizai Inc.

1993. A Non-utilitarian Interpretation of Pigou's Welfare Economics, in Koslowski, P. and Y. Shionoya, eds., *The Good and the Economical*. Berlin: Springer-Verlag, 7–24.

Singer, P. 2011. *Practical Ethics*, 3rd ed. Cambridge: Cambridge University Press.

Sumner, L. W. 1996. *Welfare, Happiness, and Ethics*. Oxford: Clarendon Press.

Suzumura, K. 1999. Welfare Economics and the Welfare State, *Review of Population and Social Policy*, 8, 119–38.

2000. Welfare Economics beyond Welfarist-Consequentialism, *Japanese Economic Review*, 51 (1), 1–32.

2002. Introduction to Social Choice and Welfare, in Arrow, K. J., A. K. Sen, and K. Suzumura, eds., *Handbook of Social Choice and Welfare*, Vol. I. Amsterdam: Elsevier, 1–33.

2007. On the Non-welfaristic and Non-consequential Foundations of Normative Economics – Or, What Is the Connecting Link between Pigou and Sen via Hicks? [in Japanese], *Economic Review*, 58 (2), 97–109.

2010. Shigeto Tsuru as the Practitioner of Welfare Economics [in Japanese], in Odaka, K. and T. Nishizawa, eds., *The Retrospection of Shigeto Tsuru: Capitalism, Socialism, and Environment*. Tokyo: Keiso Shobo, 99–114.

Yamazaki, S. 2011. *Pigou's Ethical Thought and Welfare Economics: Well-Being, Justice, and Eugenics* [in Japanese]. Kyoto: Showado.

2012. Need and Distribution in Pigou's Economic Thinking. Paper presented at 12th Conference of International Society for Utilitarian Studies, New York, 9–11 August 2012.

Yamazaki, S. and N. Takami. 2018. The Cambridge Welfare Economics, in Nishizawa, T. and T. Hirai, eds., *Cambridge Pursuit of Wisdom: Economics, Philosophy, and Literature* [in Japanese]. Kyoto: Minerva, 89–132.

5

To Which Kind of Welfare Did Léon Walras Refer?

The Theorems and the State*

Richard Arena

5.1 Introduction

Léon Walras is often assumed, at least implicitly, to be a welfarist on the grounds that his work is generally considered to be the origin of the first social welfare theorems and therefore a forerunner of Pareto optimality (Sections 5.1 and 5.2). This chapter argues that such a view contradicts the basic foundations of Walras's economic and social philosophy and especially his conceptions of society (Section 5.3) and of individuals (Section 5.4). If we take seriously Walras's distinction between "general social conditions" ("conditions sociales générales") and "specific personal positions" ("positions personnelles particulières"), we can develop an alternative interpretation of his views on welfare (Section 5.5), which leads in turn to a different, non-welfarist, conception of the Walrasian view of the state (Sections 5.6 and 5.7). But first, it is helpful to consider the standard view in a little more detail.

The modern Theory of General Economic Equilibrium (GEE) has always considered the contribution of Léon Walras as one of its main sources of inspiration. This view is expressed, for instance, by Kenneth Arrow and

* I would like to thank the participants of the Workshop "Welfare Economics and the Welfare State: Historical Re-examination," March 18–20 2013, Hitosubashi University, Tokyo and of the Workshop "Between Economics and Ethics: Welfare, Liberalism and Macro Economics," March 18–20, 2017, Le Saint-Paul, Nice, France, for their useful and valuable comments, criticisms and suggestions.

This chapter is also a friendly tribute to our kind colleague, Tamotsu Nishizawa, who allowed a splendid cooperation during so many years between historians of economic thought and economic methodologists coming from various countries and continents.

Translations of Walras's texts from French to English are mine if no other translator is mentioned.

Frank Hahn at the very beginning of their book, *General Competitive Analysis*. Characterizing their own kind of approach, they wrote that their contribution belonged to

a long and fairly imposing line of economists from Adam Smith to the present who have sought to show that a decentralized economy motivated by self-interest and guided by price signals would be compatible with a coherent disposition of economic resources that could be regarded, in a well-defined sense, as superior to a large class of possible alternative dispositions. (Arrow and Hahn, 1971: vi)

They also added that their book and therefore this "line of economists" was "concerned with the analysis of an idealized, decentralized economy. In particular, it is supposed, in the main, that there is perfect competition and that the choices of economic agents can be deduced from certain axioms of rationality" (Arrow and Hahn, 1971: v).

In 1995, Roger Guesnerie also noted:

It is useful to come back to what I consider an exemplary effort and a success story of contemporary mathematization, namely the studies of competitive equilibrium in the tradition – already formalized – of the Lausanne School. The exacting rigour applied to examining the logical validity and scope of the propositions has transformed the Walrasian model into the Arrow-Debreu model, thus making it what is in a certain way a construction without equivalent in the social sciences. ... In my opinion, the results of this study belong to the heritage of the discipline. ... And even more essentially, by purifying and clarifying the message of the Lausanne School models, contemporary formalization has even more clearly brought out its central position in the economist's "software." (Guesnerie, 1995/1997: 97–98/90)

General equilibrium theorists such as Arrow, Hahn and Guesnerie did not praise Léon Walras only for his use of rational choice, his mathematical formalization and for his representation of decentralized market economies. He was also credited with having developed a theory of the maximization of social satisfaction that today is widely interpreted as one of the first formulations of the first theorem of welfare economics, once it is assumed that a competitive GEE was also a Pareto-optimal or efficient state (see, for instance, Rebeyrol, 1999: 74). However, although it is widely held, this interpretation of Walras is far from being obvious and was criticized a long time ago by Jaffé (1977/1983). It needs to be revisited in order to draw out its consequences in the light of recent works that have contributed to the reconsideration of Walras's broader contribution to economics and social science. In particular, it has important implications for the way we view Walras's conception of welfare.

5.2 The Limits of the Usual Interpretation of Walras's Maximization of Social Satisfaction

Jaffé (1977/1983), Steiner (1994) and Béraud (2011) reconsidered the critiques addressed by Pareto (see Steiner, 1994), Launhardt (1885), Bortkiewicz (1889), Edgeworth (1889), Wicksell (1899), Samuelson (1947) and Baumol (1952) to Walras's approach of the maximization of social satisfaction.

In the first edition of the *Eléments d'Economie Pure*, Walras indeed considered the problem of social satisfaction maximization in a production economy while in the second edition (see his correspondence [Walras, 1965] with Bortkiewicz and Edgeworth in 1889) the results were extended to the theory of capitalization. In both cases, he tried to show that free competition yields a higher social maximum of satisfaction for the agents of the economy. Most of Walras's critical commentators denied this result. Some of them were not convinced by the apparent logical consistency of Walras's demonstration and they were right: more than one hundred years after, in spite of some differences of interpretation, Van Daal and Jolink (1993) and above all Mouchot (1994) confirmed and agreed that a solution to the problem raised by Walras's theorem of maximal satisfaction (at least in the case of the theory of capitalization in the second and subsequent editions of the *Eléments d'Economie Pure*) was impossible. Other commentators pointed out noncompetitive systems that offer to agents a superior maximal satisfaction. They considered however that Walras's demonstration of the existence of a social satisfaction maximum was an essential first step toward the elaboration of the first social welfare *theorem* (Baumol, 1952, for instance).

The problem is that most of all these commentators underestimated the importance of two specific assumptions made by Walras in this context, namely the zero profit and the price uniformity ones. Now, the consideration of these assumptions deeply changes the real meaning of Walras's attempt and paves the way to a rather different conception of social welfare. As Jaffé perfectly stressed,

Uniformity of competitively determined price represented for Walras not only an analytical ideal, but an ethical ideal as well, constituting an indispensable pillar of social justice. In the "Théorie de la propriété," Walras defined justice in exchange (or "commutative justice") in terms of two conditions: first, the complete freedom of every trader to pursue his own advantage in the market; and second, the complete elimination from the market of any chance for a trader to profit by exchange at the expense of his counterpart or anyone else. The first condition is satisfied by the assumed perfection of the market mechanism, and the second by the stipulated universality of the budget restraint from which no trader is exempt in the Walrasian general equilibrium schema. (Jaffé, 1977/1983: 330)

Béraud (2011: 366, 367) also emphasized the importance of these two conditions and Jaffe's, Béraud's and Rebeyrol's contributions certainly help to highlight the meaning of the following remark of Léon Walras:

> Production in a market ruled by free competition is an operation by which services can be combined and converted into products of such a nature and in such quantities as will give the greatest possible satisfaction of wants within the limits of the double condition: [1] that each service and each product have only one price in the market, namely the price at which the quantity supplied equals the quantity demanded and [2] that the selling price of the products be equal to the cost of the services employed in making them. (Walras quoted and translated into English by Jaffé [1977/1983: 331])

Now, condition (1) expresses the principle of *commutative justice*, which excludes the possibility of distributional effects or redistributional back-wash from exchange, while condition (2) is related to *distributional justice*, which excludes injustices of the existing distribution of property. If we accept this interpretation first advanced by Jaffé, it is clear that we cannot consider Walras's maximization of social satisfaction as a first formulation of the first welfare theorem but as a genuine and specific analysis of the conditions that allow to match justice, pure competition and social efficiency in a market economy. Therefore, according to this view, social and pure economics cannot be disconnected since the *Etudes d'Economie Sociale* define justice that has to be matched with pure competition in the *Eléments d'Economie Pure*. As Jaffé, Dockès, Rebeyrol and Béraud also stressed, Walras's discussion and comparison of two types of barter he attributed to Gossen and Jevons (Jaffé, 1977/1983: 333; Dockès, 1996: 119; Rebeyrol, 1999: 75 and Béraud, 2011: 366) confirm the idea that his main contribution was not to build a pre-Paretian theory of welfare but to study if a market economy *could conciliate economic efficiency and social justice*: the first of these types allowed a better optimum but was not compatible with social justice, while if the second was not the best optimum, it permitted however to realize the ideal of justice. This is the reason why Pareto considered that Walras's demonstration of the existence of the maximum of social satisfaction was logically circular (Steiner, 1994: 66). He never thought that Walras's *Economie Sociale* could be considered as a serious scientific contribution and this is why he did not even perceive the social/ethical meaning of the assumptions of uniform prices and zero profit.

5.3 From Social Satisfaction Maximization to Welfare: Walras's Specific Conception of Society

Walras considered that his contribution to the social satisfaction maximum only concerned *private* and not public goods: according to him, the "principle of free trade" could not be applied to goods related to *public* and not to *private interest*. The reasons of this point of view are not to be found in a neo-classical/Paretian conception where collective utility or social preferences have to be the result of some form of *social aggregation*.

They are related to Walras's specific *conception of the society*. According to this conception, individual members of a given society are not only rational agents, namely agents behaving according to the sole rules or rational choice theory. Let us start from the *Cours d'Economie Sociale*. In these lectures Walras defended the idea that social states are also and before all *natural states*. Why? Because, for Léon Walras, "man is characterized by his ability for the division of labour and by his moral personality" ("l'homme se caractérise par l'aptitude à la division du travail et par la personnalité morale") (Walras, 1886/1996: 94). Now both these human features allow human beings to be different from and superior to animals.

Thus, *division of labor* is not the result of a learning process as it is for instance in Alfred Marshall's *Principles* (Arena, 2002). It is a basic human feature. Referring to it, Walras wrote:

It is certainly a *natural fact* insofar as it does not depend on us to divide or not to divide labour, as it does not depend on us to be bipedal or four-legged, two-handed or four-handed (C'est assurément *un fait naturel* en ce sens qu'*il ne dépend pas* plus *de nous* [italics added] de diviser le travail que de ne le point diviser qu'il ne dépend de nous d'être bipèdes ou quadrupèdes, bimanes ou quadrumanes). (Walras, 1886/1996: 119)

Division of labor does not therefore result from individual rational choices or from agent optimizing processes; it is a characteristic and "natural" feature of human beings: "Division of labour is a natural and not a free fact" (La division du travail est un fait naturel et non point libre) (Walras, 1886/1996: 120). Why is division of labor a "natural fact" too? Walras's answer is straightforward:

The specialization of employments is not for man a conventional process and an optional resource but it is also for him the first and unavoidable condition of his existence and subsistance (Non seulement la spécialité des occupations n'est point pour l'homme un procédé conventionnel et une ressource facultative mais encore c'est pour lui la condition première et inéluctable de son existence et de sa subsistance). (Walras, 1886/1996: 120)

The concept of "personnalité morale" also contributes to distinguish human beings from animals. Far from being defined as the bearers of some form of free will, individual agents or rather "moral persons" are the result of psychology and sociology:

Moral personality is therefore a plant the development of which requires two necessary elements: a germ which is the psychological man, namely the human soul including all his faculties and a ground that is society including its institutions and traditions (La personne morale est donc une plante au développement de laquelle deux éléments sont nécessaires: un germe qui est l'homme psychologique, c'est-à-dire l'âme humaine avec ses facultés, et un terrain qui est la société avec ses institutions et ses traditions). (Walras, 1886/1996: 143)

Now, one of the reasons that explains why moral personality as well as division of labor provide the foundations of the distinction between animals and men derives from the fact that men's will is "conscious and free," while animals' one is "instinctive and fatal" (Walras, 1896/1990: 101). In other words, nature and not free will or free choices explain division of labor and moral personalities. Only a second stage can allow to set apart "humanitarian" from natural facts: division of labor is independent from human will but the existence of their moral personality paves the way to free and reasonable will, even if it is not sufficient to explain it fully:

It is often said that man is a reasonable and a free being, namely a moral person distinct from all the other beings who not being either reasonable or free are only *things* (L'homme, dit-on est un être raisonnable et libre, c'est-à-dire une personne morale par opposition à tous les autres êtres qui n'étant ni raisonnables, ni libres, ne sont que des *choses*). (Walras, 1896/1990: 34)

Thus, division of labor and "personnalité morale" "are also two natural facts but simultaneously they also provide the double foundation of all the humanitarian facts" (sont encore deux faits naturels, mais ils sont en même temps le double principe de tous les faits humanitaires) (Walras, 1896/ 1990: 91).

5.4 From Social Satisfaction Maximization to Welfare: Walras's Specific Conception of Individuals

At this stage of our contribution, it is time to investigate more thoroughly the determinants of individual behavior in Walras's economics. We noted that in relation with their moral personalities, Walrasian agents were "reasonable and free." This does not mean however that Walras accepted what he called the approach of "*spiritualism*":

According to spiritualism, man deliberates, decides and only acts according to his free will, his acts can only be imputed to him and he is personally liable for them. From this standpoint, the moral destiny of man is entirely individual and each human destiny is entirely independent from any other one; the individual is the only theater of moral facts which are all individual facts and he also is the only social type (Pour le spiritualisme, l'homme délibère, se résout et agit exclusivement en raison de sa volonté libre, ses actes lui sont personnellement imputables, et il en est personnellement responsable. A ce point de vue, la destinée morale de l'homme est absolument individuelle, et en même temps toutes les destinées humaines sont indépendantes les unes des autres; l'individu est le seul théâtre des faits moraux qui sont tous des faits individuels, et il est en même temps le seul type social). (Walras, 1896/1990: 82)

To this "spiritualist" approach, Walras opposed his own "rationalist" conception:

For rationalism, in contrast, man deliberates, decides and only acts partly according to his own will and in a complete freedom; but he also decides in relation with the *social conditions* which influence his own will and in relation with an unavoidable necessity; his acts are partially imputable to him personally but they are also *imputable to the community or the social collectivity which he is a member of*; therefore, he is personally responsible for his acts but he is also *collectively and commonly responsible* [italics added] (Pour le rationalisme, au contraire, l'homme délibère, se résout et agit, pour une part seulement, en raison de sa volonté propre, et dans une liberté absolue, et, pour une autre part, en raison des *conditions sociales* dans lesquelles sa volonté s'exerce, et sous l'empire d'une nécessité inévitable; ses actes lui sont, en partie, imputables personnellement, mais ils sont aussi, en partie, *imputables à la communauté ou à la collectivité sociale dont il est membre*; il en est, en partie responsable personnellement, mais il en est aussi, en partie, *responsable en commun ou collectivement* [italics added]). (Walras, 1896/1990: 82)

Within this approach therefore individuals provide the foundations of society but society also influences individuals (Walras, 1896/1990: 82).

It is however necessary to go further if we wish to understand how the agent's individual will and social conditions of life are combined by Walras to generate economic behavior. Walras first clearly rejects what he calls "l'individualisme absolu, soit matérialiste, soit spiritualiste" (Walras, 1896/ 1990: 82). His "rationalism" implies a conception of the society and the economy where it is impossible to consider the "ocean" as the mere "sum of the life of the water drops which it includes" (Walras, 1896/1990: 83):

We must call an *individual* a man considered independently from the society which he belongs to or each moral person living out a destiny which is independent from all other ones.

And we must call *general social conditions* the society considered independently from the men who constitute it or in other words the social environment of individual activity. But it is easy to argue that these two first terms imply the introduction of two other ones.

The first is the *state* which is the natural and necessary agent representing the institution of social general conditions. This definition of the state implies that it is supposed to represent the set of all moral persons who live out connected and interdependent destinies.

Finally we must call *specific personal positions* the natural and necessary result of individual activity when it takes place in the environment of social general conditions.

(Il faut appeler *individu* l'homme considéré abstraction faite de la société à laquelle il appartient, ou chaque personne morale envisagée comme accomplissant une destinée indépendante de toutes les autres.

Et il faut appeler *conditions sociales générales* la société considérée abstraction faite des hommes dont elle est formée, autrement dit, le milieu social de l'activité individuelle. Mais il est aisé de reconnaître que ces deux premiers termes en appellent deux autres.

En effet, il faut appeler *Etat* l'agent naturel et nécessaire de l'institution des conditions sociales générales. Ainsi défini, l'Etat représentera l'ensemble de toutes les personnes morales envisagées comme accomplissant des destinées solidaires les unes des autres.

Et enfin, il faut appeler *positions personnelles particulières* le résultat naturel et nécessaire de l'activité de l'individu s'exerçant dans le milieu des conditions sociales générales.) (Walras, 1896/1990: 134)

This quotation from Walras's *Etudes d'Economie Sociale* needs to be clarified. We first find again the notion of "personne morale." Let us come back once more to Walras's methodological foundations in his *Cours d'Economie Sociale*. The division of labor and the existence of a "personne morale" are the two "natural facts" "which provide simultaneously the dual foundation of all the humanitarian facts" (Walras and Walras, 1870/1996: 118).

Division of labor defines what Walras called "l'homme physiologique" (Walras and Walras, 1870/1996: 121) and concerns the division of labor as "the first and unavoidable condition of his existence and subsistence" (120).

Division of labor is thus a natural necessity and not the result of some form of rational choice. How can we then characterize the notion of "personnalité morale"? Moral personality implies three human psychological faculties: sensibility, intelligence and will. These faculties generate *enjoyable and esthetic love* for sensibility; *understanding and reason* for intelligence; *freedom* for will (Walras and Walras, 1870/1996: 123).

Let us here focus on *reason* and *freedom*. For our author, freedom is not a philosophical but a scientific concept:

We shall mention *freedom* as the chemist mentions *atoms* and *molecules* without assuming for it the metaphysical value of mind as well as the metaphysical value of matter (Nous parlerons de *liberté* comme le chimiste parle d'*atomes* et de *molécules* sans plus affirmer pour cela la valeur métaphysique de l'esprit que l'on affirmera la valeur métaphysique de la matière). (Walras and Walras, 1870/1996: 142)

Now, observation and experience show that two elements explain the contents of human freedom. The first was already stressed: in relation with their moral personalities, Walrasian agents were "reasonable and free"; and this reasonable and free will is related to what Walras called the "positions personnelles particulières." The second is related to social education and learning and to the influence of the social context, namely to what is called the "conditions sociales générales" by Walras.

This characterization of human behavior is somewhat surprising since it explicitly refers to two different causes that are entirely distinct and not to one which could be identified as individual and rational choice theory. This clearly means that Walras rejected pure methodological individualism. To better understand the reasons of this rejection, let us consider successively both these causes.

5.5 General Social Conditions, Specific Personal Positions and General Economic Equilibrium

The existence and influence of these social general conditions allows Walras to show that society and/or the economic system cannot be described as a simple set or even a *simple aggregation* of individual agents. Society *as such* does exist and influence individual agent behavior. Why? Because the existence of moral persons and of the division of labor implies the necessity of coordinating them.

Animals behave according to "instinctive, blind and fatal" factors and their respective "destinies" are independent (Walras and Walras, 1870/1996: 190). Quite the contrary, when human beings act in order to consume, produce and survive, they cannot ignore the existence of the division of labor and therefore the interdependence and the solidarity among all human destinies.

Thus, the so-called general social conditions provide a *purely social* factor that influences any individual behavior and implies for agents the necessity of social or inter-individual behavior coordination. This view totally differs from the one defended by modern GEE theorists and based on pure methodological individualism.

Walras located the degree of freedom that remains to individual agents within what he called the "positions personnelles particulières." Therefore, there indeed exists a space for agent free will but this space is strictly limited by human physiology and psychology and constrained by the social context. We have however still to explain if this limited and constrained free will generates rational choice in Walras's *economic theory*.

We must now come back to Walras's well-known interpretation of exchange as a "natural fact" (Walras, 1900/1976: 26–27). We know that, using their free wills, agents can influence it but only to some extent. Fundamentally and to repeat what Walras wrote concerning this "fact" in his *Eléments d'Economie Pure*, in any case, "we cannot change its contents and its laws" ("nous ne pouvons changer son caractère et ses lois.") The analysis of the fact of exchange implies the necessity to cope with two main problems. The first is not surprising; it is the problem of market general economic equilibrium:

It is first necessary within as well as without the division of labour, for the industrial production of social wealth to be *well proportioned* and not only *abundant*. Some scarce goods have not to be multiplied excessively while some others would be unsufficiently produced (Il faut d'abord qu'au sein de la division du travail, comme cela aurait lieu en dehors de la division du travail, la production industrielle de la richesse sociale soit non seulement *abondante*, mais bien *proportionnée*. Il ne faut pas que certaines choses rares soient multipliées en quantité excessive pendant que d'autres ne seraient multipliées qu'insuffisamment dans leur quantité). (Walras, 1900/1976: 34)

The second problem is more original since it is related to *social justice*: "Within as without the division of labour the distribution of social wealth among men within the society has also to be *fair* (Il faut ensuite qu'au sein de la division du travail, comme en dehors, la répartition de la richesse sociale entre les hommes en société soit *équitable*)" (Walras, 1900/1976: 34).

In other terms, the natural fact of exchange has to be compatible with both the requirements of *market clearing* and *equity*. Now, how is this compatibility achieved? It is achieved with the help of the natural foundations related to the division of labor and the existence of "moral persons." But we noted that these natural foundations also provided a framework for humanitarian facts (Walras, 1900/1976: 36).

Walras therefore drew the conclusion that market clearing or equity *could not be obtained with the mere help of a simple aggregation of individual free wills*. One element was missing: a mechanism of coordination of these free wills. Now, within this context, Walras only mentioned the conditions of both these analytical requirements but did not try to build a priori micro-foundations of general economic equilibrium and welfare. In other words, Walras tried to show how the mathematical solutions provided by general equilibrium prices were compatible with the respect of *both individual interests and social justice*, but not directly how individual rational choices could help to reach these prices. This is what we also found in the context of the search for a maximum of social satisfaction. Thus, in the conclusion of the first section of the *Eléments d'Economie Pure*, he wrote:

The theory of property sets and determines the relations between men considered as moral persons concerning the appropriation of social wealth, or the conditions of a fair distribution of social wealth between men in the society.

The theory of industry sets and determines the relations between men considered as workers devoted to specific activities dedicated themselves to the multiplication and the transformation of social wealth; or the conditions of an abundant production of social wealth among men in the society.

The first conditions are moral conditions which will be set from the standpoint of justice. Others are economic conditions which will be generated from the standpoint of interest. But both are also social conditions indications to organize society.

(La théorie de la propriété fixe et détermine les rapports des hommes comme personnes morales entre eux à propos de l'appropriation de la richesse sociale, ou les conditions d'une répartition équitable de la richesse sociale, ou les conditions d'une répartition équitable de la richesse sociale entre les hommes en société.

La théorie de l'industrie fixe et détermine les rapports des hommes considérés comme travailleurs adonnés à des occupations spéciales avec les choses en vue de la multiplication et de la transformation de la richesse sociale, ou les conditions d'une production abondante de la richesse sociale entre les hommes en société.

Les premières conditions sont des conditions morales qui seront déduites au point de vue de la justice. Les autres sont des conditions économiques qui seront déduites au point de vue de l'intérêt. Mais les unes et les autres sont également des conditions sociales, des indications en vue de l'organisation de la société.) (Walras, 1900/1976: 39–40)

This quotation shows that for Walras the respect of interest and justice is equivalent to the respect of social norms that are part of the very foundations of the *organization of society*. The necessary respect of individual self-interests is not interpreted as the result a contractual compromise between rational agents but as the realization of one of these *organizational* foundations.

5.6 Individual Agents and the State: A Different Conception of Social Welfare?

Contrary to what the *Eléments d'Economie Pure* could suggest, individual behavior is not sufficient to understand the working of the economic system and the society. The reason of this statement is obviously related to the influence played by the existence of general social conditions common to various agents. According to Walras, it is therefore impossible to understand individual behavior without taking into account the effects social conditions exert on him (Walras, 1896/ 1990: 83).

These conditions do not depend on contracts or social interactions but on social rules or institutions that preexist agents and must be respected by them. A large part of them are protected by law and therefore by the state. According to Walras, the state is not "the pure and simple set of individuals" (Walras, 1896/1990: 136) but much more than this set:

The state has its own existence which exceeds the sum of the existences of all individuals who are a part of it . . . . As far as I am concerned I argue that when the state is creating and applying laws, when it is building a road or digging a canal, when it is opening libraries and museums, *it is acting for the interest of all the members of a society, some being alive and others, more numerous, being still out of this world; this interest has to be connected to its own nature and not to the individuals which it includes* [italics added]. Society being a natural and necessary fact (and not a conventional and free one), the individual and the state are two equivalent social types and for all the social categories, the state natural law is as important as the individual natural state. (L'Etat a une existence qui lui est propre et qui dépasse même la somme des existences de tous les individus qui en font partie . . . . Je soutiens, pour ma part, que quand l'Etat fait des lois et les applique, quand il perce des routes et creuse des canaux, quand il ouvre des bibliothèques et des musées, il agit *dans l'intérêt de tous les membres d'une société desquels les uns sont vivants, mais desquels un plus grand nombre d'autres ne sont point encore de ce monde, et, par suite, en vertu d'un droit qu'il tient non point du tout des individus dont il se compose, mais de sa nature même* [italics added]. C'est ainsi, Messieurs, qu'il résulte de ce que la société est un fait naturel et nécessaire, et non point conventionnel et libre, que l'individu et l'Etat sont deux types sociaux équivalents, et que, dans toutes les catégories sociales, le droit naturel de l'Etat vaut le droit naturel de l'individu). (1896/1990: 137)

This conception of the relation between individuals and the state has important economic consequences.

First, state rationality is not based at all on standard individual rationality but on *public interest*. The state is therefore considered as an organization guided by a collective or public form of rationality and by the preoccupation of social justice. Second, public interest is defined by the state and not as some form of social welfare based on some type of agent preferences aggregation.

Third, the state has its own ends but also its own incomes (land rent essentially) and, among its main objectives, it must include the implementation of the conditions of social justice through the equality of individual initial positions.

Fourth, public and individual morals have to be clearly distinguished, the first one being dedicated to the achievement of what Walras called the "Idéal Social." Walras therefore introduced in his picture of pure, social and applied economics a conception of the state that strongly contrasts with modern views on standard public economics.

Moreover, it is clear that for Walras, the process of equalization of *raretés* or ratios of marginal utilities – that provides the unique foundation of the use of rational choice theory in Walras's economic analysis – is not always possible; it requires the use of the context of "a perfectly organized market from the standpoint of competition" (Walras, 1900/1976: 45). Therefore, rational choice as such, namely marginal utility maximization, can only be used as a norm in order to show which are the conditions of achievement of what Walras called the "Idéal Social." But the state has to play its role in this context and help to the practical realization of this norm.

As Jaffé stressed it, "uniformity of competitively determined price represented for Walras not only an analytical ideal, but an ethical ideal as well, constituting an indispensable pillar of social justice" (Jaffé, 1977/1983: 330). This uniformity implied two conditions: "first, the complete freedom of every trader to pursue his own advantage in the market; and second, the complete elimination from the market of any chance for a trader to profit by exchange at the expense of his counterpart or anyone else" (Jaffé, 1977/1983: 330–331). We find again the issue of the real meaning of Walras's attempt of finding a maximum of social satisfaction. We will not revisit here the old debate on the normative contents of Walras's *économie pure*, even if we share the major part of Jaffé's interpretation of the Walrasian message. There is only one issue to consider here: if Walras's view of welfare is not only based on an individualistic approach, we must consider more thoroughly Walras's view of the state.

This view is first related to a French national tradition that we could call Colbertism and considers the state as both a supervisor and a mediator. But it also foreshadows some of the features of the usual conception of the welfare state of the twentieth century, especially, the principles of *equality of opportunity* and of *equitable distribution of wealth* that are explicitly and deeply investigated by Walras through the difference between *justice commutative* and *justice distributive*. It strongly contrasts with the Utilitarian and the Paretian conceptions of the state (Dockès, 1996: ch. II).

First, social justice is the main foundation of society far before utility. For instance, even if slavery could increase the social satisfaction (of free individuals!!) it still had to be blamed and forbidden because it is contrary to the principle of social justice.

Second, in Walras's conception, there is nothing analogous to a classification of societies according to their types of social optimum or their aggregated utility function: as we already noted, society is autonomous and different from individuals. According to Dockès, "Léon Walras is at the Antipodes of the construction of a collective utility function based on individual utilities as well as of the Pareto optimum. It is useless to still regret that he missed such a definition! He used to reject it explicitly even before it might have been formulated!" (Dockès, 1996: 82). Dockès characterized this autonomous state and its role of supervisor and mediator using the concept of "state rationality" (Dockès, 1996: 226).

Third, in Walras, the state is first a supervisor since it determines the rules of market economies, and secures and controls their application, provided that these rules are not contrary to justice and interest. It is a supervisor because no other "collective person" (distinct from "individual persons") or organization has the abilities and the means of supervision. The state not only corrects market failures, it has its own area of intervention in favor of a public interest because it disposes of the maximal scientific knowledge and the maximal clear-sightedness ("clairvoyance") to avoid short-termism and takes the best decisions for purposes related to long-run and social general conditions.

Finally, the state is also a mediator because it is not submitted to specific individual own interests. It expresses the real social needs ("moral" as well as "utilitarian"). This is why it also disposes of its own means and resources. This explains the kind of economic policy defended by Walras in his *Economie appliquée* and based on social justice: payment of the state for land in order to give back to society what are its common resources (Dockès, 1996: 169); no direct and progressive tax on individuals (173); monopolistic supply of public services (210).

5.7 Concluding Remarks

Our conclusion is rather simple. There are two ways of considering the Walrasian conception of welfare economics and of the welfare state.

The first derives from the interpretation Pareto and Schumpeter gave of Walras's contribution to economics in their days: pure economics *has to be entirely* disconnected from social and applied economics; it is the only field in Walras's works that deserves to be considered as a major source of future advances, in spite of Walras's errors and hesitations. This is the route that paved the way to the usual interpretation of Walras's theorem of social satisfaction maximization.

A second way, arguably more faithful to Walras, was opened up by William Jaffé and consists in trying to understand the consistency and unity of Walras's global economic and social message. In this context, pure economics *cannot be disconnected* from social and applied economics; this necessary connection is the only way to really understand the methodological, philosophical and analytical foundations of pure economics. If we adopt this route, then there is little to be found in Walras concerning welfarist welfare economics. Paradoxically, however, it leads us to find in Walras some of the first characteristics of the *welfare state* in a period, in a country and in a kind of political economy that were entirely dominated by the French Liberal School of the time (Breton and Lutfalla, 1991). This conception of the welfare state is present in Walras's *Economie appliquée* and concerns many issues compatible with the French notion of "Etat-Providence" born in France in the 1860s and developed after World War II. For example, when discussing competition and markets Walras argues that it is necessary to distinguish *private* goods that concern individual agents within markets, and *public* goods that concern individuals as members of the community or the state itself. This distinction also generates the difference between "*economic*" and "*moral* monopolies" (translation from the French expression "*monopoles moraux*" used by Walras in *L'Etat et les Chemins de Fer* in 1875). Another issue to be considered is related to *taxation* as well as *nationalization of land*: both issues are connected and they influence Walras's view of state financing. *Monetary* and *social issues* could also be evoked. Several valuable contributions have been written in this respect (Steiner, 1994; Dockès, 1996; Béraud, 2011; Potier, 2011).

A systematic and unified investigation of all these themes would enable us to understand better Walras's conception of the state and view of economic policy, but such an investigation is beyond the scope of this chapter because much of the necessary work has still to be done. However, what we have done in this chapter is enough to make a strong case that the main preoccupation of Walras in this field is more closely related to the twentieth-century concept of the welfare state than it is to the so-called welfare theorems. It concerns people not just as rational individual agents but as members of communities (note the parallel with Richard Musgrave's focus on communities, discussed in this volume, Chapter 10). Hence Walras should not be seen as welfarist, not least because he took seriously the practical conditions for the realization of the "Social Ideal."

References

Arena, R., 2002. "Organisation and knowledge in Alfred Marshall's economics," in Arena, R. and Queré, M. (eds.), *The economics of Alfred Marshall: Evolution and the organisation of industry*, Palgrave Macmillan, London, pp. 221–239.

Arrow, K. and Hahn, F., 1971. *General competitive analysis*, North Holland, Amsterdam.

Baumol, W., 1952. *Welfare economics and the theory of the state*, LSE, G. Bell and Sons, London.

Beraud, A., 2011. "Walras et l'économie publique," *Oeconomia History/Methodology/Philosophy*, 1(3), September, 351–392.

Bortkiewicz, L., von, 1889. Correspondence with Walras in Walras, 1965.

Breton, Y. and Lutfalla, M., 1991. *L'économie politique en France au XIX ieme siècle*, Economica, Paris.

Dockès, P., 1996. *La société n'est pas un pique-nique – Léon Walras et l'économie sociale*, Economica, Paris.

Edgeworth, F. 1889. Correspondence with Walras in Walras, 1965.

Guesnerie, R., 1995/1997. "La modélisation en économie théorique," in Cartelier, J. (ed.), *L'économie deviant-elle une science dure?*, Economica, Paris, 1995, pp. 92–98; English ed. and trans.: "Modelling and economic theory: Evolution and problems," in d'Autume, A. and Cartelier, J. (eds.), *Is Economics Becoming a Hard Science?*, Edward Elgar, Cheltenham, 1997, pp. 85–91.

Jaffé, W., 1977/1983. "The normative bias of the Walrasian model: Walras versus Gossen," *Quarterly Journal of Economics*, no. 91, August 1977, in Walker, D. (ed.),*William Jaffé's Essays on Walras*, Cambridge University Press, Cambridge, 1983, pp. 371–387.

Launhardt, W., 1885. *Mathematical principles of economics*, Edward Elgar, Cheltenham, 1993, English translation from the German first edition.

Mouchot, C., 1994. "L'impossible théorème de l'utilite maxima des capitaux neufs," *Economie et Sociétés*, series Histoire de la pensée économique, no. 10–11.

Potier, J.-P., 2011. "Marché du travail et législation sociale dans la pensée de Léon Walras," *Oeconomia*, no. 1-3, 437–458.

Reyberol, A., 1999. *La pensée économique de Walras*, series "Théories Economiques," Dunod, Paris.

Samuelson, P., 1947. *Foundations of economic analysis*, Harvard University Press, Cambridge, MA.

Steiner, P., 1994. "Pareto contre Walras: le problème de l'économie sociale," *Economies et Sociétés – Cahiers de l'ISMEA*, XXVIII, no. 10–11, 53–73.

Van Daal, J. and Jolink, A., 1993. *The equilibrium economics of Léon Walras*, ch. 12, Routledge, London.

Walras, L., 1886/1996. *Cours d'Economie Sociale*, in Dockès, P., Goutte, P.-H., Hébert, C., Mouchot, C., Potier, J. P. and Servet, J.-M., *Oeuvres Economiques Complètes, volume XII*, Economica, Paris, 1996.

Walras, L., 1896/1990. *Etudes d'Economie Sociale*, in Dockès, P., Goutte, P. H., Hébert, C., Mouchot, C., Potier, J. P. and Servet, J. M., *Oeuvres Economiques Complètes, volume IX*, Economica, Paris, 1990.

Walras, L., 1900/1976. *Eléments d'Economie Politique Pure ou Théorie de la Richesse Sociale*, Librairie Générale de Droit et de Jurisprudence, Paris, 1952, first publication and 1976, new printing; Pichon, R. and Durand-Auzias, R. (eds.), Paris, 1900, final version revised by the author.

Walras, L., 1965. *Correspondence of Leon Walras and related papers, volume II*, edited by Jaffé, W., North Holland, Amsterdam.

Walras, L. and Walras, A. L., 1870/1996, *Oeuvres économiques complètes*, Tome 12, (Cours d'économie sociale; Cours d'économie politique appliquée; Matériaux du cours d'économie politique pure), Economica, Paris.

Wicksell, K., 1899. "Leon Walras. Etudes d'économie sociale appliquée: théorie de la production de la richesse sociale," *Jahrbucher fur Nationalokonomie und Statistik*, in Wicksell, K., *Selected essays in economics*, edited by Sandelin, B., Routledge, London, 1999.

6

Value Judgement within Pareto's Economic and Sociological Approaches to Welfare

Rogério Arthmar and Michael McLure

6.1 Introduction

The new welfare economics developed by John R. Hicks examined the welfare implications of exchange and production without resort to interpersonal comparisons of utility or, indeed, to any value judgement predicated on interpersonal comparison. On that basis, 'new welfare economics' was crafted around the 'Pareto test' (i.e. a welfare improvement in a community is achieved when no one is harmed by a change and at least one person gains) and the 'Kaldor-Hicks' compensation principle.

The 'New Welfare Economics' of a later generation – by which I mean not only the so called 'Kaldor-Hicks' compensation principle, but the whole body of work by Hotelling, Kahn, Bergson, Scitovsky, Little and many other besides Kaldor and myself – takes its name from Pigou (the 'Economics of Welfare') but its distinguishing mark is its use of the Pareto test. (Hicks 1975 [1999: 427])

Within that context, the Paretian origins of the 'New Welfare Economics' are largely evident from Hicks and Allen (1934) and Hicks (1939).

As Kotaro Suzumura (2016) has pointed out, however, when Hicks introduced his *Essays in World Economics* with a 'Preface – and a Manifesto', he presented what is now regarded as a manifesto of 'non-welfarism' (see Suzumura, Chapter 7 in this volume). In that document, Hicks appears to characterise 'economic welfarism' by the relationship between value propositions and economic analysis described above for the 'New Welfare Economics'; plus, issues related to distribution that fall within the scope prescribed by A. C. Pigou (1920) in *The Economics of Welfare*. While non-welfarism is not defined clearly in the Manifesto, its main characteristic appears to be the withdrawal of the economists' prohibition on value judgements, such as those associated with interpersonal comparisons of utility, when advising public authorities on the practical development of policy.

Vilfredo Pareto's approach to welfare theory too went through a substantial transformation. In 1894, he started a theoretical investigation of the topic in 'The Maximum of Utility Given by Free Competition' (Pareto 1894), which set his path for an economic analysis of collective welfare in which individuals are treated as egocentric in the sense that they do not act with regard to others except for respecting their property rights. By 1913 he started theoretical investigation of 'The Maximum of Utility for a Collective in Sociology' (Pareto 1913 [1999]), in which people are treated as social beings, in that one's own welfare also depends on the welfare of others.

The purpose of this chapter is twofold. First, to track Pareto's contributions to the stream of 'economic welfarism' associated with the 'new welfare economics', commencing from Pareto (1894) and continuing to his subsequent studies on the economics of welfare. Particular consideration is given to Pareto's treatment of values within that approach, which Vincent Tarascio (1968) characterised as methodological commitment to 'ethical neutrality'. Second, to identify the treatment of values within his sociology of collective welfare, from Pareto (1913) until his *Sociologia* (1916 [1935]), and to establish the extent to which his sociology of welfare constitutes a move in the direction of non-welfarism as envisaged by Hicks.

To meet these objectives, the chapter is structured in four parts including this introduction. Section 6.2 considers the development of Pareto's economics of collective welfare as an early example of economic welfarism. Particular attention is given to his exclusion of interpersonal comparisons of utility from the study of collective economic welfare and the introduction of a division between the roles of the Ministry of Production and the Ministry of Justice. Section 6.3 examines Pareto's sociological analysis in relation to values and the extension of his approach from a limited notion of economic welfare to the very much broader notion of social welfare. The non-welfarism dimension to Pareto's sociology of welfare concerns his reintroduction of interpersonal comparisons of utility and his withdrawal of the Pareto test. The study concludes in Section 6.4 that Pareto's treatment of values in his economics of welfare is an early and typical case of economic welfarism in the sense that he does not deny the importance of values, rather, he attempts to have them isolated and confined as *extra-economic* considerations. In contrast, Pareto's sociology incorporates individuals' values within the analytical process. But as Pareto also retains the requirement of ethical neutrality for policy advisors, his sociological approach to welfare does not extend to Hicks's notion of non welfarism.

6.2 Pareto's Approach to Economic Welfare as 'Economic Welfarism'

Pareto (1894) investigates the relationship between efficient production and utility maximisation. The *Cours d'Économie Politique* (Pareto 1896–7 [1971]), published a few years later, includes the proof of the main propositions presented in Pareto (1894), but, for our purposes here, the primary importance of the *Cours* is that it situated the issues of economic equilibrium and economic welfare within a broader context that reflects value propositions.

6.2.1 Policy Problem That Culminates in Analysis of Efficiency in Production

The theoretical exposition of the relationship between production, competition and economic welfare presented in Pareto (1894) was written with a practical problem in mind. Specifically, Pareto wanted to develop a general analysis capable of challenging the following proposition, which he appeared to associate with the labour movement: consumers experience a gain when entrepreneurs adopt more labour-intensive methods of production because this increases the aggregate value of wages, which, in turn, fund expenditure on consumer goods. To test, and ultimately reject, this proposition, Pareto presented three basic problems for resolution, which, for convenience, are labelled in this paper as the problem of *production and distribution*, the problem of *utility maximisation* for society as a whole and the problem of *utility maximisation without interpersonal comparisons*.

Pareto (1894) was published in two distinct parts, with the problems of *production and distribution* and the *utility maximisation* considered in the first part of the paper without raising the issue of the interpersonal comparison of utility implied by the analysis. It is only in the second part of the paper, drafted in response to concerns raised by Maffeo Pantaleoni and Enrico Barone, that Pareto extended his analysis to make it explicit that his solution to the problem of utility maximisation does not depend on an interpersonal comparison of utilities, which is, of course, a critical plank of 'economic welfarism'.

The problem of *production and distribution* is formalised by introducing variable coefficients of production within the Walrasian system of general equilibrium. Pareto succinctly presented that system as three sets of equations, which indicate that: (i) from the demand side, the prices for each good are given at the point where relative prices equal relative marginal utilities, provided the sum of the excess demands is zero; (ii) from the supply side, the prices for each good are given by the cost of production;[1] and, to close the system, (iii) the total quantity of each productive service required to produce the total quantity of each consumer good demanded is available to entrepreneurs.

Given the above system, prices and quantities are influenced by the coefficients of production, which, in turn, are determined by the prevailing production technologies. More specifically, Pareto treats relative prices, the quantities that individuals demand and the total quantity of goods available as functions of the coefficients of production. He then solves his *production and distribution* problem by finding the marginal conditions under which variable coefficients of production will minimise the unit costs of production for each good on the assumption that each entrepreneur is a price taker.

In regard to the problem of *utility maximisation*, Pareto's initial assessment (in part one of the paper) considered the net effect of utility gained from consumer good consumption 'for society as a whole' and the utility expended in production for 'society as a whole', with utility 'reckoned' in terms of the numeraire good A. The net impact on utility can, on that basis, be considered for a variation in the quantity of labour used in the production process (∂a_s), with the marginal condition for maximisation given by equation (1):

$$0 = \frac{\partial R_a}{\partial a_s} + p_b \frac{\partial R_b}{\partial a_s} + \ldots - p_t \frac{\partial R_t}{\partial a_s} - p_s \frac{\partial R_s}{\partial a_s} - \ldots \qquad (1)$$

Where:

R_a, R_b are the aggregate quantities of the two goods a and b for society as a whole.

R_t, R_s are the aggregate quantities of productive services t (land) and s (labour) for society as a whole.

---

[1] For example, the price of commodity A is given by the coefficient of production for a particular productive service used to produce A multiplied by the price of that particular productive service; and so on until the value of all productive services used in the production of A are accounted for in the unit cost equation for Commodity A.

∂a_s an infinitesimal variation in the production coefficient for labour, i.e. variation in the quantity of labour used in the production of one unit of numeraire good a.[2]

p_b the price of economic good b, given by the ratio of the final degree of utility of good b to the final degree of utility of numeraire good a.

p_s the price of productive services s, given by the ratio of the final degree of utility of the services of labour to entrepreneurs (or the final degree of utility sacrificed by workers) to the final degree of utility of numeraire good a.

The quantity demanded for each factor of production alters following a variation in the production coefficient for labour. The change in the quantity of each factor of production is then multiplied by its price to estimate the change in the value of the factors of production in terms of the numeraire. The resulting equation reduces to equation (1) when it satisfies the conditions for unit cost minimisation, which reflects the production coefficients determined under free competition. From this result, Pareto presents the following 'theorem': 'The fabrication coefficients determined by free competition have values identical with those obtained by determining those coefficients subject to the condition that they produce the maximum utility with minimum sacrifice' (Pareto 1894 [2008: 393]). The second part of the paper commences with Pareto noting that Pantaleoni and Barone had warned him that the first part of the paper was 'too imperfect and incomplete': 'The observations of these distinguished gentlemen applied to those parts of the demonstration in which . . . it appeared that my approach ran counter to the principle that the different individual utilities are reckoned in different units and cannot therefore, at least without special precautions, be added' (Pareto 1894 [2008: 395]).

Pantaleoni's and Barone's comments to Pareto are not extant, but it is certain they advised Pareto that equation (1) treats utility, which is not subject to interpersonal comparison, in terms of values based on the numeraire good, which are comparable across individuals. Pareto therefore added a second part to his paper to explicitly address the *utility problem without interpersonal comparisons*. He addressed this concern by defining all elements of production and utility with respect to each individual; and by identifying and isolating the objective and the subjective aspects of each individual's change in utility as a result of a change in the method of

---

[2] Variations in the labour production coefficient can be considered for any good, not just the numeraire good a.

producing. The term λ_i is specified as the quantitative change in individual i's income expenditure, as valued in units of the numeraire, following a change in the production coefficients; and φ_{ia} is individual i's final degree of utility[3] of the numeraire (i.e. good A). Each individual's variation in utility from a change in the production coefficients is, therefore, the product $\lambda_i\varphi_{ia}$. The first term, λ_i, is the objective and observable element of utility and the second term, φ_{ia}, is the subjective element of utility that is explicitly reckoned in different units by different individuals.

As the numeraire is an economic good, its final degree of utility is positive. Consequently, individuals with positive λs will have experienced a gain in utility following a change in production coefficients for labour (da_s);[4] whereas individuals with negative λs will have experienced a loss in utility. In regard to the *problem of utility maximisation*, when every individual's λs is positive, each individual's utility is necessarily enhanced by a small positive change in the quantity of labour used to produce one unit of the numeraire good da_s. Conversely, when every individual's λs is negative, each individual's utility can be enhanced by reversing the variation in da_s to provide for a small negative change in the quantity of labour used to produce one unit of the numeraire good (see footnote 11). Whenever every individual's λ is positive, or whenever every individual's λ is negative, it is always possible to alter production coefficients so that everyone experiences an increase in utility, thereby eliminating any need to compare the utilities of different individuals.

At this point, Pareto needed a criterion that does not require interpersonal comparisons of utility yet still accounted for the possibility of improvements in welfare as productivity being concurrent with harm to some individuals. He settled on a compensation criterion, another of the key concepts of economic welfarism, under which a welfare gain is obtained when the numeraire value of the gain, to those with a positive λ, exceeds the numeraire value of the loss, to those with a negative λ. In that case, the change in production coefficients would create a positive economic 'residual' for society as a whole. With an appropriate distribution of that residual, it is, therefore, possible to realise the maximum of the utility of each individual in society up to the point where the sum of the positive and

---

[3] In the 1894 'Maximisation of Utility' paper, Pareto employs the terminology of Stanley Jevons (and not Léon Walras's *rareté* or Alfred Marshall's marginal utility).

[4] Constant final degrees of utility in welfare analysis are implicitly assumed. But, of course, the welfare gain will still stand when the relative fall of each individual's final degree of utility is less than the relative increase in each individual's increase in consumption (as implied by the law of diminishing final degree of utility).

negative λs from any change in production coefficients is zero. At that point, utility is maximised for all individuals as further change will mean that someone is necessarily harmed because those who gain no longer have the capacity to pay full compensation to those who lose.

In regard to the problem of *utility maximisation without interpersonal comparisons*, Pareto contended that the maximisation of production of economic goods is, once again, matched with the maximisation of individual's welfare via the introduction of a compensation criterion. If an increase in the quantity of labour reduces the unit cost of production, an economic 'residual' measured in terms of the numeraire good will be produced that can be distributed among the community in a manner that increases the welfare of everyone. If an increase in the quantity of labour increases the unit cost of production, the numeraire value of output will be reduced (wealth will be 'destroyed') and economic welfare will be diminished. The point of production maximisation coincides with the point of utility maximisation given by equation (1) when compensation is provided to the point where the sum of individuals' positive and negative λs is equal to zero: 'the value of the coefficient a_s ensures that the different commodities will be produced in quantities such that, when they are suitably distributed, they give each individual the maximum utility (that is, the sum of the positive utilities less the negative ones) compatible with the economic conditions under consideration' (Pareto 1894 [2008: 398]). Pareto (1894) is, therefore, important for laying the foundation for the theory of economic welfare, under which free competition is shown to yield an economic maximum in welfare terms, without resorting to interpersonal comparisons of utility.

6.2.2 Values When Economic Welfare Is a Production Problem

The most distinct consequence for economic welfarism, especially the aspect associated with the 'new welfare economics', derives from Pareto's dichotomisation between the problem of producing goods that people value and the problem of distributing those goods among society. This led Pareto to posit that, if the goal of a socialist state was to maximise utility, it should differentiate between the roles of the 'Minister of Production', to establish the production coefficients that minimise unit cost and maximise the production of economic goods, and the 'Minister of Justice', to distribute economic goods in the manner that obtains distributive justice. If, for example, the 'Minister of Justice' wishes to advantage a certain group of workers at the expense of others in society, it would be inefficient for the

'Minister for Production' to alter the production coefficients to achieve that goal. Rather, efficient redistribution would be achieved by the 'Minister for Production' adopting production coefficients that are identical to those adopted by entrepreneurs under free competition;[5] and the 'Minister for Justice' then directly taking the product from individuals and transferring it to the favoured workers.

In other words, Pareto took his theorem, in conjunction with the compensation criterion to avoid interpersonal comparisons of utility, as the basis for achieving the desired redistribution at the minimum cost. But given the partial treatment of exchange in Pareto (1894), there was little prospect of him fully deriving the second law of welfare economics. Even though the general interdependence of Pareto's own equations for *production and distribution* actually suggest that the same pattern prevails for demand and the associated equilibrium price system, Pareto's verbal account is predicated on an implied direction of causation that runs from the coefficients of production to quantities produced and exchanged as well as equilibrium prices. At that stage, then, Pareto appears to have conceived of an economic maximum as a point in commodity space irrespective of the distribution of goods between individual members of the society.[6]

In terms of laying a foundation for economic welfarism, however, especially the part associated with new welfare economics, the most important point is that Pareto (1894) provided the distinct assignment of roles between the ministers of production and justice. And he did so in a manner that contemplated the demarcation between the economic analysis of welfare and the value judgements later associated with Hicksian economic welfarism. In other words, the domain of 'welfare economics' concerns the efficiency of free competition in terms of welfare; and the mechanism by which 'extra-economic redistribution', as determined by the 'Minister for Justice', can be achieved in an efficient manner. The value

---

[5] Pareto's formal welfare analysis does not explicitly consider savings or variations in capital formation. When discussing the role of the 'Minister for Production', however, Pareto concedes that that Minister must also consider the part of production that is to become working capital and 'decide to what uses the new capital must be put and what transformations the old capital must undergo' (Pareto 1894 [2008: 402]). If the Minister wishes to maximise utility, then Pareto contends that decisions on the use and transformation of capital have to mimic those made by entrepreneurs under free competition.

[6] In Pareto (1913), however, he makes it clear that economic maxima are a locus of points, not a single point (see Section 6.3 of this chapter). The oversight in Pareto (1894) is that he did not consider the implications for the equilibrium price system as the change in the initial endowment, through redistribution introduced by the direction of the Ministry of Justice, alters the final degree of utility for each economic good.

propositions in Pareto (1894) associated with the domain of welfare economics are:

(i) that an increase in an individual's utility is good and the maximisation of each individual's utility is best;

(ii) to avoid interpersonal comparisons of utility, maximisation of each individual's utility is determined via the compensation criterion; and

(iii) the individual's property rights are preserved (such that exchange is either voluntary or, if involuntary, compensation is paid for that harm) unless extra-economic goals for redistribution are set by the Minister of Justice, in which case the task of welfare economics is to minimise the cost of such redistribution.

However, when setting the 'extra-economic' goals for redistribution, the role of the 'Minister for Justice' is formally unconstrained and may undertake interpersonal comparison of utility or use of any type of value proposition deemed fit.

The main additional contribution of the *Cours* was to set the analysis of Pareto (1894) in a much broader context. Pareto achieved that by replacing his Jevonian focus on utility by distinguishing between utility and (his neologism) 'ophelimity'. Utility, in the *Cours*, involves judgement as to whether an action is useful, especially in the long term. More specifically, utility concerns ultimate ends, of which Pareto highlights two classes: 'individual utility', which relates to the abstract qualities of things likely to procure the physical, intellectual and moral development of an individual while assuring, and prolonging, his or her existence; and utility of the aggregate,[7] which relates to the abstract qualities of things that can assure the reproduction of the aggregate (or of the species) and the reproduction of physical, intellectual and moral prosperity of the aggregate (Pareto 1896–7 [1971: 1085]). In contrast, ophelimity is simply concerned with the pleasant sensations derived from the satisfaction of desires or needs without regard to physical, intellectual or moral well-being or the legitimacy, or otherwise, of satisfying desires or needs (Pareto 1896–7 [1971: 1086]).

When Pareto (1894) is read in light of the scheme presented in the *Cours*, the word utility should be read as 'ophelimity' (and the phrase 'final degree of utility' would be read as 'elementary ophelimity'). That is, his 1894 discussion of the 'maximum of utility' must be read as a reference to the

---

[7] Utility of the aggregate may be so broadly defined to be concerned with the utility of the species.

'maximum of ophelimity'; and the prohibition on interpersonal comparisons of utility becomes a prohibition on interpersonal comparisons of ophelimity. The intuition behind this is clear: although Pareto regards welfare in its fullest sense as dealing with the physical, intellectual and moral development of an individual, as well as the physical, intellectual and moral prosperity of the community in aggregate, he recognised such issues cannot be treated without resort to value judgement of some kind involving interpersonal comparisons of utility. So ophelimity is a concept created to facilitate the form of simplification that culminates in abstract modelling. The method of concrete deduction is employed to consider *homo œconomicus* as a molecule that responds to the force of *elementary ophelimity* and nothing else. On that basis, Pareto's theorem of welfare economics and his tentative developments towards what is now known as the second law of welfare economics were 'first approximations' under which the 'extremely varied and complex motivations of human action' are replaced by a one-dimensional *homo œconomicus*, for whom interpersonal comparisons of ophelimity were simply not necessary.

But the context for a more comprehensive welfare analysis is evident from the *Cours*, which introduces different classes of utility so that branches of knowledge within the social sciences could be developed. In that regard, Pareto (1896–7 [1971: 129]) identifies three different types of utility: economic utility, which assures 'material wellbeing'; moral utility, which furnishes more perfect morals; and religious utility, which provides more perfect religious beliefs. The problem that Pareto points to is that none of these categories, including economic utility, lend themselves well to scientific investigation, which typically breaks ideas and notions into smaller and less vague terms with an objective meaning that can be related to the observable world. While Pareto's own theoretical analysis stopped at economic equilibrium and welfare based on ophelimity, he implied in the *Cours* (Pareto 1896–7 [1971: 129]) that it may be possible to undertake studies of moral ophelimity, dealing with the relationships between pleasurable sensations and acts motivated by morals, and religious studies, dealing with the relationship between pleasurable sensation and acts motivated by religious beliefs. Indeed, in the *Manual of Political Economy*, he even coined the phrases *homo ethicus* and *homo religiosus* (Pareto 1906 [1909; 2014: 9]) as possible subjects of moral and religious theories.

In Pareto's subsequent economic works, the relationship between welfare analysis and value propositions outlined in Pareto (1894) was continued. Indeed, in some respects, his position on the matter became more ardent and less compromising. Notably, notwithstanding the introduction of his clear distinction between ophelimity and utility in the *Cours*, in the preface to the *Manual of Political Economy* Pareto chastised himself for letting his values intrude into science.

[T]hroughout the *Cours*, it can be seen that here and there the author regards peace and economic and political freedom as the best means of obtaining people's welfare. But he does not and cannot provide any scientific proof of that proposition, that is, a proof which is based solely on facts; hence that belief transcends, at least for the time being, objective reality, and seems to originate largely in sentiment. Precisely for that reason, it should have been absolutely excluded from a work whose sole aim was to study the facts scientifically. (Pareto 1906 [2014: xiv])

But it should also be noted that the increased importance he assigns to the distinction between logical and non-logical actions in the *Manual* also provided the platform from which he subsequently ruled out any prospect of welfare economics, based on the economic ophelimity of *homo œconomicus* as a logical actor, being complemented by concrete deductive studies of the logical actions of *homo ethicus* and *homo religiosus*. In his *Treatise on General Sociology* (1916 [1935]), actions motivated by morals and religion, or values more generally, are fundamentally non-logical in character – and, from an analytical perspective, the underlying non-logical character of ethical and religious propositions trumps the actual form that specific ethical and religious propositions take (see Section 6.3).

6.2.3 'On a New Error' and the Manual of Political Economy

After the *Cours*, Pareto's contributions to economic welfare mainly concerned theoretical formalism, as he continued to utilise the relationship between welfare economics and values associated with the 'economic welfarism' of Pareto (1894).

'On a New Error in the Interpretation of the Theories of Mathematical Economics' (1902 [2008]) was Pareto's response to Gaetano Scorza's criticism of Pareto's theorem of welfare economics.[8] In that paper Pareto investigated whether it is possible to improve economic welfare by moving away from a point of general equilibrium, which he labelled 'position (I)'. When Walras's law holds, such that income equals expenditure in aggregate, and production and exchange are constrained by the initial endowment, Pareto established that 'position (I)' is a maximum of ophelimity that satisfies equation (2):

---

[8] The Pareto-Scorza polemic is discussed by Chipman (1976[1999]), with some errors and misinterpretation in that account identified in McLure (2000).

$$0 = \frac{1}{\varphi_{1a}}\delta\Phi_1 + \frac{1}{\varphi_{2a}}\delta\Phi_2 + \frac{1}{\varphi_{3a}}\delta\Phi_3 + \dots \qquad (2)$$

Where:

φ_{ia} the elementary ophelimity (marginal utility) of individual i for the numeraire good a;

$\delta\Phi_i$ individual i's increment of total ophelimity. When δq_{ia} indicates an infinitesimal change in quantity of good a held by individual i, that individual's increment of total ophelimity is given by:

$$\delta\Phi_i = \varphi_{ia}\delta q_{ia} + \varphi_{ib}\delta q_{ib} + \varphi_{ic}\delta q_{ic} + \dots .$$

He then demonstrated that for any movement away from position (I), due to a very small change in prices, relative prices would no longer be equal to relative elementary ophelimities. As a consequence, at least one person must be harmed when the endowment constraint is not violated and total income is equal to total expenditure. Consequently, Pareto now referenced his proposition that free competition yields an economic maximum to the Pareto test, rather than the compensation criterion used in Pareto (1894). 'It follows from all this that the equilibrium position of maximum ophelimity... is such that we cannot, with infinitesimal variations in quantities, depart from it by increasing (or decreasing) all ophelimities, ... if certain ophelimities increase, other necessarily decline; if some individuals are favoured, other will be penalized' (Pareto 1902 [2008: 524]).

This above definition of the Pareto test is substantively the same as that adopted in the *Manual*.[9] Again, as in Pareto (1902), he considered efficiency with the initial point of reference being equilibrium and does so only with the aid of the Pareto test (i.e. without having to resort to the compensation criterion). Within that context, Pareto made at least three

---

[9] The *Manual* defines the 'Pareto test' in the following terms: 'We shall say that the members of a community enjoy, in a certain situation, maximum ophelimity when it is impossible to move slightly away from this position in such a way that the ophelimity enjoyed by each member of the community increases or decreases' (Pareto 1906 and 1909 [2014: 179]). John Chipman criticised the ambiguity of this definition because 'if one moves along the equilibrium price line in the "Edgeworth box" away from the equilibrium point, both traders will lose' (Chipman in Pareto [2014: 443]). But Pareto (1894 [2008: 397] and (1902 [2008: 525]) had previously made it clear that a state in which all members of society have suffered a loss is actually a state in which all members of society have the potential to experience a gain – all that is required is a reversal of the variation that harmed everyone.

notable contributions to the study of economic welfare in the *Manual*. He enhanced Francis Y. Edgeworth's work by introducing what is now known as the 'Edgeworth box' diagram to economics.[10] He also qualified his theorem of welfare economics through the introduction of the 'line of complete transformation'; and, finally, he introduced welfare analysis in terms of distributable surplus in the 1909 French edition. In this section, only the last of these three contributions is discussed.

6.2.4 The 'Economic Meaning' of 'Economic Welfare'

The French edition of the *Manual of Political Economy* provided a discussion of the economic meaning of equation (2) in terms of the change in numeraire value that each individual will gain or lose following an arbitrary variation. Specifically, $\frac{1}{\varphi_{ia}}\delta\Phi_i$ from equation (2) is the numeraire value of individual i's infinitesimal change in total ophelimity, so it is related as δs_1 and the economic change in welfare becomes δS. As such, the economic meaning of welfare is given by:

$$\delta S = \delta s_1 + \delta s_2 + \delta s_3 + \ldots = 0 \tag{3}$$

Equation (3) and equation (2) are, of course, equivalent in a mathematical sense. But equation (3) underlines the concrete aspect of material gain, resulting from a move from a state of disequilibrium to a state of equilibrium, without sacrificing welfare properties of the analysis. In view of that, Maurice Allais contends that the above relation may be called 'equivalent surplus' (1975 [1999: 447]). This makes perfect sense because, when moving to a state of equilibrium, equation (3) indicates the quantity of the numeraire that each individual will gain as a result of that change as well as the numeraire value of that change for the community in aggregate. But, from the definition of δs_i, the numeraire is also an indicator of individual i's utility so, although the δs_1 can be summed, that sum does not indicate aggregate value of utility, as each individual's utility cannot be compared.

Allais (1975 [1999: 448]) notes that individuals i's δs_i from the French *Manual* is defined 'using ordinal indexes of preference only'. This is, of course correct, but it must be recognised that inclusion of the initial numeraire in equation (1) by Pareto (1894) predates his formalisation of equilibrium using a preference-based ordinal system (Pareto 1900); and his treatment of welfare maximum subsequent to that (Pareto 1902) still

[10] See McLure and Montesano (2019) for a new history of Edgeworth's and Pareto's respective contributions to development of the box diagram.

reflected a formalism that referenced elementary ophelimity (marginal utility). In Pareto's mind, establishing the existence of an identifiable link between the abstract (ophelimity or welfare) and the concrete (the numeraire) was evidently far more important than the use of ordinal preferences in theory because that link gave mathematical formalism its concrete economic meaning. The other important aspect of the abstract-concrete linkage in welfare economics was that that linkage does not provide a way of sidestepping Pareto's 'no bridge' rule. That is, an economist cannot indirectly compare the ophelimity or welfare of person A with person B by comparing their respective wealth or income in terms of the numeraire, because each individual still evaluates the elementary ophelimity of the numeraire in different units.

In summary then, beyond the implicit proposition that an increase in ophelimity is good and a reduction in ophelimity is bad, the development of Pareto's welfare economics between 1894 and 1909 was fundamentally 'ethically neutral'. That neutrality was attained by: differentiating the role of the Ministry of Production from that of the Ministry of Justice; recognising that there is 'no bridge' by which economists can make comparisons of ophelimity between individuals;[11] subjecting welfare analytics to the Pareto test or the compensation criterion; and providing an ordinal link between the outcome of welfare analysis, as represented by ophelimity, and the economic meaning of that analysis, as represented by the numeraire good.

6.3 From Economic to Social Welfare: A Move towards Non-welfarism?

The *Manual* included an introductory chapter on the social sciences, which was an important step towards Pareto's attempt to create a general theory of non-logical actions. The next substantive step in that direction materialized in his article 'Le azioni non logiche' (Pareto 1910), in which the relationship between logical and non-logical action are discussed in terms of a relationship between the objective and the subjective ends of action. In the *Treatise on General Sociology* (henceforth, *Sociology*) he introduced the third aspect on non-logical action, namely, the aspect of utility. In so doing,

---

[11] 'Ophelimity, or its index, for one individual and ophelimity, or its index, for another individual are heterogeneous quantities. They may neither be added together, nor compared: *No bridge* as the English say. A sum of ophelimities enjoyed by different individuals does not exist; such an expression has no meaning' (Pareto 1909 [2014: 133]).

it is clear that his sociology steps outside the strict confines of 'economic welfarism' associated with the concept of ophelimity; and considers the difficult question of what is useful in a social context.

In switching his focus from ophelimity to utility, Pareto explicitly considered how an individual's faith and sentiments affect their judgement of what is good in relation to their behaviour and the behaviours of others. But, the sociologist, in Pareto's mind, still practises 'ethical neutrality' when seeking to act scientifically in the study of how interaction between people, with similar and different values, impacts on social outcomes. In a step towards understanding how sentiment influences social action, Pareto considered how doctrinal theory is created and used to alter action. 'Certain individuals evolve a theory because they have certain sentiments; but then the theory reacts in turn upon them as well as upon other individuals to produce, intensify or modify certain sentiments' (Pareto 1916 [1935: 11]).

About the derivation of a sociological approach to collective welfare, the above has at least three implications for Pareto. First, utility is influenced by the force associated with sentiment that leads a person to action; but that force is also linked to changes with the form of a theory that rationalises a particular sentiment, which Pareto later labels as 'derivations'. Second, both the 'derivation' and its underlying sentiment must be considered from the perspective of those asserting a particular derivation, and its underlying sentiment, and from the perspective of those assenting to that derivation, and its underlying sentiment. Third, although utility is necessarily in a continual state of variation due to the variable force associated with derivations and modifications to aspects of the institutional form of the social states, at some very general level the social state is either preserved or it collapses. This has implications for both the broad character of the social state, which Pareto tends to call the social equilibrium, and the application of social welfare analysis under conditions of a given social state.

Pareto's sociological assessment of continuity and change in social equilibrium is a 'relative' assessment: every force for continuity or change is considered relative to the prevailing social state. The subjective assessment of ends is based on information available at the time; and the aspect of utility, which is given as a quantity (i.e. is cardinal) is calibrated in the context of the prevailing social equilibrium. In that context, the interaction between political elites, as they seek to either change or preserve the prevailing balance of political authority, and the masses, is all considered with reference to the prevailing balance of political authority (political elites) as well as the prevailing distribution of wealth and the access to funds (economic elites). Interaction between economic elites primarily concerns the balance struck between the interests of high-risk speculators and the interests of low-risk rentiers. The political and the economic balances – which are revealed over time as a circulation of political and economic elites tentatively linked through a patron-client relationship – are constrained by the prevailing sentiment among the masses for continuity or change. In substantive terms, Pareto's social equilibrium is an abstract notion of the prevailing economic and political balances, the stability of which is conditional on its compatibility with the balance in the sentiment for continuity or change among the masses that comprise a society.

The aspect of utility, as it pertains to political and economic action, is influenced by 'derivations' that support certain types of social action. A 'derivation' is essentially a doctrine that provides a rationale, that is grounded in a blend of sentiment and quasi-logic, for actions that favour a subset of society at the expense of another. Values in their purest form (before values are supported by a philosophical evaluation and rationalisation) are simply sentiments in Pareto's scheme. But sentiments are not amendable to direct positive analysis, as they cannot be observed directly. To move his enquiry into the realm of the observed, Pareto introduced the term 'residues' to refer to the objective manifestations of doctrines or actions inspired by sentiment.[12] '[I]n activity based on residues human beings use derivations more frequently than strict logical reasonings ... Residues are not, like tastes, merely sources of conduct; they function throughout the whole course of the conduct developing from the source, a fact which becomes apparent in the substitution of derivations for logical reasonings' (Pareto 1916 [1935, 1442–3]).

Social welfare is, in Pareto's system, simply given in reference to the current state of the social equilibrium, and given by the views of individuals within society that are subject to the forces that maintain social equilibrium. The utility of Pareto's sociology, which is something useful to society, is, therefore, almost always path dependent because preferences over social states evolve as they are created through social interactions 'that function through the whole courses of conduct'. Pareto (1913 [1999]), which was followed by Pareto's grand three-volume *Sociologia* (1916 [1935]), was an

---

[12] All the logically sound aspects of a doctrine can be stripped away to leave an unexplained 'residual' or residue. Social theories and doctrines become the objective data that Pareto interrogated to identify the objective 'residues' that reveal something of the 'sentiment' that underlines doctrines and human action.

attempt to derive a general solution to the problem of welfare on the presumption that the individuals' assessment of utility is calibrated under the prevailing social equilibrium. As such, Pareto's general solution is intended to control for the endogenous and path-dependent character of utility by making his sociological assessment conditional on the prevailing social equilibrium.[13]

The starting point for Pareto's sociological assessment of welfare is his economic assessment of welfare given by equation (2). From the *Cours* onwards, his emphasis had been on the point of equilibrium, so economic welfare tended to be considered in reference to a point. For example, he did not fully develop the second law of welfare economics, as he regarded an efficient socialist collective as using the same coefficients of production as those under free competition, whereas the optimal point on the locus of potential Pareto optimal points will change with the initial endowment. But Pareto (1913) is clearly aware that the economic maximum changes with the initial allocation, indicating that there is a locus of 'points *p*' associated with equation (2) (Pareto 1913 [1999: 308]).

The move to the sociological approach to equilibrium starts by removing the role of the numeraire good so that the utility of individual *i*, Φ_i, is a quantity that is a cardinal value and a homogeneous quantity, and a socially determined weight, M_i, is used to give individual *i* weighting in the overall social welfare function. On that basis, the economic maximising relationship for the collective given by equation (2) is replaced by the sociological maximising relationship given by equation (4), in which

$$0 = M_1\delta\Phi_1 + M_2\delta\Phi_2 + M_3\delta\Phi_3 + \ldots \qquad (4)$$

A critical point in Pareto's approach to 'social utility' concerns the two-step process by which weights M_i are derived. In the first step, each individual undertakes interpersonal comparison of utility to establish their own interpretation of social welfare. Formally, α_i^j is the coefficient for each individual's 'social utility' function, with subscript *i* indicating the person whose utility is being weighted, and superscript *j* indicating the person who is undertaking the weighting. The government then assigns its own coefficients, β^j, to each weight of an individual's contribution to the social welfare of the collective. The combination of these coefficients gives the weighting designated by the M_i coefficients in equation (4), which are determined by the set of equations (5):

---

[13] This matter is discussed in more detail in McLure (2001).

$$\begin{cases} M_1 = \alpha_1^1\beta^1 + \alpha_1^2\beta^2 + \alpha_1^3\beta^3 \dots \\ M_2 = \alpha_2^1\beta^1 + \alpha_2^2\beta^2 + \alpha_2^3\beta^3 \dots \\ M_3 = \alpha_3^1\beta^1 + \alpha_3^2\beta^2 + \alpha_3^3\beta^3 \dots \end{cases} \tag{5}$$

Pareto also differentiates between two types of sociological maxima. A 'maximum *for* the community', which is predicated on the Pareto test being satisfied, reflects an image of society as a group of individuals, with each individual's position representing a veto on policy that results in harm for some. A 'maximum *of* the community' is not subject to the Pareto test. It effectively represents society as if it were a single social entity, so social maximisation of that entity is not constrained to prohibit harm to individuals. The lack of 'Paretian' preference ordering, the use of a 'sociological bridge' to facilitate interpersonal comparisons of utility and the removal of the Pareto test for the maximum of the community ensures that Pareto's sociological approach to 'social utility' did not anticipate the social welfare function of the Bergson-Samuelson variety. That is, while equation (4) involves maximisation of a function – and the associated maximisation constitutes a first step towards a 'theory of social utility' – that function is not 'Paretian' in the sense of an analysis associated with 'economic welfarism'.

In the *Sociologia*, Pareto also produced an additional reflection on social welfare, a point which was first underlined by Vincent Tarascio (1969). This involved a shift away from analysis of utility fields that are implicitly referenced to the commodity space, as in equation 4, towards utility being referenced to individual behaviour relative to the behavioural precepts, or 'norms', that prevail in a society. In Figure 6.1 (Pareto 1916 [1935: 1473]), the x axis is behaviour relative to the social norm, with extreme point A representing complete compliance with every social precept and extreme point B representing violation of every social precept. The y axis shows utility. Curve *mnp* maps an individual's utility as his or her behaviour moves from complete compliance with social norms (point A) to complete violation of social norms (point B); and curve *srv* maps the utility to the collective from the behaviour of that individual.

The obvious point to note is that the utility enjoyed by the collective from the behaviour of an individual does not necessarily match the utility that an individual experiences from their own behaviour. In regard to maximisation in Figure 6.1, this individual will maximise their utility at point q, which is relatively conformist (closer to A than B), whereas the welfare of the collective is maximised if that individual behaves in a less conformist way.

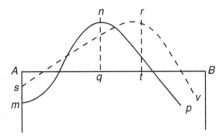

Figure 6.1 Utility from behavior relative to social norms

In short then, Pareto sees social utility as related to two dimensions: (i) the material wealth in the community and its distribution; and (ii) the distribution of behaviour by individual members of a community around the degree of conformity (or non-conformity) that is revealed by individuals' actions. The two dovetail together through his sociological contention that social equilibrium is fundamentally constrained by the balance in the psychological disposition of the people that make up the general masses for either social continuity or social change.

6.4 Conclusion

Pareto's work on welfare theory for policy purposes treated the role of values with both clarity and caution.

In the economics of welfare theory, the most significant value attributes are excised from economics and assigned to the Ministry of Justice, which is an 'extra-economic' institution. But even within this economic theory of welfare, the role played by the Ministry of Production still reflects some basic value principles, including the propositions that: private property rights should be retained (except for the case of taxation to fund the activities of the Ministry of Justice), that an increase in economic welfare is good and that the Pareto test and the compensation principle are acceptable value propositions that can be employed when determining economic maximisation. But interpersonal comparisons of utility are prohibited from economic assessments of welfare. In the sociology of welfare theory, however, the two distinct roles allocated to the Ministry of Production and the Ministry of Justice in the economics of welfare collapse to form a single analytical assessment of welfare by removing the prohibition on interpersonal comparisons for the purposes of analysis.

A significant question in this chapter is: Did Pareto, in moving from an economic analysis of welfare to a sociological analysis of welfare, anticipate Hicks's movement from economic welfarism to non-welfarism? He did so to the extent that the prohibition on interpersonal comparisons of utility is abandoned and the behaviour of individuals relative to social norms is admitted in the *Sociologia*. Notwithstanding this, however, Pareto's sociological approach to welfare does not abandon the requirement for the policy advisor to take an ethically neutral approach to his or her consideration of the values of others when providing advice on improving welfare, which is an important feature Hicks has in mind for his non-welfarism. As a result, Pareto's sociology of welfare does not fully reflect Hicks's non-welfarism. Hicks's approach emphasised the transition from the general to the particular or practical problem, whereas Pareto's sociology of collective welfare was a highly abstract general theory. Hicks was of the view that law and other social sciences will fill the policy void if economists treat practical matters with the framework of economic welfarism. There is, however, very limited scope for Pareto's sociological formulation of collective welfare, formalised using abstract mathematical symbols, to help economists compete against lawyers and other social scientists when providing advice on the minutiae associated with the detail of concrete policy matters.

References

Allais, Maurice. 1975. The General Theory of Surplus and Pareto's Fundamental Contribution, *Convegno Internazionale Vilfredo Pareto (Roma 25-27 ottobre 1973), Atti dei Convegni Lincie 9*, Rome: Accademia Nazionale Dei Lincei, 109–63; Reprinted in J. C. Wood and M. McLure, eds., 1999. *Vilfredo Pareto: Critical Assessments*, London: Routledge, Vol. 1, 428–73.

Chipman, John S. 1976. The Paretian Heritage, *Revue Européene des Sciences Sociales*, no. 37, 65–173; Reprinted in J. C. Wood and M. McLure, eds., 1999. *Vilfredo Pareto: Critical Assessments*, London: Routledge, Vol. 2, 157–257.

Hicks, John R. 1939. *Value and Capital*, Oxford: Oxford University Press.

Hicks, John R. 1975. Pareto and the Economic Optimum, *Convegno Internazionale Vilfredo Pareto (Rome 25-27 October 1973)*, Atti dei Convegni Lincie 9, Rome: Accademia Nazionale dei Lincei, 19–28; Reprinted in J. C. Wood and M. McLure, eds., 1999. *Vilfredo Pareto: Critical Assessments*, London: Routledge, Vol. 1, 417–27.

Hicks, John R. and Allen, Roy G. D. 1934. A Reconsideration of the Theory of Value, Parts 1 and 2, *Economica*, 1-1, 52–76 and 1-2, 196–219.

McLure, Michael. 2000. The Pareto-Scorza Polemic on Collective Economic Welfare, *Australian Economic Papers*, 39-3, 345–69.

McLure, Michael. 2001. *Pareto, Economics and Society*, London: Routledge.

McLure, Michael and Montesano, Aldo. 2019. Thinking Outside the Box: Edgeworth, Pareto and the Early History of the Box Diagram, *Economic Record*, 95–310, 301–11.

Pareto, Vilfredo. 1894. Il Massimo di Utilità dato dalla Libera Concorenza, *Giornale degli Economisti*, 4–9, 48–66; English translation in John Chipman, ed., 2008. The Maximum of Utility Given by Free Competition, *Giornali degli Economisti e Annali di Economia*, 67–3, 387–403.

Pareto, Vilfredo. 1896-7. *Cours d'Économie Politique*, Lausanne: Rouge; Italian translation, 1971. *Corso di Economia Politica*, Torino: Unione Tipographico-Editrice Torinese.

Pareto, Vilfredo. 1900. Sunto di Alcuni Capitoli di un Nuovo Trattato di Economia Pura del Prof. Pareto, *Giornali degli Economisti*, 2–20, March and June, 216–35 and 511–49; English translation in John Chipman, ed., 2008. Summary of Some Chapters of a New Treatise on Pure Economics by Professor Pareto, *Giornali degli Economisti e Annali di Economia*, 67–3, 453–504.

Pareto, Vilfredo. 1902. Di un Nuovo Errore nello Interpretare le Teorie dell'Economia Matematica, *Giornale degli Economisti*, 12–15, 401–33; English translation in John Chipman, ed., 2008. On a New Error in the Interpretation of the Theories of Mathematical Economics, *Giornali degli Economisti e Annali di Economia*, 67–3, 515–44.

Pareto, Vilfredo. 1906. *Manuale di Economia Politica*, Milan: Società Editrice Libraria; Revised French translation, 1909. *Manuel d'Économie Politique*, Paris; English variorum translation in A. Montesano, A. Zanni, L. Bruni, J. S. Chipman and M. McLure, eds., 2014. *Manual of Political Economy: A Critical and Variorum Edition*, Oxford: Oxford University Press.

Pareto, Vilfredo. 1910. Le Azioni Non Logiche, *Rivista Italiana di Sociologia*, May–August, 305–64; Reprinted in Giovanni Busino, ed., 1980. *Vilfredo Pareto Œuvres Complètes 22: Écrits Sociologiques Mineurs*, Genéve: Librairie Droz, 345–408.

Pareto, Vilfredo. 1913. Il Massimo di Utilità per una Collettività in Sociologia, *Giornale degli Economisti e Rivista di Statistica*, 23–46, 337–41; English translation reprinted in J. C. Wood and M. McLure, eds., 1999. *Vilfredo Pareto: Critical Assessments*, London: Routledge, Vol. 3, 307–10.

Pareto, Vilfredo. 1916. *Trattato di Sociologia Generale*, Florence: Barbara; English translation, 1935. *The Mind and Society*, New York: Harcourt, Brace and Company.

Pigou, A. C. 1920. *The Economics of Welfare*, London: Macmillan.

Suzumura, Kotaro. 2016. Pigou's 'Old' Welfare Economics, Hicks's Farewell to Welfarism, and Sen's Non-consequentialist Economics of Well-Being and Freedom, International Workshop on Economic Thought of Cambridge, Oxford, LSE, and the Transformation of the Welfare State, 5–7 September 2016, Sano Shoin, Hitotsubashi University, Kunitachi, Tokyo, Japan.

Tarascio, Vincent J. 1968. *Pareto's Methodological Approach to Economics*, Chapel Hill: University of North Carolina Press.

Tarascio, Vincent J. 1969. Paretian Welfare Theory: Some Neglected Aspects, *Journal of Political Economy*, 77–1, 1–20.

PART II

DEVELOPING MODERN WELFARE ECONOMICS

7

John Hicks's Farewell to Economic Welfarism

How Deeply Rooted and Far Reaching Is His *Non-welfarist Manifesto*?

Kotaro Suzumura[1]

A study of the history of opinion is a necessary preliminary to the emancipation of the mind. I do not know which makes a man more conservative – to know nothing but the present, or nothing but the past.
John Maynard Keynes, *The End of Laissez-Faire*, 1926

God, give us Grace to accept with serenity the things that cannot be changed, Courage to change the things which should be changed, and the Wisdom to distinguish the one from the other.
Richard Niebuhr, *Serenity Prayer*, 1943

7.1 Introduction

John Hicks is one of the major actors in the eventful evolution of welfare economics after its birth by the hands of Arthur Pigou in his magnum opus, *The Economics of Welfare* (1920). It is all the more puzzling that Hicks left a *non-welfarist manifesto* in Hicks (1959/1981) to the following effect: "Though Welfare Economics appears to have settled into the position of a regular, accepted, branch of economics ... it remains to some extent a mystery. It has often been criticized, and its critics have

[1] First Draft November 30, 2016; Second Draft January 7, 2018; Final Draft March 30, 2018. The author is grateful to Roger Backhouse, Antoinette Baujard, Walter Bossert, Tamotsu Nishizawa, Amartya Sen, Koichi Tadenuma, and Yongsheng Xu for their helpful comments on earlier drafts of this paper as well as their discussions with him over the years on this and related issues. Thanks are due to the financial support from the *Research Project on Normative Economics with Extended Informational Bases and Its Doctrinal History* through the Grant-in-Aid for Scientific Research by the Ministry of Education, Culture, Sports, Science and Technology of Japan (the grant number 16H03599). He also appreciates The University of Hyogo for its kind permission to scrutinize two unpublished documents (Hicks no date; c. 1955; Hicks no date; c. 1963) kept as a part of the Library and Papers of Sir John Hicks.

never been fully answered; yet it survives. There is a problem here; I propose ... to make yet another attempt to clear it up" (Hicks 1975/ 1981, p. 218). His repeated attempts notwithstanding, the mystery Hicks posed and tried to resolve seems to remain not fully settled yet, and very much alive. This paper is a fresh challenge to Hicks's mystery by scrutinizing his manifesto. To circumscribe the arena of this attempt, two preliminary remarks are in order.

In the first place, by welfare economics we mean the branch of normative economics, which is concerned with the critical examination of the performance of actual or imaginary economic systems, as well as with the critique, design, and implementation of alternative economic policies. Social choice theory is the complementary branch of normative economics, which is concerned with the evaluation of alternative methods of collective decision-making, and logical foundations of welfare economics.[2] What we are going to discuss in this paper will be relevant not only to welfare economics, but also to social choice theory.

In the second place, there seems to be a logical chain, starting from Pigou's "old" welfare economics, so-called, going through the interim proposals of the "new" welfare economics on the basis of hypothetical compensation principles and social welfare function à la Abram Bergson and Paul Samuelson, Hicks's non-welfarist manifesto, and terminating in Sen's (2009) acute contrast between the *comparative assessment approach* and *transcendental institutionalism*. Recollect that these two contrasting approaches were identified by Sen in the context of the *ideas of justice*, but they are also acutely relevant to normative economics as well.[3] The meaning of Hicks's manifesto will be made clearer if we keep this underlying chain in mind.

Without any further ado, let us begin our challenge to Hicks's mystery.

---

[2] This definition of welfare economics and social choice theory capitalizes on the author's introduction to social choice theory and welfare economics in Suzumura (2016, chapter 25).

[3] Sen (2009) identified two basic lines of reasoning about justice among leading philosophers associated with the European Enlightenment. One approach concentrated on the identification of *perfectly just institutional arrangements* for a society. Sen christened this approach transcendental institutionalism. Another approach focused on comparing feasible societies, all of which fall short of the ideals of perfection, and aimed at finding some criteria for an alternative being less unjust than another. Sen christened this approach the comparative assessment approach, which both commonly focused on making comparisons between different ways of life. It paid due attention to the influence not only of institutions, but also of people's actual behavior, social interactions, and other significant determinants of people's lives.

7.2 Pigou's "Old" Welfare Economics and Its Ordinalist Critics

To locate Hicks's mystery in its proper perspective, let us begin with the minimum overview of the historical evolution of welfare economics since Pigou.

Capitalizing on the long Cambridge tradition of moral philosophy, Pigou opened a gate toward a new research area called welfare economics, which is named after his treatise, *The Economics of Welfare* (Pigou 1920/1932/1999). The spirit of this inauguration is crystallized in Pigou's *Preface*: "The complicated analyses which economists endeavor to carry through are not mere gymnastic. They are instruments for the bettering of human life."

Although Pigou was a utilitarian in the tradition of Jeremy Bentham (1776), the scenario of Pigou's welfare economics was *not* a straightforward attempt to design an institutional framework of the economic system that maximizes the social sum-total of individual utilities under constraints. Careful reading of Pigou reveals that the task of his welfare economics was intended *not* to draw a radical blueprint of an ideal first-best economic system or economic policy, *but* to scrutinize the down-to-earth – imperfect and defective – economic system so as to discover feasible instruments for the bettering of human life. It should be clear that there is a substantial cleavage in between the constrained maximization paradigm and the paradigm in search of instruments for the bettering of human life. To locate these contrasting scenarios within the broad category of normative economics, and to reorient the future research program of welfare economics and social choice theory in awareness of this cleavage seems to be an important agenda.

The next problem to be posed and settled is whether the vulgar scenario of Pigouvian welfare economics by means of the maximization of the social sum-total of individual utilities can be regarded as a legitimate "scientific" research program of welfare economics in its own right. It is in this context that the well-known criticism on the informational basis of this scenario was raised by Lionel Robbins (1932/1935; 1938), which triggered a large stir in the economics profession.

On reflection, the common identification of the maximization of the social sum-total of individual utilities with the Benthamite dictum of *the greatest happiness of the greatest number* leaves in itself a wide room for reasonable doubts.[4] As a matter of fact, the criticism by Robbins was

---

[4] Bentham himself had doubts on the possibility of interpreting the greatest happiness principle by means of the social sum-total of individual utilities. Indeed, as Wesley Mitchell quoted in his "Bentham's Felicific Calculus" (Mitchell 1937, p. 184), Bentham

based *not* on this doubt, *but* on the informational basis of the maximization of the social sum-total of individual utilities per se. Indeed, it boiled
down to the categorical denial of the "scientific" possibility of interpersonal comparisons of individual utilities with interobserver validity.
Careful scrutiny of Robbins (1932/1935, pp. 138–150; 1938, pp.
636–637; 1981, p. 5) reveals that he had never rejected the possibility
of "subjective" interpersonal comparisons of utility, nor had he ever
claimed that an economist should not make "subjective" interpersonal
comparisons of his/her own. The gist of his criticism is the assertion that
"subjective" interpersonal comparisons of individual utilities do not
have any "objective" interobserver validity whatsoever.

In "Bergsonian Welfare Economics" (Samuelson 1981, p. 226), which
is meant to "set the record straight as only a living witness and
participant can," Paul Samuelson testified to the impact of Robbins's
criticism as follows:

When Robbins sang out that the emperor had no clothes – that you could not
prove or test by any empirical observations of objective science the normative
validity of comparisons between different persons' utilities – suddenly all his
generation of economists felt themselves to be naked in a cold world. Most of
them had come into economics seeking the good. To learn in midlife that theirs
was only the craft of a plumber, dentist, or cost accountant was a sad shock.

By the end of 1930s, it became widely recognized that the informational
basis of "old" welfare economics was hopelessly eroded. To salvage something valuable from the vestige of Pigou's edifice, new foundations had to
be found for welfare economics solely on the basis of *interpersonally non-
comparable* and *ordinal* utility information.

7.3 The Advent of Two Schools of the "New" Welfare Economics

Two schools of the "new" welfare economics emerged in response to
this call for relief. They were based commonly on the informational
basis of interpersonally non-comparable and ordinal utilities, but their
similarity ends precisely there.

---

observed that " 'Tis in vain to talk of adding quantities which after the addition will
continue distinct as they were before, one man's happiness will never be another man's
happiness: a gain to one man is no gain to another: you might as well pretend to add 20
apples to 20 pears." We may mention in this context that Walter Bossert and Kotaro
Suzumura (2016) attempted to reinterpret the Benthamite dictum within the informational framework of interpersonally non-comparable and ordinal utilities.

7.3.1 The Bergson-Samuelson School of the "New" Welfare Economics

The first step toward construction activities of the "new" welfare economics was taken by Abram Bergson (1938), who introduced the fundamental concept of the *social welfare function*. Samuelson (1947/1983, p. 221), who had been the most powerful disseminator of Bergson's idea, expounded this contrivance as follows:

> Without inquiring into its origins, we take as a starting point for our discussion a function of all the economic magnitudes of a system which is supposed to characterize some ethical belief – that of a benevolent despot, or a complete egoist, or "all men of good will," a misanthrope, the state, race, or group mind, God, etc. Any possible opinion is admissible . . . . We only require that the belief be such as to admit of an unequivocal answer as to whether one configuration of the economic system is "better" or "worse" than any other or "indifferent," and that these relationships are transitive . . . . The function need only be ordinally defined . . . .

Two remarks on the nature of the Bergson-Samuelson contrivance may be in order.

In the first place, the standard scenario of the Bergson-Samuelson "new" welfare economics may be phrased as follows: Design an institutional framework of the economy so as to identify and implement a social alternative x^* that maximizes the value of the social welfare function f at the profile $(u_1(x), u_2(x), \ldots, u_n(x))$ of individual utilities within the set of feasible alternatives.[5] Observe that the Bergson-Samuelson scenario and that of maximizing the social sum-total of individual utilities have a conspicuous family resemblance. Indeed, the two scenarios capture in common the essence of welfare economics by means of the *constrained maximization paradigm*. Their crucial difference can be reduced to the difference in their respective objective functions, viz. the *ordinal index of social welfare provided by a Bergson-Samuelson social welfare function*, on the one hand, and the *social sum-total of individual utilities*, on the other.

Although the transition from the scenario based on the social sum-total of individual utilities to the alternative scenario based on the Bergson-Samuelson social welfare function was once considered to be a quantum

---

[5] For any pair x, y of social states, x is judged socially at least as good as y according to the social welfare function f if and only if the value of f at x is at least as high as that at y. The social welfare function f is *individualistic* if and only if it ranks x vis-à-vis y in accordance with the profile of individual utilities at x vis-à-vis y. Thus, x is judged socially at least as good as y according to the individualistic social welfare function f if and only if $f(u_1(x), u_2(x), \ldots, u_n(x)) \geq f(u_1(y), u_2(y), \ldots, u_n(y))$ holds, where u_i is the ordinal and interpersonally non-comparable utility function of individual $i = 1, 2, \ldots, n$.

leap in the history of welfare economics, they share the conspicuous feature of focusing on the *maximization of some social welfare index subject to resource constraints*. It is this common feature of these scenarios that brings them into one and the same subclass of welfare economics. Pigou's "old" welfare economics is in clear contrast with the "new" welfare economics of the Bergson-Samuelson family in that the former is concerned with the down-to-earth – less than perfect and defective – economy with a view to finding feasible instruments for the bettering of human life.

In the second place, there exists an important difference of opinions between Bergson and Samuelson with respect to the nature and origin of the Bergson-Samuelson social welfare function. Samuelson remained uncompromising in his flat denial of thinking whose value judgments the social welfare function embodies, and how the social welfare function is generated or constructed from individual value judgments. The reason that lies behind Samuelson's insistence is not hard to surmise. He wanted to separate what belongs to the "scientific" world of *objective facts* from what belongs to the "normative" world of *ethical values,* thereby solidifying the scientific status of the "new" welfare economics of the Bergson-Samuelson family. However, it is doubtful if indeed we can separate the realm of "what is" from the realm of "what should be" even in principle. Suffice it to recollect Hilary Putnam's (2002, p. 44) skepticism, who went as far as to assert as follows: "The worst thing about the fact/value dichotomy is that in practice it functions as a discussion-stopper, and not just a discussion-stopper, but a thought-stopper." In sharp contrast, Bergson (1976, p. 186) was ready to be concerned with the nature of the values to be embodied in the social welfare function:

The practitioner of welfare economics is in principle free to take any values as a point of departure, but the resulting counsel as to economic policy is not apt to be too relevant unless the values in question are held by, or can plausibly be imputed to, one or more officials concerned with the policies in question. Should the practitioner for any reason disapprove of those values, he may, of course, refrain from offering the officials any counsel at all.[6]

---

[6] Kenneth Arrow (1951/1963, p. 107) essentially concurred with Bergson on this recognition of the nature of values to be embodied in the social welfare function. But he asked further the nature of the process or rule through which social values are democratically composed on the basis of individual values. His justly famous *general impossibility theorem* on the existence of an eligible process or rule under several reasonable axioms served as an unambiguous signal to call for serious investigations into the prerequisites under which the Bergson-Samuelson social welfare function is generated through democratic methods of collective decision-making. See Suzumura (2005/2011, p. 340, footnote 4) for more detailed documentation of this point.

7.3.2 The Kaldor-Hicks School of the "New" Welfare Economics

The second school of the "new" welfare economics is based on the *hypothetical compensation principles* introduced by Nicholas Kaldor (1939) and John Hicks (1940/1981), and elaborated further by Tibor Scitovsky (1941), Paul Samuelson (1950), William Gorman (1955), and many others.[7] The informational basis of this school is interpersonally non-comparable and ordinal utilities, which is common with the first school, but otherwise the two schools are diametrically contrasting. Unlike the social welfare function of the first school, the second school does *not* accept any ethical value *from outside* of economics. Instead, it tries to construct the ethical value *from inside* without acquiescing in the fact/value dichotomy that characterizes the first school.

The point of departure of the second school is the well-known concept of *Pareto-superiority*. According to Jan de V. Graaff (1957, pp. 84–85),

the compensation [principles] all spring from a desire to see what can be said about social welfare ... without making interpersonal comparisons of well-being. ... They have common origin in Pareto's definition of an increase in social welfare – that at least one man must be better off and no one worse off – but they are extended to situations in which some people are made worse off.

A concise articulation of the Kaldor-Hicks compensation principles may be in order.[8] As an auxiliary concept, a social state a is said to be *compensatory equivalent* to another social state b if and only if we can move from a to b by means of the hypothetical payments of compensation among individuals. Two hypothetical compensation principles can then be defined as follows. Consider an economic policy that turns a social state x, to be called the *status quo ante*, into another social state x^*, to be called the *status quo post*. Then (a) the status quo post x^* is *Kaldor-superior* to the status quo ante x if and only if there exists a social state x^{**}, which is compensatory equivalent to x^*, such that x^{**} is Pareto-superior to x; (b) the status quo post x^* is *Hicks-superior* to the status quo ante x if and only if there does *not* exist a social state x^{**}, which is compensatory equivalent to x, such that x^{**} is Pareto-superior to x^*.

It is easy to be wise after the event, and the present-day verdicts on the performance of these compensation principles are largely in the negative for ethical and logical reasons. The *ethical criticism* is based on the arbitrariness of using the status quo ante or the status quo post as the point of reference in

---

[7] There are influential opinions to the effect that the origin of the compensation principle can be and should be traced back at least as far as to John Stuart Mill and Francis Y. Edgeworth (Edgeworth 1881). Those who are interested are referred to Enrico Barone (1935), and Paul Samuelson in the conversation with Suzumura (2005/2011).

[8] The Scitovsky compensation principle (Scitovsky 1941) can be articulated similarly.

judging about welfare distributions among individuals at x vis-à-vis at y, whereas the *logical criticism* is based on the lack of transitivity, or its weaker variants, of the social preference judgments generated by various compensation principles.[9] These criticisms notwithstanding, it should not be overlooked that the second school of the "new" welfare economics is a successor of Pigou's research scenario in that this school focuses on the search of "instruments for the bettering of human life" rather than on the search of the first-best social welfare maximization.[10]

7.4 Hicks's Non-welfarist Manifesto: Its Depth and Reach

Capitalizing on many twists and turns in the brief history of welfare economics, "old" and "new," an unsympathetic wind blew toward welfare economics in the late 1950s. In his survey of welfare economics over the past twenty years, Edward Mishan (1960, p. 197) left the following cynical verdict:

While it continues to fascinate many, welfare economics does not appear at any time to have wholly engaged the labours of any one economist. It is a subject which, apparently, one dabbles in for a while, leaves and, perhaps, returns to later in response to a troubled conscience – which goes some way to explain why, more

---

[9] Those who are interested in the precise reasons behind this sweepingly negative verdict are referred in Suzumura (1999/2016, essay 26).

[10] A few remarks on Samuelson's (1950) hypothetical compensation principle may be in order. A social state x is said to be *Samuelson-superior* to another social state y if and only if, for any social state y^*, which is compensatory equivalent to y, there exists a social state x^*, which is compensatory equivalent to x, such that x^* is Pareto-superior to y^*. Intuitively speaking, the Samuelson-superiority is defined by means of the uniform upward shift of the utility possibility frontier. As such, the piecemeal welfare criterion based on his principle is free from any bias in favor of the status quo ante as well as of the status quo post. Indeed, it is free from *any* bias in favor of *any* specific social state whatsoever. Being based on the uniform upward shift of the utility possibility frontier, it is also clear that the Samuelson superiority satisfies the strong requirement of logical consistency in the form of transitivity. It may be thought that the sweepingly negative verdicts on the performance of the second school is premature in view of these positive performances of the Samuelson compensation principle. It may also be surmised that the fact that Samuelson belongs to both schools of the "new" welfare economics sends a signal that there is something dubious in my sharp distinction between these two schools within the post-Pigou "new" welfare economics. I dare to disagree. In the first place, although the Samuelson superiority relation yields a transitive social preference relation *in isolation*, it cannot but generate a cyclic social preference relation *in combination with* the Pareto principle. See Suzumura (1999/2016, essay 26, p. 728) for this verdict. In the second place, although the Samuelson compensation principle does not hinge upon the welfare distribution at any specific social state, thereby securing its ethical neutrality, this apparent merit is purchased at very high price of restricting the applicability of his compensation principle only to the rare situation of uniform upward shift of the utility possibility frontier.

than other branches of economics, it suffers from an unevenness in its development, a lack of homogeneity in its treatment and, until very recently, a distressing disconnectedness between its parts.

Almost simultaneously, Hicks (1959/1981, essay 6) published an intriguing reflection on the contemporary state of welfare economics by declaring an emotional farewell to what he called *economic welfarism*:

The view which, now, I do *not* hold I propose . . . to call "Economic Welfarism"; for it is one of the tendencies which has taken its origin from that great and immensely influential work, the *Economics of Welfare* of Pigou. But the distinction which I am about to make has little to do with the multifarious theoretical disputes to which the notion of Welfare Economics has given rise to. One can take any view one likes about measurability, or additivity, or comparability of utilities; and yet it remains undetermined whether one is to come down to one side or other of the Welfarist fence. The line between Economic Welfarism and its opposite is not concerned with what economists call utilities; it is concerned with the transition from Utility to the more general good, Welfare (if we like) itself.

7.4.1 Consequences, Opportunities, and Procedures

As an auxiliary step in our analysis of Hicks's intriguing *manifesto*, let us examine an agent who is engaging in normative social evaluations on alternative economic systems or economic policies. In order to form sensible evaluations, the agent will require some informational inputs concerning these economic systems or economic policies. Most, if not literally all, agents will require information on *consequential outcomes*, which are brought about by the use of the economic system or economic policy in question. If the agent requires nothing else, his/her stance is called *consequentialism*. In contrast, if the agent requires additional information beyond consequential outcomes pure and simple, such as the *opportunity set* from which to choose consequences, or the *procedure* through which consequences are chosen, his/her stance is called *non-consequentialism*.

Lest we should be misunderstood, let us observe that the non-consequentialist stance does *not* mean that *all* information on the consequence of economic system or economic policy is completely excluded from consideration. Quite to the contrary, it simply means that at least *some* non-consequentialist information is invoked along with consequentialist information.[11]

---

[11] If an agent focuses exclusively on the non-consequentialist information and neglects the consequentialist information altogether, his stance will be called the *deontological stance*, which is an extreme special case of the non-consequentialist stance.

There are alternative methods of describing consequential outcomes. If we depend on the description of consequences only by means of the ex post welfare accruing to individuals, our stance will be called *welfarist consequentialism*, or *welfarism* for short. Alternatively, if we require some further information on consequences beyond ex post welfare, our stance will be called *non-welfarist consequentialism*, or *non-welfarism* for short.[12]

The next point of bifurcation is whether a welfarist agent adheres to the *ordinal* concept of welfare, or he/she accepts the *cardinal* concept of welfare. In the former case, he/she stands on the informational basis of *ordinalist welfarism*, whereas in the latter case, he/she stands on the informational basis of *cardinalist welfarism*.

This classification of informational bases can be further elaborated by means of the nature of the welfare concepts involved, viz., whether welfares are interpersonally comparable or non-comparable, and whether welfares are ordinal or cardinal in nature. In combination, we can identify four categories within the welfaristic stance, viz., *ordinalist welfarism without interpersonal comparability*, *ordinalist welfarism with interpersonal comparability*, *cardinalist welfarism without interpersonal comparability*, and *cardinalist welfarism with interpersonal comparability*.

The discriminating power of this classification may be illustrated as follows. The informational basis of the "new" welfare economics, viz., the social welfare function school of Bergson and Samuelson and the compensationist school of Kaldor and Hicks, is based in common on ordinalist welfarism without interpersonal comparability. It is also noteworthy that the vulgar variant of Pigou's "old" welfare economics, which utilizes the social sum-total of individual utilities as its flag mark, is the conspicuous example of cardinalist welfarism with interpersonal comparability.

We may now resume our inquiry into Hicks's non-welfarist manifesto.

7.4.2 What Sense Can We Make of Hicks's Non-welfarist Manifesto?

To cut our way through this territory, we decompose our query into two subqueries:

(Q_1) Did Hicks's manifesto focus on economic welfarism as such, but not on welfarism in general? In other words, was Hicks resigned to stay

---

[12] In this case too, the informational stance of non-welfarism need not be fully insensitive to *any* welfarist information. What characterizes non-welfarism is that it is sensitive to *some* non-welfarist information without being totally insensitive to welfarist information.

within welfarism even after liquidating his commitment to economic welfarism, or was he ready to cross over even the welfarist fence and proceed toward non-welfarism?

(Q_2) Supposing that Hicks was ready to leave the familiar kingdom of welfarism, to what extent was he ready to make his farewells to the informational straitjacket of welfarism? In other words, was he resigned to remain within consequentialism, or was he prepared to cross over even the consequentialist fence and proceed toward non-consequentialism?

The first step in answering the subquery (Q_1) is to scrutinize the concept of welfare vis-à-vis that of economic welfare in Pigou (1920/1932/1999, pp. 10–11). In Pigou's own parlance:

Welfare ... is a thing of very wide range. ... It will be sufficient to lay down more or less dogmatically two propositions; first, that the elements of welfare are states of consciousness and, perhaps, their relations; secondly, that welfare can be brought under the category of greater or less. A general investigation of all the groups of causes by which welfare thus conceived may be affected would constitute a task so enormous and complicated as to be quite impracticable. It is, therefore, necessary to limit our subject-matter.

How did Pigou try to limit his subject matter? His contrivance for simplification was straightforward:

In doing this we are naturally attracted towards that portion of the field in which the method of science seems likely to work at best advantage. This they can clearly do when there is present something measurable, on which analytical machinery can get a firm grip. The one obvious instrument of measurement available in social life is money. Hence, the range of our inquiry becomes restricted to that part of social welfare that can be brought directly or indirectly into relation with the measuring-rod of money. This part of welfare may be called economic welfare.

Pigou (1920/1932/1999, p. 11) was certainly not unaware of possible difficulties of separating economic welfare in this sense from welfare in general. These difficulties notwithstanding, Pigou argued "though no precise boundary between economic and non-economic welfare exists, yet the test of accessibility to a money measure serves well enough to set up a rough distinction. Economic welfare, as loosely defined by this test, is the subject-matter of economic science."

With this background in mind, it may be natural to surmise that Hicks's choice was to reject Pigou's contrivance of separating economic welfare from general welfare, thus joining hands with numerous contemporary critics of Pigou's idea. We contend that it is this banal misperception of the nature of Hicks's manifesto that is mainly responsible for the long neglect of his far-reaching farewell.

To see how deep-rooted is Hicks's manifesto, it may be of some help if we quote the following passage from Hicks (1959/1981, p. 137): "It is impossible to make 'economic' proposals that do not have 'non-economic aspects,' as the Welfarist would call them; when the economist makes a recommendation, he is responsible for it in the round; all aspects of that recommendation, whether he chooses to label them economic or not, are his concern." We believe that Hicks's manifesto is *not* just a resurrection of the mundane criticism on Pigou's separation of economic welfare from general welfare; it is a declaration that we should go back all the way along the informational bifurcation of normative social evaluations to the non-consequentialist node.

To substantiate this bold contention, we begin by citing the following "one strong example" due to Hicks:

One of the issues that can be dealt with most elaborately by Welfarist methods is that of Monopoly and Competition: the theory of the social optimum which would be reached in a (practically unattainable) condition of all-round perfect competition, and of the departures from the optimum which must occur under any form in which a system of free enterprise can in practice be organized, is one of the chief ways in which the Welfarist approach has left its mark. I do not question that we have learnt a great deal from these discussions; but they leave me with an obstinate feeling that they have failed to penetrate to the centre of the problem with which they are concerned. ... Why is it, for instance, that anti-monopoly legislation (and litigation) get so little help, as they evidently do, from the textbook theory? Surely the answer is that the main issues of principle – security on the one side, freedom and equity on the other, the issues that lawyers, and law-makers, can understand – have got left right out. (Hicks 1959/1981, p. 137)

Hicks's "one strong example" seems acute enough to support our reasoned answer to the subquery (Q_1) to the following effect: Hicks was not only ready to go beyond economic welfarism and move toward welfarism in general, but he was also ready to cross over the welfarist fence per se, and move toward the territory of non-welfarism.

So far so good, but Hicks went on to pose a further problem of weighing up welfarist values against non-welfarist values in the following statement: "I have ... no intention, in abandoning Economic Welfarism, of falling into the 'fiat libertas, ruat caelum' which some latter-day liberals seem to see as the only alternative. What I do maintain is that the liberal goods are goods; that they are values which, however, must be weighed up against other values" (Hicks 1959/1981, p. 139). It seems to us that Hicks thereby turned over a new leaf in the evolution of normative economics, because weighing up the liberal values against the welfarist values may lead us to the passage toward opening Pandora's Box. Indeed, these values, if juxtaposed, may bring about a serious problem of logical incompatibility between these values.

To see that this anxiety is not just a fancy mirage, but a harsh reality, it suffices if we refer to a class of the *Impossibility Theorems of a Paretian Liberal* due to Amartya Sen (1970a, chapter 6 and chapter 6*; 1970b).[13] Sen's liberal value may be phrased in terms of the pair (x, y) of social states, where the only difference between x and y consists of a personal feature of some individual. Suppose that the relevant individual prefers x to y and the society is going to make a social choice from an opportunity set S that includes x. If, in this case, the society chooses y, Sen's liberal value is violated. The reason is that, if a pair of social states are distinguished only by features personal to an individual, according to Sen's definition of liberalism, society should respect that individual's preferences over the two social states. In addition to the liberal value in this sense, Sen introduces the Paretian – hence welfarist – value to the effect that if all individuals prefer a social state z to another social state w, then the social choice from the opportunity set that includes z should not choose w. Then Sen's impossibility theorem asserts that *there exists no universally applicable social choice rule satisfying Sen's liberal value and the Paretian value*. A part of the large literature subsequently evolved tried to criticize Sen's liberal value and/or his impossibility theorem, but the basic problem of the incompatibility of liberal value and democratic value has persisted ever since.

Although Sen's *Impossibility of a Paretian Liberal* caused a persistent stir in the social choice circle, Robert Nozick (1974, p. 166) pointed out that

a more appropriate view of individual rights [than Sen's view] may go as follows. Individual rights are co-possible; each person may exercise his rights as he chooses. The exercise of these rights fixes some features of the world. Within the constraints of these fixed features, a choice may be made by a social choice mechanism based on a social ordering.

---

[13] The literature on this class of impossibility theorems is voluminous. Some of the crucial work include Amartya Sen (1970a, chapter 6 and chapter 6*; 1970b; 1976; 2017, chapter A5), Allan Gibbard (1974), Robert Nozick (1974), Robert Sugden (1985), Wulf Gaertner, Prasanta Pattanaik, and Kotaro Suzumura (1992/2016), Kotaro Suzumura (1996/2016; 2011; 2016, part IV), and Rajat Deb, Prasanta Pattanaik, and Laura Razzolini (1997).

In this alternative view, "[r]ights do not determine a social ordering but instead set the constraints within which a social choice is to be made, by excluding certain alternatives, fixing others, and so on." It is worthwhile to emphasize that this Nozickean view of libertarian rights, which assigns rights a completely different role of specifying some personal features of the world *before* the social choice mechanism starts its function, may be traced back all the way to the long libertarian tradition of John Stuart Mill, Isaiah Berlin, and many others. Furthermore, this alternative view led to the modern theory of libertarian rights in terms of *game forms* developed by Robert Sugden (1985), Wulf Gaertner, Prasanta Pattanaik, and Kotaro Suzumura (1992/2016), and subsequent social choice theorists, where the essence of individual libertarian rights are captured by the freedom of choosing admissible strategies in the game-theoretic interactions among individuals.[14]

It deserves emphasis that the *game form articulation of rights* has no intrinsic relation with individual preferences over consequential outcomes. Thus, the articulation of the game form rights by means of respecting each individual's freedom of choice in his/her private sphere of admissible strategies represents a purely procedural value, which is not only non-welfaristic, but also non-consequential in nature.[15] This crucial contrast between the Sen rights and the game form rights makes us wonder whether replacing the Sen rights with the game form rights dissipates or maintains the *Impossibility of a Paretian Liberal*. An unambiguous answer to this natural question is provided by Rajat Deb, Prasanta Pattanaik, and Laura Razzolini (1997), who proved that *the welfaristic value of the Pareto principle and the non-consequentialist value of the game form rights are incompatible in general.*

To sum up, the phantom of the logical conflict between the claim of libertarian rights and the Pareto principle cannot be exorcised even after Sen's rights are replaced by the game form rights, so that the gate opened wide by Hicks's manifesto led us into the new rich field of research of post-exodus welfare economics.

Gathering all pieces together, we are now in the position to submit our final answer to the subquery (Q_2), which goes as follows: *Hicks was in effect*

---

[14] Those who are interested in the formal definition of the game form articulation of rights and its logical implications are referred to Suzumura (2011, section 6 and section 7) and Suzumura (2016, essay 15 and essay 16), among many others.

[15] Furthermore, the game form articulation of rights is not only an alternative to Sen's view, but also a criticism against Sen's view of rights. Those who are interested are cordially referred to Gaertner, Pattanaik, and Suzumura (1992/2016), which is republished in Suzumura (2016, essay 15).

ready to go back along the informational bifurcation of normative evaluations and proceed to the non-consequentialist node by means of his emphasis on the non-consequentialist principles of "freedom and equity."

7.4.3 Whence and Whither: After the Non-welfarist Manifesto

So much for our verdict on the contents and extents of Hicks's non-welfarist manifesto. There is one further query to be asked and answered in this context. To assert that Hicks was ready to escape from the welfarist node and climb up along the informational bifurcation of social evaluations to the non-consequentialist node is one thing, and to identify and suggest the method of analysis after exodus from welfarism is another thing altogether. Let us briefly examine Hicks's own attempt of post-exodus welfare economics.[16] In Section 7.5, we will be concerned with John Rawls's (1971/1999) *theory of justice* and Amartya Sen's (1980, 1985, 1993) *capability approach to well-being, freedom, and equality* so as to exemplify the contents and extents of the post-exodus welfare economics.

To kick off his sketch of the post-exodus welfare economics, Hicks proposes to "put the Paretian theory ... on one side, and go back to Pigou. And let us now attend to the whole of his book – to the structure of the whole book, not merely to the title and to the opening chapters" (Hicks 1975/1981, p. 212). He points out that the subject of Pigou's welfare economics is *not* the Economic Welfare as in the post-Pigou welfare economics, *but* the Real Social Product, or the National Dividend in Pigou's parlance. The subject of Part I of *The Economics of Welfare* is the definition and measurement of the Real Social Product, and Part II is focused on what makes the Real Social Product large or small, and what makes it grow. In Hicks's opinion, Part III on Industrial Relations between employers and employees "is loosely attached and may ... be disregarded," whereas part IV "sets the crown upon the whole work" by discussing the question of the Distribution of Real Social Product. A conspicuous feature of this skeleton of Pigou's treatise is that it does *not* refer to welfare at all. According to Hicks (1975/1981, pp. 222–223), Pigou took over this framework "from his predecessors, economists who did not think that they were doing 'welfare economics' at all. It was the *classical* theory of Production

---

[16] Hicks made serious efforts to reconstruct the foundations of welfare economics in Hicks (no date; c. 1955) and Hicks (no date; c. 1963), which remained unpublished for many years, but the essence of these unpublished materials was eventually published in Hicks (1975/1981). It is this published work that is the source of our explanation of, and commentary on, the Hicksian approach to the post-exodus welfare economics.

and Distribution which Pigou was taking over and turning into the Economics of Welfare. *The Economics of Welfare* is *The Wealth of Nations* in a new guise."

It is true that Adam Smith was thought by later scholars to have underemphasized distribution, but Hicks points out that David Ricardo rectified this alleged lacuna in his *Principles of Political Economy and Taxation*, by declaring in the Preface that the determination of "the laws which regulate distribution is the principal problem of Political Economy." To fortify this point of view, Hicks adds that "Mill begins his *Principles* with Book I on Production and Book II on Distribution; Distribution in Mill is well to the fore. There is continuity between the shape of Pigou's book and the shape of Mill's" (Hicks 1975/1981, p. 224).

Hicks's insight into the parallel nature of the classical theory of Production and Distribution, on the one hand, and Pigou's *Economics of Welfare*, on the other, is not an atavism, but an attempt to locate Pigou's "old" welfare economics in proper historical perspective. What role can Hicks legitimately assign to utility, or more generally welfare in this scheme? Since Pigou's *Economics of Welfare* in Hicks's recapitulation does not refer to welfare at all, this is a proper question to ask. Recollect that "the point of the 'labour theory of value', which Ricardo largely (but by no means entirely) uses, is that it gives him a means of reducing heterogeneous commodities to a common measure *in terms of cost.*" Although Pigou was also concerned with Production and Distribution just as the classical economists, he chose to differ from them in his method of valuation: "Instead of valuing by cost, he valued by utility – marginal utility" (Hicks 1975/1981, pp. 225–226). Thus, "[t]he questions that were asked by the Classics in their theory of Wealth and those which were asked by Pigou in his theory of Welfare were broadly the same; so the Cost theory and the Utility theory fall into corresponding parts" (Hicks 1975/1981, pp. 227).

So far so good. I have no hesitation in accepting Hicks's statement to the following effect: "I have tried ... to put 'welfare economics' back into the frame in which it was set by Pigou; for I think that when it is reinserted, we understand it better" (Hicks 1975/1981, p. 230). However, we found very little, if any, constructive suggestions in Hicks (no date; c. 1955), Hicks (no date; c. 1963), and Hicks (1975/1981) that orient the future research of post-exodus welfare economics in clear awareness of Pigou's founding philosophy of welfare economics as well as the logical and ethical difficulties encountered by the "old" and "new" welfare economics, neither are we aware of any work that explored this vista of the post-exodus welfare economics. For this reason, we now leave the Hicksian ground and explore elsewhere for some alternative attempts.

7.5 Post-Exodus Welfare Economics: John Rawls and Amartya Sen

In contrast with Hicks's attempt to reorient the post-exodus welfare economics on the basis of the classical tradition, there are two modern developments that have been exerting influence on the post-exodus welfare economics, viz., John Rawls's theory of justice (Rawls (1971/1999) and Amartya Sen's capability approach to well-being, freedom, and equality (Sen 1980, 1982, 1985, 1993). In what follows, we examine briefly these two approaches one by one.

7.5.1 Rawls's Theory of Justice by Means of Social Primary Goods

According to Rawls (1971/1999, p. 54), two principles of justice on the basic institutional structure of society, which governs the assignment of rights and duties in major social institutions and determines the appropriate distribution of the benefits and burdens of social life, should be chosen in the *original position* of primordial equality.[17,18] The first principle may be called the *principle of maximal equal liberty*, which requires that each individual should be assured of an equal right to the most extensive liberty compatible with similar liberty for all individuals. The second principle is widely known under the title of the *difference principle*, and it maintains that inequalities are arbitrary unless it is reasonable to expect that they would work for every individual's advantage. To make the difference principle operational, Rawls paraphrased it as follows: Social inequalities should be arranged so as to make the worst-off individual best-off. We must further ask: How can we identify the worst-off individual for each social state? This further question is answered by Rawls (1971/1999, p. 54 and pp.

---

[17] This set-up of the problem of justice by Rawls clearly suggests that his theory of justice is a salient example of transcendental institutionalism in the sense of Sen (2009).

[18] The original position is the hypothetical situation of equality among individuals, under which a certain conception of justice will be spontaneously agreed on. The principles of justice will be chosen behind a veil of ignorance. In this hypothetical situation of primordial equality, no one is advantaged or disadvantaged in the choice of principles by natural chance or contingency of social circumstances. No one is able to design principles to favor his particular condition, so that the principles of justice cannot but be the result of a fair agreement or bargain.

60–65) by means of the concept of *social primary goods,* which are defined to be general-purpose *means* for pursuing various *ends* including such diverse things as *rights, liberties, opportunities, income and wealth,* and the *social basis of self-respect.* Rawls asserts that all social primary goods have use value whatever an individual's rational life plan may be. Thus, the second principle is rephrased that all social primary goods should be distributed equally among all individuals unless an unequal distribution of any, or all, social primary goods is to everyone's advantage.[19]

With this understanding of the universal use value of social primary goods, Rawls crossed the Rubicon by choosing social primary goods as the informational basis of his theory of justice. Rawls's focus on the means rather than on the ends in the pursuit of rational life plans of individuals in society dissociated him from welfaristic theories of social judgments.

Two insidious features of Rawls's informational basis should be noted. On the one hand, as Rawls himself enumerated, there are multiple components of social primary goods. Thus, if we want to compare the well-being of two individuals in terms of the relative richness of social primary goods at their respective disposal, we must compare two vectors of social primary goods and decide which vector is richer than the other. Even if all individuals agree that more of each social primary good is better, there is no clear criterion for judging if one vector of social primary goods is better or worse than the other, or both are indifferent, neither is there any obvious method of defining an index of social primary goods. On the other hand, as Sen (1980; 1982, p. 368) points out, "[social] primary goods suffer from fetishist handicap in being concerned with goods, and even though the list of [social primary] goods is specified in a broad and inclusive way, ... it still is concerned with good things rather than with what these good things *do* to human beings."

It was this observation that led Sen to replace the Rawlsian theory of justice in a non-fetishist direction by means of his own capability approach to well-being, freedom, and equality. It is to this alternative approach that we now turn.

---

[19] In addition to these social primary goods, there are other goods such as *health, vigor, intelligence,* and *imagination* that are also of primary value in everybody's life, but they are *natural* – in contrast with *social – primary goods.* The possession of natural primary goods is also under the influence of the basic social structure, but, unlike social primary goods, they are not subject to direct social control.

7.5.2 Sen's Capability Approach to Well-Being, Freedom, and Equality[20]

Sen's capability approach started from abandoning the classical informational basis of *opulence* or *utility* in the evaluation of the state of persons, and replacing it with the Aristotelian basis that consists of the *achievement* of valuable *functionings*, and the *capability* to achieve them.[21,22] These basic components of his approach are explained as follows:

Functionings represent parts of the state of a person – in particular the various things that he or she manages to do or be in leading a life.[23] The capability of a person reflects the alternative combinations of functionings the person can achieve, and from which he or she can choose one collection. The assessment of welfares and of freedoms can be related to the functionings achieved and to the capability to achieve them. (Sen 1996, p. 57)

Three intermediate concepts must be introduced at this juncture. Commodities are clearly of *instrumental value* in enabling individuals to function, so that the human command over commodities is the natural point to kick off our analysis. To dig deeper into what is of *intrinsic value*, Sen introduced *characteristics, characteristics function,* and *utilization function* in between commodities and functionings.

According to William Gorman (1956/1980) and Kelvin Lancaster (1966, 1971), the characteristics are desirable properties that commodities embody. The essence of the Gorman-Lancaster approach is that it is *not* the

---

[20] In this paper, we will focus on the informational basis of Sen's capability approach, leaving the full articulation of Sen's approach to the companion paper, viz., Suzumura (2020).

[21] As has already been observed, Sen is explicitly against the use of opulence or material affluence as the informational basis of the analysis of human well-being and freedom due to its vulnerability to "what Marx called the 'commodity fetishism' – to regard goods as valuable in themselves and not for (and to the extent that) they help the person" (Sen 1985, p. 28). Utility is also criticized by Sen for its adaptive nature in the sense that "[o]ur mental reactions to what we actually get and what we can sensibly expect to get may frequently involve compromises with a harsh reality" (Sen 1985, p. 21).

[22] In his contribution to Nussbaum and Sen (1993, p. 30, footnote 2), Sen observed as follows: "Though at the time of proposing the [capability] approach, [he] did not manage to seize its Aristotelian connections, it is interesting to note that the Greek word *dunamin*, used by Aristotle to discuss an aspect of the human good, which is sometimes translated as 'potentiality', can be translated also as 'capability of existing or acting.'"

[23] A functioning is distinguished from the commodity that is used to achieve this functioning. For example, cycling is a functioning, and it should be distinguished from possessing a bicycle. Likewise, a bicycle should be distinguished from the happiness or desire-fulfillment attained by means of the act of cycling. Thus, a functioning should be distinguished both from having a commodity, to which it is posterior, and having utility from that functioning, to which it is prior. See Sen (1985, p. 10).

possession of commodities per se, *but* the accession to the corresponding characteristics that makes the command over commodities valuable to individuals. To formalize this idea, a commodity vector possessed by an individual is converted into a characteristics vector by means of a function to be called the characteristics function.[24] A characteristics vector, in turn, allows individuals to have access to certain functionings vector through a utilization function, which he/she chooses from the set of accessible utilization functions. Although the characteristics function is common for all individuals and given from outside,[25] the utilization function is an endogenous choice variable for each individual from the set of admissible utilization functions, which reflects social rules and conventions that prevail in society.

From the point of view of the system designer or the person in charge of policy-making, who will be called the "government" for brevity, there are two channels through which the government can exert influence on the attained individual functionings, viz., *either* through (a) the design and choice of a set of rules that regulates the allocation of commodities among individuals; *or* through (b) the design and choice of a set of rules that affects the set of admissible utilization functions, from which each individual can freely choose.

Given the government's design and choice of these sets of rules, each individual is provided with a set of commodity vectors, to be called his/her *entitlement set*, from which he/she is able to choose freely as well as a set of admissible utilization functions, from which he/she is able to choose freely. By exercising these double freedoms of choice, each individual is able to attain his/her functionings vector from the set of admissible functionings vectors, to be called his/her *capability set*.[26]

The next order of our business is to describe how these individual choices can be described. In this context, three related, but distinct

---

[24] The conversion of commodity vectors into characteristics vectors may also be variable in the long run due to the interim technological change. In the short run, however, it may be sensible to assume that the characteristics function is fixed and given exogenously.

[25] The concept of characteristics function and that of utilization function are due to Sen (1985). Unlike the characteristics function, the utilization function and the set of accessible utilization functions may differ in accordance with the nature of the society and the identity of individuals. For example, in a society with gender prejudice or racial discrimination, individuals may have different sets of accessible utilization functions, depending on their respective gender or race.

[26] Up to this stage, my articulation of Sen's capability approach followed his own account in Sen (1985, chapter 2) almost literally, but the articulation in the next stage will contain slight deviations from his own account. See Suzumura (2020) for the reasons why this modified articulation is found necessary.

concepts of utility functions or preference orderings should be distinguished. The first concept is that of individual *utility functions*.[27] Each individual is assumed to have a utility function defined on the space of functionings vectors. It represents his/her *subjective preferences*, which is distinct from, and may well be incoherent, with his/her *ethical preferences*.[28] Observe that there is nothing schizophrenic in this dual structure of individual preferences. Suffice it to quote the case of a heroin addict who feels happier with the functionings vector that allows him/her free access to heroin, than with the functioning vector that allows nobody any legal access to heroin. However, the same individual may judge differently in calm and reflective moments in which he/she evaluates the goodness of human life from the impartial and socially conscious standpoint. Thus, it makes good sense to assume that each individual has an *evaluation function* on the space of functionings vectors that judges in accordance with his/her ethical judgments. Utility functions and evaluation functions provide us with complementary informational bases for judging about the goodness of human life. However, they fall much short of providing full informational basis in the sense that not only utility functions, but also evaluation functions keep silence on the intrinsic value of freedom of choice as such, which the relevant individual entertains from the richness of his/her capability set. Recollect that welfarism in general, and utilitarianism in particular, are conspicuously indifferent not only to *negative freedoms* à la J. S. Mill and Isaiah Berlin, but also to *overall* (or *positive*) *freedoms*.[29] In contrast, Sen's capability approach assigns an important role to negative freedoms as well as to positive freedoms. Indeed, as Sen (1996, p. 59) points out, "[a]s a first approximation it is plausible to argue that well-being achievement depends only on the achieved functionings, whereas the freedom to achieve well-being is correspondingly associated with the capability to function." Careful scrutiny reveals that

freedom may have intrinsic importance for a person's well-being also. Acting freely and being able to choose may be directly conducive to well-being, not just because more freedom may make better alternatives available. This view on the direct

---

[27] Unlike the concept of utility functions used in the standard theory of consumer behavior, which is defined on the space of commodities vectors, the utility function used in the present context is defined on the space of functionings vectors, which is similar in spirit to what Sen (1985, p. 11) called the *happiness function*.

[28] The concept of subjective preferences and that of ethical preferences are introduced by John Harsanyi (1955).

[29] See Berlin (1969) for the distinction between negative freedom and positive freedom.

relevance of freedom is contrary to the one typically assumed in standard economic theory, in which the contribution of a set of feasible choices is judged exclusively
by the value of the best element available.

In sharp contrast,

if choosing is seen as a part of living . . ., then even the achievement of well-being
need not be independent of the freedom reflected in the capability set. The "good
life" is partly a life of genuine choice, and not one in which the person is forced into
a particular life – however rich it might be in other respects. With this additional
consideration, the assessment of well-being as well as that of the freedom to achieve
well-being would depend on the person's "capability set."

As an analytical vehicle for capturing the intrinsic value of opportunities for choice, let us introduce the concept of an *extended evaluation ordering*.[30] The ordering $\succcurlyeq$ is defined over the ordered pairs of
functionings vectors s, t and opportunity sets S, T such that $(s, S) \succcurlyeq (t,
T)$ means that choosing a functioning vector s from an opportunity set
S is judged at least as good as choosing a functioning vector t from an
opportunity set T.[31] This concept enables us to capture an individual's
intrinsic preference for freedom of choice as follows: If

$(s, S) \succ (s, \{s\})$ holds true for some (s, S) such that $s \in S$ and $\{s\} \subsetneq S$,[32]

then the agent prefers having freedom of choosing s from S rather than
being forced to choose s from the singleton opportunity set $\{s\}$ with no
effective freedom of choice.[33]

Let $\succcurlyeq$ be the extended evaluation ordering of an individual $i \in N :=
\{1, 2, \ldots, n\}$, where n is the total number of individuals in the society,
together forming a profile $\succcurlyeq := (\succcurlyeq_1, \succcurlyeq_2, \ldots, \succcurlyeq_n)$ of individual extended evaluation orderings.

This completes the brief articulation of basic ingredients of Sen's
capability approach. It describes several channels through which the
government can exert influence on the economic and social environment

---

[30] This concept is due to Kotaro Suzumura and Yongsheng Xu (2001), by means of which an
axiomatic characterization of consequentialism and non-consequentialism is presented,
which plays in turn an instrumental role in Suzumura and Xu (2004) to verify how the
existence of non-consequentialists along with consequentialists affects Arrow's general
impossibility theorem.

[31] In order for this definition to make sense, it is required that s, t and S, T should satisfy $s \in
S$ and $t \in T$.

[32] $\succ$ is the asymmetric part of $\succcurlyeq$, where $s \succ t$ if and only if $(s \succcurlyeq t$ & not $t \succcurlyeq s)$.

[33] For the sake of consistency between the evaluation function ω and the extended evalu-
ation ordering $\succcurlyeq$, it is assumed that $(s, \{s\}) \succcurlyeq (t, \{t\})$ if and only if $\omega(s) \geq \omega(t)$ for all s, t.

for each individual to pursue valuable human life to him/herself; it also helps us identify instruments for improving human well-being and freedom. Observe that this approach accepts thorough diversity of human beings, and it makes use not only of subjective preferences and ethical preferences, both being defined on the set of accomplished functionings, but also of extended evaluation orderings that pay due attention to the intrinsic value of the freedom of choice. In this sense, Sen's capability approach to well-being and freedom is an attempt to escape from the narrow cage of welfarism and proceed toward non-consequentialism, as it assigns a crucial role to the *intrinsic*, as distinct from *instrumental*, value of the freedom of choice. Full justification of these claims requires rather involved analysis, the exploration of which must be relegated to the companion paper, viz. Suzumura (2020), where the conceptual framework of the capability approach is set in motion in the context of giving substance to the Rawlsian notion of the *equitable allocation of maximal overall freedom* in the non-fetishist way. It is our hope that the present incomplete description of the basic structure of the capability approach may still suggest a possible avenue to explore in the post-exodus welfare economics.

7.6 Two Concluding Remarks

Let us conclude with two brief remarks.

In the first place, this paper is a humble attempt to identify the services rendered by Hicks in the history of welfare economics since Pigou. He was one of the major leaders of the ordinalist renovation of the crumbling "old" welfare economics in the form of the "new" welfare economics. In our judgments, the "new" welfare economics, not only of the compensationist school of Kaldor, Hicks, Scitovsky, and Samuelson, but also of the social welfare function school of Bergson and Samuelson, is hardly sustainable as the foundation of welfare economics of well-being, freedom, and equality. Hicks also caused a stir in the profession by proclaiming an esoteric non-welfarist manifesto. In this paper, we tried to argue that his manifesto has far-reaching implications in that it recommends us to escape from the narrow cage of welfarism and of consequentialism, and adopt the richer informational basis of non-consequentialism in order to make progress in the analysis of well-being, freedom, and equality. Furthermore, Hicks was a historian of welfare economics who tried to locate Pigou's "old" welfare economics in historical perspective by identifying the parallelism between the classical theory of Production and Distribution and Pigou's *Economics of Welfare*. Although the parallelism he identified is intellectually interesting, Hicks was reticent on the effect of this recognition on the construction of post-exodus welfare economics.

In the second place, two major contributions to the contemporary analyses of well-being, freedom, and equality, viz., the theory of justice by Rawls, and the capability approach by Sen, are briefly expounded and critically examined. The informational basis of Rawls's theory focuses on the general purpose means to be called the social primary goods rather than on the ends in the pursuit of rational life plans of individuals, which dissociates him from welfaristic theories of social evaluation. The informational basis of Sen's capability approach is Aristotelian in nature, which consists of the achievement of valuable functionings, and the capability to achieve them, where functionings are various things that he/she manages to do or be in leading a life, whereas his/her capability consists of the alternative combinations of functionings he/she can achieve, from which he/she can choose one combination. The assessment of an individual's welfare and of freedom is based on the functionings achieved, as well as on the capability to achieve these functionings. Although our treatment of these non-welfarist approaches to well-being and freedom remains sketchy, it is hoped that it may still be of some use in exemplifying the possibility of the post-exodus welfare economics.

The purpose of this paper will be served well if it can constitute at least a part of the reasonable answer to the mystery of welfare economics, which Hicks (1975/1981) posed and left unresolved.

References

Arrow, K. J. (1951/1963/2012): *Social Choice and Individual Values*, New York: John Wiley & Sons, 1st ed., 1951; 2nd ed., with "Notes on the Theory of Social Choice, 1963," New York: John Wiley & Sons, 1963; 3rd ed., New Haven, CT: Yale University Press, 2012.

Barone, E. (1935): "The Ministry of Production in the Collectivist State," in F. A. von Hayek, ed., *Collectivist Economic Planning*, London: Routledge, pp. 245–290.

Bentham, J. (1776): *A Fragment on Government*, London: T. Payne.

Bergson, A. (1938): "A Reformulation of Certain Aspects of Welfare Economics," *Quarterly Journal of Economics*, Vol. 52, pp. 310–334.

Bergson, A. (1976): "Social Choice and Welfare Economics under Representative Government," *Journal of Public Economics*, Vol. 6, pp. 171–190.

Berlin, I. (1969): *Four Essays on Liberty*, Oxford: Oxford University Press.

Bossert, W. and K. Suzumura (2016): "The Greatest Unhappiness of the Least Number," *Social Choice and Welfare*, Vol. 47, pp. 187–205.

Deb, R., P. K. Pattanaik, and L. Razzolini (1997): "Game Forms, Rights, and the Efficiency of Social Outcomes," *Journal of Economic Theory*, Vol. 72, pp. 74–95.

Edgeworth, F. (1881): *Mathematical Psychics: An Essay on the Application of Mathematics to the Moral Sciences*, London: Kegan & Paul.

Gaertner, W., P. K. Pattanaik, and K. Suzumura (1992/2016): "Individual Rights Revisited," *Economica*, Vol. 59, pp. 161–177. Reprinted in Suzumura (2016), pp. 423–446.

Gibbard, A. (1974): "A Pareto-Consistent Libertarian Claim," *Journal of Economic Theory*, Vol. 7, pp. 388–410.

Gorman, W. M. (1955): "The Intransitivity of Certain Criteria Used in Welfare Economics," *Oxford Economic Papers*, Vol. 7, pp. 25–35.

Gorman, W. M. (1956/1980): "The Demand for Related Goods: A Possible Procedure for Analysing Quality Differentials in the Egg Market," *Review of Economic Studies*, Vol. 47, 1980, pp. 843–856. First circulated as Journal Paper No. 2319, Iowa Agricultural Experiment Station, November 1956.

Graaff, J. de V. (1957): *Theoretical Welfare Economics*, London: Cambridge University Press.

Harsanyi, J. C. (1955): "Cardinal Welfare, Individual Ethics and Interpersonal Comparisons of Utility," *Journal of Political Economy*, Vol. 63, pp. 309–321.

Hicks, J. R. (1940/1981): "The Evaluation of the Social Income," *Economica*, Vol. 7, 1940, pp. 105–124. Reprinted in Hicks (1981), pp. 78–99.

Hicks, J. R. (no date; c. 1955): "Another Shot at Welfare Economics, Lecture I and Lecture II," unpublished typescript, 19 pages folio + 21 pages, diagrams in the text.

Hicks, J. R. (1959/1981): "Preface – and a Manifesto," in his *Essays in World Economics*, Oxford: Clarendon Press, 1959. Reprinted in Hicks (1981), pp. 135–141.

Hicks, J. R. (no date; c. 1963): "The Real Product – A Revision of Welfare Economics," unpublished manuscript.

Hicks, J. R. (1975/1981): "The Scope and Status of Welfare Economics," *Oxford Economic Papers*, Vol. 27, 1975, pp. 307–326. Reprinted in Hicks (1981), pp. 218–239.

Hicks, J. R. (1981): *Wealth and Welfare: Collected Essays on Economic Theory*, Vol. 1, Oxford: Basil Blackwell.

Kaldor, N. (1939): "Welfare Propositions in Economics and Interpersonal Comparisons of Utility," *Economic Journal*, Vol. 49, pp. 549–552.

Lancaster, K. J. (1966): "A New Approach to Consumer Theory," *Journal of Political Economy*, Vol. 74, pp. 132–157.

Lancaster, K. J. (1971): *Consumer Demand: A New Approach*, New York: Columbia University Press.

Mishan, E. J. (1960): "A Survey of Welfare Economics, 1939–1959," *Economic Journal*, Vol. 70, pp. 197–265.

Mitchell, W. C. (1937): *The Backward Art of Spending Money and Other Essays*, New York: McGraw-Hill.

Nozick, R. (1974): *Anarchy, State and Utopia*, Oxford: Basil Blackwell.

Nussbaum, M. C. and A. K. Sen, eds. (1993): *The Quality of Life*, Oxford: Clarendon Press.

Pigou, A. C. (1920/1932/1999): *The Economics of Welfare*, London: Macmillan, 1st ed., 1920; 4th ed., 1932. Reprinted in Vol. 3 of Pigou's *Collected Economic Writings*, London: Macmillan, 1999.

Putnam, H. (2002): *The Collapse of the Fact/Value Dichotomy and Other Essays*, Cambridge, MA: Harvard University Press.

Rawls, J. (1971/1999): *A Theory of Justice*, Cambridge, MA: Harvard University Press, original ed., 1971; revised ed., 1999.

Robbins, L. (1932/1935): *An Essay on the Nature and Significance of Economic Science*, London: Macmillan, 1st ed., 1932; 2nd ed., 1935.

Robbins, L. (1938): "Interpersonal Comparisons of Utility," *Economic Journal*, Vol. 48, pp. 635–641.

Robbins, L. (1981): "Economics and Political Economy," *American Economic Review*, Vol. 71, pp. 1–10.

Samuelson, P. A. (1947/1983): *Foundations of Economic Analysis*, Cambridge, MA: Harvard University Press, 1st ed., 1947; enlarged 2nd ed., 1983.

Samuelson, P. A. (1950): "Evaluation of Real National Income," *Oxford Economic Papers*, Vol. 2, pp. 1–29.

Samuelson, P. A. (1981): "Bergsonian Welfare Economics," in S. Rosefielde, ed., *Economic Welfare and the Economics of Soviet Socialism: Essays in Honor of Abram Bergson*, Cambridge, Cambridge University Press, pp. 223–266.

Scitovsky, T. (1941): "A Note on Welfare Propositions in Economics," *Review of Economic Studies*, Vol. 9, pp. 77–88.

Sen, A. K. (1970a): *Collective Choice and Social Welfare*, San Francisco: Holden-Day.

Sen, A. K. (1970b): "The Impossibility of a Paretian Liberal," *Journal of Political Economy*, Vol. 78, pp. 152–157.

Sen, A. K. (1976): "Liberty, Unanimity and Rights," *Economica*, Vol. 43, pp. 217–245.

Sen, A. K. (1980): "Equality of What?" in S. McMurrin, ed., *The Tanner Lectures on Human Values*, Vol. 4, Cambridge: Cambridge University Press, pp. 195–220.

Sen, A. K. (1982): *Choice, Welfare and Measurement*, Oxford: Basil Blackwell.

Sen, A. K. (1985): *Commodities and Capabilities*, Amsterdam: North-Holland.

Sen, A. K. (1993): "Capability and Well-Being," in Nussbaum and Sen, pp. 30–53.

Sen, A. K. (1996): "On the Foundations of Welfare Economics: Utility, Capability and Practical Reason," in F. Farina, F. H. Hahn, and S. Vannucci, eds., *Ethics, Rationality and Economic Behaviour*, Oxford: Clarendon Press, pp. 50–65.

Sen, A. K. (2009): *The Idea of Justice*, London: Allen Lane.

Sen, A. K. (2017): *Collective Choice and Social Welfare*, expanded ed., London: Penguin Books.

Sugden, R. (1985): "Liberty, Preference and Choice," *Economics and Philosophy*, Vol. 1, pp. 185–205.

Suzumura, K. (1996/2016): "Welfare, Rights, and Social Choice Procedure: A Perspective," *Analyse & Kritik*, Vol. 18, pp. 20–37. Reprinted in Suzumura (2016), pp. 447–467.

Suzumura, K. (1999/2016): "Paretian Welfare Judgments and Bergsonian Social Choice," *Economic Journal*, Vol. 109, pp. 204–220. Reprinted in Suzumura (2016), pp. 709–730.

Suzumura, K. (2002/2016): "Introduction" to K. J. Arrow, A. K. Sen, and K. Suzumura, eds., *Handbook of Social Choice and Welfare*, Vol. 1, Amsterdam: Elsevier Science B. V., North-Holland, pp. 1–32. Reprinted in Suzumura (2016), pp. 671–708.

Suzumura, K. (2005/2011): "An Interview with Paul Samuelson: Welfare Economics, 'Old' and 'New', and Social Choice Theory," *Social Choice and Welfare*, Vol. 25, pp. 327–356. Reprinted in Murray, J., ed., *The Collected Scientific Papers of Paul A. Samuelson*, Vol. 6, Cambridge, MA: MIT Press, 2011, pp. 843–872.

Suzumura, K. (2011): "Welfarism, Individual Rights, and Procedural Fairness," in K. J. Arrow, A. K. Sen, and K. Suzumura, eds., *Handbook of Social Choice and Welfare*, Vol. 2, Amsterdam: Elsevier Science B. V., North-Holland, pp. 605–685.

Suzumura, K. (2016): *Choice, Preferences, and Procedures: A Rational Choice Theoretic Approach*, Cambridge, MA: Harvard University Press.

Suzumura, K. (2020): "The Capability Approach from the Viewpoint of Welfare Economics and Social Choice Theory," in Enrica Chiappero, Siddiq Osmani, and Mozaffar Qizilbash, eds., *The Cambridge Handbook of the Capability Approach*, Cambridge: Cambridge University Press, pp. 106–125.

Suzumura, K. and Y. Xu (2001): "Characterizations of Consequentialism and Non-consequentialism," *Journal of Economic Theory*, Vol. 101, pp. 423–436. Reprinted in Suzumura (2016), pp. 505–519.

Suzumura, K. and Y. Xu (2004): "Welfarist-Consequentialism, Similarity of Attitudes, and Arrow's General Impossibility Theorem," *Social Choice and Welfare*, Vol. 22, pp. 237–251. Reprinted in Suzumura (2016), pp. 537–556.

8

Individualism and Ethics

Samuelson's Welfare Economics

Roger E. Backhouse

8.1 Introduction

Possibly more than any other economist, Paul Samuelson is associated with what became the standard approach to the theory of welfare economics after 1945. The relevant chapter of his *Foundations of Economic Analysis* (1947) was written after it had been shown that compensation tests could generate contradictory conclusions, thereby undermining the so-called new welfare economics of John Hicks and Nicholas Kaldor. Samuelson clarified what was valid in the previous literature using the concept of a social welfare function, attributed to his friend from his student days, Abram Bergson, in which welfare is written as a function of all relevant economic variables. In its most general form, such a social welfare function is without content, doing no more than state that social welfare depends on the factors that determine social welfare. However, it could be given content by introducing ethical judgments that restricted its form. Central among these was "individualism," the idea that the factors that affected welfare were the factors that affected individuals' appraisals of their own welfare. The result was that although he argued that a social welfare function could represent any set of ethical values, his focus was on what he called an individualistic welfare economics, based on the assumption that welfare depended on individuals' preferences. Samuelson did not coin the phrases "Pareto optimality," "Pareto optimum" or "Pareto efficiency" – that honor is due to Ian Little (1950) – but he emphasized that the genealogy of his approach led back to Pareto, if not earlier.

Samuelson repeatedly claimed that the idea of the social welfare function was Bergson's, but, as Suzumura (Chapter 7, this volume) points out, Samuelson used the concept in a subtly different way from Bergson. For

Bergson the social welfare function represented the views of a community, whereas Samuelson argued that it could represent any set of ethical values, and that these values had to be given from outside. They could therefore be the shared values of a community or the values of a dictator or simply a hypothetical set of values that the analyst wished to explore. This is why, after Kenneth Arrow's *Social Choice and Individual Values* (Arrow, 1951) questioned the possibility of deriving a social welfare function from the preferences of individuals in an ethically acceptable way, Samuelson continued to hold that Arrow's theorem did not apply to his own social welfare function. He argued that Arrow's function should more appropriately be called a constitutional function being concerned with the process by which communities' views were formed.

This paper is not concerned with the ongoing and frustratingly opaque debate between the two economists on the merits of their conceptually very different welfare functions, surveyed by Herrade Igersheim (2017). Instead it explores the origins of Samuelson's ideas about welfare that led him to an approach in which social welfare did not necessarily rest solely on individuals' judgments of their own welfare. Samuelson claimed that assessments of social welfare needed to take account of the distribution of income, and on some occasions he argued that other clearly non-welfarist judgments could legitimately be made.

8.2 Under the Spell of Knight

Samuelson was exposed to welfare thinking as an undergraduate at the University of Chicago. In the interdisciplinary social science course that he took in his sophomore year, he was exposed to ideas about the "human costs" of industry and the "human utility" of consumption on which the required reading was John A. Hobson's *Work and Wealth: A Human Valuation* (1914; see Backhouse, 2017, p. 49). In this book, Hobson drew on resources from John Ruskin to differentiate between "economic" and "human" costs, imposing ethical judgments that were not necessarily those of the people whose activities were being analyzed (see Shionoya [Chapter 1) and Cain [Chapter 2], this volume). Samuelson's response to this material is unknown, but such ideas would have resonated with those of Frank Knight, who never taught him in a for-credit course, but with whom he became obsessed. He claimed that when he left Chicago he had read everything that Knight had ever written. Knight's ideas on welfare economics were brought together in a collection of his essays that four graduate students assembled to mark his fiftieth birthday, published as

The Ethics of Competition ([1935]1997) in the year that Samuelson graduated. Samuelson was not involved in this project but, given his infatuation with Knight, his voracious reading habits and his friendship with George Stigler, one of the editors, it is inconceivable that he was not familiar with these essays. Given his love for Knight's iconoclasm, which was exhibited clearly in the essays, Samuelson would have read them carefully.

A repeated theme in Knight's writings was that wants were not to be taken as given. They were in large part determined by the economic system. Thus while Knight found much to admire in Pigou's work, he was critical of the idea that welfare should be calculated by adding up the total of satisfied wants. He accepted the argument that individualism and the free market would place resources in the hands of those who valued them most, and maximize the social dividend, but he denied that this constituted "a sound ethical social ideal" (Knight, 1923, p. 588; 1997, p. 40). Social ideals had to come from ethics, not from arguments about the efficiency of the economic system.

We contend not merely that such ideals are real to individuals, but that they are part of our culture and are sufficiently uniform and objective to form a useful standard of comparison for a given country at a given time. . . . In what follows we shall appeal to what we submit to be the common-sense ideals of absolute ethics in modern Christendom. (Knight, 1923, p. 583; 1997, p. 36)

Knight made no attempt "to 'settle' moral questions or set up standards" but sought merely to "bring out the standards involved in making some familiar moral judgments in regard to the economic system, and to examine them critically" (Knight, 1923, pp. 583–4; 1997, pp. 36–7).[1] Knight summarized his methodological position as being "any judgment passed upon a social order is a value judgment and presupposes a common measure and standard of values, which must be made as clear and explicit as possible if the judgment is to be intelligent. Economic efficiency is a value category and social efficiency an ethical one" (Knight, 1923, p. 623; 1997, p. 66).

Knight thus took into account the need for physical goods and the implications of the process of competition. His conclusion was that, irrespective of whether or not it was possible to find a better form of social organization, the competitive system had weaknesses. "There is," he wrote, "a certain ethical repugnance attached to having the livelihood of the masses of the people made a pawn in such sport [i.e. 'business considered purely as a game'], however fascinating the sport may be to its leaders,"

---

[1] A similar position was taken by Gunnar Myrdal (1932). Further analysis of Knight's position is provided in Emmett (2009, ch. 8).

contrasting action motivated by rivalry with "the Pagan ethics of beauty or perfection and the Christian ideal of spirituality" (Knight, 1923, p. 624; 1997, p. 67).

8.3 Collaboration with Bergson

Samuelson has argued that credit for developing what has come to be known as the Bergson-Samuelson social welfare function rests squarely with Abram Bergson, then Abram Burk (he changed his name as a matter of principle because he did not consider it sounded sufficiently Jewish, the opposite of the normal practice). "Mine," he wrote, "was the spectator's seat for Bergson's creative travail. I was the stone against which he honed his sharp axe – the semiabsorbing, semireflective surface against which he bounced off his ideas" (Samuelson, 1981, p. 223). In conversation with Kotaro Suzumura (2005, p. 334), Samuelson went slightly further in claiming that he was the "helpful midwife" who helped pull the baby out, denying emphatically that he was a co-author of the crucial paper.

Bergson and Samuelson came to the idea of a social welfare function whilst attending courses as graduate students at Harvard in 1935–7 (see Backhouse, 2017). They both wrote articles on consumer theory and on the measurement of utility (Burk (Bergson), 1936; Samuelson, 1937; Samuelson, 1938c). In these papers, they noted, Bergson implicitly and Samuelson explicitly, that there was a gap between that field and welfare economics. Thus Bergson wrote that utilities, as calculated by Ragnar Frisch, whose work he was criticizing, could "in no sense be considered measurements of real money utility" (Burk (Bergson), 1936, p. 42, n. 1). If it did not measure real money utility then, *a fortiori*, utilities could not have welfare implications. Samuelson went further, writing at the end of his first paper: "[A]ny connection between utility as discussed here and any welfare concept is disavowed. The idea that the results of such a statistical investigation could have any influence upon ethical judgments of policy is one which deserves the impatience of modern economists" (Samuelson, 1937, p. 161). He made exactly the same point in his next publication: "[N]othing said here in the field of consumer's behaviour affects in any way or touches upon at any point the problem of welfare economics, except in the sense of revealing the confusion in the traditional theory of these distinct subjects" (Samuelson, 1938c, p. 71).

Implied in Samuelson's brief remarks is a criticism of virtually all existing literature on welfare economics for confusing two completely different concepts. "Utility," as used in the theory of the consumer, was a device for analyzing how consumers behaved – for modelling the choices they made when confronted with prices and incomes – but it had been widely assumed that it could also be used to form welfare judgments. Modern writers avoided committing themselves to utilitarianism, with its suggestions of hedonism (that people were mechanical seekers of pleasure and avoiders of pain) but the connection between welfare and the consumer had not been abandoned. A. C. Pigou, whose *Economics of Welfare* (1920, 1932) had by then been through four editions and whose work dominated discussions of welfare in the English-speaking world in the 1920s, argued in terms of "satisfactions" rather than utilities, and he pointed to many limitations of the utilitarian criterion, but he still grounded his analysis of welfare on his theory of the consumer. Pareto (1909) also refused to argue in terms of utility, preferring the term "ophelimité," but though he was willing to distance himself further from an aggregative notion of welfare, he still saw a close connection between the two. So too did most of the literature on welfare economics with which Samuelson and Bergson were engaging.

In contrast, though the idea was not developed, Samuelson described welfare economics as "ethical judgments of policy." He had not forgotten what he had learned from Knight. Given the timing, it seems plausible to conjecture that in writing these brief remarks, both tacked on at the very end of the paper, he was responding to reactions to Bergson's article, published shortly before.[2]

Their starting point for more substantial work on the problem of welfare was Pareto (see Arthmar and McLure, Chapter 6, this volume). At some point in 1937, during the second year of Samuelson's coursework, Bergson kept asking Samuelson, "What can Pareto mean by this 1898 use of the French singular when he speaks of 'the social optimum'?" (Samuelson, 1981, p. 224). Their conclusion was that Pareto's writings were ambiguous and that he meant different things. Samuelson explained this to Suzumura (Suzumura, 2005, p. 334) in the following way.

I had to read Pareto in the Italian original, and my command of Italian was very poor. Nevertheless, I had a feeling when I read the 1913 article – I say this with diffidence – that he may momentarily have had the notion of an imposed-from-outside social welfare function .... But I thought I detected in it also a positivistic real political function of certain elites in any society. Each one of these elites has different power, like the powers of father and mother, oldest son, younger sons in

---

[2] This remains a conjecture, for the precise timing of these articles, and the lags between submission and publication, are not known.

a family. If you try to get a demand function for the family, you must combine these different influences. Generally speaking, when you do that, you don't get an integrable function. To me, that was what Pareto was talking about in the 1913 article.

Samuelson makes two points here. The first is that he thought Pareto glimpsed the idea of "a positivistic real political function of certain elites in society," an idea he no doubt expressed diffidently as he could have been reading Arrow's social welfare function into his memory of Pareto. The second is the idea that he and Bergson developed: the notion of "an imposed-from-outside" function that represented a particular set of ethical values. Welfare was a normative judgment conceptually completely different from propositions about behavior. However, in Bergson's paper on the subject (Bergson, 1938) such points were not made explicitly.

8.4 Bergson's Use of the Social Welfare Function

Bergson (Bergson, 1938, p. 310) described the object of his paper as being "to state in a precise form the value judgments required for the derivation of the conditions of maximum economic welfare which have been advanced in the studies of the Cambridge economists [Marshall, Pigou, Kahn and Edgeworth], Pareto and Barone, and Mr. Lerner." In other words, he was not challenging their approach, merely explicating it. He then simplified his notation by assuming there were two consumption goods, two types of labor, two non-labor inputs into production and that each commodity was produced in a single production unit. Ignoring non-economic variables that might affect welfare, he focused on an Economic Welfare Function (EWF), in which economic welfare was a function of each person's consumption of each of the two consumption goods (x and y), each person's supply of each type of labor in producing each consumption good (a^x, b^x, a^y, b^y) and the quantities of non-labor inputs (C, D) used in producing each consumption good.

$$E = E(x_1, y_1, a_1^x, b_1^x, a_1^y, b_1^y, \ldots x_n, y_n, a_n^x, b_n^x, a_n^y, b_n^y, C^x, D^x, C^y, D^y)$$

He then discussed the conditions under which Economic Welfare would be maximized, including the conditions derived by the three groups of economists mentioned earlier.

It was only when Bergson discussed the Pareto-Barone conditions that he referred to individuals' judgments of their own welfare. They assumed that if the quantities of consumption goods and labor supplied were constant for all except the ith individual, "if the ith individual consumed the various commodities and performed the various types of work in combinations which were indifferent to him, economic welfare would be constant" (Bergson, 1938, p. 318). This implied that the EWF must take the form

$$E = E[S^1(x_1, y_1, a_1^x, b_1^x, a_1^y, b_1^y), \ldots S^n(x_n, y_n, a_n^x, b_n^x, a_n^y, b_n^y)]$$

where the functions $S^i(.)$ are individuals' indifference loci.

It is notable, given more recent discussions, that Bergson did not discuss where his EWF might come from. It is simply a mathematical statement, the explanation of which is initially left open pending discussion later on, when he explains that welfare principles have to be based on the prevailing values of the community being discussed.

[O]nly if the welfare principles are based upon prevailing values, can they be relevant to the activity of the community in question. But the determination of prevailing values for a given community, while I regard it as both a proper and necessary task for the economist, and of the same general character as the investigation of the indifference functions for individuals, is a project which I shall not undertake here. (Bergson, 1938, p. 323)

This suggests not so much an imposed-from-outside welfare function as one that reflects the values of the community being analyzed, which is potentially vulnerable to Arrow's critique.

As he had promised at the outset, Bergson analyzed the value judgments implicit in the conditions others had developed. He was particularly critical of the Cambridge economists' use of the concept of utility that, he stressed, did not avoid the need to introduce ethical judgments. Rather, reference to utility served to conceal the role of value judgments.

[It] does not provide an alternative to the introduction of value judgments. First of all, the comparison of the utilities of different individuals must involve an evaluation of the relative economic positions of these individuals. No extension of the methods of measuring utilities will dispense with the necessity for the introduction of value propositions to give these utilities a common dimension. Secondly, the evaluation of the different commodities cannot be avoided, even tho this evaluation may consist only in a decision to accept the evaluations of the individual members of the community. (Bergson, 1938, p. 327)[3]

Utilitarianism introduces value judgments in a way that Bergson considered misleading, the reason being that statements about "the aggregative

---

[3] Bergson added a third objection but these two are sufficient for the point being made here.

character of social welfare" or about "equality of marginal utilities when there is an equal distribution of shares, provided temperaments are about the same" sound like factual propositions even though they are not. Such language serves to conceal the value judgments being introduced. On the other hand, Bergson found difficulties in the writing of those, such as Pareto, Enrico Barone and Abba Lerner, who, in refusing to add up utilities, had turned their back on utilitarianism (Bergson, 1938, pp. 329–30). In rejecting utilitarianism they effectively excluded certain distributional issues from their analysis, without providing any justification for doing so.

8.5 Debating Welfare Economics

Though the social welfare function was Bergson's, it was Samuelson who defended the underlying approach to welfare economics during the next decade. Bergson's publications were confined to issues relating more directly to problems confronting the government agencies for which he was working during the war – price flexibility and the economics of the Soviet Union. The first context for Samuelson's application, and hence defense, of the approach was international trade. "Welfare economics and international trade" (Samuelson, 1938b) opened with the observation that the theory of international trade had been developed in order to answer normative questions. Given that the theory of welfare economics was going through a period of controversy, it was, he contended, appropriate to determine whether conclusions reached in trade theory were valid.

Samuelson's starting point was that welfare economics implied making ethical judgments.

At the outset, it is understood of course that every discussion of welfare economics implies certain ethical assumptions. I do not propose, however, to discuss the philosophical grounds for holding or rejecting different ethical precepts or assumptions. Rather will the discussion be confined to the implications of different ethical assumptions and the necessary and sufficient presuppositions or the truth of various theorems. (Samuelson, 1938b, p. 261)

He simplified the argument, avoiding the issues that arguably made welfare economics so difficult, by considering trade between two individuals, so that no aggregation problems arose within each of the parties engaging in trade. This meant that he could represent each trader's behavior by a set of indifference curves. He made the assumption that if one trader preferred one outcome to another, this was better. This left the problem of measuring welfare when one of the two parties to trade was made better off and the other worse off, for there was no way to measure or add their utilities. Failing to solve this problem meant that Samuelson could not show that free trade was optimal from a welfare point of view, though he could show that some trade was better than no trade. The following year he developed this argument, arguing that if the introduction of trade resulted in relative prices that were different from those prevailing with no trade, all parties to trade would be better off than if trade did not take place (Samuelson, 1939, p. 200). This result might be familiar, but he claimed that this was the first rigorous proof.

Samuelson's discussion of the case where countries are not composed of identical individuals makes it clear that he was thinking in terms of what became Pareto optimality. Indifference curves are taken to denote well-being and the problem of evaluating welfare is simply that of comparing different people's gains and losses. Perhaps implicitly responding to John Hicks's attempts to reinstate the concept of consumers' surplus, Samuelson noted that "constructs such as consumers' surplus are in general inadmissible" and that in the special cases where they could be used, they were "perfectly arbitrary and conventional, adding nothing to the analysis" (Samuelson, 1939, p. 205).

Shortly after Bergson's article,[4] Samuelson restated its conclusion in arguing that a line of theory initiated by Oskar Lange, and involving Roy Allen, Hicks's co-author in their articles on indifference curves, about the determinateness of the utility function was misconceived. "As Mr. Burk [Bergson] has shown," Samuelson argued, "it is only necessary in order to make welfare judgments that we agree upon the definition of an ordinal function involving as variables the quantities of goods consumed by all individuals; and that even if we permit the individual's own preferences to 'count,' there is still no need for any cardinal measure of utility" (Samuelson, 1938a, p. 65). Assuming cardinal utility added "literally nothing" to welfare analysis. Notwithstanding this, he felt able to conclude by agreeing with Lange that earlier mathematical economists had been very inconsistent in their work.

The occasion for a more explicit assessment of what he now called "the new welfare economics," in which his work was placed alongside those of Hicks, Harold Hotelling, Nicholas Kaldor, Lerner and others, was a critique by his friend from his Chicago student days, George Stigler. Stigler published a paper that claimed that the "new welfare economists"

---

[4] The evidence for this statement on timing is that Samuelson cites Bergson's paper and his was published in the same year.

(including Samuelson in the paper on international trade cited above) claimed that "many policies can be shown ... to be good or bad without entering a dangerous quagmire of value judgments" (Stigler, 1943, p. 355). Claiming that the new theory, though usually presented using formidable mathematics, was simple enough to be summarized in half a page, he offered what he believed was a strong critique. If the precepts of the new welfare economics were followed, thieves would be rewarded for their crimes and wars should be fought with checkbooks (Stigler, 1943, p. 356).[5] The problem was, he contended, that societies were concerned with more than maximizing national income. Policy changes would lead to changes in individuals' indifference curves (to changes in their preferences), making it impossible to use them as the basis for welfare analysis. What societies required, Stigler contended, was consensus on the ends that society is to seek. Without such consensus, and a belief that the system is fair, the social system will disintegrate.

Samuelson (1943) responded to this by saying that he agreed with much of what Stigler was saying – economic welfare was not necessarily the main goal in society and tastes would change – but Stigler had got the new welfare economics completely wrong. The new welfare economics was not intended to displace the old but to derive necessary conditions for social welfare, basing them on the very mild assumptions that it is better to have more than to have less, and that "individual tastes are to 'count' in the sense that it is 'better' if all individuals are 'better' off" (Samuelson, 1943, p. 605). This is all entirely consistent with the claim that ethical judgments have to be imposed but the emphasis is, as in his work on trade, on what is now called Pareto efficiency. In saying that the new welfare economics is no substitute for the old, he implied that stronger ethical judgments can and should be made, though it is not a point he chose to stress.

8.6 A General Theory of Welfare Economics

Samuelson's PhD thesis (Samuelson, 1940), written in 1940 after he had left the Society of Fellows and was now free to work toward a higher degree, and examined in February 1941, contained material on the measurement of marginal utility, but did not discuss welfare. The fifty-page chapter on welfare included in *Foundations of Economic Analysis* (1947) was written later. It began with what was effectively a long defense of the historical claim he had made in his *Econometrica*

---

[5] Note that this was published during a crucial year in World War II.

article about the process whereby ethical and, later, psychological elements had been removed from consumer theory.

Economics had, Samuelson claimed, always been associated with the notion that "in some sense perfect competition represented an optimal situation," albeit expressed in different ways (Samuelson, 1947, p. 203). It was exemplified by the case for free trade. This clearly normative idea was bound up with teleology, whether ideas of natural rights, natural selection or the Malthusian doctrine that competition was necessary to bring out the best in people. But though these were generally conservative ideas, used to defend the status quo, Samuelson noted that arguments about perfect competition could also be used to challenge the status quo, as when they were used to justify anti-monopoly legislation.

More convincing were arguments that did not depend on teleology. The argument that some trade was better than no trade could easily (albeit illegitimately) become an argument for free trade. This was reinforced by the argument that in an equilibrium every agent is doing the best they can for themselves. So by the end of the nineteenth century, economists, including Walras, Jevons, Launhardt, Wicksell and Marshall, were in a position to construct proofs that competitive equilibrium was optimal. Some went further, trying to argue that the distribution of income produced under competition was optimal and though John Bates Clark's (1899) view that people were morally entitled to their own marginal product was attractive to many in a frontier society, such notions were inconsistent with widely held ethical views. Generally, economists concluded that, subject to some caveats, perfect competition was optimal provided that the distribution of income was appropriate. However, Samuelson did not find any of their arguments convincing. For example, Walras barely went beyond the assertion that people did what was best for themselves, Jevons assumed he could add up utilities and Marshall made the mistake of assuming that he could measure utility with consumers' surplus, an idea Samuelson discussed at length because Hicks had recently sought to revive it.

The economist who went further was Pareto, who argued that competition produced "a *maximum d'utilité collective* regardless of the distribution of income, and indeed even if the utilities of different individuals were not considered to be comparable" (Samuelson, 1947, p. 212). This maximum position "*was defined by the requirement that there should not exist any possible variation or movement which would make everybody better off*" (p. 212). Pareto's exposition was not ideal, partly because he worked with infinitesimal changes – one of the main features of Samuelson's dissertation was that he also analyzed finite changes – but the main defect in his exposition was that he failed to make it clear that the optimum he had defined was not unique. What remained was to work out the conditions that it implied, a process that writers from Barone to Lerner and Hotelling had undertaken. This development culminated in the work of Bergson.

> The last writer to be mentioned is Professor A. Bergson. He is the first who understands the contributions of all previous contributors, and who is able to form a synthesis of them. In addition, he is the first to develop explicitly the notion of an ordinal social welfare function in terms of which all the various schools of thought can be interpreted, and in terms of which they for the first time assume significance. (Samuelson, 1947, p. 219)

The stage was thus set to introduce the idea of the social welfare function, which Samuelson was adopting as his own approach to the problem.

    Samuelson's defense of the notion of a social welfare function began with the charge made by Lionel Robbins (Robbins, 1932) that value judgments had no place in scientific analysis. However, whilst such a view was useful in culling bad reasoning, it went too far. "It is a legitimate exercise of economic analysis to examine the consequences of various value judgments, whether or not they are shared by the theorist, just as the study of comparative ethics is itself a science like any other branch of anthropology" (Samuelson, 1947, p. 220). Contrary to Robbins and many proponents of the new welfare economics, Samuelson contended that even propositions that rely on interpersonal utility comparisons have "real content and interest for the scientific analyst" even though the economist may not wish to deduce or verify the ethical judgments on which they rest, "except on the anthropological level." He summed this up when he explained his use of a social welfare function.

> Without inquiring into its origins, we take as a starting point for our discussion a function of all the economic magnitudes of a system which is supposed to characterize some ethical belief – that of a benevolent despot, or a complete egoist, or "all men of good will," a misanthrope, the state, race, or group mind, God, etc. Any possible opinion is admissible, including my own, although it is best in the first instance, in view of human frailty where one's own beliefs are involved, to omit the latter. (Samuelson, 1947, p. 221)

All he assumed about such ethical beliefs was that they provided an ordering of possible states of the world and that they were transitive (that if A was better than B, and B better than C, then A was better than C).

    At this point, even though Samuelson's position might be read into Bergson's formulation of the problem, he was, as Suzumura (Chapter 7, this volume) has noted, taking a more radical stance. Where Bergson assumed that his EWF reflected the consensus of the relevant community, other functions not being relevant, Samuelson argued that the economist could analyze *any* set of ethical judgments, completely separating the problem from that of discerning the views of the community whose welfare was being analyzed.

To this point, Samuelson's analysis led up to Bergson's formulation of the problem of welfare, though he provided a more substantial historical context and he cut the analysis free from the tangled debates of the 1930s. This freedom from engaging closely with the terms in which welfare had been discussed in the 1930s meant that Samuelson could outline, far more clearly than Bergson had done, various ethical judgments that might be used to give structure to the social welfare function and make it possible to derive substantial results. His starting point was a function that was even more general, and with less content, than Bergson's, for it simply stated that social welfare, $w = w(z_1, z_2, \ldots)$ where the z's are variables that are thought relevant to social welfare. This formalized the problem but added no content whatsoever, because nothing was said about either the z's or the form of the function W. Anything more specific than this involved making ethical judgments.

After observing that the z's were not normally taken to include prices (itself a value judgment) he explained that many of the variables would be specific to individual households. It mattered what different households consumed, and the services different households provided were not interchangeable. The crucial assumption was, however, the fifth, that individuals' preferences "count." Yet, important as this assumption was, and though it was, in the context of the 1940s, ideologically charged as Samuelson implicitly noted when he referred to the attitude of the "soap box speaker" who said, "When the revolution comes, you will eat strawberries and cream, and like it!" (Samuelson, 1947, p. 224),[6] there were still objections that could be raised to it. One of these was handled by a further assumption that individuals' preferences were to depend only on their own consumption and not that of others, so as to rule out Veblenian conspicuous consumption, envy and related phenomena.

Samuelson contended that the ethical judgments he had made up to this point were held by most economists. He then explored more controversial ones: that the social welfare function be nearly symmetric with respect to

---

[6] The importance of individual rationality as a distinction between the United States and the Soviet Union has been discussed by Amadae (2003).

the consumption of all individuals (that everyone counts for approximately the same); and that welfare was the sum of individuals' cardinally measurable utilities. These involved judgments about the distribution of resources. It is important to note that Samuelson was not arguing about the merits of such judgments: his claim was merely that they did involve value judgments even though they might appear to be mere technical assumptions.

Samuelson then turned to the mathematical analysis of welfare, using this list of value judgments first to narrow down the z's to quantities of commodities and productive services, to render the social welfare function as $w = w(U_1(.), U_2(.), \ldots)$ – that social welfare is a function of the utilities of all the individuals in the society – from which he could derive the now-familiar conditions relating to production and exchange. More unusually, given subsequent developments, he had a section discussing interpersonal optimum conditions. The point here is that he did not claim that interpersonal comparisons could not be the subject of scientific analysis. His first point was that the previously derived optimum conditions defined an infinite number of points: to use Ian Little's terminology, there was an infinite number of Pareto optima. All that the production and exchange conditions could do was to establish that there was an equation relating the well-being of different people in the system, $0 = P(U_1(.), U_2(.), \ldots U_n(.))$: a utility possibility function. Using this device, he proceeded to make sense of the concepts of marginal social costs and benefits that Pigou (Pigou, 1932) had used to construct a case for government intervention.

Samuelson used this to mount a brief discussion of public policy, noting that the lump-sum taxes and subsidies, favored by some economists as a way to separate issues of resource allocation from issues of distribution, might not always work. For example, we might wish everyone to have a minimum income, but such a policy could easily provide an incentive not to work. His own view, which took him away from welfarism, was that it might be possible to avoid this problem by creating new motivations for work. "However," he continued, "this will not provide comfort to those who wish to utilize a parametric pricing system with algebraic lump-sum allowances, since these same considerations undermine the 'individualistic' assumptions upon which their analysis is based." The issues of resource allocation and distribution could not be separated: "from a consistent ethical point of view decisions should be made concerning the welfare function itself. Beliefs concerning the distribution of income are derivative rather than fundamental" (Samuelson, 1947, p. 248).

8.7 After *Foundations*

Ch. 8 of *Foundations* was long, and containing much more verbal explanation of the mathematics than was to be found elsewhere in the book, but Samuelson considered it "particularly condensed," added to the book because of the "rather scandalous state of confusion and ignorance" found in the current literature (Samuelson, 1948a). This no doubt explains why he took up several opportunities to repeat and elaborate on the ideas he had presented there. One of the first points he made was the need to go beyond the judgments implicit in individualism. In 1949, in a review of a book by the LSE economist Hla Myint, Samuelson wrote, "freed from the obscurities of geometry and Paretian French, the new welfare economics stands revealed as being merely a set of *incomplete necessary* conditions whose whole *raison d'être* disappears if the additional ethical conditions are not adjoined" (Samuelson, 1949, p. 372). This is a very strong statement in that he was claiming that it was *essential* to make ethical judgments that went beyond those that economists were generally willing to make. It was a deliberate, considered remark. A year earlier he had criticized Melvin Reder for "never going beyond the weakest interpersonal ethical axioms" (those of the new welfare economics) (Samuelson, 1948b, p. 399). A year later he wrote of the new welfare economics that, not only did it not go all the way to solve problems of what policy makers should do, "taken by itself, and without supplementation, it goes *virtually none* of the way" (Samuelson, 1950a, p. 11). The reason was that it analyzed *potential* welfare improvements but if these were not translated into actual improvements, they were hardly relevant for policy. Thus Samuelson argued that a competitive equilibrium would be socially optimal only if there was an optimal distribution of income and making judgments about the distribution of income involved in making ethical judgments.

A second point, crucial to understanding Samuelson's writing, is that he considered some ethical judgments to be uncontroversial. In "Evaluation of Real National Income" (1950a) his concern was whether a change in real national income indicated a change in the welfare of a community of possibly heterogeneous individuals.[7] There was an extensive literature on this problem but Samuelson believed it was confused: "most people who have seen the recent discussion between Kuznets, Hicks and Little must find their heads swimming, and must be

---

[7] This was an important problem because of the recent explosion of work on creating national accounts.

in considerable doubt as to what the proper status of this vital matter is."[8] Samuelson's main point was that one situation could be said to be unambiguously better than another only if it was better for all possible distributions of income. Hicks and others had considered only the distribution of income prevailing before and after a policy change, but this was insufficient. Samuelson explained this using a "utility possibility frontier" (UPF), a curve showing how the utilities of two parties would change as the distribution of income between them changed. Only if one UPF is completely inside the other (i.e., if the two curves do not cross) is it possible to say that one situation is better than another: "The only consistent and *ethics-free* definition of an increase in potential real income of a group is that based upon a uniform shift of the utility-possibility function for the group" (Samuelson, 1950a, pp. 19–20). This claim, resting on the Pareto criterion – that if at least one person is better off and no one is worse off, there has been an increase in social welfare – could be described as "ethics-free" only because it rested on ethical judgments that were uncontroversial. Elsewhere in the paper, he wrote with greater precision, adding qualifications, as when he wrote that the "new welfare economics" (of Kaldor, Hicks and Scitovsky) "attempts to clear the way of all issues that can be disposed of in a non-controversial (relatively) ethical-free fashion" (Samuelson, 1950a, p. 11).

A third point concerns the relationship between welfare economics and the theory of the consumer. Since his first papers on the subject, Samuelson had been adamant that "utility" had no welfare implications, for it did no more than describe the choices people made. He repeated this point in "The Problem of Integrability in Utility Theory" (Samuelson, 1950b, p. 375):

A last argument might be built up against non-integrability: if people lack the consistency of behaviour that integrability implies, then that attractive branch of individualistic welfare economics which says people's tastes should count loses most of its content; hence, we should rule out non-integrability. I am afraid that this is an illegitimate intrusion of wishful thinking by the would-be political philosopher into the facts of life.

The furthest Samuelson would go toward linking consumer theory to welfare economics was to argue that if people did not behave rationally then it weakened the case for individualist welfare economics.

---

[8] Samuelson (1950a, p. 2). The references are to Simon Kuznets, John Hicks and Ian Little. Little had just completed a doctorate on the subject at Oxford, the material being published as a series of articles and as Little (1950).

If people do not behave as if it matters to them just what they consume, that is a weakness (but not necessarily a fatal one) for the Pareto-type compensationist new-welfare economics. We must not bias our view of the facts to fit our wishes and prejudices, however pretty their pattern. On the other hand if integrability should turn out to be the best hypothesis to explain the empirical facts of the market-place, this makes a belief in individualistic ethics possible but still not mandatory. (Samuelson, 1950b, p. 375)

In other words, if people do not behave as if they were maximizing an ordinal utility function, there is no justification for an individualistic or welfarist welfare economics. However, this does not turn the problem of establishing a social welfare function into an empirical one because, even if behavior could be shown to be consistent with utility maximization, ethical judgments would still be needed to justify an individualistic or welfarist social welfare function.

Samuelson's most comprehensive reflection came in a lecture apparently delivered in 1951, in which he reflected on the position taken by Lionel Robbins in *The Economic Problem in Peace and War* (1950), first delivered as a series of lectures in 1947. The lecture, titled "Politics, Ethics, and Economics," was never published, but it was not without influence. Francis Bator (1960, p. 113), a widely read author on welfare economics and a former student of Samuelson's, acknowledged its importance for his thinking. What most interested Samuelson in these lectures was that consideration of practical problems of planning in war and peace had led Robbins to reflect on the theoretical issues of welfare economics that were involved. Robbins noted that people might not know what was best for them, raising the issue of paternalism. More serious was the problem that there was no clear division between public and private goods, for many purchases affected people other than the purchaser. An important issue in postwar Britain was saving, but the paternalism involved in government control of saving had to be balanced against arguments that a nation's saving might bear little connection with what consumers wanted. Robbins's conclusion was that, at least in peacetime, "it is the dispute about ends which matters most" (Robbins, 1950, p. 28).

Samuelson explained that, in scrutinizing Robbins's views, he was investigating his own self-doubts: he was re-examining the Chicago individualist faith in which he had been brought up. His starting point was a non-welfarist judgment: "[L]ike Robbins, I have an ethical preference for the use, wherever possible and efficient, of a decentralized price-enterprise system" (Samuelson, 1951, p. 1). However, although he shared Robbins's dislike of paternalism, there were complications. Suppose that an individualist regime required "tolerance and indifference," and people could be vaccinated against intolerance? And what about the person choosing suicide even though, if he remained alive, he would soon change his mind? The answers were not clear: "[T]he differences between childhood, maturity, and senility – between sanity, insanity, and neuroticism – between care and carelessness are all of degree. In a thousand ways in everyday life we impose upon others and we impose upon ourselves temporary and lasting *trusteeships* that limit freedom" (Samuelson, 1951, pp. 6–7). Perhaps the reason why people did not go further in limiting their freedom to make mistakes was not that this was undesirable, but that the means of doing so efficiently were not available. The provision of public goods raised questions of ethical inter-personal comparisons, just as did the provision of private consumption goods to different individuals. Further problems arose from much consumption being "*conventional* rather than *necessitous* in any physiological sense." Samuelson asked whether it was possible for even "the most refined theoretician ... to identify a consistent and invariant indifference-curve field for even the most rational individual?" (Samuelson, 1951, p. 8).

This was where the politics of his title entered, for he could address some of these issues only through bringing in "non-economic political ethical axioms" (Samuelson, 1951, p. 8). For example, one might say "We don't really care a bit what things we happen to consume, but we will fight for the death for the right to choose them freely on competitive markets," a position he attributed to Stigler. To take such a stance was to see the pricing mechanism as an end, not as a means. Samuelson distinguished between the "economic well-being" of individuals (resulting from consuming goods that they want to consume) and "any subtractions, additions, or modifications to this purely economic well-being that stems from the political and economic mechanisms by which their actual consumption is brought about and determined" (Samuelson, 1951, p. 10). He claimed that the first could be summarized by "an Economic Welfare Function a la Bergson," and he coined the phrase "Political Welfare Function" to describe the second. However, having written as though economic and political welfare could be added together, he immediately qualified this, denying that they were independent of each other:

Because of the interactions between these two aspects of welfare and for other reasons too, it would not be proper *simply to add* the two together in order to arrive at the larger total of welfare. Rather it is a case where changes in either aspect of life – economic or political – will cause (ordinal) changes in welfare most broadly conceived. (Samuelson, 1951, pp. 10–11)

The political problem on which he then focused was that of an ethically acceptable distribution of income. The complication this raised was that changes in distribution (political welfare) would have implications for efficiency and hence economic welfare, meaning that the two needed to be considered together.

Samuelson then took up Robbins's discussion of the optimal level of saving. He criticized both Robbins and the Cambridge mathematician Frank Ramsey (1928) who had analyzed the problem of a planner maximizing the discounted sum of utility over an infinite time horizon. Ramsey had used some interesting methods but his theory was completely unacceptable because it involved individuals evaluating their own consumption (their own utility) in relation to that of future generations. This raises a political-ethical problem:

> Just as it is a political-ethical problem to decide how much today's Peters share with today's Pauls, so it is a political-ethical problem to decide how much we present-day Peters must share with the Peters that will come after us. A welfare function must have been defined before normative appraisals are meaningful. ... The young Peter has no more right to rob old Peter than to rob his unborn great-great grandchildren. (Samuelson, 1951, p. 18)

8.8 Assessment

In *Foundations* and in the articles he wrote to develop and support the claims he made in the book, Samuelson developed a justification for what became the standard approach to welfare economics, based on the concept of Pareto efficiency. This makes him appear to be a supporter of an individualist welfare economics in which welfare was presumed to be an increasing function of individuals' well-being – a welfarist. However, to draw that conclusion would be a mistake. Samuelson made it clear that individualist welfare economics – or indeed any other welfare economics – rested on ethical judgments that had to be provided from outside economic science. Samuelson (1951, p. 18) cited Maurice Allais as having made the point that people changed over their lifetimes, which would have been consistent with what he had learned from Knight. People were not always rational and it might sometimes be possible to make a case for decisions that appeared to involve paternalism, not least because the division between those qualified to make their own decisions and those not so qualified was not black and white. In addition, the distinction between private and public goods was imprecise, there being many externalities in consumption, and it was necessary to form judgments about income distribution. Some problems, notably the optimal level of saving for a society, involved interpersonal comparisons of utility that could be made only by making additional ethical or political judgments. The ethical values needed to justify an individualistic or welfarist welfare economics might be widely accepted – so much so that one might describe such welfare economics as *relatively* value-free – but they were neither sacrosanct nor sufficient to draw conclusions about welfare. His own view was that it was important to go beyond the ethical and political judgments involved in individualism.

Samuelson's own views were clearly non-welfarist in that he attached importance to the distribution of income and he took an ethical stance on means – the merits of freedom and of the market mechanism, but he did not construct a formal non-welfarist theory. In his writings on policy issues (not discussed in this chapter) he often held back from making normative judgments, recognizing that these were matters on which people legitimately held different views. That is consistent with his social welfare function being "imposed" and not explained. He saw the derivation of a social welfare function from the different views held by different people as a political, not an economic problem and he did not want political differences to make it harder for people to understand the economic arguments he was making. Because of this, when he was writing about welfare economics, he generally confined himself to what he hoped were generally accepted ethical judgments, focusing on Pareto efficiency. This gave the impression that his perspective was welfarist, even though it was not.

References

Amadae, S. M. (2003) *Rationalizing Capitalist Democracy: The Cold War Origins of Rational Choice Liberalism*. University of Chicago Press, Chicago.

Arrow, K. J. (1951) *Social Choice and Individual Values*. Wiley, New York.

Backhouse, R. E. (2017) *Founder of Modern Economics: Paul A. Samuelson*. Oxford University Press, Oxford and New York.

Bator, F. M. (1960) *The Question of Government Spending: Public Needs and Private Wants*. Harper and Row, New York.

Bergson, A. (1938) A Reformulation of Certain Aspects of Welfare Economics. *The Quarterly Journal of Economics*, 52, 310–34.

Burk (Bergson), A. (1936) Real Income, Expenditure Proportionality, and Frisch's "New Methods of Measuring Marginal Utility." *The Review of Economic Studies*, 4, 33–52.

Clark, J. B. (1899) *The Distribution of Wealth*. New York, Macmillan.

Emmett, R. B. (2009) *Frank Knight and the Chicago School in Modern Economics*. Routledge, London.

Hobson, J. A. (1914) *Work and Wealth: A Human Valuation.* Macmillan, London.

Igersheim, H. (2017) The Death of Welfare Economics: History of a Controversy. *CHOPE Working Paper,* 2017-03, 1–37.

Knight, F. H. (1923) The Ethics of Competition. *The Quarterly Journal of Economics,* 37, 579–624.

Knight, F. H. (1997) *The Ethics of Competition.* Transaction Press, New Brunswick, NJ.

Little, I. M. D. (1950) *A Critique of Welfare Economics.* Oxford University Press, Oxford.

Myrdal, G. (1932) *Das Politisches Element in der Nationaloekonomischen Doctrinbildung.* Juncker und Duennhaupt, Berlin. English translation: *The Political Element in the Development of Economic Theory.* London: Routledge and Kegan Paul, 1953, translated by Paul Streeten.

Pareto, V. (1909) *Manuel d'economie politique.* Giard et Briere, Paris.

Pigou, A. C. (1920) *The Economics of Welfare.* Macmillan, London. 1st ed.

Pigou, A. C. (1932) *The Economics of Welfare.* Macmillan, London. 4th ed.

Ramsey, F. P. (1928) A Mathematical Theory of Saving. *The Economic Journal,* 38(152), 543–59.

Robbins, L. C. (1932) *An Essay on the Nature and Significance of Economic Science.* Macmillan, London.

Robbins, L. (1950) *The Economic Problem in Peace and War: Some Reflections on Objectives and Mechanisms.* Macmillan, London.

Samuelson, P. A. (1937) A Note on Measurement of Utility. *The Review of Economic Studies,* 4, 155–61.

Samuelson, P. A. (1938a) The Numerical Representation of Ordered Classifications and the Concept of Utility. *The Review of Economic Studies,* 6, 65–70.

Samuelson, P. A. (1938b) Welfare Economics and International Trade. *The American Economic Review,* 28, 261–6.

Samuelson, P. A. (1938c) A Note on the Pure Theory of Consumer's Behaviour. *Economica,* 5, 61–71.

Samuelson, P. A. (1939) The Gains from International Trade. *The Canadian Journal of Economics and Political Science / Revue canadienne d'Economique et de Science politique,* 5, 195–205.

Samuelson, P. A. (1940) *Foundations of Analytical Economics: The Observational Significance of Economic Theory.* PhD thesis, Harvard University.

Samuelson, P. A. (1943) Further Commentary on Welfare Economics. *The American Economic Review,* 33, 604–7.

Samuelson, P. A. (1947) *Foundations of Economic Analysis.* Harvard University Press, Cambridge, MA.

Samuelson, P. A. (1948a) Letter to Jacob Viner. Paul A. Samuelson Papers, Rubenstein Library, Duke University, Box 74.

Samuelson, P. A. (1948b) Review of *Studies in the Theory of Welfare Economics* by Melvin W. Reder. *American Economic Review,* 38, 397–400.

Samuelson, P. A. (1949) Review of Hla Myint, *Theories of Welfare Economics. Economica,* 16, 371–4.

Samuelson, P. A. (1950a) Evaluation of Real National Income. *Oxford Economic Papers,* 2, 1–29.

Samuelson, P. A. (1950b) The Problem of Integrability in Utility Theory. *Economica,* 17, 355–85.

Samuelson, P. A. (1951) Politics, Ethics, and Economics. Unpublished paper, in Paul A. Samuelson Papers, Rubenstein Library, Duke University, Box 133.

Samuelson, P. A. (1981) Bergsonian Welfare Economics. In *Economic Welfare and the Economics of Soviet Socialism: Essays in Honor of Abram Bergson* (ed. Rosefielde, S.). Cambridge University Press, Cambridge, pp. 223–66.

Stigler, G. J. (1943) The New Welfare Economics. *The American Economic Review*, 33, 355–9.

Suzumura, K. (2005) An Interview with Paul Samuelson: Welfare Economics, "Old" and "New," and Social Choice Theory. *Social Choice and Welfare*, 25, 327–56.

9

Non-welfarism in the Early Debates over the Coase Theorem

The Case of Environmental Economics*

Steven G. Medema

9.1 Introduction

The modern theory of externalities developed simultaneously with welfare economics and has typically embodied its welfarist orientation.[1] In fact, it is the traditional welfarist approach to the subject that has generated resistance to the economic approach to external effects, such as pollution, among non-economists. The primacy of efficiency, the individualism underlying welfarist approaches, and the lack of attention to larger "social" goals or other non-individualistic or utility-grounded first principles have all been identified as culprits.

While economists typically eschewed non-welfarist arguments in the post-WWII period, there is at least one prominent instance in which such arguments were very much in play, both directly and as underpinnings for welfare-related arguments: the debate over the Coase theorem. This debate saw the Coase theorem regularly challenged on both welfarist (whether the result is efficient, with efficiency being variously defined) and non-welfarist grounds. This then raises the question of what it was about the Coase theorem that led economists into the latter territory. The present paper revisits the early debates over the Coase theorem, where non-welfarist

* The financial support of the Institute for New Economic Thinking, the Earhart Foundation, and the National Endowment for the Humanities is gratefully acknowledged, as are comments on a previous draft of this paper provided by Roger Backhouse, Antoinette Baujard, Elodie Bertrand, Anna Carabelli, Masahiro Kawamata, Tamotsu Nishizawa, and participants in the workshops on "Economic Thought of Cambridge, Oxford LSE and the Transformation of the Welfare State" held at Hitotsubashi University in September 2016 and on "Between Economics and Ethics: Welfare, Liberalism, and Macro Economics" held in Nice in March 2017.
[1] There are exceptions, of course. See, e.g., Kapp (1950).

arguments featured prominently, in order to bring out the nature of those arguments and attempt to understand the rationale(s) for their deployment. We must acknowledge from the outset that it can be difficult, at least at times, to disentangle welfarist and non-welfarist arguments. The starting point for the analysis here is Sen's (1979, p. 464) definition of "welfarism" as "the principle that the goodness of a state of affairs depends ultimately on the set of individual utilities in that state." As Kaplow and Shavell (2003) have emphasized, goals such as "fairness" can have both welfarist and non-welfarist components – the former if "fairness" affects individual utilities and thus social welfare, and the latter if "fairness" is considered an end in itself, or an independent evaluative principle, apart from any influence on individual utilities. In the discussion that follows, our attention is confined to aspects of the Coase theorem debate that appear to explicitly raise non-welfarist concerns.

9.2 Background

The result that we now know as the Coase theorem (Coase 1960; Stigler 1966) was developed as a critique of Pigovian welfare theory and, in particular, of the Pigovian view that efficiency in the presence of externalities could not be assured apart from the governmental imposition of tax, subsidy, or regulatory remedies. That is, externalities were perceived as impediments to efficiency, and Pigovian remedies were conceived as means by which efficiency could be assured.[2]

One piece of Coase's challenge to the Pigovian position involved a demonstration that the externality-generated inefficiency was the result of an absence of property rights over the relevant resources. Once such rights were established, Coase argued, efficiency would follow if the costs of transacting were zero. Using his now well-known illustration of a farmer and cattle raiser, Coase (1960, pp. 2–8) showed that it would be in the interests of the parties to negotiate a resolution of the externality problem, and that the outcome would be both efficient, in the sense of

---

[2] On the larger themes of "The Problem of Social Cost" and of Coase's use of the negotiation result within it, see, e.g., Medema (1996) and Bertrand (2010). Coase's commentary was targeted both at Pigou (1920) and at the "Pigovian tradition" that ostensibly emerged from Pigou's analysis. Coase (1960, p. 40) did allow that the Pigovian tradition was primarily an oral one, and Medema (2020) argues that the subject of externalities largely disappeared from economics between the 1920s and the late 1950s. On Pigou's welfarism, see Yamazaki, Chapter 4, this volume.

maximizing the value of output, and independent of whom rights were initially assigned.

Lying at the heart of Coase's analysis here is his view that externalities are reciprocal in nature (1960, p. 2). If *A* imposes harm (or costs) on *B*, the imposition of a rule that reduces the harm on *B* has the effect of imposing costs on *A*. For example, while it is true that the chemicals a factory dumps into a river as byproduct of its production process cause harm to the downstream farmer who uses the river water for irrigation, forcing him to substitute a higher-cost source of water supply, it is equally the case that a prohibition on such dumping makes the factory's production process more costly. The Pigovian approach, Coase argued, focused only on the former path of causation and so ignored the possibility that the least-cost method of dealing with the issue may, in fact, be to allow the dumping to continue.[3] Once one recognizes the reciprocal nature of the problem, Coase said, "The real question that has to be decided is: should *A* be allowed to harm *B* or should *B* be allowed to harm *A*? The problem is to avoid the more serious harm" (1960, p. 2). For Coase, then, it was wrongheaded to even speak in terms of causation in these contexts, given the reciprocal nature of harm.[4] And, in failing to recognize this essential reciprocity, the economist was at risk of mis-applying the efficiency criterion.

This reciprocity is brought out neatly in Coase's analysis of the process by which negotiation between affected parties will bring about an efficient and invariant resolution of externality problems in a world of zero transaction costs. Suppose that the aforementioned chemical plant saves 100 dollars by dumping its waste into the river rather than filtering the discharge, and that the alternative water supply costs the farmer 200 dollars. Efficiency then dictates that the plant should abate, as this generates a net savings of 100 dollars. If the owners of the plant are made liable for damage, they will abate the pollution, since the 100-dollar cost of abatement is lower than the 200-dollar damage payment associated with dumping waste into the river. If the plant owners are given the right to pollute, however, the same result obtains. The farmer, faced with the prospect of paying 200 dollars for the alternative water supply, will be willing to offer the owners of

---

[3] That is, if the cost to the farmer of using the alternative water supply source is lower than the cost to the factory of installing pollution abatement technology, the value of output will be higher (or costs of remedying the pollution damage will be lower) if the factory is allowed to continue its dumping practices.

[4] In the hands of some later law and economics commentators, causation then became an empirical question, the answer to which is grounded in efficiency. See, e.g., Landes and Posner (1983).

the chemical plant up to 200 dollars to filter its discharge. As the plant owners would be willing to undertake this abatement for any price greater than 100 dollars, a deal will be struck. Thus, Coase argued, bargains among affected agents will efficiently resolve externality problems, and the outcome will be identical regardless of which party is assigned the rights over the relevant resources.

The upshot of Coase's negotiation analysis is that the Pigovian contention that tax or regulatory instruments are necessary to efficiently resolve externality problems in a neoclassical framework was in error. If coordination is costless, private action can generate efficiency just as well as can state action. Moreover, if one wishes to counter that exchange is a costly process, one must allow that state action, too, has its costs. And, in fact, it is possible that the least-cost way of dealing with the externality is to do nothing at all about the problem, as the costs of remedies may exceed the harm done by the external effect itself. The appropriate means for dealing with divergences between private and social costs, then, comes down to an evaluation of which among these imperfect remedies will maximize the value of output.

It is fair to say that Coase's analysis in "The Problem of Social Cost," as elsewhere in his policy-related writings, was conducted on typical welfarist principles – wealth maximization or the Kaldor-Hicks criterion – the very principles that were standard fare in the discussion of externalities over the nearly five decades prior to the publication of Coase's article.[5] It is usually not noticed, however, that, when winding up his discussion in "The Problem of Social Cost," Coase emphasized that his approach in the article was "confined, as is usual in this part of economics, to comparisons of the value of production, as measured by the market." "But," he continued,

> it is, of course, desirable that the choice between different social arrangements for the solution of economic problems should be carried out in broader terms than this and that the total effect of these arrangements in all spheres of life should be taken into account. As Frank H. Knight has so often emphasized, problems of welfare economics must ultimately dissolve into a study of aesthetics and morals. (1960, p. 43)

Coase's own view of the role that these factors should play is unclear, as he did not elaborate on this line of argument in "The Problem of Social Cost" or elsewhere in his writings. Little did he know, however, that

---

[5] Helm (2005, p. 210n.10) notes the welfarist thrust of Coase's analysis as against Sen's non-welfarism. On Sen's non-welfarism, see also the essays by Binder (Chapter 12) and Gilardone (Chapter 13), this volume.

considerations of "aesthetics and morals" would become a major point of emphasis in the reactions to his analysis over the next few decades.

9.3 The Environmental Turn

The earliest responses to Coase's analysis in "The Problem of Social Cost" were largely affirming, though this affirmation centered on the negotiation result rather than the larger message of the paper – his call for a comparative institutional approach to economic policy issues. And, as is now well known, George Stigler (1966, p. 113) considered this result sufficiently important to label it the "Coase theorem."[6] While the relevance or applicability of the negotiation result to the real world of costly transacting was questioned with regularity, there was little objection to its correctness as a proposition in economic theory.

In formulating the Coase theorem as he did, Stigler seems to have been intentionally drawing a parallel to the First Fundamental Theorem of Welfare Economics, which asserts the optimality of competitive equilibrium under certain conditions – one of which is the absence of external effects. The Coase theorem, then, suggests that externalities are *not* inevitably an impediment to optimality. Given the slight literature on the theory of externalities extant, Stigler's rendering is sensible. The focus of the limited discussion of externalities in the period since Pigou penned *The Economics of Welfare* (1920) had been on ascertaining the effect of externalities on competitive equilibrium and the reasons for the resulting inefficiencies (Medema 2019).[7] And, indeed, this was the basic frame through which Coase's result was viewed for the first decade following its publication. With a couple of prominent exceptions (Wellisz 1964; Mishan 1967b), it was generally accepted that negotiation could, under the assumed conditions, result in the maximization of the value output, though commentators typically stressed that this was not relevant to the problem under consideration in the paper at hand owing to the prevalence of transaction costs.

In the 1970s, however, the tide began to turn, and to turn sharply. The Coase theorem was assailed seemingly from every side and on a variety of

---

[6] Stigler's specific formulation of the "Coase theorem" was this: "[U]nder perfect competition private and social costs will be equal" (1966, p. 113). On Stigler and the Coase theorem, see Medema (2011), Bertrand (2018), and Marciano (2018).

[7] Pigou had focused on externalities as real phenomena rather than impediments to optimality. It was not until the late 1950s that we saw the phenomenological approach begin to reemerge. See Papandreou (1994) and Medema (2020).

grounds, theoretical and otherwise. The argument here is that it is the "otherwise" that provided much of the impetus for the controversy, including the theoretical part of it. Specifically, the Coase theorem's logic and implications – both real and perceived – for policy struck a chord, and on at least two fronts.

First, the Coase theorem and its implications for externality policy intersected, externally, with an increased societal concern about the effects of large-scale pollution and, internally, with the related genesis of the field of environmental economics (Medema 2014). In the process, the traditional externality-related concern with the efficiency of market outcomes became enmeshed with, and at times gave way to, non-welfarist considerations driven by attitudes toward pollution and what should be done about it. Second, the Coase theorem became a, and perhaps *the*, bedrock principle of the emerging economic analysis of law (e.g., Calabresi 1970; Posner 1973). Here, its implications intersected with traditional behavioral norms and perceptions of justice, offending the sensibilities of both legal scholars and economists. Given the subject matter of this paper and the fact that the great majority of these concerns were raised by lawyers rather than economists, we will not treat this literature directly. But as there are common threads of argument across these two fronts, we will at times make note of the legal-economic commentary.[8]

The association of externalities with pollution is a long one. Though, as noted above, the externality literature prior to the late 1950s is extremely thin, such discussions as we do see regularly invoke pollution – typically a factory dumping waste into a stream – to illustrate the problem. Even so, the focus of the analysis, post-Pigou, was not on devising mechanisms to restrain the polluter's activity, or on remedies generally. Instead, it was on devising an explanation for why the presence of these external effects led to deviations from efficiency (Medema 2020). And for these harmful effects, of course, the deviation was in a particular direction – too much of the harmful activity, relative to what is optimal.

When economists began to take up the analysis of environmental problems in the latter half of the 1950s, they did so via the theory of externalities handed down from Pigou and, as the field developed over the next two decades, the Pigovian approach became entrenched as the dominant paradigm. The focus was on Pigovian tax and regulatory remedies (with some attention to subsidies), all justified based upon the standard welfare

---

[8] For an interesting set of discussions on the legal side, see the "Symposium on Efficiency as a Legal Concern," published in the *Hofstra Law Review* (1980), and Fiss (1986).

prescriptions of orthodox economics – that pollution led to divergences from the marginal conditions for an optimum, divergences that could be effectively eliminated via Pigovian instruments.

Despite this Pigovian emphasis, the Coase theorem was slowly becoming a staple of the externalities literature. As we move through the 1960s, we find Coase's result discussed more and more in theoretical treatments of the subject, as well as in applied discussions of externalities and the policies available for dealing with them. Even so, there was no groundswell of support in the literature for negotiated solutions to externality problems. Instead, as noted above, we find Coase's result mentioned, but quickly pushed to one side in favor of Pigovian remedies on the grounds that transaction costs preclude the operation of the theorem's mechanics.

The explosion of literature on the economics of the environment in the 1970s, however, brought a radical change to the nature and tone of the discussion. Suddenly, the Coase theorem was perceived as a threat to the proper analysis of and policy formation with respect to externalities and, in particular, the problem of large-scale pollution. Though Coase (1960, p. 18) himself had specifically noted that the negotiation result could not be expected to apply to such situations, a substantial body of theorem criticism emerged suggesting that many economists took seriously the notion that the Coase theorem offered a means for dealing with pollution externalities.

If the goal of externality policy is to generate efficient outcomes – and this had been the theme in the literature for some four decades – economic theory provided no reason to prefer Pigovian instruments to Coase theorem solutions. Each assured efficient outcomes under idealized conditions but could promise no more than that. To get at the hostility to the theorem, then, we must look to other considerations. Two such considerations emerge from the environmental economics literature of the 1970s: a concern with fairness, or equity, in the allocation of the costs associated with reducing pollution damage and a view of the environment as an end in itself.

9.3.1 Equity, Fairness, and the Rejection of Reciprocity

In what is typically regarded as the first major statement of a neoclassical economic approach to the environment, Allen Kneese, writing in *The Economics of Regional Water Quality Management* (1964), put Coase's negotiation result front and center in the environmental discussion.[9]

---

[9] Kneese's discussion of Coase's result was not the first in an environmental context (see Milliman 1962), but it was by far the most extensive and influential to that point.

Kneese devoted several pages to Coase's result and accepted the theoretical validity of both the efficiency and invariance claims. Having gone this far, however, he suggested that, in the case of a firm whose pollution damages fishing stocks, "on equity grounds it might be considered justifiable to compensate the fisherman for his loss of fish," as opposed to having the fisherman pay the polluter to induce a reduction in or the elimination of pollution emissions (1964, p. 44). Kneese's concern that equity matters in the determination of who is made to bear the costs related to environmental harms would echo time and again in the discussions of the Coase theorem within the environmental economics literature. The underlying message here, implicit in Kneese's argument but a recurrent theme in the environmental Coase theorem literature through the 1970s, was that there are "injurers" and "victims," and it would be unfair to require "victims" to bribe polluters to reduce their emissions. Because their actions visit injury on other agents, polluters should be forced to bear the costs of the harm and of reductions in it.

The strongest voice on this front was LSE welfare economist E. J. Mishan, who wrote extensively on welfare economics in general and externalities in particular during the 1960s and 1970s.[10] His views, expressed across a range of books and articles – including his 1971 *Journal of Economic Literature* (*JE:*) survey of externality theory (1971b) and *The Costs of Economic Growth* (1967a), written for a broader public – received wide exposure. Though his initial reaction to Coase's negotiation result was largely affirming (Mishan 1965), his attitude toward it changed as externality theory increasingly became synonymous with pollution control in the late 1960s and early 1970s. Mishan's concern for ethical issues on this front comes through forcefully already in *The Costs of Economic Growth*, but the connection to the Coase theorem was driven home in his 1971 *JEL* survey, where, in the course of analyzing the Coase theorem's invariance claim, he took pains to emphasize that while the claims of competing resource users in situations of externality "are indeed Pareto symmetric," they "may not be ethically symmetric" – that there is something ethically wrong with an assignment of rights under which the victim pays (Mishan 1971b, p. 24).[11] As Baumol (1972, p. 309) put it, under this line of reasoning, "the murder victim too, is then always an accessory to the crime."

[10] See, e.g., Mishan (1965; 1967a; 1967b; 1971a; 1971b).
[11] See also Mishan (1967a, pp. 65–66), Head (1974, pp. 5–6), and Boll-De Cock (1976, p. 31). It should be noted that this was not the only fairness-related concern raised in the literature. There was also concern that pollution costs fall disproportionately on the poor, and so should be mitigated by more wealthy polluters who are better able to bear

While Mishan was concerned about the potential distributional consequences of Coasean bargains – in other words, that the poor may be harmed for the benefit of the wealthy through pollution – he placed greater emphasis on "the inequity per se of a law that countenances the inflicting of a wide range of damages on others without effective means of redress." Absent a set of sanctions against those who would "trespass on the citizen's amenity," he believed that "existing institutions lend themselves inadvertently to a process of blackmail in so far as they place the burden of reaching agreement on the person or group whose interests have been damaged" (1967b, p. 278). In light of this, Mishan argues for "amenity rights," which force the injurer, as traditionally defined, to compensate the victim for harm (1967a, pp. 71–73).

The message that emerges here is that holding "victims" liable is simply *wrong*, or, as Mishan put it in 1967, contrary to "social justice" (1967a, p. 68). These arguments represent a clear-cut rejection of the reciprocal view of externalities laid out by Coase in "The Problem of Social Cost."[12] Indeed, given this reciprocity – which we find emphasized not just in Coase, but in, for example, Hohfeld (1913) and Commons (1924) – the very rhetoric of "polluter"/"injurer" and "victim" speaks to the non-welfarist underpinnings implicit in economists' discussions of these issues. One prominent illustration of this, and of the problematic nature of such assertions, can be found in Mishan's argument for the priority of rights of non-smokers, made on the grounds that "the freedom to breath fresh air does not, of itself, reduce the welfare of others." In like manner, he said, "the freedom desired by members of the public to live in clean and quiet surroundings," as against having noisy vehicles or polluting factories operating nearby "does not, of itself, reduce the welfare of others" (1971b, p. 25). But these statements are patently false; freedom for the non-smoker reduces the welfare of the smoker and the freedom of the residents

these (e.g., Mishan 1967a, pp. 60–61), though Common (1988), in contrast, later argued that this conventional story of wealthy polluters and poor victims may well not be true in certain instances. Problems associated with the long-term nature of certain forms of environmental degradation, too, were raised in this context, with the argument being that the interests of future generations are not likely to be sufficiently taken into account in Coasean negotiations carried out by members of the present generation and that governmental solutions were more likely to be framed with these intergenerational issues in mind (Mishan 1971b, pp. 24–26).

[12] Interestingly, others, including some not favorably disposed to the Coase theorem as a mechanism for dealing with externality problems, suggested that alerting economists to the reciprocal nature of externalities was one of the major contributions of Coase's article. This is a theme that Samuels, for one, emphasized repeatedly. See, e.g., Samuels (1974).

to enjoy amenity reduces the welfare of owners of the automobiles and of the plant, as well as the plant's employees and the customers, both of which groups are impacted by the higher costs of production associated with costly pollution abatement activities.[13]

The centrality of these fairness considerations in the literature and the seriousness with which they were taken by scholars in the field is further evidenced in the fact that they were given prominent play in the *textbook* literature of the period.[14] Lloyd Reynolds (1973, p. 214), for example, instances a situation where "A chemical plant dumps wastes into a river which kill the fish in a lake located downstream, thereby depriving would-be fishermen on the lake of a pleasant recreation." Reynolds pointed out that the fishermen could band together and bribe the plant to reduce emissions sufficiently to make the lake safe for the fish. "But on second thought," he continued, "this doesn't seem very fair. Why shouldn't the company pay the fishermen for the damage inflicted on them, instead of the other way round?" It was not simply about efficiency, then, and even when it was about efficiency there was concern for how that efficiency was to be achieved.

It is worth noting that not all of those who raised the issue of fairness came down on this side of the fence. Tony Chisholm, Cliff Walsh, and Geoffrey Brennan (1974), for example, struck a rather different tone, contesting the standard dichotomy between wicked polluters and virtuous victims. Like Coase, they argued that the problem is inherently reciprocal: "The truth of the matter is that *all* consumers contribute to pollution by the very act of consumption; firms pollute, not because they derive fiendish delight from doing so, *but because the individual consumers of their products pay them to do so*" (p. 4). The argument, of course, is that if consumers, too, are a cause of the pollution, it becomes reasonable to consider the option of making them bear some amount of the cost. This, however, was very much a minority view.

9.3.2 The Environment as an End

The second major emphasis in the non-welfarist attacks on the Coase theorem was the view that environmental preservation is an end in itself

---

[13] For defense of the Coase theorem and the notion of reciprocity in the smoking context, see Tollison and Wagner (1988, ch. 5).

[14] Why textbook authors devoted significant space to a topic, the Coase theorem, the theoretical validity of which was still very much the subject of dispute in the profession at large, is another story. See Medema (2014; 2015) for further discussion of this issue.

and that the Coase theorem works as a threat to the achievement of this end. This emphasis manifested itself in a strong "pro-abatement" tone that was found in so much of the environmental economics literature during this period – a view that pollution levels must be reduced "to levels that are considered to be tolerable" (Baumol 1972, p. 307).

The perception of potentially cataclysmic effects from pollution was a driving force behind the writings of two of the theorem's staunchest critics during this period. Warren Samuels, writing in 1972, argued that other criticisms of the Coase theorem were "dwarf[ed]" by

the fact that such externalities as water and air pollution may threaten the very basis and operation of civilization both in individual industrialized nations and on the planet as a whole. We may be dealing not with the subtle marginal conditions of a maximizing equilibrium, but the even more subtle total conditions of survival, a bounded consumption set, as it were, for the entire species. The threatened wreckage is far more than welfare economics. (1972[1981], p. 67])

H. H. Liebhafsky (1973, p. 676) struck a similar chord in his essay for the *Natural Resources Journal*'s Coase theorem symposium:

We are all tenants for life of the environment and our possession is rightful. The environment is an essential part of the inheritance, and uncontrolled pollution constitutes a destruction or improper deterioration of that inheritance. Those who may from time to time be in a position to make use of governmental power to preserve the inheritance stand as trustees.

The question of the Coase theorem's applicability is front and center here, underpinned by the belief that leaving things to the market will almost certainly result in significant environmental degradation owing to the failure of the Coase theorem to work its magic in the real world (e.g., Samuels 1974, p. 22).

As Randall pointed out, those who saw the Coase theorem as relevant for dealing with environmental issues made one of two arguments. The first, grounded in the notion of allocative neutrality, was that there is no reason to move away from a system where polluters are not liable, since a change in the assignment of liability would have no allocative impact in any event (Randall 1974, p. 38). Randall referred to the doctrine of allocative neutrality as "the clincher" to the Coasean approach and argued that "its demise," owing to the various critiques of the theorem, was "disastrous to the laissez-faire people" (p. 53). As both Samuels (1974) and Randall (1975) noted, it makes the policy significance of the Coase theorem the exact opposite of what those disposed to market solutions assert – property rights assignments, in reality, affect both allocation (including pollution levels) *and* distribution, as well as "the whole range of macroeconomic variables" (Randall (1975), p. 739).[15]

The second argument made by Coase theorem supporters, most forcefully stated by Demsetz (1964; 1968), was that transaction costs are simply another form of cost, like production costs, and that exchange which exhausts all gains from trade, net of transaction costs, is Pareto optimal. The conclusion drawn from this was that externalities are efficiently internalized through the market if transaction costs are the only factor precluding further exchange. As such, it was argued, government intervention to internalize the externality is unnecessary and even efficiency-diminishing. Randall (1972a, pp. 176–177) summarized this position as follows: "[W]hen a market for an external economy does not exist it should not exist, since the benefits from such a market clearly cannot exceed the costs of its operation. The absence of an observable market is itself a market solution."

It goes almost without saying that both of these "Coasean" positions would be anathema to those who believed that pollution should be reduced from its existing levels. As Mishan put the case in his *Journal of Economic Literature* essay, "Rationalizing the *status quo* in this way brings the economist perilously close to defending it" (1971b, p. 17), and the status quo was viewed by many as wholly objectionable. The clear sentiment that emerges from the writings of the theorem's strongest critics is that the market should not be the sole arbiter of rights over resources such as air and water.

The objection here is not to the use of Coase-theorem-type legal rules of liability or property-rights solutions per se – that is to non-Pigovian (tax/regulatory) remedies – but to the notion that failing to directly restrict the activities of polluters will lead to unacceptable levels of environmental degradation.[16] Randall (1974, p. 54) even went so far as to ask whether one can adopt the Coasean invariance position "without appearing blatantly anti-environment" (Randall 1972b, p. 47; 1971, p. 867) and Dick (1976, p. 194) made the achievement of "higher levels of environmental quality" (Randall) or "environmental gains" (Dick) a goal and advocated polluter liability on that basis, though both were willing to countenance the possibility of market arrangements that allow polluters to purchase the right to pollute.[17] Mishan's case for "amenity rights," referenced above,

---

[15] See also Randall (1974, p. 53). Dick (1976, p. 194) argued this same point.

[16] In fact, we do not see in the literature critical of the Coase theorem arguments against assigning property rights (e.g., in clean air) to those considered to be victims.

[17] Paul Burrows (1970, p. 48) made a similar point in the context of law, arguing the case for assigning rights based on notions of "legal equity" and leaving it to negotiation to sort out economic considerations.

similarly was grounded in his view that they would "promote . . . a rise in standards of environment generally" by reducing activity levels or promoting abatement or, if necessary and feasible, the compensation of victims (Mishan 1967a, pp. 71–73). Daniel Bromley (1978, p. 57), for his part, took a still stronger position, going so far as to suggest that it may be best to *rule out* the possibility of market transactions in certain situations, asserting that a rule of inalienability "would seem most appropriate" for externality situations that are "detrimental to human health or to long-run ecological integrity."

In short, there can be no question that the Coasean approach was perceived – by environmental economists and others – as a real threat to the long-accepted status of the Pigovian tradition, an approach that *guaranteed* reductions in pollution emissions from market-generated levels and did so in a way that imposed costs on emitters rather than "victims." Mishan made this explicit, characterizing what he labeled a "consensus" on the Coase theorem (1971b, pp. 16–17) as the launching point for "an iconoclastic movement to edge the master [Pigou] from his niche in the hall of fame" (1974, p. 1288n.1),[18] the blame for which he laid squarely at the feet of Coase and, to a lesser extent, Buchanan and Stubblebine (1962). In adopting such a stance, however, economists put themselves at odds with "politicians, administrators, and the general public," as this latter group, in Randall's view, "seems to have more faith in systems of standards" to achieve the desired level of pollution reduction (1972a, p. 176).[19]

9.4 Coase's "Amoralization" of Externalities

Underlying both the "fairness/equity" and "environment as an end" considerations was, in Randall's (1974, p. 53) words, Coase's effective

---

[18] See also Samuels (1974, pp. 27–28). That said, not everyone saw things in this way. Horner (1975, p. 34) noted that, in the period since Coase raised the possibility of negotiated solutions, "most of the literature has defended policies based on Pigovian taxes and subsidies to correct the inefficiencies caused by externalities." Fisher and Peterson (1976, p. 25), in like manner, tell us that environmental economists "usually recommend Pigovian taxes to internalize the externalities associated with pollution." Horner went on, though, to play into the hands of those disposed to Coasean solutions (with transaction costs, à la Demsetz, Cheung, and the Coase of pages 15 onward in "The Problem of Social Cost") in saying that Pigovian policies "eliminate the need to consider the transactions costs preventing negotiations and the ambiguity of property rights associated with natural resources such as air and water" (1975, p. 34), thus tacitly admitting that the exclusive focus on Pigovian remedies forecloses the investigation of whether market solutions might entail lower costs than the Pigovian ones.
[19] See also Randall (1974, pp. 40–41).

"amoralization of the externality issue," grounded in his emphasis on the reciprocal nature of harm and the suggestion the problem is to avoid the more serious (in value of output terms) harm. Yet, we noted in Section 9.2 that Coase had argued in "The Problem of Social Cost" that it is "desirable" that policy decisions over issues such as these "be carried out in broader terms" than just efficiency, including "aesthetics and morals" (1960, p. 43). Given this, Randall's charge against Coase himself is likely too strong, though it may have validity against others – for example, within the property rights tradition – who built upon Coase's work.[20]

Whether or not one agrees with Randall's contention that Coase amoralized the externality issue,[21] it is difficult to disagree with his assessment that ethical concerns raised by the Coase theorem, particularly in the environmental and legal contexts, played a significant role in the hostility expressed toward it. Stigler no doubt added fuel to the fire when, rather than carrying through Coase's emphasis on the reciprocal nature of the problem, said, in his introduction of the "Coase theorem," that "When a factory spews smoke on a thousand homes, *the ideal solution* is to arrange a compensation system whereby the homeowners pay the factory to install smoke reduction devices up to the point where the marginal cost of smoke reduction equals the sum of the marginal gains to the homeowners" (1966, p. 113, emphasis added). Demsetz's emphasis on efficiency net of transaction costs likely only exacerbated the problem.[22]

---

[20] Of all of the commentators on the equity issue during this period, only Weld (1973, p. 596) appears to have noticed (albeit rather dismissively) this aspect of Coase's discussion.

[21] Apart from Coase's above-cited comment about larger criteria informing policy decisions, one could argue, for example, that wealth maximization is simply an alternative moral structure.

[22] One of the interesting features of the literature during the 1970s is that one finds no claims that the Coase theorem offers a way forward for dealing with large-scale pollution problems. Yet, as Alan Randall, Emery Castle, and Robert McCormick have pointed out in correspondence with this author, the Coase theorem was very much "in the air" during the 1970s, discussed in department hallways and seminar rooms, in addition to the scholarly literature. And among those talking about externality issues, there was a not insubstantial cadre suggesting that the theorem showed that tax and regulatory remedies, such as the Clean Air Act, were not necessary for an efficient resolution of environmental problems – that Coasean mechanisms would effectively internalize – or had already – the relevant costs. Thus, while the environmental economics literature would suggest that the critics were reacting against an invisible straw man, attention to the larger background against which this emerging literature played out reveals a different picture and gives credence to the claims made by scholars such as Mishan and Randall that the theorem had a degree of support among economists generally as a framework through which one could do environmental policy analysis.

But was "amoralization" the problem? It could certainly be argued that the Pigovian approach was no more inherently moral than the Coasean. After all, the thrust of the Pigovian discussion was efficiency. It just so happened that, on the road to efficiency, the Pigovian approach provided ways of dealing with pollution and other harmful acts that resonated with social norms (including traditional legal notions of causation)[23] and with the interests of those who considered environmental preservation an end worth pursuing. The Coasean approach, on the other hand, raised the prospect of putting efficiency on a collision course with these larger concerns, as Randall brought out starkly:

In essence, Coase seemed to be saying that in cases where two parties have conflicting interests there are no moral precepts to guide the resolution of the conflict. Viscous criminals being bribed to desist and of little children being regarded as "hitting" automobiles in pedestrian crossings, with Coasians failing to be morally offended, were evoked . . .[24] Mishan scored early points with the issue of income distribution. Surely decent people could see a moral problem in poor citizens bribing an affluent producer of effluents, while Coasians looked on benignly. (1974, p. 53)

John Weld went even further, defending the traditional approach to causation and liability by arguing that polluter liability and similar restrictions exist for a reason – they reflect social norms, an "evolved consensus," embodied in the common law, that you should "use your land as not to injure another" (1973, pp. 598–599). These norms, then, take precedence over efficiency and override the indifference suggested by the Coase theorem's invariance claim.

While supporters of the Coasean approach extolled its avoidance of fuzzy concepts such as fairness, Randall (1978, p. 12) held to a very different view, that "The amorality of [this] scholarship is not viewed by critics as a welcome escape from normative methodological traps, but as symptom of failure to understand the fundamental nature of institutions." Sounding a note from the old institutionalist tradition, Randall argued that "Institutions express a society's value system and give it effect in the form of working rules" and, in doing so, "tend to shape the individual's habits of thought and action and his expectations." This, said Randall, presents a problem in that institutional stability requires that these institutions be

---

[23] On causation, see, e.g., Cooter (1987, p. 546).

[24] Randall here was making reference to a paper by John Weld entitled, "The Social Cost of the Coase Theorem," presented at the Symposium on Environmental Economics and the Law, held at the University of California, Riverside in February 1972. Weld's paper is referenced in several articles from the 1970s but never appeared in print.

"broadly consistent with the ethical values of the society." The presence or absence of such consistency has powerful effects:

Man responds positively to institutions he sees as ethically right and openly or surreptitiously undermines those he sees as wrong. When institutions are in harmony with a broad social consensus about what is right and wrong, the day-to-day transactions of individuals and groups will proceed smoothly; when that is not the case, defiance and perhaps social upheaval and insurrection will result. (p. 12)

While assessments such as those made by Randall and Weld focused on Coase and the Coaseans as the primary source of the inattention to broader social and ethical concerns, Mishan, for all of his criticism of the Coase theorem, laid the blame more broadly – at the feet of economists and the economic method generally. In his view, economists' fixation on the Coase theorem was but one example of what he saw as their excessive preoccupation with efficiency at the expense of equity:

It is not, of course, hard to understand the somewhat exaggerated weight attached by economists to the allocative aspects of an economic problem as distinct, say from those concerned with equity. For the former aspects lend themselves nicely to formal theorizing and, with patience and a little finesse, impressive measures of social losses and gains can be foisted on credulous civil servants and a gullible public.

Yet, the priority given to allocative aspects in real economics problems cannot, I think, be justified; certainly not by recourse to welfare economics. The more "affluent" a society becomes, the less important is allocative merit narrowly conceived. And in a society in the throes of accelerating technological change (one in which, of necessity, pertinent knowledge of the human, social, and ecological consequences of what we are doing is generally slight and partly erroneous) complacency on the part of any economist, guided in his professional discussions by considerations alone of allocative merit or economic growth potential, is both to be envied and deplored. (1971b, p. 26)

Samuels (1974, p. 12) offered a similar challenge, questioning why the efficiency criterion should be given privileged status over any other. Yet, in spite of these ethically grounded critiques of the Coase theorem, economists, environmental or otherwise, continued to frame their discussions of externalities largely in terms of efficiency – whether for ideological reasons or out of professional habit.[25] Even so, the fact that the Pigovian subsidy remedy, like requiring victims to bribe polluters to reduce emissions, was and continues to be so roundly panned in the literature – also on fairness grounds – suggests that ethical issues have loomed fairly large in the calculus of environmental economists.

[25] On this see Bromley (1990).

9.5 Dueling Non-welfarisms: The Primacy of the Market

Though the thrust of this paper has been on the role of non-welfarist considerations in the attacks made on the Coase theorem, it is by no means clear that non-welfarism was confined to one side of the debate. On the environmental side, there was, as we have seen, the felt need to reduce environmental damage irrespective of the implications for economic welfare as traditionally defined and to avoid victim liability. But there is also an argument to be made – and the theorem critics frequently made it – that Coase and those who defended the Coase theorem and its potential relevance did so in part, at least, because of an a priori preference for the market as an allocative device.

The Coase theorem was (and is) a proposition in economic logic with no direct normative (or "ought") implications. It does not say that markets are superior to government or should be used in place of it. Indeed, in a world of zero transaction costs, markets and direct state action function equally well in efficiency terms; Coasean and Pigovian remedies are identical in their allocative effects. Yet, that is anything but the picture painted by the critics, who objected to what they perceived as the theorem's normative thrust. Samuels (1974), for example, pointed to what he saw as "the laissez faire, non-interventionist tenor of the usual Coasian discussions" (p. 13), as evidence that the Coase theorem was little more than a "part of the apologetics and theology of the market" (p. 27).[26] As such, he said, "the Coasian analysis is but an attempt to lend the credo of science to normative justification of the market and its fantasies of markets everywhere, and to have everything seen in that light" (p. 11).

Randall described the Coasean position in similar terms: "If there is one normative statement which sums up their position, it is this: The opportunity for trades, of all types, should be maximized," and private trading is "the solution to any and all perceived economic and/or institutional problems" (1978, p. 7). The role of government here, then, is reduced to "allocative impotence" (Randall 1974, p. 37).[27] We even find this point of view reflected in the textbook literature, with David Pearce, for example, associating the Coasean position with

---

[26] In a similar vein, Bensusan-Butt (1974, p. 181) contends that market-based approaches to environmental questions are "very cold comfort for the aesthetes," for "[t]hey know they have no chance in the market."

[27] Randall suggested that Coase and Demsetz seemed to be of the mind that "the role of central planning [read: government intervention] should be minimized" (1974, p. 35). Samuels (1974) made a similar argument.

"[a]dvocates of a free market" and "those who are concerned to minimize government activity" (1976, p. 84).[28]

The implication of the Coasean analysis, Randall argued, is that "any externalities which are observed to exist unmodified should not be modified"(Randall 1972a, p. 177n.3) – a notion that Samuels (1974, p. 5) rejected on the grounds that it assumes "the propriety of allocations made through market adjustments" and which Randall (1972a, p. 177n.3) labeled a "fallacy" because it ignores the possibility that other corrective actions (e.g., Pigovian instruments) may be less costly than the market solution.[29] Todd Lowry's perspective is perhaps more telling against the welfare implications of Coase theorem's view of the world: "in the context of a relationship composed of only two parties, each of whom is guided only by self-interest, *we may not define any action as antisocial behavior since a social reference has been excluded by our definition*" (1976, p. 5, emphasis added).

We see in the strong critiques of the theorem leveled by Randall, Samuels, and Mishan the suggestion – essentially confirmed by Mishan in the above quotation (see also Mishan [1971a]) – that these critics put a great deal of stock in the idea that economists were very attracted to the Coase theorem owing to their predisposition toward decentralized market solutions, and in the potential for the continuation, and even increase, of that attachment (Randall 1972a, p. 176; 1974, pp. 37–38). Indeed, Randall felt that no small amount of the support for the Coase theorem and its perceived implications for policy lay in its "combination of neoclassical orthodoxy with [the Coaseans'] fascinating and somewhat heretical habit of visualizing potential trades in situations where trading is illicit or, at least, not customary" (1978, p. 7). One gets the sense from reading these works that there was a perceived need to "demolish" the theorem (to use Randall's term) in order to put an end to fantasies about market solutions and, perhaps more importantly, any prospective attempts to make status-quo-favorable efficiency judgments that would deflect attention from the goal of achieving a reduction in environmental pollution, which Mishan (1971b, p. 26) labeled "the most urgent economic problem of our fragile civilization."

One of the oddities of these "primacy of the market" critiques lies in the fact that Pigovian taxes, which had significant support among those hostile

---

[28] Matthew Edel (1973, p. 98) sounded similar concerns in his environmental economics textbook.

[29] See also Randall (1974, pp. 45–46; 1975, p. 735) and Samuels (1974, pp. 4–5).

to the Coase theorem, were viewed by environmental economists at that time as a *market* instrument for resolving externality problems. The tax put a price on, for example, pollution emissions and allowed market forces to take matters from there. What distinguished these taxes from Coase theorem solutions was that they essentially guaranteed a reduction in pollution emissions and imposed the costs of these reductions on the polluters. In short, Pigovian instruments satisfied the non-welfarist considerations preferred by the theorem critics and, one could argue, environmental economists generally.[30]

While the in-depth treatments of the Coase theorem that we do find in the literature from this period are almost wholly critical of the theorem and the policy conclusions that some drew from it, we find nothing like the same level of critical attention focused on Pigovian remedies. Dick's (1974) treatment of the Coase theorem and of Pigovian remedies in his monograph on environmental economics is illustrative of the attitude found in the environmental economics literature. He provides a lengthy critique of the Coase theorem, surveying and affirming every argument that has been raised against it in the literature. But when he comes to an analysis of Pigovian instruments, his presentation consists of a defense of it against various theoretical attacks and an acknowledgment that there may be some information problems with determining the optimal Pigovian tax. The transaction costs that loomed so large in his critique of Coase's result are nowhere in evidence in his analysis of the efficacy of State action.

9.6 Conclusion

Non-welfarist arguments loomed large in debates over the Coase theorem in the 1970s, particularly within the literature of environmental economics. The invocation of such arguments is unusual in and of itself, but even more so – and perhaps singularly unique – given what the Coase theorem tells us. The Coase theorem is a proposition in economic logic, a statement with no direct implications for how to go about dealing with externality issues. It

---

[30] Dan Bromley and Alan Randall have both suggested to this author in correspondence related to this paper that what one might call the "pro-environment" view present in much of the environmental economics literature during this period may be the result of self-selection: that the individuals most likely to be attracted to this emerging field were those who had an interest in doing something about the environmental conditions of the day. The title of Donald Thompson's textbook, *The Economics of Environmental Protection* (1973) is suggestive of this viewpoint.

says, simply, that under assumed set of conditions *A*, result *B* will follow.[31] In this respect, it is no different than the Fundamental Theorems of Welfare Economics. But this is not how it was interpreted by many who encountered it. Instead, it was seen as a potential prescription for externality, including environmental, policy.

Understood as a policy prescription, the Coase theorem was thought by some to legitimate a system that could make "victims" liable for harm and allow imperfect market processes to determine the level of environmental damage. Such outcomes ran afoul of certain values that could only be brought into play via non-welfarist arguments. Curiously, though, these arguments were not used to build a case for a particular assignment of rights or liability in a Coase theorem world – that is, to suggest that polluters should not be given the right to pollute or that they should be made liable for damages. Instead, they were used to criticize the theorem itself. As Randall pointed out in 1974, "many of those who have worked so hard to pierce the Coasian balloon have invested that effort mainly because they found the policy implications of the Coase Theorem rather offensive" (1974, p. 35).

There can be no question that some of those predisposed to markets found in the theorem a justification for private or market-based solutions to externality problems and even a reason for believing that the status quo can be deemed efficient – both of these obviating the need for direct State action via Pigovian instruments that would (further) reduce pollution. But if one is to pretend that the Coase theorem is actually applicable to environmental problems, the argument cuts both ways. One of the many ironies found in the Coase theorem debate is that the theorem, by ensuring efficiency, leaves the door wide open for non-welfarist criteria – indeed, almost demands them as a method of choosing among alternative measures for dealing with external effects in a world of zero transaction costs. There is no need to worry about sacrificing efficiency when indulging one's non-welfarist values.[32]

---

[31] Assume that there are two driving routes to the office. Taking route 1, where one can average 60 mph if roads are clear, involves driving 30 miles. Taking route 2, where one can average 30 mph if roads are clear, involves driving 15 miles. If roads are clear, I will arrive at the office in 30 minutes' time regardless of which road I drive. This proposition says nothing about *which* route I *should* drive, whether I should instead take the train (which also takes 30 minutes) or whether I should go to the office at all. The Coase theorem is a proposition of this variety.

[32] As was first pointed out by Ralph Parish in 1972, because, in a zero transaction costs world, the assignment of liability does not matter from an efficiency perspective, "the question of liability for pollution damage could be decided *entirely* on the grounds of equity" (1972, p. 34, emphasis added).

The implications of this argument are striking: it makes the Coase theorem at least as strong a weapon in the hands of those concerned with victim liability and environmental damage as in the hands of those concerned with efficiency or the virtues of markets. But rather than employing this line of argument, these authors instead attempted to discredit the theorem. One is left to wonder whether the fear that the theorem's efficiency and invariance claims could be used to justify granting polluters the right to pollute in unrestricted fashion may have blinded many environmental economists to this insight. In commenting on the raging debate over the theorem in 1974, Randall said that: "At almost every stage in the debate which sprang up around 'The Problem of Social Cost,' it is unclear whether theory fathered policy viewpoints or vice-versa" (1974, p. 36). Our analysis of the non-welfarist attacks on the Coase theorem suggests that "vice-versa" is at least part of the answer to the question.

References

Baumol, William J. 1972. "On Taxation and the Control of Externalities." *American Economic Review* 62–3, 307–322.

Bensusan-Butt, D. M. 1974. "Political Economy for Aesthetes." *Australian Economic Papers* 13–23, 178–187.

Bertrand, Elodie. 2010. "The Three Uses of the 'Coase Theorem' in Coase's Works." *European Journal of the History of Economic Thought* 17–4, 975–1000.

⎯⎯ 2018. "George Stigler: The First Apostle of the Coase Theorem." In *Understanding the Enigmatic George Stigler: Extending Price Theory in Economics and Beyond*, edited by Craig Freedman. London: Palgrave Macmillan, 445–475.

Boll-De Kock, Suzan. 1976. "A Critical View on Liability Rules in Theory and Practice: The Belgian Case." *Recherches Économiques de Louvain / Louvain Economic Review* 42–1, 23–36.

Bromley, Daniel W. 1978. "Property Rules, Liability Rules, and Environmental Economics." *Journal of Economic Issues* 12–1, 43–60.

⎯⎯ 1990. "The Ideology of Efficiency: Searching for a Theory of Policy Analysis." *Journal of Environmental Economics and Management* 19–1, 86–107.

Buchanan, James M. and Wm. Craig Stubblebine. 1962. "Externality." *Economica* 29–116, 371–384.

Burrows, Paul. 1970. "On External Costs and the Visible Arm of the Law." *Oxford Economic Papers* 22–1, 39–56.

Calabresi, Guido. 1970. *The Cost of Accidents: A Legal and Economic Analysis*. New Haven, CT: Yale University Press.

Chisholm, Tony, Cliff Walsh, and Geoffrey Brennan. 1974. "Pollution and Resource Allocation." *Australian Journal of Agricultural Economics* 18–1, 1–21.

Coase, Ronald H. 1960. "The Problem of Social Cost." *Journal of Law and Economics* 3–1, 1–44.

Common, Michael. 1988. *Environmental and Resource Economics*. London: Longman.

Commons, John R. 1924. *Legal Foundations of Capitalism.* New York: Macmillan.

Cooter, Robert D. 1987. "Torts as the Union of Liberty and Efficiency: An Essay on Causation." *Chicago-Kent Law Review* 63, 523–551.

Demsetz, Harold. 1964. "The Exchange and Enforcement of Property Rights." *Journal of Law and Economics* 7–1, 11–26.

1968. "The Cost of Transacting." *Quarterly Journal of Economics* 82–1, 33–53.

Dick, Daniel T. 1974. *Pollution, Congestion and Nuisance.* Lexington, MA: Lexington Books.

1976. "The Voluntary Approach to Externality Problems: A Survey of the Critics." *Journal of Environmental Economics and Management* 2–3, 185–195.

Edel, Matthew. 1973. *Economics and the Environment.* Englewood Cliffs, NJ: Prentice-Hall.

Fisher, Anthony C. and Frederick M. Peterson. 1976. "The Environment in Economics: A Survey." *Journal of Economic Literature* 14–1, 1–33.

Fiss, Owen M. 1986. "Death of the Law." *Cornell Law Review* 72–1, 1–15.

Head, John G. 1974. "Public Policies and Pollution Problems." *FinanzArchiv / Public Finance Analysis* 33–1, 1–29.

Helm, Dieter. 2005. "Economic Instruments and Environmental Policy." *Economic and Social Review* 36–3, 205–228.

Hohfeld, Wesley. 1913. "Some Fundamental Legal Conceptions as Applied in Judicial Reasoning." *Yale Law Journal* 23–1, 16–59.

Horner, Gerald L. 1975. "Internalizing Agricultural Nitrogen Pollution Externalities: A Case Study." *American Journal of Agricultural Economics* 57–1, 33–39.

Kaplow, Louis and Steven Shavell. 2003. "Fairness versus Welfare: Notes on the Pareto Principle, Preferences, and Distributive Justice." *Journal of Legal Studies* 32–1, 331–362.

Kapp, K. William. 1950. *The Social Costs of Private Enterprise.* Cambridge, MA: Harvard University Press.

Kneese, Allen V. 1964. *The Economics of Regional Water Quality Management.* Baltimore, MD: The Johns Hopkins Press.

Landes, William M. and Richard A. Posner. 1983. "Causation in Tort Law: An Economic Approach." *Journal of Legal Studies* 12–1, 109–134.

Liebhafsky, H. H. 1973. "The Problem of Social Cost: An Alternative Approach." *Natural Resources Journal* 13–4, 615–676.

Lowry, S. Todd. 1976. "Bargain and Contract Theory in Law and Economics." *Journal of Economic Issues* 10–1, 1–22.

Marciano, Alain. 2018. "Why Is 'Stigler's Coase Theorem' Stiglerian? A Methodological Explanation." *Research in the History of Economic Thought and Methodology* 36A, 127–155.

Medema, Steven G. 1996. "Of Pangloss, Pigouvians, and Pragmatism: Ronald Coase on Social Cost Analysis." *Journal of the History of Economic Thought* 18–1, 96–114.

2011. "A Case of Mistaken Identity: George Stigler, 'The Problem of Social Cost,' and the Coase Theorem." *European Journal of Law and Economics* 31–1, 11–38.

2014. "The Curious Treatment of the Coase Theorem in Environmental Economics, 1960–1979." *Review of Environmental Economics and Policy* 8–1, 39–57.

2015. "How Textbooks Create Knowledge and Meaning: The Case of the 'Coase Theorem' in Intermediate Microeconomics, 1960–1979." Working Paper, University of Colorado Denver.

2020. "'Exceptional and Unimportant'? Externalities, Competitive Equilibrium, and the Myth of a Pigovian Tradition." *History of Political Economy* 52–1, 135–170.

Milliman, Jerome W. 1962. "Can People Be Trusted with Natural Resources?" *Land Economics* 38–3, 199–218.

Mishan, E. J. 1965. "Reflections on Recent Developments in the Concept of External Effects." *Canadian Journal of Economics and Political Science / Revue Canadienne d'Economique et de Science Politique* 31–1, 3–34.

1967a. *The Costs of Economic Growth.* New York: Frederick A. Praeger.

1967b. "Pareto Optimality and the Law." *Oxford Economic Papers* 19–3, 255–287.

1971a. "Pangloss on Pollution." *Swedish Journal of Economics* 73–1, 113–120.

1971b. "The Postwar Literature on Externalities: An Interpretative Essay." *Journal of Economic Literature* 9–1, 1–28.

1974. "What Is the Optimal Level of Pollution?" *Journal of Political Economy* 82–6, 1287–1299.

Papandreou, Andreas A. 1994. *Externality and Institutions.* Oxford: Oxford University Press.

Parish, Ross M. 1972. "Economic Aspects of Pollution Control." *Australian Economic Papers* 11–18, 32–43.

Pearce, David W. 1976. *Environmental Economics.* London; New York: Longman.

Pigou, A. C. 1920. *The Economics of Welfare.* London: Macmillan.

Posner, Richard A. 1973. *Economic Analysis of Law.* Boston, MA: Little, Brown.

Randall, Alan. 1971. "Market Solutions to Externality Problems: Theory and Practice." *American Journal of Agricultural Economics* 53–5, 867.

1972a. "Market Solutions to Externality Problems: Theory and Practice." *American Journal of Agricultural Economics* 54–2, 175–183.

1972b. *On the Theory of Market Solutions to Externality Problems.* Corvallis, OR: Oregon State University Agricultural Experiment Station Special Report 351.

1974. "Coasian Externality Theory in a Policy Context." *Natural Resources Journal* 14–1, 35–54.

1975. "Property Rights and Social Microeconomics." *Natural Resources Journal* 15–4, 729–747.

1978. "Property Institutions and Economic Behavior." *Journal of Economic Issues* 12–1, 1–21.

Reynolds, Lloyd G. 1973. *Microeconomic Analysis and Policy.* Homewood, IL: Richard D. Irwin.

Samuels, Warren J. 1972. "Welfare Economics, Power, and Property." In *Perspectives of Property*, edited by G. Wunderlich and W. L. Gilson. University Park, PA: Institute for Research on Land and Water Resources, 61–127. Reprinted in Warren J. Samuels and A. Allen Schmid, eds., *Law and Economics: An Institutionalist Perspective.* Boston, MA: Nijhoff, 1981, pp. 9–75.

1974. "The Coase Theorem and the Study of Law and Economics." *Natural Resources Journal* 14–1, 1–33.

Sen, Amartya. 1979. "Utilitarianism and Welfarism." *Journal of Philosophy* 76–9, 463–489.

Stigler, George J. 1966. *The Theory of Price*, 3rd ed. New York: Macmillan.
Thompson, Donald N. 1973. *The Economics of Environmental Protection*. Cambridge, MA: Winthrop Publishers.
Tollison, Robert D. and Richard E. Wagner. 1988. *Smoking and the State: Social Costs, Rent Seeking, and Public Policy*. Lexington, MD: D. C. Heath.
Weld, John. 1973. "Coase, Social Cost and Stability: An Integrative Essay." *Natural Resources Journal* 13-4, 595–613.
Wellisz, Stanislaw. 1964. "On External Diseconomies and the Government-Assisted Invisible Hand." *Economica* 31–124, 345–362.

10

Musgrave and the Idea of Community

Maxime Desmarais-Tremblay

Human beings live in groups. They share values with other members of their community, values that they transmit to new members. In turn, these values shape their expectations and the way they interact with other members of their community as well as with individuals of other groups. A truism in sociology, the previous statement would have been alien – or even dangerous – to some economists in the middle of the twentieth century. Richard A. Musgrave (1910–2007) was not one of them. Born and educated in Germany before he moved to the United States in 1933, Musgrave was a widely read intellectual who, throughout his long career, fought attempts to narrow the scope and methods of economics.[1] Faithful to the traditions of public finance, he kept a broad view of the economic functioning of the state, drawing ideas from works that would nowadays belong to other disciplines such as sociology and political philosophy (Sturn 2016a). Musgrave had always been critical of what we now call welfarism, and more generally of strict methodological individualism. For instance, without being a vocal opponent of the New Welfare Economics, he nonetheless raised serious doubts about the claim that it was impossible to make meaningful interpersonal welfare comparisons.

In this chapter, I review the history of Musgrave's engagement with the idea of community. Musgrave's modest opening – often implicit – for the

This chapter was presented at the workshop 'Between Economics and Ethics: Welfare, Liberalism, Macro Economics' in Nice in March 2017, and at the Associazione Italiana per la Storia del Pensiero Economico annual conference in Rome in November 2017. I thank the participants of these events for their positive feedback. I am especially indebted to Marianne Johnson, Roger Backhouse, and Antoinette Baujard for providing me with detailed recommendations that have improved this work.

[1] For biographical elements on Musgrave, see Sinn (2009); Read (2016); Sturn (2016b) and Desmarais-Tremblay (2017b).

232

idea of community provides a basis for an alternative conception of welfare. Musgrave came to realise the importance and originality of a social or communal frame only late in his life and left readers with at most cursory remarks to ponder. He never fully articulated a coherent vision of what the idea of community belonging might entail for a democratic theory of the government's budget. Yet, securing an ontological status for societies or communities, besides individuals, allowed him to theorise a larger scope for legitimate public interventions than other economic models of the state allowed, such as can be found in Public Choice.[2] For instance, his *Theory of Public Finance* (1959) accounts for the government's role in income redistribution, both in cash and in kind through the provision of goods to satisfy merit wants. Moreover, the broad foundation of his *Theory*, synthesising different national traditions, is a reminder of the fruitfulness – and an invitation to renew – cross-cultural and interdisciplinary dialogues between economics and other disciplines.

Musgrave (1959) theorised three functions for public expenditures: allocating public goods, redistributing income, and stabilising the economy. Public goods fulfil social wants and merit wants. In Musgrave's subsequent terminology (1969), the government should provide social goods because the private market fails to satisfactorily allocate such goods, given that they are non-rival and non-excludable. Merit wants are individual needs of high importance which should not be left to market allocation. Education, health, and basic nutrition are cases in point for which the government can guarantee a minimal level of satisfaction through transfers in kind. Such interventions, however, were deemed paternalistic by many economists, and the concept of merit wants was rejected by economists such as Charles E. McLure and James M. Buchanan who thought Musgrave should have been more careful to respect individual preferences in his theoretical construct. Musgrave acknowledged that the provision of merit goods violated the norm of consumer sovereignty, but he needed this concept to build a comprehensive and realistic theory of the public sector; the concept of social or collective goods would not be sufficient. In other words, the practical problems faced by governments and their administrations could not be solved by relying exclusively on information from individual subjective preferences. For instance, governments do behave paternalistically, and Musgrave thought it was not always

---

[2] On the contrasting visions of the state of Musgrave and James M. Buchanan, see Musgrave and Buchanan (1999). For further references, see also Desmarais-Tremblay (2014). For elements of a history of Public Choice, see Medema (2000).

a bad thing, considering the high level of poverty prevalent in the post-war United States (Desmarais-Tremblay 2017a).

Musgrave was of two minds about the status of merit wants in his normative theory of the public household. The normative underpinnings of the concept were not clearly formulated in his *Theory* (1959), which led to a long debate about the nature of merit wants (or merit goods) and how they could be justified in modern public finance (Desmarais-Tremblay 2019). Late in his life, Musgrave provided what he came to see as the most appropriate explanation of the provision of merit goods:

[C]onsider a setting where individuals, as members of the community, accept certain community values or preferences, even though their personal preferences might differ. Concern for maintenance of historical sites, respect for national holidays, regard for environment or for learning and the arts are cases in point. Such acceptance in turn may affect one's choice of private goods or lead to budgetary support of public goods even though own preferences speak otherwise. By the same token, society may come to reject or penalize certain activities or products which are regarded as demerit goods. Restriction of drug use or of prostitution as offences to human dignity (quite apart from potentially costly externalities) may be seen to fit this pattern. Community values are thus taken to give rise to merit or demerit goods. The hard-bitten reader regards this as merely another instance of fashion which may be disposed of accordingly. But such is not the case. Without resorting to the notion of an 'organic community', common values may be taken to reflect the outcome of a historical process of interaction among individuals, leading to the formation of common values or preferences which are transmitted thereafter. (Musgrave 1987, 452)

The goal of this chapter is twofold. First, it aims to understand how Musgrave came to propose this 'communal' reading of merit goods in his *New Palgrave* entry of 1987. Musgrave gave this direction to the concept despite the attempts by many economists to justify merit goods in an extended welfarist framework accounting for information asymmetries, irrationality, and psychic externalities. Second, this chapter aims to reconstruct the place that collective concepts play in Musgrave's normative theorisation of the public sector in order to unlock its (often implicit) criticism of standard welfare economics. This chapter follows Musgrave's interaction with the idea of community during three periods of his career. During the early years, he was much influenced by the German economic tradition, as reflected in his 1937 dissertation. In the second part of his career – from the fifties to the early seventies – Musgrave rose to prominence in the academic community and in policy circles. Although he rarely explicitly criticised the mainstream methodological perspective, he nevertheless held that the state (and not the individual) was the correct vantage point to deal with two problems in particular: fiscal policy and the distribution of the tax burden according to ability-to-pay. I take this as an implicit epistemological commitment to a notion of the collective as not being reducible to individuals. Then, in the seventies, important philosophical works by Harvard professors, as well as the responsibility for a new graduate seminar on 'Economy and Society', provided Musgrave with an opportunity to revisit the social and philosophical foundations of economics, as I discuss in Section 10.3. In Section 10.4, I present Musgrave's mature comments on merit goods.

10.1 The German Roots

Musgrave's dissertation, defended at Harvard in 1937, synthesised different traditions in public finance. He attempted to reconceptualise the burden of taxation as a *net* burden to account for the positive effect of governmental expenditures. Musgrave put forward a 'rational model of the public economy' composed of rules to be followed by the budget planner. For Musgrave, the public economy and the market economy were particular economies, part of the larger national economy. This way of conceptualising economic relations had been typical of nineteenth-century German thought and went back at least to Karl Heinrich Rau (on which see Tribe 1988, 195). It found a very developed expression in Gustav Schmoller's *fin de siècle* exposition. For Schmoller, the national economy (*Volkswirtſchaft*) related to the collective, like the nation, society, or the state (Schmoller 1900, 10). He saw the national economy as a system of economic relations dominated by the spirit of the people and embedded in the social (*gesellschaftlichen*) life (Schmoller 1900, 18–19). In other words, the national economy was structured by the institutions of the whole community.

What could constitute the model for the public economy? In his dissertation, Musgrave (1937, 76) suggested that the public economy was 'the economy of the community'. This point had been made by Hans Ritschl whose 1931 book Musgrave (1937) was discussed at length. Ritschl defended a community-based view of the state, but for an economic and fiscal theory, distancing himself from nineteenth-century idealistic philosophy. He argued that 'the principle of social cohesion in the State is not that of society, but of community' (Ritschl 1931, 234). Ritschl explicitly borrowed Ferdinand Tönnies's conception of community (*Gemeinschaft*) and used it as a basis for his theory of the state. In his famous essay, Tönnies (1887) contrasted the organic kin-based relationships of the community with the artificial and interest-based interactions of the society (*Gesellschaft*). The natural bond of love in a family was progressively extended to communities of places, such as neighbourhoods and towns, but they were of a structurally different kind from the instrumental interactions of individuals in civil society. For Ritschl, the community of reference for an economic theory of the state was, unsurprisingly, the nation. Musgrave always repudiated the organic view of the state (see 1937, 49; 1959, 87).[3] Yet, through this German literature, he was exposed early on to radically different conceptions of the relations between individuals, society, community, and the state from the mainstream British and American ones.

Musgrave's (1937, 73) model of the public household aimed at achieving 'optimum satisfaction of wants with given scarce resources'. Once again, the idea that the purpose of an economy is to satisfy wants was commonplace in German economics by the middle of the nineteenth century (Tribe 1988, 149). Following Emil Sax (1924), Musgrave assumed that there were individual wants and 'social wants proper'. From the point of view of the state, both types of wants had to be homogenised in order to plan public expenditures. For Musgrave, optimal planning required that wants be satisfied in the order of their intensity. Moreover, the public economy being a complement to the market economy, the planner had to arrange fiscal processes to minimise disturbances with the satisfaction of wants by the market (Musgrave 1937, 76). The 'social wants proper', or collective wants, posed for Musgrave the problem of calculating the benefits that individuals derived from public expenditures because benefits could not be divided.

Rau was one of the first modern exponents of the idea that economic activity is first and foremost a matter of satisfying human needs by the consumption of material goods. By extension, he also postulated that the state had its own needs, the satisfaction of which became the object of the public economy (*öffentliche Wirthschaftslehre*, or *Staatswirthschaftslehre*) (Rau 1837, 2). Towards the end of the century, Adolph Wagner refined the argument by postulating communal needs (*Gemeinbedürfnisse*) rather than needs of the state. Communal needs were differentiated from simple individual needs, but in the end, they were also felt by individuals. They resulted from the social nature of human life (Wagner 1892, 270 ff.). Some arose from the conditions of

---

[3] Raised in a liberal and cosmopolitan family of Jewish background, Musgrave would not have been enthusiastic about the strongly nationalistic flavour of some passages of Ritschl's text (e.g. p. 234).

life in natural communities, while others resulted from life in larger groups. Examples of such communal goods were public hygiene facilities and transportation infrastructure, especially as urban density increased with the division of labour. Wagner argued that communal provision of these goods had to be achieved by coercive organisations like the state or local authorities because the market could not satisfy them properly. Wagner observed a secular growth in public expenditures that reflected the political and social evolution of western nations. The state was thereby partaking in a civilisation process by providing goods and services that promoted the physical, moral, intellectual, and religious interests of the nation (Wagner 1892, 369). Hence, for Wagner, the explanation of collective wants mostly followed the history of communities.

The 'communal needs' of Wagner and the 'collective needs' of Sax were called social needs by Musgrave (1937). Besides, Musgrave remarked that governments were also providing goods to satisfy *individual* wants that were considered especially important from a *social* point of view (336, 348). In order to compare the benefits of public expenditures for the satisfaction of individual and social wants, one had to assume a 'common denominator' and allow for the construction of a 'social value scale' (349).

Thus, Musgrave's economic model of the state adopted a social point of view, one that was not reducible to the summation of individual values. The construction of a social value scale to prioritise public expenditures required a comparison of the social urgency of different individual needs. Following Arthur Cecil Pigou (1932), Musgrave adopted an objective conception of social welfare that did not shy away from interpersonal comparisons of welfare, at least as a 'working hypothesis': 'The capacity to enjoy benefits is after all but part of the general nature of "man". It being the generally accepted procedure to define certain general characteristics of men, there is no reason why no *typical* degree of intensity for the enjoyment of benefits could be assumed' (Musgrave 1937, 274 n. 2).[4] Musgrave assumed that the economist and the budget planner could rely on social and political knowledge about the national community to which the model would be applied. Information about socially important needs was not something that can be directly found in the world. It required a thorough sociological analysis:

---

[4] On the objective conception of welfare, see Cooter and Rappoport (1984).

The sociological problem of the theory of the model economy in turn consists of explaining how and according to what standards this system of relative wants is formulated: Its actual content will at any given time depend upon the entire complex of cultural, political and social forces prevailing. No consideration can here be given to this aspect of the problem, but it is to be emphasised that even in the theory of the model economy the sociological sector of the problem forms an essential part. (77)

In a Weberian frame of mind, Musgrave argued that political factors can explain a deviation of actual practices from the rational model, such as traditionally oriented action:

Public Economy . . . is in its rational execution limited by a variety of institutional factors: historical, though on economic grounds 'unrational' institutions are maintained for the sake of tradition; the conduct of the revenue-expenditure process is affected by constitutional rules concerning the power to tax or the power to spend in certain fields of government endeavour, et cetera. (71)

To put it differently, in his dissertation, Musgrave did not provide a welfarist account of the revenue-expenditure process of the public economy. He did not think that a universal mapping of individual subjective preferences into a social value scale (later named social welfare function) could in itself determine which goods should be provided by the state, to whom they should be made available, nor who should pay for them. Methodologically, politicians took decisions in a given institutional setting, they had their own agency and they made judgements based on qualitative social information.

In his first paper, published twelve years after Musgrave's dissertation, James M. Buchanan (1949) argued that fiscal theories could be classified as either 'organismic' or 'individualistic'. According to Buchanan, an individualistic theory of the state could not accept vague terms such as 'social welfare'. Only an organismic approach could assume that the state was a separate decision-making unit. Musgrave's approach avoided this strict dichotomy since it rejected any organic view and assumed that the community was composed of individuals the welfare of whom was the ultimate objective of policy, yet it relied on social value scales. In these social scales, stress should be put on the *social* basis.

In a nutshell, with the teaching he received in Munich and in Heidelberg, as well as with the literature he engaged with while working on his dissertation at Harvard, Musgrave was receptive to the importance of the social dimension of life, how it played out historically, and how it impacted economic questions. To some extent, it reflected on his conceptualisation of the problem of the public budget, although the concrete implications were not spelled out in his dissertation.

10.2 The *Theory of Public Finance* (1959) and the Cold War Era

After teaching as an instructor for a few years at Harvard, Musgrave was recruited in 1941 by the research department of the Federal Reserve, where he spent the war years. In the 1950s, he wrote his magnum opus while at the University of Michigan. At the same time, he participated in fiscal expertise missions in Colombia and in Germany, as well as providing behind-the-scenes advice on tax policy to Democratic presidential candidate Adlai Stevenson. This practical experience must have influenced his views of public finance problems, although it is hard to measure its impact in *The Theory of Public Finance*, which he completed in 1958. Musgrave wanted to move back to the East Coast, and a few months after the publication of his book, he accepted a position at Johns Hopkins, where he stayed for a brief time before moving to Princeton and then back to Harvard in 1965.

The intellectual space for criticising methodological individualism and the norm of consumer sovereignty was very limited in the United States during the cold war. Ideas of social planning and community-belonging would have been suspicious to many economists. Already during the Second World War, Friedrich Hayek had argued that invoking communal needs could only be a means for the ruling elite to impose their preferences on the community (Hayek 1944, 106). While organic visions of society were especially unpopular in the post-war period, economists, among other intellectuals, could appeal to a broad liberal consensus (Forrester 2019, xx).

The spectrum of social and psychological foundations for economic theory narrowed, thanks in part to the rise of mathematical formalism. Arrow's impossibility theorem frontally attacked the idea that an extended society could produce a rational social choice that would be compatible with (his reading of) the normative principles of liberalism. His framing of the problem already reduced social choice to a mechanical aggregation of individual preferences, casting out any conception of a 'shared social world' (Amadae 2003, 119). A few years later, Buchanan and Tullock (1962, 19 ff.) argued that the self-interested model of human agency should be applied in all spheres of life, in particular in regard to political decision-making. Even if Buchanan and Tullock's radical individualism did not convince all economists in the 1960s, they contributed to the demise of thick conceptions of political agency in social sciences. In the 1960s, the Vietnam war, racial unrest, and student protests brought to light increasing cultural divisions in American society (Cherrier and Fleury 2017). Appealing to shared values would increasingly sound optimistic, if not disconnected from the real world. The cumulative effect of these cold war economic theories was to put forward a reduced vision of the polity as a mechanical aggregation of individual self-centred preferences. In other words, with respect to the ideal types of Tönnies (1887), the cold war rational choice view of man was the triumph of *Gesellschaft* over *Gemeinschaft* and its conceptual extension to all collective life.

In this context, it is not surprising that Musgrave did not refer to a substantial notion of community throughout the major part of his career. Without a broad consensus on values, it is difficult to talk convincingly about the importance of community life. Yet, I show how an *implicit* idea of a community, or society, was still central to his specific approach to public finance. I focus on his *Theory* (1959) because it is the theoretical matrix through which we can read Musgrave's work from the 1950s to the end of this life. As a grand synthesis of different traditions, Musgrave's *Theory* combined elements of New Welfare Economics with utilitarian calculus (old welfare) and other norms of liberal democracy. The three branches of Musgrave's theory of the budget have something to do with the notion of community.

First, the stabilisation branch, which dealt with fiscal policy to guarantee full employment, price stability, and growth, conceptualised the economy using a Keynesian framework. It dealt with macroeconomic aggregates that were not reducible to individual variables. Variables such as the propensity to consume were attributes of a national community.[5]

Second, the redistribution function of the budget was meaningless without at least an implicit understanding of a community of reference. The conceptual separation of public goods allocation and income redistribution allowed Musgrave to demarcate the legitimate application of two funding principles. Contrary to what he argued in his dissertation, Musgrave now held that social (public) goods could be provided according to individual demand, thereby respecting the benefit principle.

---

[5] Fiscal policy and debt policy were always part of Musgrave's public finance, but as the field of 'public economics' emerged in the 1970s, it restricted itself to microeconomic problems of the public sector. On Musgrave's first contact with fiscal policy at Harvard, see Desmarais-Tremblay and Johnson (2019).

Third, the distribution branch secured the socially desired distribution of income by taxing individuals according to their ability-to-pay. For Musgrave, there was no optimum level of redistribution; it depended on the 'accepted mores' in the society of reference and how they were revealed in the political process. In other words, redistribution was not Pareto-improving and the government planners had to make decisions on the distribution of the tax burden based on their understanding of the social views held by the citizens. Musgrave discussed at length different interpretations of the idea of equity. According to his own terminology, justice in taxation required horizontal equity, that is, everyone must be treated equally by the taxman irrespective of how his/her ability was measured. If income was the accretion index, then it meant treating individuals irrespective of the sources of their income.[6] In addition, the budget planner needed to implement an interpretation of vertical equity, that is, how differently unequal incomes would be treated. In other words, it must provide arguments for the proportionality or the level of progressivity of the fiscal structure. Here Musgrave followed the subtle refinements of the discussion on equality of sacrifice which culminated in Pigou (1928). Musgrave acknowledged the problematic nature of interpersonal comparisons of utility in the discussion on the fiscal burden as a sacrifice to share between members of the political community:

This assumption is basic to a subjective view of the ability-to-pay doctrine. Yet it is an assumption generally rejected by the 'new' welfare economics. If such rejection is valid, the entire concept of equal sacrifice becomes so much nonsense and must be discarded – lock, stock, and barrel. I hesitate to go this far. While we cannot assume that the utility schedules of individuals are known, the new welfare economics may have gone too far in its categorical rejection of interpersonal utility comparisons. Such comparisons are made continuously, and in this sense have operational meaning. Surely, there is such a thing as utility from the receipt of income. Evidence on measurable characteristics of people – physical, mental or emotional – lends credence to the assumption that there is a fair degree of similarity among individuals living in a given society. (Musgrave 1959, 109)

As long as utility was a subjective attribute, it could hardly be compared between two individuals, but this epistemic problem was avoided if one postulated a 'social value'. According to Musgrave, in a democracy, such values had to be 'traced to the preferences of the individuals' through a political mechanism such as majority, plurality, or point voting (109). In the 1950s, Musgrave was still using utilitarian tools. Therefore, as an

---

[6] For a genealogy of Musgrave's concept of horizontal equity, see Desmarais-Tremblay (in press).

objective measure of welfare, he reiterated the idea of his PhD thesis of a social utility of public expenditures schedule. Combined with a social disutility of taxes schedule, the two curves could, in theory, determine a socially optimum level of public expenditures and a corresponding distribution of the fiscal burden provided by the tax formula (based on the constructed social income utility schedule) (113). Thus, in the 1950s, Musgrave's theory of public goods was now welfarist according to the first definition, but it violated the second definition of welfarism to the extent that it relied on information beyond subjective ordinal preferences (see the introduction to this volume).

Third, merit wants are better understood with respect to a community of reference. Although this fact was only explicitly acknowledged by Musgrave decades later, one can find hints of it in the first exposition of 1959. Musgrave argued that the allocation branch should generally provide public goods according to individual preferences following the benefit principle, but he conceded that not all public services respected consumers' sovereignty: merit goods were 'sensible' exceptions to a 'position of ex-treme individualism' (1959, 14). Musgrave suggested that a direct register-ing of individual preferences was not and should not be the political norm of democracy. One had to make room for the 'role of leadership': 'While consumer sovereignty is the general rule, situations may arise, within the context of a democratic community, where an informed group is justified in imposing its decision upon others' (14). In responding to Gerhard Colm's criticism of his conversion to an individual preference-based view of social goods, Musgrave conceded that one should not forget the 'political character of the budget process and the essentially social nature of its objectives' (88).[7] Musgrave recognised that individuals are influenced by their social environment when deciding which goods to support publicly:

[T]he voter's attitudes and preferences may be conditioned by his image of the good society and by influences extending far beyond matters of his immediate environment. His choices may be determined by what he considers altruistic motivations rather than by the self-interest in the narrower sense that under-lies typical consumer choices in the market. (88)

---

[7] A German *émigré* who was influential in Washington policy circles, Colm rejected the Samuelson-Musgrave individualistic approach to social/collective goods. In other words, Colm refused to conceptualise the government responsibilities in terms of individual benefits. Musgrave might have coined the concept of merit goods partially as a concession to the views of his senior colleague and friend. See Desmarais-Tremblay (2017a).

Throughout these writings, Musgrave used community and society as synonyms. He had a modern understanding of the latter term influenced by Max Weber as a generic group of people sharing institutions, historically and geographically located. Moreover, the society was ultimately responsible for fiscal decisions which entailed a trade-off between efficiency and equity, for instance when choosing between different tax instruments (159). Musgrave added that the higher the social cohesion in a country, the less arbitrary such collective decisions by majority vote would be (128).

Upon reviewing Musgrave's *Theory* which formed the matrix for his thinking throughout his career, we found an implicit use of collective notions that were not reducible to individuals, at least at the level of an economic theory of the government's budget. Even if Musgrave did not yet argue for the importance of community belonging, his use of collective notions went beyond strict methodological individualism.

10.3 The Revival of Moral Philosophy and Musgrave's 'Economy and Society'

Musgrave's late remarks on merit goods and the idea of community were influenced by the revival in moral and political philosophy which became visible in the early 1970s. In their quest for the foundations of moral thinking that would be compatible with modern social sciences, philosophers provided intellectual tools with which to criticise welfare economics. From 1967 onwards, a group of American philosophers, lawyers, and political theorists which included John Rawls, Robert Nozick, and Michael Walzer gathered once a month on the East Coast under the heading of the Society for Ethical and Legal Philosophy. Although they had quite contrasting views, members of the Society were united by their rejection of utilitarianism and a commitment to save moral questions from the subjectivist and relativistic perspective that had been dominant for part of the century (Nagel 2013; Forrester 2019, 40). In fact, logical positivism, and its empiricist cousin, emotivism, had already started to decline in philosophy departments after the Second World War (Forrester 2019, 4). Yet, they continued to form the – often implicit – philosophical backbone of economists' view of science at least until the 1970s (Davis 1990; McCloskey 1994, 3 ff.).

The reception of Rawls's *Theory* by economists focused mostly on some technical points such as the maximin rule and the index of primary goods (see Roemer 1996, 163 ff.; Hawi 2016, 291 ff.). The fact that Rawls's argument relied on a rational choice framework and that he borrowed many elements from economic theory helped to start a fruitful dialogue between economists and philosophers on the normative basis of society in a democracy.[8]

By mid-decade, the influence of Rawls on economists was already substantial. It can be perceived, for instance, in the way Robert D. Cooter framed the problem he dealt with in his PhD dissertation at Harvard, a dissertation that was supervised by Jerry Green and none other than Musgrave and Rawls themselves. Cooter criticised the narrow psychological, sociological, and moral foundations of economic theory:

[W]elfare economics has limited itself to identifying Pareto efficient changes, which is a narrow, stifling concept of rational ethics. This arbitrary demarcation of economics has been maintained by dedicated theorists whose motive is to preserve the scientific rigor of the subject, and by vulgar technicians who curry favor by apologizing for whatever those in power wish to do. (Cooter 1975, ii)

Cooter argued that welfare economics was 'captive of a defunct philosophical theory, namely positivism and its cousin [behaviorism]'. In a prophetic statement, he remarked that in recent years 'the conditions have become favorable for writing good moral philosophy. As the various ethical schools recover their vitality, welfare economics will be the beneficiary' (iii). For Cooter, 'the proper foundation of welfare economics is a characterization of the fundamental principles embodied in the moral and legal framework'.[9]

A year later, Musgrave started to teach a graduate seminar to Harvard PhD students titled 'Economy and Society' in which he discussed and contrasted various sociological and philosophical underpinnings of economics.[10] The course was named in honour of Max Weber, whom Musgrave greatly admired. Part of the course was dedicated to methodological issues, addressing for instance Weber's position on value

---

[8] Even before the publication of the *Theory of Justice*, Amartya Sen (1970b, 187–200) had discussed the relevance of Rawls's work for solving the economists' problem of interpersonal comparison of welfare. Sen (1970a) was one of the first to address systematically the problem posed by Robbins for collective choices. 'Interpersonal Aggregation and Partial Comparability' was published just after Sen visited Harvard, where he taught a graduate seminar together with Arrow and Rawls. In his entry on merit goods, Musgrave (1987) quoted Sen's famous essay 'Rational Fools' (1977). Sen's criticisms are beyond the scope of this chapter. Still, one can note that for Sen (1977, 344), groups and communities provide a focus for commitments.

[9] Before embarking on his PhD, Cooter read Philosophy, Politics, and Economics at Oxford.

[10] Syllabuses for the following semesters, as well as some reading notes and reprints of articles, are kept in the Richard A. Musgrave Papers at Princeton University (Box 7, sub-box 'Social Philosophy and 2080'): s1976, s1977, f1978, f1979, s1981. Musgrave retired from Harvard in 1981.

judgements and on objectivity in the social sciences. Moreover, Musgrave also presented the fundamentals of Weberian sociology. He stressed how Weber conceptualised society as a multidimensional social structure. Economic phenomena had to be understood in historical processes, yet individual action was basic. In this respect, Weber (1922) identified different types of individual social action, of groupings, and of relationships. Among the latter, Weber presented a modified version of the typology of Tönnies as communal versus associative relationships – one which Musgrave mentioned in his course.[11] The seminar provided Musgrave with an opportunity to revisit some authors of his youth which he had stopped referring to in the central part of his career.

According to the first course syllabus for 1976, Musgrave planned to devote the largest part of the semester to the philosophical underpinnings of society, including an assessment of 'recent formulations' of more or less classical doctrines by Rawls (1971), Nozick (1974), and Unger (1975). Among his three Harvard colleagues, Musgrave was definitely more sympathetic to Rawls. Nozick and Unger presented extreme visions: a rigorously individualistic Lockian political philosophy on one side, and a Hegelian theory of organic groups culminating in an appeal to God on the other side.

In what follows I highlight passages from texts that Musgrave must have read since he assigned them to his students of the Economy and Society seminar. Musgrave did not leave annotations of his readings, so it is impossible to assert with certainty to what extent he was influenced by them. These passages, together, suggest a genealogy of Musgrave's later remarks on merit goods (Section 10.4).

Rawls envisioned society as a 'cooperative venture for mutual advantage'. One of Rawls's challenges was to make room for the value of community in human life, but from an individualistic basis: 'The essential idea is that we want to account for the social values, for the intrinsic good of institutional, community, and associative activities, by a conception of justice that in its theoretical basis is individualistic' (Rawls 1971, 264).[12]

---

[11] 'Notes on Weber', 18 April 1977, 'Economics 2080', Box 7, RAM Papers.

[12] In his undergraduate thesis on the meaning of sin and faith, Rawls argued that morality was located in interpersonal human relations: 'Christian morality is morality in community, whether it be the earthly community or the heavenly community. Man is a moral being because he is a communal being.' (Rawls [1942] 2009, 122). For the young Rawls, the plural associations to which persons belonged (family, church, firm) characterised their moral life (Bok 2015). Rawls tossed aside these ideas in his mature work, but, ironically, his communitarian critics returned to them in the 1980s (Forrester 2019, xvii, 241).

In the third part of the book, Rawls formulated a theory of the development of the sense of justice which drew from Jean-Jacques Rousseau, Immanuel Kant, John Stuart Mill, Jean Piaget, and notably his Harvard colleague, Lawrence Kohlberg. Between the first stage of the morality of authority and the highest stage of the morality of principles, Rawls discussed the morality of association. Through participation in a web of associations, humans developed a sense of the importance of friendship, trust, and fairness, all of which are important for the stability of society as a cooperative venture: 'Thus we may suppose that there is a morality of association in which the members of society view one another as equals, as friends and associates, joined together in a system of co-operation known to be for the advantage of all and governed by a common conception of justice' (1971, 472). For Rawls, a sense of justice came normally with being human: 'a person who lacks a sense of justice, and who would never act as justice requires except as self-interest and expediency prompt, not only is without ties of friendship, affection, and mutual trust, but is incapable of experiencing resentment and indignation' (487).

From this anthropological viewpoint, Rawls condemned the 'simplifying motivational assumptions' of the 'so-called economic theory of democracy' (492). Referring to Buchanan and Tullock and to Downs, among others, Rawls remarked that the 'constraints of a competitive market' cannot be applied in the case of constitutional procedures:

The leading political actors are guided therefore in part by what they regard as morally permissible; and since no system of constitutional checks and balances succeeds in setting up an invisible hand that can be relied upon to guide the process to a just outcome, a public sense of justice is to some degree necessary. It would appear, then, that a correct theory of politics in a just constitutional regime presupposes a theory of justice which explains how moral sentiments influence the conduct of public affairs. (493)

In 1977, Musgrave reorganised his lecture on the philosophical underpinnings around four traditions: the utilitarian tradition, the Kantian tradition, the contractarian tradition, and the communal tradition. The first one was subdivided in philosophical works (Bentham, Mill, Sidgwick) and welfare economics (Edgeworth, Pigou, Bergson, and Samuelson). The second one comprised Kant and Rawls; the third one, Locke, Nozick, and Buchanan. The communal tradition was presented as a utopian strand of thought embracing Rousseau, Hegel, and Marx. The precise impact of these readings of the 'communal tradition' on Musgrave's idea of community is impossible to identify, since he did not leave detailed notes. Whether Musgrave was reading these classics for the first time or not, they constituted rich intellectual resources to challenge the standard neoclassical conceptualisation of the relation between individuals, society, and the state.

10.4 Musgrave's Late Writing

In the 1970s, Musgrave wrote an undergraduate textbook on public finance with his wife and former PhD student, Peggy B. Musgrave.[13] In the second edition of their textbook, Musgrave and Musgrave (1976) presented a standard interpretation of merit goods that extended the welfarist framework to account for cases of misinformation, irrationality, and interdependent preferences (Desmarais-Tremblay 2019). In a different part of the book where they explained 'fiscal politics', the authors introduced a discussion on 'the community interest'. Rejecting out of hand the idea of an organic group and that of a dictator, Musgrave and Musgrave (1976) entertained the hypothesis that there might exist a community interest beyond the addition of individual interests. Such an interest might emerge through social interaction:

[B]y virtue of sustained association, people come to develop common concerns. A group of people, for instance, share a historical experience with which they identify, thereby establishing a common bond. Individuals will join in defending the borders of 'their' territory or to protect the beauty of 'their' countryside. At the same time, it is difficult to extend this existence of common concern to the contention that resource allocation should, generally speaking, be based on consensus rather than on individual preference. X and Y may join in defending 'their' territory even though each wishes to make an independent choice regarding his consumption of apples and oranges. (122)

Musgrave and Musgrave also argued that accounting for a community interest might call for a change of perspective on social interaction, substituting a competitive view for a 'cooperative approach'. They claimed that interindividual co-operation towards the realisation of common goals might even be 'more conducive to human dignity and fulfillment' (123). Musgrave and Musgrave reminded their readers that 'economic welfare narrowly defined, after all, is not the only objective in life; and efficiency (as a criterion for rational action) should be interpreted to include all objectives that matter'. To put it differently, economists should account for the fact that individuals might have non-selfish motivations and a realistic theory of fiscal processes should make room for other values that individuals might want to defend

---

[13] British born, Peggy Musgrave (1924–2017) was herself a distinguished public finance scholar, specialised in the taxation of international investment.

through public means. Contrary to the welfarist interpretation, this interpretation of merit wants did not appear in the first edition of their textbook, thus indicating a change of mind over the 1970s. Yet, the consequences of this short discussion of a 'cooperative approach' for fiscal theory were not developed by Musgrave and Musgrave in the 1970s.

In the third edition of the book, the newly renamed 'communal wants' were discussed side by side with 'merit wants' (Musgrave and Musgrave 1980, 83–6). Compared to the previous edition, the authors added the following comment on the idea of community interest:

> This community interest then gives rise to communal wants, wants which are generated by and pertain to the welfare of the group as a whole. . . . [B]y virtue of sustained association and mutual sympathy, people come to develop common concerns. A group of people, for instance, share an historical experience or cultural tradition with which they identify, thereby establishing a common bond. (84)

Their conclusion echoed a point already acknowledged by Musgrave (1959): the 'individual preference approach does not tell the entire story' (Musgrave and Musgrave 1980, 84).

That communal wants could be a type of merit want was only explicitly spelled out by Musgrave in his entry on 'merit goods' for the *New Palgrave Dictionary of Economics* in 1987. One reason for this late integration of the two concepts might be that from the 1960s onwards, merit *wants* came to be called by the goods which satisfy them – merit *goods*. This transition suited well the evolution of social wants to social goods, but not the notion of merit wants, as Musgrave (1986, 39) eventually admitted. Communal wants arose because of human interaction. They capture the needs of social beings, not specific commodities. If the concept of merit goods was more fruitful in the discussion on 'fair shares' of primary goods, of 'higher values', and of 'community values', as Musgrave (1987) claimed, then it would be more appropriate to talk of merit *wants*. Going back to the label of *wants* brought the concept closer to the newly (re)discovered idea of 'community preferences', or 'communal wants'.

Thus, contrary to the 1960s and the 1970s when Musgrave tried to minimise the relevance of merit wants, from the 1980s onwards, he started to commend more and more his concept because he found better philosophical underpinnings. Moreover, the communal wants rationale was a positive argument to support public provision of some goods and services; it did not rely on a negative view of human agency or markets such as the market failure argument. Rather than relying on a qualification, or an exception to the norm of consumer sovereignty, it suggested an alternative principle for the allocation of some resources (Musgrave 1987).

Besides the philosophical opening of the 1970s, another reason for Musgrave's renewed interest in his concept of merit wants might be the 'swing of the pendulum' towards more negative attitudes to the government among economists in the 1970s and eventually the rise of neoliberal politics in the 1980s. In justifying extended transfer programmes, the concept of merit goods could serve as a reminder of the plural functions of government in a democratic society. As Samuelson later remarked: 'Since about 1980, under the influence of libertarians like Milton Friedman, the quasi-paternalistic "merit wants" of Musgrave have too often become forgotten' (Samuelson in Atkinson et al. 2008, 167).

Reiner (2011, 302) makes a similar point to explain the contributions of Michael Walzer and Michael Sandel to the so-called communitarian doctrine in political philosophy. He argues that they have to be understood as a response to the rise of Reaganomics in the 1980s. There is a striking proximity between Musgrave's ideas on community and communitarian philosophy. Each in their own way, Charles Taylor, Michael Walzer, Alasdair MacIntyre, and Michael Sandel have criticised the individualistic basis of Rawlsian liberal egalitarianism. They insisted on the centrality of community ties in human life. Their different anthropological starting point led to a different vision of the polity, one that did not shy away from a substantial conception of the common good. Whereas defending the importance of communities could have passed as conservative talk in the post-war period, in the neoliberal politics of the 1980s, it could be used to defend state intervention. There is no evidence that Musgrave was knowledgeable about this communitarian literature when he reframed his ideas on merit goods in the 1970s and early 1980s.[14] Yet, in the 1970s Musgrave read Unger, who was influenced by Hegel, just as the other communitarian critics of philosophical liberalism (Gutmann 1985, 308). In the end, the communitarian critiques probably arrived too late on the scene for Musgrave to benefit from them in his reformulation of merit wants as communal wants.

After his retirement from Harvard in 1981, Musgrave moved to California, where his wife was teaching. During the 1980s and 1990s, he wrote a few history of economics papers, as well as more personal retrospective accounts. In contrasting German and Anglo-American

---

[14] Apart from the fact that Musgrave participated in a workshop in Canberra in 1986 where Charles Taylor presented a paper on 'irreducibly social goods' (Taylor 1990).

public finance, he explicitly distinguished issues of 'public goods' in the market failure tradition from 'communal wants' concerns in *Finanzwissenschaft*:

Membership in the community also implies values and imposes obligations which transcend self-interest. Communal wants and obligations, evidently, are not amenable to ready analysis by the economist's tools as are public goods. It does not follow, however, that Finanzwissenschaft was mistaken in raising the issue of communal concerns, and of motivations which transcend self-interest. Public finance may well have taken too narrow a view by holding that self-interest-based action is all there is. While the state or community 'as such' cannot be the subject of wants, a distinction between the private and communal concerns of individuals cannot be rejected that easily. Nor can the role of communal concern be resolved in the utilitarian frame by allowance for inter-personal utility interdependence. There remains an uneasy feeling that something is missing. The concep[t] of merit wants ... address[es] this gap, but much remains to be done to resolve the problem of communal wants in a satisfactory fashion. Such remains the case, uncomfortable though the community concept may be to economics, and dangerous though it becomes when abused. (Musgrave 1996, 73)

A few years earlier, Musgrave had participated in a conference in Germany organised by Harald Hagemann on German *émigré* economists. In his retrospective account of his youth, Musgrave indicated that a 'concern with a communal want approach had remained much in the air during [his] Heidelberg years':

Though non-rival consumption is the core of the public goods problem, it does not follow that self-interested exchange (be it via market or vote) is the only meaning-ful form of social interaction. Admittedly difficult to define and dangerous to entertain, communal concerns have been part of the scene from Plato on, and my concept of merit goods (applicable to private and social goods alike) was to provide a limited opening for their role (Musgrave 1958 and 1987). Dutiful performance of civil service remains a constructive concept, as does that of responsible public leadership. Though they now tend to be ridiculed, both these alternative modes are essential to make democracy work. Nor are issues of entitle-ment and distributive justice reducible to principles of exchange, issues which have to be resolved before that mode can be given its role. The broad-based roots of the German tradition, its linkage to the theory of state and to fiscal sociology (Musgrave 1980) helped to provide awareness of these issues, and could have done so quite consistently with a private-want-based theory of public goods. (Musgrave 1997, 77)

Hence, for Musgrave communal wants, a type of merit wants, had their place in a broad-based view of the public household. At the expense of a fully consistent and simple view of human agency, Musgrave assumed that individuals in a democracy held different values, some of which needed to be directly supported by public institutions, while others motivate them to work for their self-interest in the market sphere – but this also called for governmental intervention to correct the resulting inefficiencies, for instance by providing public goods.

10.5 Conclusion

Contemplating Musgrave's long intellectual life has allowed us to identify recurrent themes in his writing. The concept of merit wants that he coined in his middle age acquired an original meaning as 'community wants' only in his old age. This late reframing of the problem benefited from a revival of moral and political philosophy in the 1970s, yet it also connected directly to ideas Musgrave had been exposed to during his formation in Germany and in the United States in the interwar years. In his dissertation, Musgrave (1937) employed the concepts of individual wants and social wants. As the concept of a social/public/collective good acquired its definitive – and restrictive – meaning in the 1960s, a host of legitimate concerns were left out. Musgrave wanted to remind economists about these concerns, which did not fit the narrow category of collective goods. Even many arguments that commentators understood to justify merit goods could be explained by other categories found in the market failure literature. What did not fit were the communal concerns.

More generally, the New Welfare Economics was too narrow a methodological perspective to achieve the aims of public finance and public economics. As Musgrave remarked: 'The "new welfare economics", by definition, excludes distributional issues, limiting its attention to situations where everybody's welfare can be raised. Welfare economists thus save their scientific conscience but, alas, are of only slight use in solving policy problems' (1964, 2). In other words, a comprehensive normative theory of public finance must have a conception of justice that goes far beyond Pareto-efficiency. For Musgrave, the moral dimensions of the public budget could not be derived in the abstract, but had to be related to the values of the social group or community to which the theory would be applied: 'Distributive justice, as seen by most people, is not divinely preordained but depends on society's sense of entitlement and fairness' (Musgrave 1981, 221). Welfare economics could satisfy itself with unrealistic welfarist assumptions, but public finance being an applied field, Musgrave wanted to design a framework that could be used to improve policy decisions and fiscal administration.

Individuals are always the ultimate valuation reference, but social groups or communities need to enter the theoretical framework. This is the message we can extract from analysing Musgrave's engagement with the notions of community and society. Musgrave did not provide a fully fledged alternative to individualistic welfare economics. Nonetheless, he warned us against the danger of building an unrealistic construction based on isolated individuals. Such a model might be appropriate for a pure market price theory, but it will be insufficient for a theory of the public household. The first proponents of methodological individualism were conscious of this limitation – one that was forgotten in the middle of the twentieth century. As Schumpeter put it: '[A]s soon as we go beyond the limits of the pure theory, the whole thing looks different. For example, in the organization theory and in the sociology in general, individualism would not get us very far' (Schumpeter 1908, 183). Likewise, Pareto (1898) argued that the *homo œconomicus* assumption was useful only in pure economics. Yet, pure economics was only a first approximation of complex human behaviour. This behaviour could only be fully apprehended by an extended sociological analysis. To put the matter differently, Musgrave's message is that a narrow reading of the *Gesellschaft* sociability does not provide wide enough foundations for an economic theory of the state. Two alternatives remain: enlarge the bases of economics, or draw from sociology, law, and from moral and political philosophy, other sources of normativity. Group belonging can be one such source of normativity.

References

Amadae, Sonja M. 2003. *Rationalizing Capitalist Democracy: The Cold War Origins of Rational Choice Liberalism*. Chicago: The University of Chicago Press.
Atkinson, Anthony B., Sijbren Cnossen, Helen F. Ladd, Peter Mieszkowski, Pierre Pestieau, and Paul A. Samuelson. 2008. 'Commemorating Richard Musgrave (1910–2007)'. *FinanzArchiv: Public Finance Analysis* 64(2): 145–70.
Bok, P. Mackenzie. 2015. 'To the Mountaintop Again: The Early Rawls and Post-Protestant Ethics in Postwar America'. *Modern Intellectual History*: 1–33.
Buchanan, James M. 1949. 'The Pure Theory of Government Finance: A Suggested Approach'. *The Journal of Political Economy* 57(6): 496–505.
Buchanan, James M., and Gordon Tullock. 1962. *The Calculus of Consent*. Ann Arbor: University of Michigan Press.
Cherrier, Beatrice, and Jean-Baptiste Fleury. 2017. 'Economists' Interest in Collective Decision after World War II: A History'. *Public Choice* 172(1–2): 23–44.
Cooter, Robert D. 1975. 'What Is the Public Interest'. PhD dissertation. Harvard University.

Cooter, Robert D., and Peter Rappoport. 1984. 'Were the Ordinalists Wrong about Welfare Economics?' *Journal of Economic Literature* 22(2): 507–30.

Davis, John B. 1990. 'Cooter and Rappoport on the Normative'. *Economics and Philosophy* 6(1): 139–46.

Desmarais-Tremblay, Maxime. 2014. 'Normative and Positive Theories of Public Finance: Contrasting Musgrave and Buchanan'. *Journal of Economic Methodology* 21(3): 273–89.

2017a. 'A Genealogy of the Concept of Merit Wants'. *The European Journal of the History of Economic Thought* 24(3): 409–40.

2017b. 'Musgrave, Samuelson, and the Crystallization of the Standard Rationale for Public Goods'. *History of Political Economy* 49(1): 59–92.

2019. 'The Normative Problem of Merit Goods in Perspective'. *Forum for Social Economics* 48(3): 219–47.

in press. 'Généalogie du principe d'équité horizontale: Une contribution à l'histoire de la normativité en théorie des finances publiques'. *Revue de philosophie économique.*

Desmarais-Tremblay, Maxime, and Marianne Johnson. 2019. '"The Fiscal Policy Seminar: Its Early Stages" by Richard A. Musgrave'. *Research in the History of Economic Thought and Methodology* 37 C: 147–79.

Forrester, Katrina. 2019. *In the Shadow of Justice: Postwar Liberalism and the Remaking of Political Philosophy*. Princeton, NJ: Princeton University Press.

Gutmann, Amy. 1985. 'Review: Communitarian Critics of Liberalism'. *Philosophy & Public Affairs* 14(3): 308–22.

Hawi, Rima. 2016. *John Rawls – Itinéraire d'un libéral américain vers l'égalité sociale*. Paris: Classiques Garnier.

Hayek, Friedrich A. 1944. *The Road to Serfdom*. Chicago: The University of Chicago Press.

McCloskey, Deirdre N. 1994. *Knowledge and Persuasion in Economics*. Cambridge: Cambridge University Press.

Medema, Steven G. 2000. '"Related Disciplines": The Professionalization of Public Choice Analysis'. *History of Political Economy* 32 (Supplement): 289–324.

Musgrave, Richard A. 1937. 'The Theory of Public Finance and the Concept of "Burden of Taxation"'. PhD dissertation. Harvard University.

1959. *The Theory of Public Finance: A Study in Public Economy*. New York: McGraw Hill.

1964. 'Efficiency vs. Equity in Public Finance'. *Review of Social Economy* 22(1): 1–8.

1969. 'Provision for Social Goods'. In *Public Economics: An Analysis of Public Production and Consumption and Their Relations to the Private Sectors*, edited by Julius Margolis and H. Guitton, 124–44. London: Macmillan.

1981. 'Leviathan Cometh – Or Does He?' In *Public Finance in a Democratic Society. Volume II: Fiscal Doctrine, Growth and Institutions*, 200–32. Brighton: Wheatsheaf Books.

1986. *Public Finance in a Democratic Society. Volume I: Social Goods, Taxation and Fiscal Policy*. New York: New York University Press.

1987. 'Merit Goods'. *The New Palgrave Dictionary of Economics*, edited by John Eatwell, Murray Milgate, and Peter Newman, 1958–60. London: Palgrave, 452–3.

1996. 'Public Finance and Finanzwissenschaft Traditions Compared'. In *Public Finance in a Democratic Society*. *Volume III*, 2000, 33–80. Cheltenham: Edward Elgar.

1997. 'Crossing Traditions'. In *Zur Deutschsprachigen Wirtschaftswissenschaftlichen Emigration Nach 1933*, edited by Harald Hagemann, 63–79. Marburg: Metropolis-Verlag.

Musgrave, Richard A., and James M. Buchanan. 1999. *Public Finance and Public Choice: Two Contrasting Visions of the State*. Cambridge, MA: MIT Press.

Musgrave, Richard A., and Peggy B. Musgrave. 1976. *Public Finance in Theory and Practice*. 2nd ed. New York: McGraw Hill.

1980. *Public Finance in Theory and Practice*. 3rd ed. New York: McGraw Hill.

Nagel, Thomas. 2013. 'Foreword'. In *Anarchy, State, and Utopia*, by Robert Nozick, xi–xviii. New York: Basic Books.

Nozick, Robert. 1974. *Anarchy, State, and Utopia*. New York: Basic Books.

Pareto, Vilfredo. 1898. 'Comment se pose le problème de l'économie pure'. Reprinted in *Cahiers Vilfredo Pareto* 1(1): 121–30 (1963).

Pigou, Arthur Cecil. 1928. *A Study in Public Finance*. 3rd ed., 1960. London: Macmillan.

1932. *The Economics of Welfare*. 4th ed. London: Macmillan.

Rau, Karl Heinrich. 1837. *Lehrbuch der Politischen Oekonomie. Grundsätze der Volkswirtschaftslehre*. French translation of the 3rd ed. *Traité d'économie nationale*. 1839. Brussels: Société Belge de Librairie. Hauman et cie.

Rawls, John. 1971. *A Theory of Justice*. Cambridge, MA: Harvard University Press.

2009. *A Brief Inquiry into the Meaning of Sin and Faith: An Interpretation Based on the Concept of Community*, edited by Thomas Nagel. Cambridge, MA: Harvard University Press.

Read, Colin. 2016. 'The Early Life of Richard Musgrave'. In *The Public Financiers*, 144–9. Basingstoke: Palgrave Macmillan.

Reiner, Toby. 2011. 'The Sources of Communitarianism on the American Left: Pluralism, Republicanism, and Participatory Democracy'. *History of European Ideas* 37(3). 293–303.

Ritschl, Hans. 1931. *Gemeinwirtschaft und Kapitalistische Marktwirtschaft*. Tübingen: J. C. B. Mohr (Paul Siebeck).

Roemer, John E. 1996. *Theories of Distributive Justice*. Cambridge, MA: Harvard University Press.

Sax, Emil. 1924. 'Die Wertungstheorie der Steuer'. *Zeitschrift für Volkswirthchaft und Sozialpolitik* 4(4–6): 191–240.

Schmoller, Gustav. 1900. *Grundriß der Allgemeinen Volkswirtschaftslehre*. French translation *Principes d'économie politique*. 1905. Paris: V. Giard et E. Brière.

Schumpeter, Joseph A. 1908. *The Nature and Essence of Economic Theory*. New Brunswick, NJ: Transaction Publishers. Translated by Bruce A. McDaniel from *Das Wesen und der Hauptinhalt der theoretischen Nationalökonomie*. 2010.

Sen, Amartya K. 1970a. 'Interpersonal Aggregation and Partial Comparability'. *Econometrica* 38(3): 393–409.

1970b. *Collective Choice and Social Welfare*. London: Penguin. 2017 Extended Edition.

1977. 'Rational Fools: A Critique of the Behavioral Foundations of Economic Theory'. *Philosophy and Public Affairs* 6(4): 317–44.

Sinn, Hans-Werner. 2009. 'Please Bring Me the New York Times: On the European Roots of Richard Abel Musgrave'. *International Tax and Public Finance* 16(1): 124–35.

Sturn, Richard. 2016a. 'Public Economics'. In *Handbook on the History of Economic Analysis. Volume III: Developments in Major Fields of Economics*, edited by Gilbert Faccarello and Heinz D. Kurz, 480–98. Cheltenham: Edward Elgar.

2016b. 'Richard Abel Musgrave (1910–2007)'. In *Handbook on the History of Economic Analysis. Volume I: Great Economists since Petty and Boisguilbert*, edited by Gilbert Faccarello and Heinz D. Kurz, 634–37. Cheltenham: Edward Elgar.

Taylor, Charles. 1990. 'Irreducibly Social Goods'. In *Rationality, Individualism, and Public Policy*, edited by Geoffrey Brennan and Cliff Walsh, 45–63. Canberra: Centre for Research on Federal Financial Relations, the Australian National University.

Tönnies, Ferdinand. 1887. *Gemeinschaft und Gesellschaft*. Translated as *Community and Civil Society* by Jose Harris. 2001. Cambridge: Cambridge University Press.

Tribe, Keith. 1988. *Governing Economy: The Reformation of German Economic Discourse 1750–1840*. Cambridge: Cambridge University Press.

Unger, Roberto Mangabeira. 1975. *Knowledge and Politics*. New York: The Free Press.

Wagner, Adolph. 1892. *Lehr- und Handbuch der Politischen Oekonomie. Grundlegung der Politischen Oekonomie*. 3rd ed. Translated in French as *Les fondements de l'économie politique*. 1904. Paris: V. Giard et E. Brière.

Weber, Max. 1922. *Wirthschaft und Gesellschaft*. Tübingen: J. C. B. Mohr (Paul Siebeck). A new English translation of *Economy and Society* by Keith Tribe. 2019. Cambridge, MA: Harvard University Press.

11

Non-welfaristic Features of Kenneth Arrow's Idea of Justice

Nao Saito[1]

Introduction

This paper characterizes Kenneth Arrow's contribution to justice issues in economics. Arrow is famous for establishing the fundamental theorems of welfare economics (Arrow and Debreu 1954), according to which general equilibrium in competitive market satisfies Pareto optimality under some conditions, and the general impossibility theorem (hereafter, Arrow's theorem), which is the foundation of social choice theory (Arrow 1963). The latter discusses the existence of desirable aggregation of individual preferences as the criterion of individual welfare in order to create a social preference as the criterion of social welfare. To prove his theorem, Arrow defined a criterion of social welfare as a consequence restricted to a function of individual preferences, and stressed that only non-comparable utilities are considered. Because of these two important restrictions, his approach was regarded as "welfarist."[2]

Gradually, however, Arrow transitioned to stating that the consequences of both economic and political decision-making are not always just, even when they are Pareto optimal. Arrow ultimately concluded that social choice theory can be useful in deducing a standard of justice with non-welfaristic aspects.

This paper clarifies the non-welfarist features of Arrow's idea of justice,[3] beginning with some of his contributions to formal theory:

[1] The author is grateful to Roger Backhouse, Antoinette Baujard, and Tamotsu Nishizawa for their helpful comments on earlier drafts of this paper. This work was supported by JSPS KAKENHI Grant Number JP 19K23174.
[2] See the definition of welfarism in the introduction to this volume.
[3] Famous previous studies on the philosophical aspect of Arrow's theorem include Mackay (1980), Riker (1982), Pildes and Anderson (1990), Amadae (2003), and Mackie (2003). In

Arrow's theorem and the fundamental theorems of welfare economics (Section 11.1). Second, this paper illustrates how Arrow designed political and economic decisions using the same framework in the 1950s (Section 11.2), and how he gradually realized that the consequences of both economic and political decisions justified in this narrow framework are not always just in the real world. He notably appreciated the differences among welfare, equality, freedom, and fundamental rights by considering a variety of different case studies of public actions. Accordingly, he recognized that the significance of justice cannot be reduced to economic efficiency, neither could it be properly or sufficiently defined in the strict welfarist informational framework (Sections 11.3 and 11.4). Finally, this paper argues that Arrow insisted that a criterion of justice can be deduced from the collective decision-making process in the hypothetical original position, because this position assumes equality (Section 11.5). We conclude that Arrow's idea of justice is based on a variety of values beyond utility, including non-welfaristic aspects such as freedom, equality, and fundamental rights.

11.1 New Welfare Economics and Arrow's Contribution to Formal Economic Theory

This section clarifies Arrow's two most famous contributions to formal economic theory and their normative implication.

Welfare economics was established by Arthur Cecil Pigou in 1920. In this field, new welfare economics gained traction after Lionel Robbins' criticism of how old welfare economics did not satisfy the condition of scientific objectivity (Robbins 1969). In 1938, Abram Bergson successfully formalized the economic welfare function that can deduce a criterion of social welfare from a set of economic variables (Bergson 1938; Backhouse, Chapter 8 in this volume). His study was pivotal because it allowed new welfare economists to formally analyze a criterion of social welfare. Arrow tried to rationalize the construction of a social welfare function solely on the basis of individual preferences. To achieve this, he inquired into the collective decision-making process that deduces a criterion of social welfare from a set of individual orderings as a criterion of individual welfare. He did this in the following two ways.

addition, Saito (2018) focuses on the theoretical change in Arrow's view of democracy and his attitude toward war. These studies, however, do not analyze the theoretical change in Arrow's view of the market and his idea of justice.

In his book *Social Choice and Individual Values*, Arrow proved a theorem that is generally regarded as proof of the logical impossibility of a collective-choice rule. He states that "we ask if it is formally possible to construct a procedure for passing from a set of known individual tastes to a pattern of social decision-making, the procedure in question being required to satisfy certain natural conditions" (Arrow 1963, p. 2). To prove this question, first, he assumes that all the members in a society are rational. This means that each member has an ordering of all possible alternatives. It is defined that an ordering satisfies two conditions: completeness and transitivity. They then choose their top alternatives in the ordering over a set of feasible alternatives at each step, acting to maximize their welfare in their decision-making. Social ordering, which satisfies the same two conditions, is deduced from individual ordering. Second, it is assumed that an individual's ordering is the criterion for his or her individual welfare and that social ordering is the criterion for social welfare. The social welfare function is mapped from the individual orderings of the members of a society to social ordering (Arrow 1963, pp. 12–19; Saito 2018, p. 241). His theorem questions whether the collective decision process can meet the following four desirable conditions. The first is the condition of unrestricted domain, which requires the collective decision process to accept any pattern of individual ordering. The second is the Pareto principle, which dictates that society should prefer what its members prefer. The third is the condition of indifference to irrelevant alternatives, which dictates that a decision on one opportunity set should be independent of external alternatives. The fourth is the condition of non-dictatorship, which directs that no individual ordering should become a social ordering by disregarding others' individual orderings (Arrow 1963, pp. 96–103). These four conditions of the collective decision-making process are assumed to be axioms. Arrow proved that no social welfare function satisfies these four conditions.

Arrow's theorem also perpetuated the research interests of new welfare economics, especially those of Bergson. Arrow wanted to identify the criterion for social welfare in new welfare economics because he argued for a relationship between his social welfare function and Bergson's economic welfare function (Arrow 1963, pp. 22–24; Bergson 1938). The theorem, however, encompasses not only new welfare economics but also political science, because it deals with general collective decision-making, such as voting (Samuelson 1967, p. 42).

Arrow and Debreu presented the fundamental theorems of welfare economics in 1954. The first theorem specifies that if a market satisfies three assumptions – that it is a complete market, includes price-taking behavior, and contains local non-satiation of preferences – it will reach a competitive equilibrium that is Pareto optimal (Arrow and Debreu 1954). Arrow summarized his research about general equilibrium in 1971 (Arrow and Hahn 1971).

In short, Arrow proved that there is no desirable process of social decision-making that deduces a criterion of social welfare from individual orderings as a criterion of individual welfare. While he also proved that competitive equilibrium can satisfy Pareto optimality as a criterion of social welfare.

11.2 The Welfaristic Framework of Political and Economic Decision-Making

Arrow's contributions were primarily welfarist in the 1950s, using the framework of welfarism in his analyses of political and economic decision-making. According to the first fundamental theorem of welfare economics, a competitive equilibrium achieved by rational agents can satisfy Pareto optimality. The theorem regards Pareto optimality as one criterion of social welfare, which is only assessed by the consideration of individual preferences, excluding any other observations. The general impossibility theorem considers that consumer or economic choice and political choice can be generalized as a single category within a more general rational choice.[4] In other words, Arrow discusses the general, collective decision-making process, not specifically economic or political decisions (Arrow 1963, p. 5). While collective decision-making does not exist in the market, economic and political decisions have two characteristics in common.

First, Arrow considered that economic and political decision-making have rationality as their common informational basis (Arrow 1963, pp. 11–13), in that individuals are rational as long as their economic or political preferences are consistently represented by their preference orderings.

While the conception of welfare in a political decision-making is different from its conception in economic decision-making, in the consumer choice theory, individual preferences are not just represented as

---

[4] The social choice theory was established to solve Arrow's question and amend his negative conclusion. Moreover, his theorem influenced the foundation of the rational choice theory in political science.

transitive ordering; rather, they also comply with the property of monotonicity,[5] which is not required in collective decision-making contexts. Arrow, however, accepts any individual ordering[6] and excludes the assumption of the individual utility function to make individual ordering more general. He also includes non-economic matters, such as an ethical judgment on the distributive sharing of goods in society (Arrow 1963, pp. 17–18). As a result, individual ordering can be regarded as the informational basis for the general, collective decision-making process (Arrow 1963, pp. 11–17).

Second, the consequences of both economic and political decision-making are considered to improve social welfare. The reason for this is as follows. First, Arrow regarded an individual's ordering as the informational basis for both types of decision-making. He mentioned that economists can know someone's ordering by observing his or her actual choice. According to the Austrian school, in particular, one's actual choice is related to estimation and judgment. This assumes that what someone chooses must be what he or she prefers, and what is preferred must be better than what is not (Arrow 1985, p. 141).[7] Not only in economic decision-making, but also in social decision-making, Arrow's choice of the Pareto principle as one condition of collective decision-making leads to the optimization of society's welfare. Thus, Arrow considers that both types of decision-making can contribute to social welfare.

Arrow focused on common characteristics and did not account for the difference between economic and political decision-making in his analyses during the 1950s and 1960s. He regarded the type of social ordering that values social states according to their consequences as a criterion of social welfare. When regarding one's welfare judgment as the informational basis, Arrow considered it to be ordinal and regards one person's welfare as non-comparable with that of another. Because of these ideas, he was considered as an advocate of a type of welfarism.

---

[5] It means that one's utility increases as the amount of one's consumption of economic goods increases.

[6] For example, Arrow mentions that he does not distinguish between someone's preferences in foreign culture and those in personal matters. This means that, in his theory, someone's preference not to have any goods over having all goods is acceptable. This is the meaning of the condition of unrestricted domain.

[7] This idea may be criticized because it combines fact and value. Arrow believed fact and value should be separated. However, he also admitted that logical analysis makes this difference unclear (Arrow 1985, p. 141).

11.3 Limitations of the Market

Arrow notably debated with philosophers and economists on the necessary distinction between economic and political decision-making (Arrow 1970, p. 18). He initially stated that the motivation within each of the two types of decision-making is different. It can be assumed that one's moral obligations are a primary factor in political decision-making; for instance, when one votes, the opportunity cost is higher than the utility of voting.[8] In the 1960s and 1970s, however, Arrow still considered that both types of decision-making can deduce a criterion of social welfare, but he does not consider that their consequences are always just. Regarding this point, this section clarifies Arrow's view about the consequences of economic decision-making.

11.3.1 The Price System and Justice

In the 1960s, Arrow did not clearly criticize injustice of market outcomes; however, he clearly stated in the 1970s that the distribution of goods on the basis of a price system does not necessarily achieve distributive justice. On this point, there is a clear distinction between Arrow and other new welfare economists of the time, such as Little and Bergson.

Arrow refers to the condition of Pareto efficiency, wherein everyone is better off under a particular distribution than another, and so society as a whole is judged to be better off. Arrow interprets that some economists viewed such a value judgment as both efficient and just; however, if this were true, then laissez-faire policy and the consequences of the free market are both efficient and just, because they lead society to Pareto efficiency (according to the first fundamental theorem of welfare economics) (Arrow 1983, p. 176).

Arrow opposes this idea, stating that there are three drawbacks of the price system. The first of which is its imperfection, wherein something can contribute to social good but not have a price. For example, we know that it is beneficial to establish a relationship of trust to effectively deal with goods in the market. If one cannot trust one's business acquaintances, the products must be investigated and numerous transaction costs have to be borne. Similarly, honesty and faithfulness are beneficial for business efficiency; nevertheless, such qualities cannot be purchased with money (Arrow 1974, p. 14). Thus, we should establish a legal system and social norms to promote such relationships of trust if we want to promote social welfare.

---

[8] For details, see Saito (2018, pp. 247–248).

To understand Arrow's position in detail, it is worth noting that one of the assumptions of the fundamental theorem of welfare economics is the universality of the market. From this assumption, resources and goods traded on the market are based on ownership rights and any benefits or expenses arising from such transactions between individuals are settled with money. Thus, there exist no public goods, future goods, or externalities.

In order for such market universality to be achieved, one of the following conditions must be met. First, all the objects of production, consumption, and their influences are commercialized and made available on the market. In practice, this is impossible. Second, externalities that cannot be accommodated by the market are removed through law, the practice of morality, and social customs. This is because negative externalities include illegal and immoral conduct, such as fraud, theft, threats, and failure to honor contracts, as well as harm to others due to unintentional errors. Externalities, then, must be prevented in order to achieve market efficiency, which requires that certain norms are followed with respect to law, morality, and customs. The Pareto-optimal state cannot be produced only through free competition among individuals seeking their own self-interest; moral behavior is also necessary from the standpoint of positive externalities. In other words, law and morality are necessary conditions for the establishment of the first fundamental theorem (Shionoya 2005, pp. 135–137); thus, it can be inferred that Arrow's analysis is based on such considerations.

The second drawback is that even if these three assumptions are satisfied and the competitive equilibrium obtained satisfies Pareto optimality, this is not necessarily desirable for the social good. According to Arrow, market theory assumes personal ownership; however, social welfare improves when individuals use the goods they own to contribute to society. He considers the view that "the distribution of goods in a market satisfies distributive justice" overlooks the public utility of private goods. To clarify this point, it is necessary to consider Arrow's criticism of Robert Nozick.

Nozick's entitlement theory states that an individual has the right to self-property; thus, it follows that an individual has the right over the property that he or she produces by using labor and talent. An individual can exchange this property by trade that meets the following three principles: (1) the principle of justice in transfer, meaning that an owner can exchange property with others; (2) the principle of justice in acquisition, stating that one can acquire any good if no one else owns it; and (3) the principle of rectification, where one can get back goods lost by illegal means.

Individuals are entitled to goods acquired through one of these three principles (Nozick 1974, ch. 7).

Arrow points out that "Nozick's criteria are very much like the welfare economics theorem" (Arrow 1983, p. 177), because both consider that the equilibrium achieved under perfect competition in the market is desirable. Arrow admits that Nozick does not assume perfect competition by stating that "Pareto optimality is not implied in Nozick's voluntary, just transfers" (Arrow 1983, p. 177). According to Nozick's idea, however, only redistribution that improves one's satisfaction can be accepted, because rational agency would voluntarily accept only such a redistribution of goods. This idea is similar to competitive equilibrium being desirable (Arrow 1983, p. 188); therefore, it achieves just distribution for both Nozick and the welfare economists. Arrow refuses this claim, stating that Nozick assumes that one can freely use one's own property; however, from the viewpoint of social welfare, it is sometimes better to use such property collectively and socially rather than privately. Private usage of precious individual goods is not an optimal usage, because these goods become more valuable if they are used within the social system. Redistribution, then, is beneficial for maximizing social welfare (Arrow 1983, p. 188).

In short, Nozick regards an individual's talent as his or her own property, and the goods that someone acquires by his or her talent as their own private property. Arrow rejects this idea and considers one's talents and goods to be more valuable if they are used socially. For him, the redistribution of goods is recommended. It must be noted that Arrow opposes Rawls' idea that one's property constitutes common goods, and instead insists that it belongs to the individual. Arrow does consider, however, that individuals have a social obligation to contribute to maximizing social welfare by using the property they obtain through their talents. Arrow does not clarify whether one has a moral or legal obligation to make a voluntary contribution (i.e., if it is a matter of moral duty or an obligation to, for example, pay taxes to rectify an imbalance). Nonetheless, it is clear that Arrow does not regard market consequences as desirable (Arrow 1983, pp. 185–187).[9]

If Arrow criticizes Pareto optimality from only the above two viewpoints, he would be a welfarist in a broad sense, because those criticisms argue that Pareto optimality cannot always maximize social welfare.

---

[9] Although Arrow recommends the redistribution of goods to improve social welfare, Nozick opposes such consequentialism. Thus, Arrow's criticism seems to be misdirected. However, I refer to his criticism of Nozick for the sake of a complete analysis.

However, he does criticize welfarism by saying that Pareto optimality can be unjust from the non-welfarist point of view. The third drawback of the price system is that it does not provide for the fair distribution of income. Even if one accepts Pareto efficiency as a desirable criterion for the distribution of goods, many social states satisfy it (Arrow 1974, p. 11). Arrow shows that some situations that satisfy Pareto efficiency are not socially desirable if the method of distribution of individual goods is unfair. For example, Pareto efficiency sometimes contradicts other very reasonable value judgments, such as a decrease in the gap between rich and poor. Arrow insists that Pareto improvement does not become social improvement if the distribution of income becomes unbalanced (Arrow 1983, p. 35). For Arrow, one of the roles of distributive justice is the correction of this imbalance; therefore, Pareto optimality is incomplete, not only as a measure of social welfare, but also as a measure of justice.

In short, Arrow notes that the consequences of economic decision-making do not necessarily fulfill the requirement of distributive justice. According to Arrow, something beyond the market is required to achieve efficiency, social welfare, and distributive justice (Arrow 1974, p. 17). In other words, the price system cannot be the final arbiter of social welfare (Arrow 1974, p. 14). From this, it follows that Arrow cannot be regarded as a welfarist on the basis of his work in the 1970s, even when he evaluates the consequences of the market. This is because he uses non-welfaristic measures, such as fairness and equality, for the evaluation.

11.3.2 The Problem of Racial Discrimination

In the 1970s, there was a growing consensus that the theoretical development of microeconomic analysis advanced by Arrow and others could be used for purposes other than market analysis. This trend was called "economics imperialism" by researchers in other disciplines. Against this historical background, Arrow expanded the scope of economics to cover social issues and made contributions to racial discrimination issues in the 1970s by adopting formal theory to solve them (Arrow 1972b; Arrow 1972c; Arrow 1973b; Chassonnery-Zaïgouche 2015).

Arrow himself, however, argued in a 1998 article that the market and economic analysis cannot adequately handle racial discrimination because it is a statistical fact that many black people are excluded from certain jobs, residential neighborhoods, and certain aspects of social community, such as restaurants. Economic methods analyzing racial discrimination in employment include an approach that assumes that white employers prefer not to hire black employees. One of the problems with this assumption is that such a preference will neither benefit shareholders nor help companies survive competition. Next, one can also assume that white employees prefer not to have black people as colleagues; however, this assumption merely leads to the conclusion that there would be segregated factories that have either only white workers or only black workers, and it cannot explain why wage disparities occur. Yet another assumption could be that employers, by virtue of personal experience, believe that white people usually have higher productivity than black people and that their decisions are based on this experience. However, it is unlikely that employers have enough experience in this regard considering that racial segregation has existed from the outset (Arrow 1998, pp. 93–97).

The upshot of all of this is that economic analysis is unsuitable for elucidating the causes of racial discrimination. It would be better to approach the issue with an assumption that the preferences of individuals arise from social interactions that are not necessarily mediated by the market. According to Arrow, "I am going to suggest in this paper that market-based explanations will tend to predict that racial discrimination will be eliminated. Since they are not, we must seek elsewhere for non-market factors influencing economic behavior. The concepts of direct social interaction and networks seem to be good places to start" (Arrow 1998, p. 93). In other words, non-market social relationships change the allocation of resources; thus, from the methodological perspective, as well as from others, Arrow does not believe that economic analysis is universally applicable.

11.4 Political Decision and Justice

The conclusion of Section 11.3 leaves unanswered questions about the relationship between political decision-making and justice. This point is examined by tracing the changes in Arrow's theoretical stance between the 1950s and the 2000s.

11.4.1 The Will of Majority

In the 1960s, Arrow continued to insist that the consequences of political decision-making are regarded as the criteria of social welfare and obeying the socially agreed position is a moral obligation; yet, an individual need not obey it if doing so does not improve his or her welfare (Arrow 1967).

Arrow went a step further. In the 1970s, he considered that obeying social ordering is just and mentions his welfaristic idea in a paper that criticizes Rawls' *A Theory of Justice* (Arrow 1973a). Rawls considered that the voice of the majority is not always just because it may violate one's rights; however, Arrow opposed Rawls' idea. According to Arrow, a public officer can improve social welfare by following the consequences of majority decision. Improving social welfare is just. Moreover, submitting to the will of majority means that recognizing and protecting others' positive freedom. This is a moral obligation for individuals. Thus, even if one's notion is not the same as the will of majority, he or she should submit to the latter (Arrow 1973a, p. 109; cf. Saito 2018, p. 251).

In conclusion, during the 1970s, Arrow thought that obeying social preference was a moral obligation for individuals and that it could stabilize society. He points out that, despite his theorem denying the existence of an ideal democratic decision-making process, there is some agreement in real society, and one should respect it.

11.4.2 Doubts about Democratic Decisions

Arrow (1996) stated that the presence or absence of information influences the degree of social responsibility assigned to individual decision-makers. He acknowledged that there is an asymmetry of information when individuals choose medical services or schools; for example, when it comes to decisions regarding medicine, medical personnel have more expertise than patients. Similarly, when choosing schools, it is assumed that parents have more knowledge to bring to the decision-making process than children. In either case, those who have more information are in a position to make better decisions (Arrow 1996, p. 233).

Glenn C. Loury, however, argued that Arrow's assertion, when generalized, means that those with more information should be entrusted with decision-making powers. Arrow himself affirms paternalism (Arrow 1996, p. 233), and, according to Loury, Arrow's argument could be applied to the claim that decision-making on medical or educational policies should also be entrusted to individuals who have more information.[10] In fact, Arrow refers to government regulations regarding national security, stating that those directly involved in the subject matter usually make better decisions (Arrow 1996, p. 234).

---

[10] Arrow mentions that his idea is related to the principal-agent theory in mechanism design (Arrow 1996, p. 233).

When all these factors are considered, it is doubtful whether Arrow really believes that popular decisions are always preferable when it comes to voting or policymaking since there is an asymmetry of information. In an article on racial discrimination, Arrow (1994) acknowledged that discrimination is morally evil; however, discrimination is often affirmed through social practices or decisions that are made in a democratic manner. Thus, Arrow (2016) is extremely critical and pessimistic about the results of democratic decisions, as well as about democracy itself (pp. 180–181).

11.4.3 Social Welfare and Fundamental Rights

Arrow also changed his perspective on fundamental rights. In the 1970s, Arrow seemed to consider that improvement of social welfare occurs prior to the protection of one's fundamental rights. It is found from Arrow's criticism of Nozick in the 1970s that he allowed the violation of one's property rights and entitlement to improve social welfare. In another paper, he criticized Amartya Sen's theorem of impossibility of a Paretian liberal society that proves incompatibility between one's right to freedom and social welfare, revealing his utilitarian position (Sen 1970; Kelly 1987, pp. 59–60).

In the 1990s, however, Arrow does not agree to the violation of one's right in the market. Arrow refers to child trafficking as an example, insisting that this violates the fundamental rights of a child. According to Margaret Radin (1996), the market should not set any price on goods based on the violation of an individual's personality; nevertheless, it does sometimes set the price of such goods, as during child trafficking and prostitution. Such goods "contest" the setting of any price and point to a market failure (Arrow 1997, p. 765). Arrow partly agrees with this opinion but does not clarify the reason. It can, however, be interpreted that he considered that there are two types of goods, only one of which can be purchased in the market.[11]

Second, Arrow insists that the consequence of a vote should not violate certain individual rights. The individual mistakenly prefers a social state in which goods that should not be sold are sold, and thus, may form his or her individual ordering. Hence, social ordering,

---

[11] This opinion is different from his opinion in the 1970s. At that time, when Arrow took up a controversial issue, stating that we can deal with some goods (e.g., commercial blood transfusions) in the market, he justified the market mechanism (Arrow 1972a).

which is an aggregation of individual orderings, is not always considered to possess an ethical meaning.

As mentioned earlier, Arrow accepted the condition of unrestricted domain in the 1960s and 1970s and regarded the consequences of social decision as a criterion of social welfare. Accordingly, if most individuals judge child trafficking to be ethically acceptable, Arrow may have accepted this judgment and obeyed it. During the 1990s and afterward, however, Arrow rejected some types of individual ordering on ethical grounds. In Arrow's words, "[j]udicial decisions and votes are not to go to the highest bidder. Individuals cannot waive certain legal rights" (Arrow 1997, p. 765).[12]

In short, during the 1970s, Arrow insisted that obeying social preference was a moral obligation, but during the 1990s and afterward, he left room to ethically reject social preference. Arrow began to admit that such social preference is not always desirable, and it is clear that, in the 1990s, he believed that if the consequences of the market or a vote go against one's fundamental rights, one should not obey them. Arrow changed his opinion and asserted that one's right is superior to social welfare. He, therefore, became a non-welfarist.

11.5 Criteria of Justice

11.5.1 Original Position

In 1985, Arrow raised the question "What are the standards of justice?" (Arrow 1985, p. 136). First, according to Arrow, Rawls' theory of justice affirmed the redistribution of goods. Arrow agreed with Rawls' fundamental assumption, although he criticized him on many other points. Rawls' fundamental assumption is that "justice values both liberty and equality" (Arrow 1985, p. 136). For Arrow, liberty means free choice and equality means that of income and power. Accordingly, Arrow recommended the correcting of any imbalance and equalizing income (to some extent) by the redistribution of goods.

---

[12] Arrow is well aware that this perspective is incompatible with his previous idea that the consequences of the democratic decision-making process have moral meaning. He noted that he has a contradictory idea. On one hand, he trusted the ethical meaning of the consequences of the democratic decision process for a long time, and on the other, he now doubts it and wants to protect one's rights against it. He stated in his interview, "On the one hand, I feel I shouldn't impose my ethics on everybody. On the other hand, I'm not necessarily willing to take the voice of the people as the voice of God. ... I don't have a consistent answer" (Arrow 2016, p. 112).

Arrow did not believe that freedom and equality were in conflict with each other; rather, one cannot be achieved without the presence of the other. In other words, respect for one's freedom as justice means equal respect for everyone's freedom. In contrast, the biggest restriction on an individual's free choice and action in the market is the scale of his or her budget. Consequently, an individual's income decides his or her free choice regarding consumption type and occupation. Inequality of income means that many people face restrictions in getting a job and only a few enjoy freedom; thus, the consequence of the market cannot provide a just distribution of income because poverty restricts freedom.[13]

According to Arrow, "income inequality also constrains freedom in dimensions other than economics." By this, he implies the political freedom dimension. Some resources are necessary to exercise political freedom, especially freedom of expression and publication. Since the rich tend to provide extra money to help public officials operate the market politically and receive special political advantages in return, "an equalization of income will increase the political freedom of the lower-income groups" (Arrow 1985, p. 137).

Along with income equalization, the equalization of power is essential to promote freedom. Power means the authority to make a collective decision. For example, China and Cuba have achieved equality of income to some extent in 1985, but they are not idealistically equal societies, because only a few people have the authority to make collective decisions in these countries.

Next, Arrow considered that one should choose a redistributive policy to achieve such freedom and equality through the social decision process in the original position. To clarify this point, he noted the relationship between social choice and distributive justice.

Social choice theory provides a normative judgment of interpersonal relationships. In other words, it can provide the criterion of justice. For example, this theory can adopt Rawls' theory of justice, which it can interpret as the problem of social choice and an attempt to deduce "state x is more just than state y" from "state x is better than y for individuals" (Arrow 1985, p. 142).

Social choice theorists, however, have tried to identify a social welfare function that can deduce a criterion of distributive justice from individual preferences; however, they have not succeeded. There are three primary

---

[13] According to Arrow, it has been pointed out in general equilibrium theory that equal distribution is not efficient. However, the theory has made it clear that perfect employment solves the conflict between equality and efficiency.

difficulties in doing so. First, it is difficult for a theorist to truly know an individual because a theorist can only analyze individual observable actions (Arrow 1974, p. 19). Second, even if such a difficulty can be overcome, a paradox emerges when one tries to aggregate individual orderings to form social ordering, as Arrow's theorem proves (Arrow 1974, p. 24). Third, as previously mentioned, even if social ordering can be obtained successfully, it is not always just.

Nevertheless, Arrow stated that justice is not independent of the problem of social choice; rather, he only questioned whether its real consequences achieve justice. Accordingly, he insisted that rational choice in Rawls' and Harsanyi's original position was a desirable procedure to deduce a justice criterion. According to this position, parties do not know their characteristics, belongings, or their entire lives. Such a position is desirable because it provides an impersonal decision process (Arrow 1985; cf. Rawls 1971, sec. 24; Harsanyi 1975).

According to Arrow, justice is not specific to some individuals; rather, it adapts equally to any individual. It is universal and impersonal. Moreover, mutual respect is essential in society. No one can ethically defend a distributive policy unless it benefits everyone equally. Rawls' and Harsanyi's original position provided the procedure that satisfies the requirement of justice (i.e., impersonality and mutual respect).[14]

According to this position, risk-averse rational agents prefer an equal distribution. In Arrow's words, "the original-position argument shows that the impersonality that characterizes moral judgment implies that the content of that judgement is an equalization of outcomes" (Arrow 1985, p. 145). Moreover, "[w]e may similarly presume that in the original position, where the uncertainties are the outcomes of an entire life, the individuals would find it prudent and desirable to enter into a mutual insurance agreement, to redistribute the incomes they would subsequently receive to make them more nearly equal" (Arrow 1985, p. 145).

The consequences of rational choice in the original position are correct because such judgment conforms to just judgment in reality. It achieves impersonality and mutual respect; additionally, Arrow, as an economist, could deal with the problem of justice without giving up his commitment to rationality.

---

[14] Arrow uses the word "impersonality" in the sense that social choice is not affected by the preferences of a particular individual. In his words, "the original-position argument shows that the impersonality that characterizes moral judgement implies that the content of that judgement is an equalization of outcomes" (Arrow 1985, p. 145).

As explained previously, Arrow identified Rawls' original position in *A Theory of Justice* with Harsanyi's and supported it as a fair procedure. According to Arrow, it is true that Rawls' original position differed in character from Harsanyi's; however, the two scholars also had something in common in that both sought fair distribution. This similarity is more noteworthy than their differences (Arrow 1985, p. 145).

Of course, many differences exist between Arrow's position and that of Rawls. First, Arrow criticized Rawls' way of deducing the difference principle, noting that rational agency with a risk-averse tendency in the original position supports the choice of the principle of average utility (Arrow 1973a). If someone's risk-averse tendency reaches a limiting value, however, he or she will choose the difference principle. Therefore, the two principles are not qualitatively different from each other, as Rawls argued (Arrow 1983, pp. 107–108).

Second, Rawls considered that individuals or parties in their original position choose a principle of justice. By contrast, Arrow considered that an object that an individual or parties choose is a social preference, in that it satisfies mutual respect and impersonality. It can be assumed that such a social preference is a criterion of justice because it leads to a just social condition. As mentioned earlier in this subsection, Arrow considered that "justice values both liberty and equality"; thus, this condition is considered to include non-welfaristic aspects (i.e., freedom of choice and equality of power).

Third, Arrow did not clearly answer the question, "Equality of what?" He agrees with the equalization of income and power, but Rawls considered that these are just elements related to social primary goods and fundamental freedoms (Rawls 1971, sec. 11).

Fourth, Arrow's view of one's talents differs from that of Rawls, for whom it is a common asset of society. For Arrow, it is unequal and belongs to the individual (Arrow 1985, p. 146), in compliance with libertarianism: a person with great talent should use it to contribute to society.

Fifth, Arrow attached importance to the problem of incentive. According to him, maintaining one's incentive can be in conflict with the promotion of equality. It is clear that some inequality is necessary to incentivize workers; one need not, however, acquire all rewards in accordance with the productivity principle (Arrow 1985, p. 147).[15]

---

[15] Moreover, Arrow does not argue for the difference between social choice and social contract theories; however, Amartya Sen argued this difference in his *An Idea of Justice* (Sen 2009). According to Sen, social choice theory can compare relatively different social states, and the social contract theory can define the best and ideal social state. Sen insists

Many differences exist between Arrow and Rawls, but it is clear that Arrow considered that rational choice in the original position deduces a criterion of justice because of its impersonal character. He believed that the consequences of actual social decisions are not always just, but that the problems of justice and social choice are related.

We can characterize Arrow's idea as proceduralism because he regards social states as just, not because they consequently optimize social welfare, but because they are deduced by the choice in the original position. It means that he considers fairness in decision-making as important, which is a non-welfaristic aspect. Conversely, we can also say that Arrow maintains his consequentialist aspect because he mentions that the consequences of such fair process are standards of true social goods. In short, Arrow wanted proceduralism to be consistent with consequentialism.[16]

11.5.2 Criticism of Sen's Approach

In the previous section, Arrow admitted the importance of one's freedom, though he did express his doubts about the intrinsic value of freedom in his criticism against Amartya Sen.

While admitting Sen's contribution, Arrow criticized Sen's study of the ranking of opportunity sets and of "the pairs (x, A), where A is the set from which the choice is to be made ('menu' in Sen's terminology) and x belongs to A" (Arrow 2006, p. 54) as follows. On one hand, Sen considered that opportunity sets can be ranked by the number of elements they contain, but on the other, some of Sen's criteria to evaluate opportunity sets constitute consequentialism. Arrow takes up "one criterion, called Elementary Option Superiority" as an example. When one wants to compare two opportunity sets, S and T, this criterion "simply says that S is at least as good as T if there exists an element x in S, such that x is at least as good as y for every element y in T" (Arrow 2006, p. 55). However, S may have fewer elements than T, which is inconsistent with the previous criterion. In other words, Sen sometimes valued opportunity sets because they express freedom, and sometimes valued them by their outcomes. In short, Sen's idea comprised both the intrinsic value of freedom and consequentialism, meaning that he did not fully abandon the consequentialist view.

---

that the former has more relevance than the latter. However, Arrow does not note this difference, and he considers that the former can deal with the latter.

[16] See Bossert and Fleurbaey (2014).

Arrow also had doubts about the intrinsic value of freedom by saying that people sometimes want to escape from freedom because freedom implies responsibility and they consider it a burden (Arrow 2006, pp. 58–60). This means that he considers not only freedom but also the majority will as important. This idea is inconsistent with his previous idea of respect of freedom and equality. We can, however, infer the following point from this criticism. Arrow merely criticized the idea that only freedom is important, and that we do not have to consider other things (e.g., social good or the majority will). Instead, he considered how freedom and equality are compatible with welfaristic values, such as social welfare or social good, or the appropriate balance of such values. In short, Arrow advocates moral pluralism.

11.6 Concluding Remarks

When Arrow proved his theorem, he regarded only non-comparable and ordinal individual preference as the informational basis for judgment. This means that his informational basis was restricted to one value: one's own utility. He regarded social preference, which is an aggregation of individual preferences, as a criterion of social welfare, or a proper criterion to evaluate social states. The first fundamental theorem of welfare economics states that competitive equilibrium satisfies Pareto efficiency, so it was interpreted that it evaluates competitive equilibrium from a welfaristic point of view. In short, his contribution to formal economic theory was regarded as welfarism.

From the 1950s to the 1970s, Arrow still considered that social preference was a proper criterion to evaluate social states, and one should respect and follow it as a policy guide. After the 1980s, however, he came to believe that the consequences of both market and social choice are not always just, from a non-welfaristic point of view. For example, if a decision-maker does not have accurate information, he or she may not make the proper decision (e.g., there is a particular information asymmetry in decision-making on medical and educational policies). Though racial discrimination has been affirmed in the majority vote, Arrow regarded it as ethically wrong; for example, child trafficking must not be dealt with by the market and must not be affirmed by voting. Arrow, however, considered that social choice theory can be useful to deal with justice issues. He stated that it is collective choice under a veil of ignorance that can deduce a criterion of justice, because its informational basis is the individual welfare judgment that eliminates subjective viewpoints and such a procedure also satisfies both mutual respect and impersonality. A criterion of justice also includes non-welfaristic aspects (e.g., equal distribution of power and opportunity of choice and correction of inequality); therefore, we can say that, after the 1980s, Arrow's analyses contained non-welfaristic aspects. He also gradually came to believe that we must protect our fundamental rights, no matter how society tries to violate them. He did not regard rights or equality as mutually exclusive values and supported the pluralism of values; in other words, he sought a proper balance between several values.

We can learn about the limitations of welfarism from such a transition in Arrow's thought. Though he used the welfarist way as a tool to formulate market and social choice, if a number of striking examples are considered, it is clear that he did not ultimately consider welfarism as acceptable from the normative point of view.

References

Amadae, Sonia, 2003, *Rationalizing Capitalist Democracy: The Cold War Origins of Rational Choice Liberalism*, Chicago: University of Chicago Press.

Arrow, Kenneth. 1963[1951], *Social Choice and Individual Values*, 2nd ed., New York: Yale University Press.

1967, "The Place of Moral Obligation in Preference System," in Sidney Hook, ed., *Human Values and Economic Policy*, New York: New York University Press, p. 118.

1970, "Political Economic Evaluation of Social Effects and Externalities," NBER chapters, in *The Analysis of Public Output*, National Bureau of Economic Research, Inc, pp. 1–30.

1972a, "Gifts and Exchanges," *Philosophy & Public Affairs*, Vol. 1, No. 4, pp. 343–362.

1972b, "Models of Job Discrimination," in Anthony H. Pascal (ed.), *Racial Discrimination in Economic Life*, Lexington: D. C. Heath, pp. 83–102.

1972c, "Some Mathematical Models of Race Discrimination in the Labor Market," in Anthony H. Pascal (ed.), *Racial Discrimination in Economic Life*. Lexington: D. C. Heath, pp. 187–204.

1973a, "Some Ordinalist-Utilitarian Notes on Rawls's Theory of Justice," *Journal of Philosophy*, 70, pp. 245–263.

1973b, "The Theory of Discrimination," in Orley Ashenfelter and Albert Rees (eds.), *Discrimination in Labor Markets*, Princeton: Princeton University Press, pp. 3–33.

1974, *The Limits of Organization*, New York: Norton.

1983, *Collected Papers of Kenneth J. Arrow: Social Choice and Justice*, Cambridge: Harvard University Press.

1985, "Distributive Justice and Desirable Ends of Economic Activity," in George Feiwel (ed.), *Issues in Contemporary Macroeconomics and Distribution*, Albany: State University of New York Press, pp. 134–156.

1994, "Methodological Individualism and Social Knowledge," *American Economic Review*, Vol. 84, No. 2, pp. 1–9.

1996, "Information, Responsibility, and Human Services," in Victor R. Fuchs (ed.), *Individual and Social Responsibility: Child Care, Education, Medical Care, and Long-Term Care in America*, Chicago: University of Chicago Press, pp. 229–244.

1997, "Invaluable Goods," *Journal of Economic Literature*, Vol. 35, Issue 2, pp. 757–765.

1998, "What Has Economics to Say about Racial Discrimination?," *Journal of Economic Perspectives*, Vol. 12, No. 2, pp. 91–100.

2006, "Freedom and Social Choice: Notes from the Margin," *Utilitas*, Vol. 18, pp. 52–60.

2016, *On Ethics and Economics: Conversations with Kenneth J. Arrow*, New York: Routledge.

Arrow, Kenneth and Gerard Debreu, 1954, "Existence of Equilibrium for a Competitive Economy," *Econometrica*, 22, pp. 265–290.

Arrow, Kenneth J. and Frank H. Hahn, 1971, *General Competitive Analysis*, San Francisco: Holden-Day.

Bergson, Abram, 1938, "A Reformulation of Certain Aspects of Welfare Economics," *Quarterly Journal of Economics*, Vol. 52, pp. 310–334.

Bossert, Walter and Marc Fleurbaey, 2014, "An Interview with Kotaro Suzumura," Hitotsubashi University Repository.

Chassonnery-Zaïgouche, Cléo, 2015, "Crossing Boundaries, Displacing Previous Knowledge and Claiming Superiority: Is the Economics of Discrimination a Conquest of Economics Imperialism?," Working Paper 5.

Harsanyi, John C., 1975, "Can the Maximin Principle Serve as a Basis for Morality? A Critique of John Rawls's Theory," *The American Political Science Review*, Vol. 69, No. 2, pp. 594–606.

Kelly, Jerry S., 1987, "An Interview with Kenneth J. Arrow," *Social Choice and Welfare*, Vol. 4, Issue 1, pp. 43–62.

Mackay, Alfred, 1980, *Arrow's Theorem: The Paradox of Social Choice: A Case Study in the Philosophy of Economics*, New Haven: Yale University Press.

Mackie, Gerry, 2003, *Democracy Defended*, Cambridge: Cambridge University Press.

Nozick, Robert, 1974, *Anarchy, State, and Utopia*, New York: Basic Books.

Pildes, Richard and Elizabeth Anderson, 1990, "Slinging Arrows at Democracy: Social Choice Theory, Value Pluralism, and Democratic Politics," *Columbia Law Review*, Vol. 90, pp. 2121–2214.

Radin, Margaret, 1996, *Contested Commodities*, Cambridge: Harvard University Press.

Rawls, John, 1971, *A Theory of Justice*, Cambridge: Harvard University Press.

Riker, William, 1982, *Liberalism against Populism: A Confrontation between the Theory of Democracy and the Theory of Social Choice*, San Francisco: W. H. Freeman.

Robbins, Lionel, 1969[1932], *An Essay on the Nature and Significance of Economic Science*, 2nd ed., London: Macmillan.

Saito, Nao, 2018, "The Transformation of Kenneth Arrow's Attitude toward War," in Yukihiro Ikeda and Annalisa Rosselli (eds.), *War in the History of Economic Thought: Economists and the Question of War*, New York: Routledge, pp. 239–257.

Samuelson, Paul, 1967, "Arrow's Mathematical Politics," in Sidney Hook (ed.), *Human Values and Economic Policy*, New York: New York University Press, pp. 41–51.

Sen, Amartya K., 1970, "The Impossibility of Paretian Liberal," *Journal of Political Economy*, Vol. 78, No. 1, pp. 152–157.

2009, *The Idea of Justice*, Cambridge, MA: Harvard University Press.

Shionoya, Yūichi, 2005, *Economy and Morality: The Philosophy of the Welfare State*, North Hampton: Edward Elgar.

12

Beyond Welfarism

The Potential and Limitations of the Capability Approach*

Constanze Binder

12.1 Introduction

The capability approach is widely employed as a promising alternative to conventional (welfarist) approaches to the assessment of individual well-being and social states in theory and practice. It can be understood as an answer to the question as to what information is relevant for the assessment of the way society is organised and goods are allocated. The answer to this question given by capability scholars is simple: what matters is a person's freedom to pursue life paths she has reason to value. This informational shift towards freedom constitutes an important difference from other approaches to assessing a person's well-being: welfarist approaches, for instance, consider individual preferences or utility as the sole relevant information. Freedom matters only if it contributes to one's preference satisfaction. Other approaches to well-being that rely on information about the resources at a person's disposal include the Rawlsian approach (1971), based on the provision of primary goods, and the monetary indicators that are often employed in economic policy assessment. To put this slightly differently, welfarist approaches to the evaluation of policy proposals focus on how far the preferences of the individual people in society are satisfied, resource-based approaches focus on the policy's effect on resources or monetary indicators, such as GDP per capita, whereas capability approaches

* I would like to thank Antoinette Baujard and Roger Backhouse for their detailed, patient and inspiring editorial comments and support. Furthermore, I am very grateful for earlier fascinating and inspiring discussions with Antoinette Baujard and Ingrid Robeyns that shaped the argument of this chapter.

consider information on how the policy affects what people can actually do or be.

An obvious question to ask at this point is why capability scholars choose capabilities or people's real freedom as the (proper) informational basis for evaluating alternative states of the world, rather than individual preferences or people's resource endowments. Why focus on freedom to pursue valuable doings and beings rather than on the resources needed to pursue these or the preference satisfaction resulting from them? The problems faced by many preference- and resource-based approaches constitute a prominent argument for this informational broadening in the beginning of the capability approach (Nussbaum and Sen 1993). Preference adaptation (discussed in greater detail in subsequent sections) occurs when unconscious adaptation of preferences to people's constrained circumstances leads to an overestimation of their well-being. Neglect of diversity is a problem that arises in resource or means-based approaches. Because people have diverse physical characteristics and because they live in different cultural and environmental circumstances, they may need different amounts of resources to realise the same doings and beings. This means that equalising the distribution of resources among people can lead to significant differences in what they can actually do or be.

Thus, a crucial question is whether the capability approach itself succeeds in overcoming these problems. What makes an inquiry into this question difficult is the fact that the capability approach is not a well-defined and fully specified theory. It is a general framework specified in different ways in a variety of disciplines, dependent on the problem it is meant to address.[1] The open nature of the approach makes it possible to specify it in different ways and to address a variety of problems in theory and practice, such as: the assessment of states of the world in welfare economics; providing an alternative to cost-benefit analysis in policy and project assessment; or the development of a theory of justice in political philosophy. One aspect particularly relevant for the discussions about the informational basis of welfare assessments is whether these different specifications of the capability approach have the potential to overcome the problems associated with the informational basis of other approaches, such as preference-based or resource-based approaches, that motivated the move to the capability approach. Is the importance ascribed to freedom

---

[1] For an overview of the different areas of the capability literature, see Robeyns (2017). For a more detailed introduction to the plurality of capability theories, see Section 12.2 of this chapter.

sufficient to move beyond welfarism and avoid the problems associated with it?

This chapter aims to explore the potential and limits of capability theories to move beyond welfarism by drawing on the literature about the (formal) conceptualisation of the key concepts of the approach and their measurement. This area of the literature aims to formalise and axiomatise rankings of sets in terms of freedom or capability (Pattanaik and Xu in press). We shall draw on the insights and the formal clarity of this axiomatic literature in order to argue that a focus on freedom is not enough to address the problems (of welfarist/preference-based and re-source-based approaches) the capability approach was meant to address. Whether the capability approach can hold its promise to overcome the problems that motivated it will depend on the way capability, as freedom, is conceptualised and the value assigned to it.

The chapter is structured as follows. Section 12.2 outlines the origins of the capability approach, pointing to its beginning as a constructive alternative to address problems in the assessment of well-being along utilitarian or Rawlsian theories in welfare economics and political philosophy. We discuss two specific problems of resource-based and utilitarian theories that triggered the development of the capability approach, namely the neglect of diversity and preference adaptation. In Section 12.3, we give a short overview of the plurality of specifications of the capability approach that developed in recent decades. We discuss a framework developed by Robeyns (2017) that aims to categorise and systematise different versions of the capability approach by identifying a number of characterising features all capability theories share. In Section 12.4 we then explore whether two of these characterising features, namely the move from achievements to freedom and the shift from means to ends, are indeed sufficient to address the problem of diversity neglect and preference adaptation respectively. By drawing on recent developments of the freedom ranking literature we show that this is not the case and argue that whether capability theories do indeed succeed to address the problems at its origins and move beyond welfarism will depend on the way the concept of freedom underlying capability sets is conceptualised.

12.2 The Origins of the Capability Approach: Two Problems

The capability approach developed in a variety of ways to address different problems in different disciplines. Before giving some more insight into these developments in Section 12.3, we shall briefly discuss in this section what it is commonly taken to be and how it originated from criticism of existing theories. The capability framework is a claim on how human well-being and related concepts, such as development or poverty, should be conceptualised and assessed. What matters in the assessment of a person's well-being are all the different life paths that she has reason to value and that are open to her. Life paths are made up of all 'doings and beings', a person's so-called functionings, that she can realise in them. These can range from 'being well nourished' over 'having access to family and friends' or 'enjoying good health'. Dependent on a person's resource endowment, her physical requirements and the culture and environment she is living in, different life paths, or bundles of functionings might be open to her. The capability set comprises all the functioning bundles she can choose from, and reflects her freedom to pursue different life paths she has reason to value. There is great consensus among capability scholars that only those bundles of functionings that a person has reason to value will increase the freedom offered by a person's capability set and with it a person's well-being. However, it remains a matter of dispute how these valuable 'doings and beings' that matter to people can and should be identified. Some (Sen 1999) argue that they should be identified in a process of reflection, deliberation and discussion among all concerned people, while others (Nussbaum 2000) defend a list of objectively valuable functionings.

Though it has been claimed (see for example Qizilbash 2016) that its roots go back to Aristotle, Adam Smith and Karl Marx, the origins of modern capability theory lie in the writings of Sen (1980, 1985) and Nussbaum (1988) in the late 1970s and 1980s. Even at the start, writings on capability ranged over very different fields of the literature, crossing disciplinary boundaries between philosophy, economics, development studies and political science. Especially in political philosophy and in welfare economics, the capability approach emerged out of criticism of existing theories.

In welfare economics, one can see how the approach emerged out of criticism of traditional welfare economic approaches.[2,3] One of Sen's major

---

[2] In this chapter we follow the definition employed in the introduction to this volume and use the term welfarism, or welfarist approaches, to refer to approaches that restrict the informational basis of social assessments to the individual welfare of the people concerned, depicted by (ordinal and interpersonally non-comparable) preferences. For a discussion about the change in meaning of the term welfarism in the history of welfare economics, see Baujard (2016). For a more detailed discussion about the origins and historical development of welfarism, see the introduction to this volume.

[3] See Qizilbash (2007) for a discussion of the capability approach in relation to social choice theory.

concerns in his writings on welfare economics was the broadening of the informational basis for the conceptualisation of well-being and the assessment of social states. He prominently criticised the 'informational poverty' of welfarist welfare economics, that restricts the information relevant to the assessment of societal states or the market mechanism, to individual welfare, understood as the satisfaction of people's preferences (ruling out interpersonal comparisons) (Sen 1977, 1979a, 1999). Other information or values, such as the rights and freedom people enjoy in a certain state, were excluded from the informational basis of welfare economics at the time.[4]

In political philosophy, beside Nussbaum's work (1988, 2000), one of the most prominent early accounts of the capability approach was put forward by Sen (1980) as an answer to the question 'equality of what?'. He argued that all theories in political philosophy ascribe importance to the equality of human beings in some way. However, what differs is the informational space in which equality is sought. Utilitarianism aims for the utility of each person to be counted equally, whereas what matters in Nozickean accounts of justice is the equality of rights (Nozick 1974). Yet again in resource-based accounts, among which Sen includes the Rawlsian approach (Rawls 1971), equality of resources or primary goods is the goal. Sen pointed to problems that can occur if equality is sought in each of these spaces, namely preference adaptation and neglect of diversity. Nussbaum (2000, 2001) discussed the problem preference-adaptation phenomena can pose in the assessment of well-being and defended the capability approach as a promising alternative to utilitarian theories in political philosophy. Unlike Sen, however, she focused mainly on political philosophy and combined Aristotelian approaches to the good life with the capability approach in her earlier work, while gradually moving towards developing it into a theory of justice, overcoming lacunae in the Rawlsian theory of justice (2006).

Thus, both in the welfare economic literature, as well as in political philosophy, the development of the capability approach was motivated by a criticism of the informational basis of conventional approaches. In the following, we shall focus on the two problems that received particular attention: the problem of preference adaptation, which is a criticism voiced against many variants of utilitarianism, and the problem of diversity-neglect, which, according to Sen (1980), applies to resource-based approaches.[5]

---

[4] For a detailed discussion about the history of welfare economics and the informational paradigms in the 1940s, see Backhouse and Nishizawa (2010).

[5] In this chapter, we follow Sen's (1979b) definition of outcome utilitarianism that takes the goodness of societal states to solely depend on the sum of individual preference satisfaction or utilities in this state. Along this definition, utilitarian approaches are thus a particular

Problems involving preference adaptation can occur in utilitarian approaches, where utility is equated with the satisfaction of the preferences people actually have at any time (Sen 1984). Drawing on a phenomenon identified by Elster (1982, 1983), Sen described preference adaptation as a process in which people in long-term hardship unconsciously adapt their preferences to avoid cognitive dissonance.[6] More specifically, if a person perceives her goals to be beyond her reach, her preferences may unconsciously change, so that she prefers what is within her reach over her previously preferred but unattainable option. For example, consider a person growing up in a poor neighbourhood who originally aspired to become a doctor. Over the years this goal seems more and more beyond her reach and so, in order to reduce frustration and cognitive dissonance, her preferences might unconsciously change so that she comes to prefer a feasible option, such as becoming a nurse or even a shoe cleaner, over the seemingly unattainable option of becoming a doctor. If her well-being is assessed in terms of her newly adapted preferences (and she indeed became a nurse or a shoe cleaner), the result would be an overestimation of her well-being, neglecting the fact that she could not pursue her originally preferred option of becoming a doctor.

In the case of approaches that aim for an equal distribution of resources, whether this is expressed in terms of money, as when one focuses on GDP per capita, or primary goods, as is the case in Rawlsian theory, Sen (1980) pointed out the problem of diversity neglect (see also Sen 1987; Nussbaum 2001). The problem is that the diversity among human beings and their different abilities to convert resources at their command into actual 'doings and beings' is neglected by a focus on resources. Whether a person can obtain the 'doings and beings' she has reason to value, say to be well-nourished, from a certain amount of resources, such as a certain amount of meat at her disposal, will not only depend on her physical state and age and the calorie intake she requires every day, but also on the social norms of meat eating or social festivities (for which the meat can be used) in the respective society and the environmental and climate conditions (say how long meat can be preserved). Thus, if one were to focus on the equality of

---

form of welfarist approaches (along the definition adopted in this volume/chapter). All those (utilitarian) approaches that take people's actual (and thus possibly non-reflected /scrutinised) preferences as the basis of welfare assessments are taken to be vulnerable to the adaptation problem.

[6] For early discussions about the adaptation phenomenon and the capability approach, see Sen (1984, 1995) and Nussbaum (1993). For a more recent account of the literature on adaptive preference, see Khader (2011).

resources among people, a neglect of the diversity along these various dimensions between human beings would risk leading to inequalities as to what people can actually do or be given the resources at their command. The question of the proper informational basis was thus present at the origin of the capability approach both in welfare economics and in political philosophy. The capability approach can thus be understood as one answer to the question how the informational basis in welfare economics can be broadened and how the question 'equality of what?' can be answered in political philosophy, such that the problems of existing theories can be avoided. However, in the light of a large number of different variants of the capability approach that are meant to address different questions and problems in different areas and disciplines, it is not always straightforward anymore as to whether and how they succeed in addressing these problems. In the following section we shall provide a short exploration of the plurality of the various ways the capability framework is used in different disciplines and discuss proposals on how to categorise this plurality. In the subsequent section we then move to a discussion as to whether all of these variants of the approach do indeed succeed in avoiding the problems of human diversity neglect and preference adaptation.

12.3 A Plurality of Ways to Specify the Capability Framework

One of the claims that characterises the capability approach (see, e.g., Nussbaum 2011; Robeyns 2017; Sen 1985) is that the information that matters to a person's well-being is her real freedom (reflected by a person's capability set) to achieve 'doings and beings' (the so-called functionings) (s)he has reason to value.[7] Two crucial shifts are involved. One is a shift from the resources or means that are available for people to achieve well-being to well-being itself, where well-being is understood as the 'doings and beings' or functionings that a person has reason to value. The second shift is from achievements to the effective freedom to achieve, reflected by her capability set.

Even though this gives already some indication about the information relevant for the evaluation of human well-being and related concepts along

---

[7] Note that the use of the terms capability and functionings varies slightly across the capability literature: while Sen takes a person's effective freedom to be reflected by her capability set, that includes all those functioning bundles within her reach (those actually chosen he usually calls achieved functionings), Nussbaum (2011) refers to capabilities as the 'doings and beings' open to a person and to those she actually realizes as functionings. In this chapter Sen's definitions are used.

the capability approach, it does not yet specify sufficiently well which information is relevant. Which information matters and how the capability approach is specified will depend to a crucial extent on the purpose for which it is used. If the capability approach is employed for practical project or policy assessment in a specific area, say health, then it might be that some specific health-related individual functionings, such as being well-nourished or being well-sheltered, matter while others do not. If on the other hand one is interested in developing the capability approach into a theory of justice in political philosophy, in addition to specifying the relevant valuable functionings, for questions about justice it will also matter how they are distributed between different (groups of) people.

In recent decades, the capability approach has been specified in many different ways across a large number of disciplines. It became a prominent framework to conceptualise and assess well-being and related concepts in theory and practice, ranging from development and educational studies to law and political science. To give some impression of this plurality of ways in which the capability approach has been specified in recent decades, we shall discuss some of these areas in greater detail before taking up the question about the characterising features all of these theoretical and practical applications of the framework have in common.[8]

As detailed in Gilardone's chapter in this volume (Chapter 13), one particularly well-known application of the capability framework resulted in a new approach to human development, becoming the basis to measure human development by the United Nations Development Programme, replacing the GDP-focused measurement (Sen 1983). Sen and ul Haq developed the first comprehensive alternative to GDP measures of human development that gained increasing importance in assessments of human development by the UN, the World Bank and other international organisations (Fukuda-Parr 2003).

Another area in which the capability approach gained increasing prominence has been as an alternative to cost-benefit analysis in project and policy assessment. Alkire (2002) has shown for instance that the broader informational basis capability assessments provide by accounting for non-monetary impacts on valuable 'doings and beings' can lead to very different assessments of projects. For example, an Oxfam-funded project in Pakistan that supported women to start their own rose growing and selling business would not have been refunded if purely assessed in terms of its monetary

---

[8] For a more exhaustive and detailed overview of the different areas of the capability literature, see Nussbaum (2011) and Robeyns (2011, 2017).

cost-benefit balance. However, once one also accounted for the project's non-monetary influence on the women's valuable doings and beings, such as their financial independence, strengthened self-worth and joy about the beauty of the roses, the assessment pointed clearly towards a refunding of the project (Alkire 2002). Especially in such cross-cultural applications it seems of crucial importance to uphold pluralism and to make sure one does not neglect diversity. Alkire succeeds in doing so in her assessment by choosing to involve the women themselves by means of a participatory measure. However, it has been argued that by giving too much room for possible differences, one risks running into the second problem the capability approach was meant to avoid. That is, possibly problematic values that might be due to phenomena of adaptation, a lack of reflection or oppression can come on board and distort one's assessment of people's well-being.

More generally, the capability approach became very influential in development studies (Gasper 2002) and development ethics in theory and practice (Fiebiger Byskov 2018; Drydyk and Keleher 2019). A special feature of the capability framework is that it allows for theoretical discussion about existing concepts, such as well-being, development or poverty for instance, as well as their practical operationalisation and measurement. Such a bridge between conceptual discussion and practical application is a particularly strong feature of poverty measures based on the capability approach that were pioneered in recent years on a theoretical and operational level (Alkire and Foster 2011). One of the main differences to conventional poverty measures is their multidimensionality. Poverty is understood as deprivation in a plurality of dimensions, such as health, education or work for instance, allowing one to account for an interdependence between such multidimensional deprivation as well.

These are but some of the areas where the capability approach has gained prominence in recent years. Other areas where the capability framework became widely used range from educational studies (Saito 2003) and debates about the conceptualisation of health and its measurement, to legal scholarship, such as debates about legal rights (Nussbaum 2006) or minority and indigenous rights (Binder and Binder 2016; Kramm 2019; Wantene et al. 2019). Another important area is debates about justice in political philosophy, where Nussbaum (2006) developed her own capability theory of justice to address what she sees as blind spots in the Rawlsian theory. However, whilst Sen is associated with capability theory, it is not clear how far his account of justice (Sen 2009) is a variant of the capability approach. It has been argued that it is not (Baujard and Gilardone 2017).

That capability theory has been able to develop in this way is partly due to the openness and underspecification of the approach, that allows it to be completed in different ways so as to deal with specific problems. It thus lends itself to different practical and theoretical applications. Its under-specification is one of the features that gives the capability approach its appeal as a broad evaluative framework that can be used to address differ-ent problems in different areas in which the information relevant to assess a person's state might vary. The drawback of this flexibility is that it risks blurring the picture of what constitutes the approach. Nowadays, many frameworks and assessments are described as being capability approaches but it is not always clear what all of these different variants have in common or why they should be considered variants of the capability approach. So, what are the features that characterise the capability approach?

Robeyns (2017) recently developed a way to categorise and systematise these different specifications and applications. She uses the term capabil-itarianism to denote the class of all variants and specifications of the general capability framework. Her categorisation consists of a core, con-taining the characterising features shared by all of its variants, as well as a set of issues and questions that can be answered differently dependent on how the approach is used. Within the core of characterising features, identified by Robeyns, are the following: first, functionings (i.e. ends instead of resources) and capability (i.e. freedom instead of achievements) form the informational space for the evaluation of human well-being and related concepts. Second, different people have different capacities to convert resources into functionings, dependent on their personal, social and environmental conversion factors. A third characterising feature is the distinction between means and ends where the ends are reflected by the capability set that contains the functionings open to a person and the actually achieved combination of functionings. A fourth fundamental building block of the capability approach is value pluralism, which involves allowing for different conceptions of the good life in the assessment of human well-being with the capability approach.

This categorisation promises to provide much needed clarification in the current capability literature about the openness of the framework and its necessary commitments.[9] Worries could be raised that such a broad way to

---

[9] An exhaustive discussion of the different parts of Robeyns's framework and how it can contribute to its further development would exceed the scope of this chapter. Instead, we shall restrict ourselves to a discussion of whether a commitment to some of the core requirements, as identified by Robeyns (2017), is sufficient to avoid the problems the approach was originally meant to address.

characterise the class of capability theories risks erring at the other extreme by including specifications that do not succeed in addressing the problems the capability approach was originally meant to address. In this light, it seems to be a more promising route to explore whether the two main characterising features of the capability approach – that also belong to the core of Robeyns's categorization – namely the shift from means to ends (functionings) and the shift from achievements to freedom (capability), are sufficient to overcome the problem of diversity-neglect and the adaptation problem, respectively. In the next section we shall see that a move to freedom is not sufficient to address these problems. Whether certain variants in the capability approach do indeed succeed in addressing the problems it was originally meant to address and allow one to move beyond welfarism, will depend on the way freedom is conceptualised and the reason(s) why it is valued.

12.4 Can the Capability Approach Live Up to Its Promises? The Conceptualisation of Freedom Matters

In this section we shall explore whether all variants belonging to the class of specifications of the general capability framework as defined by two characterising features, identified by Robeyns (2017), can indeed live up to the promise to address and overcome the problems the capability approach was originally meant to address and to move beyond welfarism at the same time. More specifically, we focus on the move from achievement to freedom (capability) and the shift from means to ends (functionings), characterising the capability approach. At first sight it might seem that the move to the functioning and capability space for evaluation, understood as the real freedom a person enjoys to achieve well-being, as well as the importance ascribed to conversion factors, that is the personal, environmental and social factors that affect a person's conversion from resources into valuable 'doings and beings', is sufficient to address the problems other approaches and theories suffer.

However, such a move from achievements to freedom and from means and resources to ends is not sufficient to overcome the highlighted problems. As we show in this section, whether the problems can be overcome will depend on the conceptualisation and valuation of capability, reflecting the real freedom a person enjoys. In order to do so, we shall draw on the freedom ranking literature in welfare economics that can and is often interpreted as the ranking of capability sets (Sen 2002; Baujard 2007).

Despite its prominent roots in welfare economic theory, the welfare economics literature on the capability approach has remained surprisingly limited. A notable exception is the small literature on freedom rankings, that can be interpreted as the ranking of capability sets.[10] In this literature an axiomatic approach is employed to rank sets of options in terms of the freedom they offer to a person. The axiomatic method makes it possible to clarify the key concepts at stake and highlight unresolved problems. In the following we shall use it to discuss the way freedom or capability is conceptualised in greater detail. This will help clarify the conditions under which problems arise or can be avoided.

In recent decades scholars increasingly employed the axiomatic approach to clarify the limits of welfarism in general (Suzumura and Xu 2009) and the capability approach and its unresolved challenges in particular (Echávarri and Permanyer 2008; Basu and Lopez Calva 2011; Foster 2015; Pattanaik and Xu 2012, 2020; van Hees 2016). In this formal literature, the main focus is on the construction, conceptualisation and ranking of capability sets. It should be noted though that many of the scholars in the freedom ranking literature do not explicitly defend one informational basis for welfare assessments. Instead, the interest is usually directed towards gaining a deeper understanding of the core concepts of the approach and possible problems by formalising them.

The formal literature on the capability approach usually starts out from (capability) sets of (mutually exclusive) bundles of functionings a person can choose from. One of the main questions discussed is that of which conditions should be satisfied by rankings of capability sets. The axiomatic literature dealing with this issue initially focused on the general question how sets of alternatives can be ranked in terms of freedom of choice. A crucial point when interpreting the freedom ranking literature in terms of the freedom offered by a capability set, is in how far the respective conceptions of freedom are in line with the notion of real freedom employed in the capability approach. In the following we shall discuss this issue in greater detail and explore some problems related to it (van Hees 2016; Pattanaik and Xu 2020). One important issue is what are the relevant constraints that have to be absent for a person to indeed have a certain bundle of functionings at her reach. Unlike other conceptions of freedom, say negative conceptions of freedom that often focus on the absence of

---

[10] For an overview of the freedom ranking literature, see Baujard (2007, 2011), Dowding and van Hees (2009). For an overview of the formal literature on capability rankings, see among others Basu and Lopez Calva (2011) and Pattanaik and Xu (2012, in press).

constraints imposed by the government, real freedom, as used in the capability approach, considers whether a 'doing or being' is indeed open to a person. In other words, legal freedom to do things may be meaningless if a person has neither the income nor the resources to do those things. In the construction of capability sets outlined in greater detail in Sen's earlier writings (Sen 1985), it is clear that a very wide set of constraints, including societal, environmental, physical and institutional constraints is relevant to identify whether a bundle of functionings is indeed within a person's reach, that is whether it forms part of her capability set.

Once the conditions under which certain functionings are within a person's reach and thus form part of her capability set are clear, the question then becomes how such capability sets can be ranked in terms of the freedom they offer to a person. The literature on freedom rankings is concerned precisely with this question.[11] Sets of mutually exclusive alternatives, that can be interpreted as capability sets containing the bundles of functionings within reach of a person, are ranked in terms of the freedom they offer to her. The question is which conditions such rankings should satisfy. In other words, what does it mean to say that one set of functioning bundles offers more freedom or capability to a person than another one?

One of the first answers provided was the simple cardinality ranking (Pattanaik and Xu 1990), in which sets are ranked in terms of the number of options they contain: the more options available, the more freedom of choice a set offers. This ranking has been criticised for various reasons, one being that it does not account for the value of the alternatives (or functioning bundles) available to a person. As Sen (1991) influentially pointed out, a dreadful alternative such as 'being beheaded at dawn' would increase a person's freedom as much as say 'going to school', which is counterintuitive, particularly if we are concerned with the role and value freedom has for human well-being and development. In response, a number of ways were explored as to how the value of alternatives can be considered in freedom rankings. As we shall argue, dependent on the way the value of functioning bundles is considered, some of the problems that motivated the development of the capability approach can reoccur.

Pattanaik and Xu (in press) distinguish four different ways in which the value of alternatives could be incorporated in freedom rankings. For this purpose, they introduce the notion of a 'Value Based Ordering' (VBO)

---

[11] Note, however, that the conception of freedom employed in the freedom ranking literature often differs from the conception of capability and with it the plausibility of (some of) the axioms employed.

which can, but does not have to coincide with a person's actual (or possible) preference ordering(s). More specifically, they distinguish between (a) all possible VBOs a person might have in the future, (b) a person's actual VBO over functioning bundles, (c) all VBOs held by a certain group or by members of a society, (d) all VBOs a person could reasonably have (according to some perfectionistic theory of the good life), (e) all VBOs a person could possibly think of choosing herself. Whether a newly available functioning (bundle) then increases the freedom offered by a capability set will depend on whether it is ranked at least as high as all other functioning bundles available by at least one of the VBOs. For instance, whether the functioning 'being beheaded at dawn' will increase the freedom offered by a capability set will depend on whether it is ranked at least as high in at least one VBO, as all other options.

One crucial issue is whether all of these ways to account for the value of the options that are available in a person's capability set allows one to move beyond welfarism and to overcome the problems the capability approach was meant to address. I argue that this is indeed not always the case. The first four classes of freedom rankings ((a)–(d)) are, in one way or another, in conflict with either the ability of the capability approach to address the problems that motivated its development or the possibility of moving beyond welfarism. Only if (as in case (e) above) the value of options is based on the VBOs a person could possibly imagine choosing herself (that is if a person's agency is taken seriously), a possibility might open up to move beyond welfarism while overcoming the problems the capability approach was originally meant to address. To explain this, we shall consider the question whether the new functioning of 'wearing a headscarf' when going to the office would increase a woman's freedom offered by her capability set or not.

In case (a) freedom is valued instrumentally to achieve a higher preference satisfaction (if VBO is equated with preferences) in the future (Kreps 1979). Thus, what is (intrinsically valued) is preference satisfaction and freedom is a mere means to achieve that in case of uncertainty over one's future preferences. This, however, does not do justice to the original aim to move beyond a welfarist informational basis, since freedom is only valued instrumentally to achieve a higher level of preference satisfaction. In our example this would mean that the availability of the option to wear a headscarf increases freedom only if the woman might one day prefer wearing a headscarf to not wearing one, say because of religious conversion, so that being able to choose this functioning bundle would lead to a higher satisfaction of her future preferences.

In cases (b) and (c) it can be shown that the adaptation problem, one of the criticisms of certain utilitarian variants that motivated the capability approach, can reoccur. To see this, it is important to see how the value of functioning bundles identified by VBO influences freedom rankings. In many contributions (see, e.g., Pattanaik and Xu 1998) an additional option increases the freedom offered by a set only if it is at least as good as all other options available (in terms of at least one of the relevant VBOs). If, however, adaptation can influence the valuation of functioning bundles itself, the adaptation problem can reoccur on the level of freedom. Say if a person adapts her valuation in the light of her (perceived) circumstances and starts to value 'becoming a shoe cleaner' more than 'becoming a doctor', then the addition of 'going to university and becoming a doctor' to her capability set (in which 'becoming a shoe cleaner' is also available) would not increase the freedom or capability offered by it. Whether this variant of the adaptation problem also applies to case (c), that is to the case where all VBOs of a given group or society are incorporated, will depend on whether adaptation of values can be a group phenomenon. If the answer to this question is 'yes', then (c) is equally vulnerable to the discussed version of the adaptation problem.

In case of (d) one considers all VBOs a person can reasonably have (according to some perfectionistic theory of the good life). In this case there is a risk of running into a similar problem as the one that was the main criticism of resource-based approaches, namely to neglect the diversity of human beings and the plurality of their conceptions of the good life.[12] The problem that might occur is that it becomes conceptually impossible to identify acts of paternalism (Binder 2019). To see this, consider the following definition of paternalistic acts based on Dworkin (1972): paternalism refers to (i) an act (of interference) of an agent X with the freedom of another person Y, which is (ii) without the consent of Y, and (iii) promotes the good of Y.

Now, suppose we take freedom in clause (i) in the definition of paternalism to be measured along a ranking that incorporates the valuation of alternatives/functionings as in (d). This means that a particular freedom or bundle of functionings increases a person's real freedom (or capability) only if it is considered to be valuable according to some standard, independent of a person's own views. The standard could, for instance, be an objective list theory of well-being. Say the objective list theory at hand does

---

[12] Note that case (d) would thus lead to a violation of the core characteristic of value pluralism in Robeyns's (2017) categorization.

not consider the option of wearing a headscarf in the office or at school to
have any value for a woman. Next, assume person X removes some
particular freedom of wearing a headscarf (x) from the opportunity set of
person Y, motivated by the promotion of Y's good or interests, where Y's
good is defined along the lines of the objective theory under consideration,
without the consent of Y. Thus clauses (ii) and (iii) of the definition of
paternalism are satisfied. To see whether this is an instance of paternalism,
consider clause (i) in the above definition again. If interference is taken to
mean that a person interferes with another person's freedom if, and only if,
he diminishes it, we do not then speak of interference if the freedom of
a person is increased or is left untouched. Given that x, that is, the option to
wear a headscarf, is not considered to be valuable along the objective theory
employed, the removal of it does not diminish Y's real freedom. Hence
X does not interfere with Y's overall freedom, and we do not face an act of
paternalism since clause (i) in the definition above is not satisfied. In
a sense these acts of paternalism are 'defined away'. However, this would
make it *per definitionem* impossible to identify cases of paternalism, thereby making it impossible to justify such acts, opening the doors to excluding
all conceptions of the good life that deviate from the employed objective list
theory. To illustrate, consider the debate about prohibiting the wearing of
headscarves in schools that became the topic of considerable public debate
in many European countries in recent years. Such prohibitions to wear
headscarves of hijabs are often justified on paternalistic grounds, in other
words that they are for the women's own good. No matter whether one
agrees or not, it is usually considered important for such arguments to be
open to public scrutiny, debate and justification. The problem of the above
highlighted case of 'hidden paternalism', however, is that it is no longer in
need of justification, as prohibiting the wearing of headscarves would not
count as an interference in a woman's freedom and therefore not as an act
of paternalism. As a result, the diversity in valuation and conceptions of
well-being risk being severely violated (if the approach is for instance
employed in policy evaluation or design).

   This last part and the problem of paternalism deserves special attention
if one is concerned with welfarism and its alternatives. Problems of paternalism are considered particularly problematic in welfare economics. As
discussed in the introduction to this volume, avoiding paternalism or any
value judgements that do not stem from the preferences of the individuals
concerned, was considered crucial to safeguard consumer sovereignty and
autonomy in welfare economics throughout the years. Including additional
information beside a person's preferences, which is a characterising feature

of non-welfarist approaches, is thus often considered to raise suspicions of paternalism. In the literature in political philosophy, convincing arguments have been made for paternalistic policies to be justified in some cases (such as when agents are not being well equipped to take decisions on their own). To discuss whether acts of paternalism are justified, the possibility of identifying paternalistic policies is required. Note however that the problem highlighted here is even more severe, as it leads to a situation of 'hidden paternalism', that is cases of paternalism can no longer be identified (due to them being defined away) and are thus no longer even in need of justification.

This discussion thus illustrates that if freedom or capability is conceptualised along the lines (a)–(d), a number of different problems that the capability approach was originally meant to address risk re-emerging. To put it differently, the ways to conceptualise it along (a)–(d) all fail to satisfy at least one of the discussed desiderata, namely to move beyond welfarism and address the two problems at the capability approaches' origin respectively. If, for instance, sets are ranked in terms of their value to maximise uncertain future preferences (or VBOs), then freedom is valued instrumentally to achieve higher utility or preference satisfaction in the future (but not for its own intrinsic value). The information that ultimately counts is a person's utility/preference satisfaction, not freedom. If, alternatively, the valuable functioning bundles in a set are identified on the basis of a person's or group's actual valuation function (b, c) or by using a list of objectively valuation functions that are independent of the person in question (d), then we saw that a version of the adaptation problem or an impossibility of paternalism, a problem of diversity neglect, can (re)occur. The remaining avenue still open that holds the promise to satisfy all of the three criteria is the one in which functionings are valued in terms of their contribution to a person's agency, that is to the process in which a person reflects upon and chooses her preferences.[13]

These points highlight that the importance ascribed to freedom in the capability approach is not enough to move beyond welfarism and overcome the problems at its origin. Whether the approach can move beyond welfarism in the assessment of societal states and succeeds in addressing the problems at its origin crucially depends on the way freedom is conceptualised and capability sets are ranked. To move beyond achievement by including information about the freedom a person enjoys is thus neither

---

[13] For one way as to how such a process of preference formation can be formalised, please see Binder (2013).

enough to ensure that the capability approach can overcome the problems at its origins, nor does the assignment of importance to freedom in itself guarantee one to move beyond welfarism.

12.5 Conclusion

In the late 1970s and 1980s, Sen and Nussbaum introduced the notion of capability and, since then, the capability literature has increased and diversified enormously. In this chapter, we have asserted the origins of the capability approach as a constructive alternative to the informational poverty of welfarist welfare economics and as a way to address problems of the informational space of utilitarianism and resource-based theories in political philosophy. The focus on freedom rather than on utility or resources was meant to overcome the issues of preference adaptation and diversity neglect. To say this differently, we expect the capability approach to be able to respect three different desirable criteria: moving beyond welfarism (or attaching an intrinsic value to freedom), solving the issue of preference adaptation, and the luring risk of paternalism. However, we have shown that if one attaches an intrinsic value to freedom, thereby moving beyond welfarism, then one faces a tension between preference adaptation and the risk of paternalism.

Whether the capability approach does overcome the problems it was meant to solve will depend on the way the notion of freedom underlying capability is conceptualised. To put it differently, we need to appreciate more specifically what constraints on freedom or capability are relevant, why one values the availability of additional options and how their value should be identified. One promising route to escape the highlighted tension and move beyond welfarism is a focus on agency, understood as a person's capacity to reflect on the preferences she would like to be hers and to revise and change them if needed. Identifying the value of the available functionings in this light can provide a route to escape the highlighted tension.

We have shown how the underspecification of the capability approach allows it to be completed in different ways to address specific problems. When different problems and applications of capability theories are considered separately, the focus is often on overcoming one of the highlighted problems, losing sight of the others. Thus, even if each criterion is satisfied by some of the existing contributions, it remains to be shown how all of them can be satisfied. The diversity of variants of capability theory has blurred the picture, but our analysis supports the conclusion that it remains to be shown that the capability approach can indeed live up to its promises. One promising route is to take the notion of agency more seriously in theory and practice. We need to check systematically whether the desired properties are still respected when we apply these policies to real settings, and under which conditions non-welfarist approaches may overcome issues of adaption or paternalism. How agency can play a crucial role in this endeavour is the concern of the next chapter.

References

Alkire, S. 2002. *Valuing Freedoms: Sen's Capability Approach and Poverty Reduction*, New York: Oxford University Press.

Alkire, S. and Foster, J. 2011. Counting and Multidimensional Poverty Measurement, *Journal of Public Economics* 95(7–8): 476–87.

Backhouse, R. E. and Nishizawa, T. 2010. *No Wealth but Life: Welfare Economics and the Welfare State in Britain, 1880–1945*, Cambridge: Cambridge University Press.

Basu, K. and Lopez Calva, L. F. 2011. Functionings and Capabilities, in K. Arrow, A. K. Sen and K. Suzumura (eds.), *Handbook of Social Choice and Welfare, Volume II*, Amsterdam: Elsevier, 153–87.

Baujard, A. 2007. Conceptions of Freedom and Ranking Opportunity Sets: A Typology, *Homo Oeconomicus* 24: 231–54.

Baujard, A. 2011. Utilité et liberté de choix dans les classements d'ensembles d'opportunités, *Raisons politiques* 43: 59–92.

Baujard, A. 2016. Welfarism, an historical perspective. 3rd International Conference Economic Philosophy, June 2016, Aix-en-Provence, France.

Baujard, A. and Gilardone, M. 2017. Sen Is Not a Capability Theorist, *Journal of Economic Methodology* 24(1): 1–19.

Binder, C. 2013. Plural Identities and Preference Formation. *Social Choice and Welfare*: 1–18. doi:10.1007/s00355-013-0761-z.

Binder, C. B. 2019. *Agency, Freedom and Choice*. Theory and Decision Library A: Rational Choice in Practical Philosophy and Philosophy of Science. Heidelberg: Springer.

Binder, C. and Binder, C. B. 2016. A Capability Perspective on Indigenous Autonomy, *Oxford Development Studies* 44: 297–314.

Dowding, K. and van Hees, M. 2009. Freedom of Choice, in P. Anand, P. K. Pattanaik and C. Puppe (eds.), *The Handbook of Rational and Social Choice*, Oxford: Oxford University Press, 374–92.

Drydyk, J. and Keleher, L. 2019. *Routledge Handbook of Development Ethics*, New York: Routledge.

Dworkin, G. 1972. Paternalism, *The Monist* 56: 64–84.

Echávarri, R. A. and Permanyer, I. 2008. Ranking Profiles of Capability Sets, *Social Choice and Welfare* 31: 521–35.

Elster, J. 1982. Sour Grapes, in A. Sen and B. Williams (eds.), *Utilitarianism and Beyond*, Cambridge: Cambridge University Press, 219–38.

Elster, J. 1983. *Sour Grapes: Studies in the Subversion of Rationality*, Cambridge: Cambridge University Press.

Fiebiger Byskov, M. 2018. *The Capability Approach in Practice: A New Ethics for Setting Development Agendas*, New York: Routledge.

Foster, J. E. 2015. Freedom, Opportunity, and Well-Being, in K. Arrow, A. K. Sen and K. Suzumura (eds.), *Handbook of Social Choice and Welfare, Volume II*, Amsterdam: Elsevier, 687–728.

Fukuda-Parr, S. 2003. The Human Development Paradigm: Operationalizing Sen's Ideas on Development, *Feminist Economics* 9(2/3): 301–17.

Gasper, D. 2002. Is Sen's Capability Approach an Adequate Basis for Considering Human Development? *Review of Political Economy* 14: 435–61.

van Hees, M. 2016. Analysing Capabilities: Games, Groups and Effectivity, *Working Paper*.

Khader, S. 2011. *Adaptive Preferences and Women's Empowerment*, New York: Oxford University Press.

Kramm, M. 2019. When a River Becomes a Person, *Working Paper*.

Kreps, D. M. 1979. A Representation Theorem for 'Preference for Flexibility', *Econometrica* 47: 565–77.

Nozick, R. 1974. *Anarchy, State and Utopia*, New York: Basic Books.

Nussbaum, M. C. 1988. Nature, Function, and Capability: Aristotle on Political Distribution, in J. Annas and R. H. Grimm (eds.), *Oxford Studies in Ancient Philosophy*, Supplementary Volume, Oxford: Clarendon Press, 145–84.

Nussbaum, M. C. 1993. Non-relative Virtues: An Aristotelian Approach, in M. C. Nussbaum and A. K. Sen (eds.), *The Quality of Life*, Oxford: Clarendon Press, 242–69.

Nussbaum, M. C. 2000. *Women and Human Development: The Capabilities Approach*, Cambridge: Cambridge University Press.

Nussbaum, M. C. 2001. Adaptive Preferences and Women's Options, *Economics and Philosophy* 17: 67–88.

Nussbaum, M. C. 2006. *Frontiers of Justice: Disability, Nationality, Species Membership*, Cambridge, MA: Harvard University Press.

Nussbaum, M. C. 2011. *Creating Capabilities: The Human Development Approach*, Cambridge, MA: Harvard University Press.

Nussbaum, M. C. and Sen, A. K., eds. 1993. *The Quality of Life*, Oxford: Clarendon Press.

Pattanaik, P. K. and Xu, Y. 1990. On Ranking Opportunity Sets in Terms of Freedom of Choice, *Recherches Economiques de Louvain* 56: 383–90.

Pattanaik, P. K. and Xu, Y. 1998. On Preference and Freedom, *Theory and Decision* 44: 173–98.

Pattanaik, P. K. and Xu, Y. 2012. Some Foundational Issues in the Functioning and Capability Approach to the Concept of Well-Being, in *Social and Cultural Development of Human Resources* [Eds. UNESCO-EOLSS Joint Committee], in *Encyclopedia of Life Support Systems (EOLSS)*, developed under the Auspices of the UNESCO, EOLSS Publishers, Oxford, UK, [www.eolss.net] [Retrieved 24 April 2013].

Pattanaik, P. K. and Xu, Y. 2020. The Concept of Capability and Its Measurement, in E. Chiappero, M. Qizilbash and S. Osmani (eds.), *The Cambridge Handbook of the Capability Approach*, Cambridge: Cambridge University Press.

Qizilbash, M. 2007. Social Choice and Individual Capabilities, *Politics Philosophy Economics* 6: 169–92.

Qizilbash, M. 2016. Capability, Objectivity and 'False Consciousness': On Sen, Marx and J. S. Mill, *International Journal of Social Economics* 43: 1207–18.

Rawls, J. 1971/1999. *A Theory of Justice*, Cambridge, MA: Harvard University Press.

Robeyns, I. 2011. The Capability Approach, *The Stanford Encyclopedia of Philosophy* (Winter 2016 Edition), Edward N. Zalta (ed.), https://plato.stanford.edu/archives/win2016/entries/capability-approach/.

Robeyns, I. 2017. *Wellbeing, Freedom and Social Justice: The Capability Approach Re-examined*, Cambridge: Open Book Publishers.

Saito, M. 2003. Amartya Sen's Capability Approach to Education: A Critical Exploration, *Journal of Philosophy of Education* 37: 17–34.

Sen, A. K. 1977. On Weights and Measures: Informational Constraints in Social Welfare Analysis, *Econometrica* 45: 1539–72.

Sen, A. K. 1979a. Personal Utilities and Public Judgements: Or What's Wrong With Welfare Economics?, *The Economic Journal* 89: 537–58.

Sen, A. K. 1979b. Utilitarianism and Welfarism, *The Journal of Philosophy* 76: 463–89.

Sen, A. K. 1980. Equality of What?, in S. M. McMurrin (ed.), *The Tanner Lectures on Human Values*, Cambridge: Cambridge University Press, 195–220; reprinted in R. E. Goodin and P. Pettit (eds.), *Contemporary Political Philosophy, An Anthology*, Oxford: Blackwell, 473–83.

Sen, A. K. 1983. Development: Which Way Now?, *The Economic Journal* 93(372): 745–62.

Sen, A. K. 1984. Rights and Capabilities, in *Resources, Values, and Development*, Cambridge, MA: Harvard University Press, 307–24.

Sen, A. K. 1985. *Commodities and Capabilities*, Amsterdam: North-Holland.

Sen, A. K. 1987. *Ethics and Economics*, Oxford: Oxford University Press.

Sen, A. K. 1991. Welfare, Preference and Freedom, *Journal of Econometrics* 50: 15–29.

Sen, A. K. 1995. Gender Inequality and Theories of Justice, in M. C. Nussbaum and J. Glover (eds.), *Women, Culture, and Development*, Oxford: Clarendon Press, 259–73.

Sen, A. K. 1999. *Development as Freedom*, Oxford: Oxford University Press.

Sen, A. K. 2002. Rationality and Freedom, *The American Economic Review* 89: 349–78.

Sen, A. K. 2009. *The Idea of Justice*, Cambridge, MA: Harvard University Press.

Suzumura, K., and Xu, Y. 2009. Consequentialism and Non-consequentialism: The Axiomatic Approach, in P. Anand, P. K. Pattanaik and C. Puppe (eds.), *The Handbook of Rational and Social Choice*, Oxford: Oxford University Press, 346–73.

Wantene, K., Yap, M. and Bockstael, E. 2019. *Indigenous Peoples and the Capability Approach*, New York: Routledge.

13

The Influence of Sen's Applied Economics on His Non-welfarist Approach to Justice

Agency at the Core of Public Action for Removing Injustices*

Muriel Gilardone

> There is a close relationship between public understanding and awareness, on the one hand, and the nature, forms and vigour of state action in pursuit of public goals, on the other. . . . public enlightenment may, thus, have the role of both drawing attention to problems that may otherwise be neglected, and of precipitating remedial action on the part of governments faced with critical pressure. . . . It is important to see the public as an agent and not merely as a passive patient.
>
> Drèze and Sen (1989: 19)

Amartya Sen is well known for highlighting the failures of the standard framework of welfare economics, in particular what he has called 'welfarism' (Sen 1977, 1979), which can be broadly interpreted as the focus on one kind of predefined information (Baujard and Gilardone 2020). His work has greatly contributed to making normative economics and political philosophy evolve in a direction which takes seriously persons' agency (see for instance Peter 2003; Burchardt 2009; Crocker and Robeyns 2010; Alkire 2010; Davis 2012). In contrast to most of these articles, we will neither study Sen's interest in agency strictly in relation to his capability approach[1] nor argue that personal agency shall be understood as a notion of individual advantage. Our view is rather that Sen's increasing focus on agency is a means to acknowledge theoretically: (1) people's 'ability to

---

* I would like to express my gratitude to Roger Backhouse, Antoinette Baujard and Tamotsu Nishizawa for their confidence in asking me to write this chapter, and thank Roger and Antoinette for their helpful and thorough proofreading. I am also particularly grateful to Antoinette for the many passionate discussions we had on related subjects. Lastly, I would like to thank Iwona Kelly-Dagnelie for the final proof-reading.
[1] See Chapter 12 for an analysis of the way the capability approach deals with agency requirements. In line with Baujard and Gilardone (2017, 2020), we consider here that the capability approach is not the essential point in Sen's approach to justice.

reason, appraise, choose, participate and act' rather than viewing them only in terms of their needs (Sen 2009: 250); and (2) the basic human abilities 'to understand, to sympathize, to argue' rather than viewing them as 'doomed to isolated lives without communication and collaboration' (Sen 2009: 415). The scope is thus different from a mere widening of the informational base for appreciating personal situations within a social state[2] because it takes us on the territory of the procedural aspects of injustice removal.[3] If we were to consider the views of critics, such as Ben Fine (2004: 101) who has argued that 'the social, the contextual and the empirical' clashes absolutely with 'the individual, the formal and the a priori' that character-izes the reasoning within social choice theory, such a perspective would be surprising. However, Sen still claims that the 'analytical – rather mathem-atical – discipline' of social choice theory has helped him to investigate the demands of justice, along with 'general – and largely non-mathematical – political and moral philosophy' (Sen 2012: 102). Looking beyond such formal and philosophical reasonings, we believe that some of Sen's other works – which may be called empirical, applied or directly engaged with the diagnosis of concrete injustices – have also played a non-negligible role in the definition of his approach to justice, with personal agency at its heart. This is that kind of influence that we want to present here.

Before making these points, it is important to recall that Sen's non-welfarist perspective has gradually been clarified within a debate between welfare economists and political philosophers that started in the late 1960s. Arrow's (1950) pessimistic result regarding the possibility of a democratic social choice from a set of individual ordinal preferences had a profound impact. For instance, it led some authors to propose a return to utilitarian-ism (Harsanyi 1955), others to develop an ideal but anti-utilitarian theory of justice (Rawls 1971) and others to oppose a libertarian and process-oriented approach to justice instead of a consequentialist construction of welfare (Nozick 1974). Under the influence of all these contributions, Sen (1970, 1977, 1979) began to question the standard assumptions of social choice theory, that is, the search for Pareto optimality and completeness,

---

[2] We do not deny though that Sen has also advocated a wider informational base for the evaluation of social states than strict personal utility or well-being: '[t]aking note of agency achievements or agency freedom shifts the focus away from seeing a person as just a vehicle of well-being, ignoring the importance of the person's own judgements and priorities, with which the agency concerns are linked' (Sen 2009: 288).

[3] Note that Davis (2012: 171) remarks that Sen's 'strong concept of freedom' – agency – 'places considerable demands on how a just society can function', emphasizing the concept of responsibility and the central role of public reasoning. He nevertheless suggests that it may take us on an entire new continent, 'but perhaps ... too far!'.

the avoidance of interpersonal comparisons and value judgements, the exclusive focus on utility information however that is defined and the absence of considerations of justice. His long-running attempt to reformulate the latest embodiment of welfare economics ultimately resulted in the proposal of a novel theory of justice.

Although it was not Sen's purpose from the outset, his mature writings on justice (Sen 2009, 2012) clearly assume, and indeed claim, a 'social choice' approach to justice against a 'social contract' approach that characterizes mainstream theories of justice, including in the first place that of Rawls.[4] Sen above all opposes the idea that the principal task of a theory of justice is the characterization of 'just institutions' (2012: 103). He defines his own alternative approach through three main departures from the social contract theories (2012: 103): (1) 'the identification of clear cases of injustice on which agreement could emerge on the basis of reasoning' (e.g., slavery, famines, chronic undernourishment, preventable epidemics, etc.); (2) the examination of 'the nature of lives that people are actually able to lead', with a special attention to their 'quality of lives and freedom' viewed as 'social realizations'; and (3) including in the search of 'reasoned agreement' the views of 'people from anywhere in the world', making reasoning on 'global justice' possible (e.g. addressing problems such as global economic crises, global warming, global pandemics, etc.). According to us, the meaning of these three departures may be examined in the light of Sen's experience in applied or development economics dealing with pressing problems in the world, often within international institutions. More precisely, we want to show that Sen's alternative theory of justice is greatly influenced by (1) his work on famines for the International Labour Office (ILO); (2) his empirical work on gender inequalities, specifically within the Indian society, that helped him to refine his approach to hunger developed under the auspice of the World Institute of Development Economics Research (WIDER); and (3) his implication in the creation of the human development approach within the United Nations Development Programme (UNDP). All these engagements – seemingly completely separate from his contribution to theories of justice – have in fact fostered the formulation of a novel non-welfarist approach in which agency and public reasoning are the core elements.

Sen stated very early that welfare economics is concerned with policy recommendations (1970: 56). Although he has been particularly shy about

---

[4] For an exploration of the theoretical debate between the two philosophers and the progressive modification of Sen's theoretical ambition, see Gilardone (2015).

being involved in governments, he did not remain confined to Universities and accepted working for international organizations – principally for the ILO[5] and later for the UNDP.[6] In those organizations, his recommendations were directly concerned not so much with state policy as with some changes of focus to better understand extreme poverty and persistent inequalities, and thus with new types of reasoning to address these problems and provide fuel for public discussion regarding appropriate action. Sen strongly believes that 'public action is neither just a matter of state activity, nor an issue of acting from some "privileged ground"' (Drèze and Sen 1989: 61). In this sense, policy recommendations against deprivation cannot take the state 'as the great promoter and a heroic protector'; they should rather involve 'the agency of the public as well as its role as a beneficiary' (Drèze and Sen 1989: 60–1). Sen's experience of concrete and urgent problems such as famines and malnutrition made him formulate quite early the idea that 'public action will be determined by what the public is ready to do, what sacrifices it is ready to make, what things it is determined to demand, and what it refuses to tolerate' (Drèze and Sen 1989: 61). And he insists on the fact that it would be a mistake to impoverish the richness of the set of possibilities for public action by focusing on one part of the picture only – for example, state activity. The challenge was also to develop a theoretical approach adequate to reflect such a broad conception of public action, since its role is crucial in underpinning policy recommendations as well as in enlightening public reasoning. While it is fair to say that Sen's entitlement approach to famines, and then his capability approach to inequalities and development, lay the foundations of a new theory of justice, we should not forget the 'action' part of his empirical works, which is certainly the most important for removing injustice. Indeed, Sen's focus on personal agency and public reasoning reappears forcefully in his recent elaboration of a procedural social choice approach to justice (Sen 2009).[7]

---

[5] The invitation came from Louis Emmerij whose first contact with Sen goes back to 1962, when they were both working on the econometric model that Tinbergen had prepared linking educational change to economic development. Emmerij reminds: 'When I took on the ILO's WEP, one of my first thoughts was to get him involved, together with others like Tinbergen and Leontieff'(Fetherolf Loutfi 1998: 1).

[6] This time the invitation came from Mahbub ul Haq, who had been Sen's fellow student at Cambridge. Haq was put in charge by the UNDP of the newly planned 'Human Development Reports', and he insisted on Sen's collaboration in order to broaden the informational bases of development evaluations (Sen 1999a: 13).

[7] For a presentation of Sen's (2009) procedural social choice approach to justice inspired by Adam Smith's device of the impartial spectator, see Bréban and Gilardone (2020).

13.1 Analysing Famines for the International Labour Organization: Linking the Removal of Injustice to Democracy as Public Agency

Sen's (1981) seminal work on famines was prepared for the ILO within the framework of the World Employment Programme (WEP). The WEP was launched in 1969, as the ILO's main contribution to the International Development Strategy for the Second United Nations Development Decade. It was committed to help national decision-makers to reshape their policies and plans with the aim of eradicating mass poverty and unemployment. Sen actually began his work on the causation of famines in 1973,[8] at a period when Ethiopia and the Sahelian countries were experiencing important famines, and Bangladesh was nearly to suffer this way as well – chapter 7 to 9 of Sen's (1981) book are devoted to these respective famines. However, Sen wanted to give a larger scope to his study of famine, by formulating a new approach to poverty and destitution – which may be seen as an embryo of his capability approach (Gilardone 2010: 15). Above all, it seems that his idea was to change the focus from strict *food availability* to that of *direct entitlement to food* since 'something more than availability is involved' (Sen 1981: 165). In this regard, we may pay some attention to Sen's dedication of the book 'to Amiya Dasgupta who introduced me to economics and taught me what it is about', as well as to his later confession of being deeply shaken in his childhood by the agony and outrage caused by the Great Bengal famine of 1943 – to which chapter 6 is devoted.

Firstly, in a later interview with Richard Swedberg (1990: 251), Sen outlined the influence of Amiya Dasgupta, a friend of his father, in his choice to study economic theory while he was quite sceptical of its impact. At a time when he was much more concerned with things that looked immediately applicable and perspicuous in their relevance to the real world,[9] Dasgupta[10] made him aware that 'one could make a terrible

---

[8] Sen had already made important contributions for the WEP about the choice of techniques in connection with his PhD thesis; he had also studied employment in the non-wage sector. See Sen (1972, 1975).

[9] Indeed, Sen had begun his college education in the fields of mathematics and physics.

[10] Dasgupta was teacher of Economics at Dhaka University for twenty years, from 1926 to 1946. Except brief periods at the London School of Economics, during 1934–6, to earn a PhD, working with Lionel Robbins, and on Visiting Fellowship at the University of Cambridge in 1963–4, Dasgupta was based in India. This prevented him from receiving any real recognition abroad. Nevertheless, he was considered in his country as 'the economists' economist' (Sen 1994: 1149). Dasgupta was one of the pioneers of development economics and Sen remembers him as combining rigour and humanity: 'While the

mistake, even in terms of any relevance for practical concerns, by going *too directly* at it'. Sen was very concerned with politics, but he learnt from Dasgupta the crucial role that theorizing inevitably has in setting the problem right and in confronting practical problems. More precisely, there are two reasons for his gratitude to appear precisely in that book (Swedberg 1990: 251-2). The first reason is that the book concentrates on the kind of problem that really affects people in Asia or Africa, and that is neglected by standard economic theory. The second reason is that Sen presents and uses there a theoretical approach that is different from the prevalent approach of hunger and famine and, according to him, more relevant. The setting of a new theory certainly explains why it eventually took him almost ten years to publish *Poverty and Famines: An Essay on Entitlement and Deprivation*,[11] but it was critically important since he certainly already had the conviction that 'a misconceived theory can kill' (Sen 1999c: 209).

Secondly, although there is no reference in his book to his own experience when he discusses, among others, the Bengal famine he had witnessed, one can guess that his motivation for that research came from his childhood trauma – to which he first confessed in 1990 (Sen 1990a) and then recurrently presented as a decisive experience in his choice of subject study as well as on the methodological setting (e.g. Sen 1999a; Barsamian 2001). Born on a university campus,[12] the son and grandson of academics, Sen's childhood was quite protected and privileged. But this condition didn't prevent him from being deeply shaken by the Great Bengal famine of 1943. Although he was a witness, and not a victim, of this event, it left

---

reason for being interested in economics was what he called "the presence of economically remediable misery in the world", the reasoning it demanded had to be strict and exacting' (Sen 1994: 1147).

[11] In the preface, Sen (1981: vii) thanks the ILO's members 'for, among other things, their extraordinary patience; the work took a good deal longer than they – and for that matter I – imagined it would'.

[12] Sen was born in Santiniketan – which means 'the home of peace' – on the campus founded by the poet and social thinker Rabindranath Tagore in the forest, while his parents lived in Dhaka. Indeed, in the Indian tradition, the birth of the first child has to take place in the mother's parental home, in that case where his maternal grandfather worked and lived. Not only had Tagore christened Sen as 'Amartya', which means 'immortal' in Sanskrit, but he is one of the strongest influences on Sen's world view, at least for two reasons: (1) the bounds that linked the poet with Sen's family and (2) Sen's education at the school Tagore founded (see Gilardone 2008). Especially in Sen (2001) appears the proximity between the engagements of the poet and the economist. The main themes are the importance of science and education in people's lives, the reasoning in freedom, the critique of patriotism, nationalism and cultural separation.

a deep impression on him. When the Bengal famine occurred, Sen was a nine-year-old boy. He remembers he was allowed by his grandfather to give a cigarette tin of rice to anyone that came for help. But the main memory he has and on which he prefers to focus is, on the contrary, his feeling of helplessness and 'bewilderment' (Barsamian 2001: 5). He then realized that no one in his family, nor any of his friends' families, were affected by the famine. This quite transparent and brutal class-division profoundly sensitized him to the issue of inequality.[13] Moreover, he knew from his parents that 'the crop hadn't been bad in any sense so it was surprising that there would be a famine' (Barsamian 2001: 6), which maybe oriented him to postulate that the problem was not just about the availability of food. Those thoughts of his childhood returned in the work on famines he started some thirty years after the Bengal famine and without doubt influenced the opening lines of his study:

Starvation is the characteristic of some people not having enough food to eat. It is not the characteristic of there being not enough food to eat. (Sen 1981: 1)

For example, the general understanding that the famine he witnessed was taking place at a time when food supply was not insufficient – which was confirmed by empirical research on other famines as well – certainly helped him work out another hypothesis. Indeed, he found that overall food output during the Bengal famine of 1943, in which about 3 million people died according to his evaluation, was no lower than in 1941. Thus he questioned the view that famines are caused by food availability decline and showed that it 'gives little clue to the causal mechanism of starvation, since it does not go into the relationship of people to food' (Sen 1981: 151). Finally, he tackled the problem keeping in mind what he had wondered as a child:

If some people had to starve, then clearly, they didn't have enough food, but the question is: why didn't they have food? What allows one group rather than another to get hold of the food that is there? These questions lead to the entitlement approach, which has been explored in this monograph, going from economic phenomena into social, political, and legal issues. (Sen 1981: 151)

According to Sen, the entitlement approach[14] provides a general framework for analysing famines rather than one particular hypothesis about

---

[13] It is what one can deduce from Sen's autobiographical reconstruction and it is indeed quite plausible. However, as we said previously, there is inevitably a part of interpretation, imagination and commitment in this reconstructed reality from present questions and reflections.

[14] We will not enter here into the details of Sen's entitlement approach. Let us simply recall that '[a]n entitlement relation applied to ownership connects one set of

their causation. However, that view allows explanation as to why the market mechanism takes food away from the famine-stricken areas to elsewhere: 'Market demands are not reflections of biological needs or psychological desires, but choices based on exchange entitlement relations' (Sen 1981: 161). Just as Keynes had shown that a market economy could be in equilibrium with many people unemployed, so Sen showed that a functioning market economy could leave millions dead (Desai 2001: 220).

From the middle of the 1980s, Sen carried on his work on famines and chronic hunger under the auspices of WIDER in Helsinki.[15] In collaboration with Jean Drèze, he tried to focus on the appropriate public actions in facing hunger, rather than on its measurement. Their book *Hunger and Public Action* (1989) represents one of the first fruits of a programme of 'research for action',[16] and the primary focus of which is indeed on action. While they highlight the major role the state might play in eradicating famines and in eliminating persistent deprivation, they also insist from the very beginning on the decisive part of 'agency' in such action – although the term agency is not always used:

the reach of public action goes well beyond the doings of the state, and involves what is done by the public – not merely for the public. We also argue that the nature and the effectiveness of the activities of the state can deteriorate very easily in the absence of public vigilance and activism. (Drèze and Sen 1989: vii)

On the one hand, Sen argued that theoreticians have a role to play in proposing a better approach to famines[17] that would help to anticipate and

---

ownerships to another through certain rules of legitimacy' (Sen 1981: 1). And in a market economy, '[a] person will be exposed to starvation if, for the ownership that he actually has, the exchange entitlement set does not contain any feasible bundle including enough food' (Sen 1981: 2).

[15] The World Institute of Development Economics Research (WIDER) was established by the United Nations University as its first research and training centre in 1984 and started work in 1985. The principal purpose of the Institute was to help identify and meet the need for policy-oriented socio-economic research on pressing global and development problems, as well as common domestic problems and their interrelationships (see Sen 1987: 1).

[16] Lal Jayawardena – the director of WIDER and an old friend of Sen who had also studied at Cambridge in the 1950s – explains in the preface that Drèze and Sen's book is one of the first results of WIDER's programme of 'research for action'. He also insists on the fact that, since its creation in 1985, 'WIDER has consistently searched to promote research on contemporary development problems with a practical orientation' (Drèze and Sen 1989: v).

[17] To him, it means 'making better use of economic analysis that focuses on entitlement failures of particular occupation groups rather than on output fluctuations in the economy as a whole' (Sen 1987: 14).

prevent them. On the other hand, alerts given by media, non-governmental organizations, pressure groups or opposition parties are also of crucial importance – which takes us to the notion of 'agency', as Sen (1987: 14) notes. '[A]ctive journalism can fruitfully supplement the work of economic analysis, by reporting early signs of distress', and 'how soon, how urgently and how actively the government will act will also depend on the nature of the politics of the country and the forces that operate on the government to act without delay' (Sen 1987: 14). Agency here is related to two crucial elements: (1) 'public knowledge', in which economists as well as journalists have a role to play and (2) 'involvement in social issues', or political commitment of the population (Sen 1987: 15). It is now well known that one of Sen's points in his analysis of famines was that democracy – implying adversarial politics and social criticism, in addition to elections – can influence state action in the direction of greater sensitivity to extreme poverty, and indeed plays a major role in the eradication of hunger and deprivation (see Sen 1999b). For example, he and Drèze came to the conclusion that the Bengal famine of 1943 would not have occurred if India had not been under the British domination (e.g. Drèze and Sen 1989: 126). More generally, in democratic countries, even very poor ones, the survival of the ruling government would be threatened by famine, since it is not easy to withstand the criticism of opposition parties and media.[18]

It appears that Sen's contribution to the study of famines has been an important step in theorizing agency and integrating practical ideas of democracy in tackling the removal of injustice. As Alkire (2010: 212) has noted, Sen's writings on famines politicized the problem in a new way: while there is 'no law against dying of hunger' (Sen 1981), Sen's analysis, later pursued with Jean Drèze, made it clear that people's actions and protests of injustice can effectively prevent famines. His insistent focus on 'social actions taken by members of the public – both "collaborative" (through civil cooperation) and "adversarial" (through social criticism and political opposition)' (Drèze and Sen 1989: vii) not only had 'the effect of shifting the borders of development out from a narrowly economic space' (Alkire 2010: 214), but offered some insights on the way actions towards more justice can be implemented. There is no doubt it influenced his formulation of a new approach to justice, alternative both to the social contract approach and the welfarist perspective.

---

[18] 'Even the poorest democratic countries that have faced terrible droughts or floods or other natural disasters (such as India in 1973, or Zimbabwe and Botswana in the early 1980s) have been able to feed their people without experiencing a famine' (Sen 1999b: 8).

13.2 Analysing Gender Inequality: A Further Step towards Agency Considerations

We have seen that, in order to better alert people on the risks of famines, Sen thought that it was important to present 'the food problem as a relation between people and food in terms of a network of entitlement relations' (Sen 1981). He knew that such an approach needed to get into issues which were not 'so clearly economic and legal, especially the notion of legitimacy' (Swedberg 1990: 255). In the original version of *Poverty and Famines*, there were chapters in which he tackled the problem of 'perceived notions of rights', but he finally decided to leave them out, in order to go straight to his important point. However, the notion of legitimacy eventually reappeared when he developed a gendered perspective on the problem of hunger (e.g. Kynch and Sen 1983; Sen 1987: 13; Drèze and Sen 1989: ch. 4). Sen sometimes used the term 'extended entitlements' to broaden the focus of entitlement analysis 'from legal rights to a framework in which accepted social notions of "legitimacy" can be influential' (Sen 1987: 13; Drèze and Sen 1989: 50). But he also developed the problem of 'the perception bias' in terms of basic capabilities[19] within the family distribution (Sen 1983a; Kynch and Sen 1983). The idea of a 'perception bias' refers to a situation where the systematic disadvantage of a particular group is not perceived, while documented analysis shows that the different family members do not enjoy the same basic capabilities. For Kynch and Sen (1983: 364), it may be 'closely related to a sense of *priorities*, e.g. there may be magnification of the needs of the males in general and the head of the household in particular'. It may also be related to a perception bias of the respective contribution to joint prosperity, which in turn influences the respective legitimacy to benefit of it (Drèze and Sen 1989: 57). It may even be related to a bias in the perception of one's own self-interest,[20] which 'is in fact a "socially determined" perception' (Sen 1989: 65).

With the notion of legitimacy, Sen tried to raise concern about some rules in the distribution of food generally unquestioned by economic theories: the rules governed by mores, conventions and other social practices. And in this respect, he wanted to show that the class conflict was not

---

[19] In particular: the ability to survive, to be well nourished, to be free from disease and to receive medical attention.

[20] For instance, Sen (1989) mentions some studies which demonstrate that the notion of 'personal well-being' is unintelligible to typical rural Indian women, and that if they were able to reply to the question of their own well-being or interest, they might answer the question in terms of their 'understanding of the welfare of the family as a whole' (Sen 1989: 69).

the only conflict of interest that was deserving attention in the food battle; intra-family distribution was also an important issue:

> Inter-household divisions, ownership rights and the rights of transaction and bequeathing are, obviously, relevant to the determination of entitlements of families. The perceived legitimacy of these legal or semi-legal rights has a powerful influence on the nature of personal and public action related to the distributional problem. While the lines are not so sharply drawn in the case of intra-household divisions, there are important issues of perceived legitimacy in that context as well. (Sen 1987: 13)

The relative deprivation of women became a central issue in Sen's writings in the early 1980s (Kynch and Sen 1983; Sen 1983a, 1984; Sen and Sengupta 1983). This work on gender inequality was initially confined to analysing available statistics on the male-female differential in India.[21] He started looking at the pattern of the allocation of resources within a family, on the basis of some available data, but also of some 'freshly collected in India in the spring of 1983, in collaboration with Sunil Sengupta, comparing boys and girls from birth to age 5' (Sen 1999a). Sen's primary objective – and challenge given the difficulty of observation in that matter – concerned the diagnosis of sex-bias or not in the distribution of food within the family. He soon came to the conclusions that 'there is some straightforward evidence of serious comparative neglect of female children, especially in distress situation', or that the overall decline in Indian mortality rates has gone 'hand in hand with a decline in the female-male ratio . . . *since* 1921' (Kynch and Sen 1983: 370, 378). In other words:

> There is no escape from the grave tragedy of the undernourishment of children (or sharper undernourishment of female children in distress situations . . .), or the unusual morbidity of women . . . . (Sen 1984: 346)

From empirical and local analysis, he gradually moved to a general theory of gender inequality (Sen 1989, 1990b). He remarked that there were misconceived theories regarding the economics of the family, or the distribution of resources within households.[22] Before thinking about public action to remedy what Sen considered as one the biggest injustices in the world, he proposed a novel approach to the economics of the family in terms of 'cooperative conflict'. Basically the idea is that there are strong

---

[21] Notice that in *Commodities and Capabilities* (1985), he also proposed some international comparisons.

[22] For a summary of Sen's arguments against standard theory of the family and some interpretations in terms of social choice theory and capability approach, see respectively Peter (2003) or Gilardone (2009).

elements of conflict embedded in a situation in which there are mutual gains to be made by cooperation (Drèze and Sen 1989; Sen 1989, 1990b). Sen identifies four determinants of the outcomes of such cooperative conflicts: (1) the breakdown position, for example the separation of spouses or their cohabitation in a state of permanent strife; (2) perceptions of contributions to joint prosperity – often devalued when unpaid work is involved; (3) threats that the parties can respectively employ; and (4) the understanding of conflicts faced by the different parties – women sometimes value more the well-being of their family members than their own and contribute to perpetuating gender inequality. While education and politics can have a far-reaching impact on the deal women receive, Sen and Drèze above all – and very pragmatically – highlighted the undeniable importance of female participation in 'gainful' economic activities as a material factor in combating the special deprivation of women (Drèze and Sen 1989: 59).

Once again, the choice of the policy should not be confined to what the government can do. Sen demonstrates that issues of perceived legitimacy and entitlement can be deeply influenced by a re-examination of the social and political aspects of intra-family inequality and disparity. In analysing gender relations as complex cases of cooperative conflicts with female deprivation as a consequence, Sen's point is to provide 'a basis for informed and enlightened public action in the broadest sense' (Sen 1987: 13). While famines are extremely easy to politicize – 'all you have to do is to print a picture of an emaciated mother and a dying child on the front page and that in itself is a stinging editorial' – in order to bring quiet but widespread undernourishment, or the debilitating effects of lack of schooling, to public attention, 'you need a great deal more engagement and use of imagination' (Shaikh 2004).

At the theoretical level, it is also critical to be a little more imaginative and less reductive. Firstly, if we want to address adequately issues of injustice, Sen's empirical work on Indian economy and society shows that a relevant framework requires integrating the role of norms, rules and social perceptions of interests and legitimacy on behaviours. Secondly, he puts to the fore the presence of both congruent and conflicting elements in the diverse social arrangements between which we might choose:

Given the multiplicity of collusive solutions that exist, an important issue is the relation between alternative norms, rules, and perceptions and alternative cooperative solutions that may exist – some more favorable to one and others more favorable to another. (Sen 1989: 66)

While the impasse identified by narrow models of 'individual rationality' is invalidated by Sen (1989)[23] in case of cooperative conflicts, he nevertheless highlights another kind of problem related to 'isolation'. Values and perceptions need social examination and discussion, especially when it is shown that one group systematically receives a lower share of the benefits of cooperation than another. Since the inequalities between men and women observed by Sen are not seen as 'real inequalities' by most Indians, it leads Sen to conclude that the value system underlying the sense of obligation and legitimacy in a society may obliterate the sense of inequality and of exploitation. In other words, the nature of the perceptions that prevail in a cohesive and well-integrated family 'may go hand to hand with great inequalities emerging from perception biases' (Sen 1989: 68). Referring to Marx's notion of 'false consciousness', Sen considers thus that the examination of different cooperative solutions shall be done in terms of some objective criteria like functional achievements. Simultaneously, notions of who is 'contributing' how much call for closer scrutiny since the 'deal' that women get vis-à-vis men is clearly not independent of the perception problem regarding contributions made by different people. Let us remark that the perception biases or false consciousness that Sen wants to undermine are important barriers to personal agency – barriers that 'the traditional economic model which relates individual welfare to a clear introspective perception, or a choice-based concept, of advantage' (Kynch and Sen 1983: 364) cannot identify, and a fortiori remove. In contrast, Sen's study of within-family distribution tends to show that:

the perception of reality – including illusions about it – must be seen to be an important part of reality. Non-perception of disadvantages of a deprived group helps to perpetuate those disadvantages. (Kynch and Sen 1983: 365)

In a nutshell, we may say that Sen has drawn three important lessons from his analysis of gender inequality in India: (1) it is crucial to take *actual behaviours as a basis for reasoning* on cooperative conflicts, rather than some ideal or hypothetical behaviour (e.g. rational behaviour); (2) in order to assess the merits of different cooperative outcomes, *the informational basis shall be as objective as possible* to escape perception biases; (3) *if the social results* – according to some objective criteria – *are systematically*

---

[23] Sen particularly refers to the famous prisoner's dilemma, a two-person game, in which 'the pursuit of each party's own goal leads to substantial frustration for both, since each inflicts more harm on the other through this pursuit than the gain that each receives from selfishness' (Sen 1989: 63).

unfavourable towards a specific group within the society, it may be relevant to *examine the value system* that influences the behaviours that produce an unequal solution. In these matters, public reasoning is much more relevant than direct state intervention.

13.3 The Human Development Approach within the UNDP: A Focus on Agency through the Capability Approach and Public Reasoning

Just after the publication of his seminal work on famines (Sen 1981) and while he was engaging in the analysis of gender inequality in India (Kynch and Sen 1983; Sen 1983a, 1984), Sen was invited to give the Presidential Address of the Development Studies Association in 1982. It gave him the opportunity to propose a rethinking of the idea of development inspired by the methodological turns and results of his empirical studies. In 'Development: which way now?',[24] Sen clarified the relationship between his concepts of entitlements – elaborated in the context of famine analysis – and capabilities – worked out in the context of moral philosophy as more relevant than utility to address issues of inequality (Sen 1980), and he further explored within the specific issue of gender inequality.[25] On this occasion, he also brought persons' agency to the fore:

Perhaps the most important thematic deficiency of traditional development economics is its concentration on national product, aggregate income and total supply of particular goods rather than on 'entitlements' of people and the 'capabilities' these entitlements generate. Ultimately, the process of economic development has to be concerned with what people can or cannot do, e.g. whether they can live long, escape avoidable morbidity, be well nourished, be able to read and write and communicate, take part in literary and scientific pursuits, and so forth. It has to do, in Marx's words, with 'replacing the domination of circumstances and chance over individuals by the domination of individuals over chance and circumstances'. (Sen 1983b: 754)

This paper may be considered as the launching of a novel approach to development since it is the first time Sen defines development as the 'expansion of people's capabilities' (Sen 1983b: 760). It may also be noticed that Sen's quotation of Marx is a good definition of what Sen calls 'agency': 'the domination of individuals over chance and circumstances'. Not only

---

[24] The paper is the final version of Sen's 1982 Presidential Address of the Development Studies Association.

[25] For an analysis of the relationship between Sen's empirical studies of gender inequalities and the working out of the capability approach, see Gilardone (2009).

did Sen carry on his research on hunger and deprivation within WIDER through developing a capability approach (e.g. Drèze and Sen 1989), but he was a major influence on work led within the United Nations Development Programme.

It is now well known that Mahbub ul Haq, a close friend of Sen, thought that his capability approach could be very relevant to ground the new development perspective of the United Nations.[26] Sen reported that, while Haq was working on the launching of a Human Development Report (HDR) for the UNDP, he called Sen who was in Finland to include him in the project: 'he told me that I was too much into pure theory and I should drop all that now ("enough is enough"), and that he and I should work together on something with actual measurement, actual numbers, and try to make an impact on the world' (Shaikh 2004). Haq's ambition was to create a simple measure of social welfare, or human development, inspired by Sen's theoretical insights.[27] Despite his scepticism about reducing his capability approach to a single number that would go beyond Gross National Product, Sen helped to develop the Human Development Index (HDI). Haq eventually convinced Sen that such an index would certainly be 'just as vulgar as GDP, except it will stand for better things' (UNDP 2010b: 2). Above all, Sen understood that 'in order to communicate, you have to have the simplicity that GDP had' (UNDP 2010b: 3). Indeed, for the twentieth-anniversary HDR edition, Helen Clark – the administrator of the UNDP – recalls that '[t]he premise of the HDI, considered radical at the time, was elegantly simple: national development should be measured not simply by national income, as had long been the practice, but also by life expectancy and literacy' (UNDP 2010a: iv).

We should acknowledge though that the human development approach has also, and primarily, drawn a strong and direct influence from the basic needs approach, including non-material needs such as participatory

---

[26] In his autobiography, Sen (1999a) reports: 'Mahbub insisted that I work with him to help develop a broader informational approach to the assessment of development. This I did with great delight, partly because of the exciting nature of the work, but also because of the opportunity of working closely with such an old and wonderful friend.'

[27] Sen reports that Haq kept quoting his 1985 book called *Commodities and Capabilities*:

It was kind of a formal lecture – a mathematical lecture. But Mahbub would comment on the fact that I made a big distinction between judging people and how their lives are going by looking at the commodity basket they own, as opposed to the freedoms and the capability they actually enjoyed. And Mahbub tried to tell me that this is the thing to do – and obviously you have done a few things, as he pointed out, but there are other things to do. (UNDP 2010b: 4)

process and freedom (Hirai 2017: 18).[28] But the definitive form of the human development approach, as it was launched in 1990 with the first HDR (UNDP 1990), is strongly in line with Sen's capability approach[29] and his more general plea for people's agency: emphasizing the centrality of human initiative and creativity and the need to democratize the development process (Hirai 2017: 11). According to Desai, Sen's influence reappeared in 1995 when the HDR put to the fore the theme of gender:

> Here the agency theme is crucial and the human rights that women can exercise are an essential part of daily existence. Women need rights indoors to cope with domestic violence and intra-household inequalities. . . . Women's human development thus requires a broadening of the notion of freedom, and good nutrition or education presumed as given by the liberal notion of freedom become crucial. (Desai 2001: 221)

It also helped to undermine 'the presumption – often implicitly made – that the issue of gender inequality does not apply to "Western" countries' (Sen 2009: 257). For instance, the 1995 HDR revealed that 'Italy had one of the highest ratios of "unrecognized" labour by women (mostly unglamorous family work) among all the countries of the world included in the standard national accounts in the mid-1990s' (Sen 2009: 257).

In a sense, the human development index (UNDP 1990), and then the gender-related development index and the gender empowerment measure (UNDP 1995) are the translation of Sen's theoretical work influenced by his empirical results over a dozen years in terms which were to influence the largest number of policy-makers and opinion-formers. However, it is important to keep in mind that for Sen, this was just one application of his capability approach – which has its contextual relevance, but in no case the only possible implementation (Gilardone 2010: 22–3). The philosophy at the roots of the human development approach is somehow in this line. Indeed, the approach is characterized by a perpetual evolution, 'to the extent that it places importance on public discussion and participation in the process of development' (Hirai 2017: 1). More precisely, decision-making through public discussion is a core message in the human development approach, aiming to submit the values involved in development explicitly to the public (Hirai 2017: 68). Sen keeps insisting on the idea that using any particular index always needs explicit formulation to facilitate

---

[28] Hirai (2017: 11) notices that a clear change of perspective – from the basic needs approach to the capability approach – occurred during the 1988 Amman Roundtable.

[29] Chapter 1 of the first HDR is very explicit regarding the link between the idea of human development and the capability approach.

public scrutiny, criticism and correction (e.g. Sen 1997: 544, UNDP 2010a: vi). Even, at the beginning, Sen and Haq tried out different weighting systems to build the index – moving back and forth between theory and empirical results. They examined the results, keeping in mind their under-standing and knowledge of the countries, 'to try to see to what extent it tallied with the kind of implicit wisdom that [they] had' (UNDP 2010b: 2). Another persistent idea in Sen's work is the following: it is important not to see the use of any framework for evaluation as an 'all or nothing exercise' (Sen 1992: 48). In other words, we need to leave room for ambiguities or incompleteness and we cannot expect a perfect evaluation of the develop-ment level, or the inequality level of a society. However, it can help to identify situations of patent injustice.

Last but not least, it is important to point out that, for Sen, providing indexes is not the only role of HDRs. While he is conscious that 'an avalanche of tables (and a large set of related analyses) ... lacks the handy usability of the crude GNP' (UNDP 2010a: vi), he nonetheless highlights the essential role of the prose that HDRs contain, along with all the information displayed by many tables. Sen also insists upon one point very strongly: setting out indicators for everything that matters is not always relevant. For instance, he has refused to help Haq get a quantitative measure of human freedom, although freedom is the most important value in Sen's work (UNDP 2010b: 4). It seems that Sen is very clear on the fact that obtaining indexes of political democracy and political freedom is not the right way to think about it and to promote such values. It does not mean that those critical issues for any development process should not be addressed in the reports, but 'rather than trying to make nonsense out of numerical indicators and trying to put something which doesn't fit there', he considers it more relevant to 'write about it' (UNDP 2010b: 5). In other words, it would be a big mistake to reduce the human development approach to numbers like the HDI, and Sen reminds us that '[pe]ople have read prose for generations – they have read the epics, read poetry, read novels, read essays, to learn from each other' (UNDP 2010b: 5). If we agree with Sen that the goal of all scientific analysis is to provide some constructive basis for 'broader public exchanges, deliberations and in-formed agitations' (Sen 2013: 7),[30] then we should not reduce the wealth

---

[30] In this 2013 paper, Sen elaborates on the complementarities between scientific scrutiny and public involvement within a reflection on 'the ends and means of sustainability' that is quite similar to his view on the ends and means of human development: 'we have to go beyond the role of human beings specifically as "consumers" or as "people with needs", and consider more broadly their role as agents of change who can – given the

of information about how human beings in each society live and what substantive freedoms they enjoy to pure numbers.

To summarize, we may say that Sen's role in the human development approach was motivated by three important aspects of his development studies: (1) the necessity for a wider informational basis on personal situations that may reveal unfair living conditions – relative to personal agency rather than purely material conditions or purely subjective conditions; (2) the necessity for an explicit formulation of the value judgements behind each evaluation done; and (3) the significance of public discussion in making evaluations evolve according to some shared values and defining policy strategy to improve the living conditions.

13.4 Conclusion

From the middle of the 1970s, Sen's exploration of the limits of the welfarist framework began to be fuelled by the results of his research in empirical studies, notably concerning famines but also gender inequalities or the evaluation of development. Such a statement is not meant to deny that most of his work was devoted to exploring theoretical problems, especially in the fields of social choice theory and moral philosophy, which eventually gave rise to a novel approach to justice. It is rather meant to contest a common view according to which Sen is *only* a theoretician, whose ideas are difficult to 'work out' (e.g. Pressman and Summerfield 2002).[31] Indeed, we have shown that Sen's approach to justice is clearly political and impregnated with practical sense due to his research dedicated to public action.

Sen has been strongly driven by his awareness of his privileged condition in a world with much poverty and inequality as well as by the feeling that he owes something to others (Barsamian 2001: 13). His empirical research not

opportunity – think, assess, evaluate, resolve, inspire, agitate, and, through these means reshape the world' (Sen 2013: 7). This implies to have a definition of sustainability broad enough to be enliven by people seen as 'the ultimate agents of change' (Sen 2013: 9), in the same way that human development has been thought to influence public discussion with broad information on people's lives, and conversely been influenced by the priorities determined by public reasoning.

[31] For an overview of the commentators' expectations regarding what is frequently called 'operationalization' and Sen's position on this issue, see Baujard and Gilardone (2017). Like in the present chapter, but through another perspective, it is shown that Sen's contribution to the theory of justice should not be remembered for having provided a capability theory, but for something very different: a theory of human agency and public reasoning.

only persuaded him that it would be irrelevant to tackle those crucial issues directly without paying sufficient attention to the role of theorization but confirmed that public action against injustice cannot be decided from some 'privileged ground' (Drèze and Sen 1989: 61). It does not entail that theorists have no role to play in the setting of public action. On the contrary, 'a discriminating economic analysis ... can have a significant informative and activist role' (Sen 1987: 16).

While he declined numerous invitations to advise the Indian government, he considers it a part of social scientists' task to choose important subjects to work on and develop analysis that can serve public debate and put governments under pressure. It seems that for him, advising governments directly without public approbation would be counterproductive. Public understanding and appropriation of economists' results is a necessary stage in social choices. Through this strategy, Sen's work eventually had a major effect on politics. In particular, his work on the causes of famine changed public perception by showing that hunger is not caused by a failure in food supply, but by a decrease of people's ability to buy food. His analysis of inequality and poverty translated into the United Nations' Human Development Index and other similar gender-related indexes has also been very influential, providing an authoritative international source of welfare comparisons between countries, competing against the simple measure of GNP. Above all, Sen's analysis of the male-female conflict coupled with the cooperative aspects of family life urges us to make room for the perceptions underlying ideas of obligation and legitimacy in the formulation of the gender inequality problem – and more generally in the formulation of any inequality problem. When it clearly appears that one group systematically receives a lower share of the benefits of cooperation than another, there is good reason to examine the value system that implicitly leads to such unequal cooperative outcome. And in this respect, defining the so-called right informational basis for welfare evaluation like the welfarist tradition proposes would not be very helpful.

Sen's strong support for values such as personal freedom, democracy and pluralism led him to challenge welfarism by introducing the concepts of agency, public reasoning and incompleteness. In Sen's non-welfarist approach to social justice, not only do economists need to broaden their informational basis and use multidimensional criteria, but they also need to give up their 'expert' posture or paternalist views. Relevant consequential evaluations are important, but they must be preceded and followed by adequate democratic processes. Beyond mere participation, people need to be involved in identifying the problems that matter and defining public action for addressing them. All Sen's contributions to applied economic problems support the view that the economist's role is not to provide precise evaluations of how justice will be advanced or hindered. He sees the economist's role as being to offer an objective – even if potentially incomplete – basis for public reasoning in defining policy strategy and different types of public action to improve living conditions. For each empirical problem he has tackled, Sen elaborated a specific theoretical framework in order to give the most objective picture of it given his observations of people's experiences and understanding of the situation. He formulated the *entitlement* approach, and then the *capability* approach, to analyse problems of hunger and poverty. He formulated the *cooperative conflict* approach for distribution problems within the family, and a mixture of *indexes inspired by the capability approach and explicit discussion of the value judgements* for different evaluations in development studies. In this way, his work aims to inform and enlighten public action in a broad sense. Not only does Sen claim that state policy has to be supplemented by public involvement in a way that is both 'collaborative' and 'adversarial', but he also defends the idea that public understanding of common perception biases is key for a removal of injustices that relies on changes of behaviours and social norms, as well as institutional arrangements.

References

Alkire. S. 2010. Development: A Misconceived Theory Can Kill, in C. W. Morris, ed., *Amartya Sen*, New York: Cambridge University Press: 191–219.

Arrow, K. J. 1950. A Difficulty in the Concept of Social Welfare, *Journal of Political Economy*, August, 58, 4: 328–46.

Barsamian, D. 2001. Reflections of an Economist, Alternative Radio, USA, India Together, September.

Baujard, A. and Gilardone, M. 2017. Sen Is Not a Capability Theorist, *Journal of Economic Methodology*, 24, 1: 1–19.

Baujard, A. and Gilardone, M. 2020. 'Positional Views' as the Cornerstone of Sen's Idea of Justice, *Working paper of the Condorcet Center for Political Economy*.

Bréban, L. and Gilardone, M. 2020. A Missing Touch of Adam Smith in Amartya Sen's Account of Public Reasoning: The Man within for the Man Without, *Cambridge Journal of Economics*, 44, 2: 257–283.

Burchardt, T. 2009. Agency Goals, Adaptation and Capability Sets, *Journal of Human Development and Capabilities*, 10, 1: 3–19.

Chanda, A. 1998. Amartya Sen Returns to Repay His Debt to Alma Mater, *Rediff on the Net*, 21 December, http://202.54.124.133/business/1998/dec/21sen.htm.

Crocker, D. A. and Robeyns, I. 2010. Capability and Agency, in C. W. Morris, ed., *Amartya Sen*, New York: Cambridge University Press: 60–90.

Davis, J. 2012. The Idea of Public Reasoning, *Journal of Economic Methodology*, 19, 2: 169–72.

Desai, M. 2001. Amartya Sen's Contribution to Development Economics, *Oxford Development Studies*, 29, 3: 213–22.

Drèze, J. and Sen, A. K. 1989. *Hunger and Public Action*, Oxford: Clarendon Press.

Fetherolf Loufti, M. 1998. Amartya Sen, Lauréat du Prix Nobel d'Economie, et l'OIT, *Le Magazine de l'OIT*, 27 December: 1–9.

Fine, B. J. 2004. Economics and Ethics: Amartya Sen as Point of Departure, *The New School Economic Review*, 1, 1: 95–103.

Gilardone, M. 2008. Dobb, Dasgupta et Tagore: trois sources méconnues de la pensée de Sen, *Storia del Pensiero Economico*, 5, 2: 107–31.

Gilardone, M. 2009. Inégalités de genre et approche par les capabilités: quelle mise en dialogue chez Sen?, *Tiers Monde*, 198: 357–71.

Gilardone, M. 2010. Amartya Sen sans prisme, *Cahiers d'économie politique*, 56: 9–39.

Gilardone, M. 2015. Rawls's Influence and Counter-Influence on Sen: Post-Welfarism and Impartiality, *The European Journal of the History of Economic Thought*, 22, 2: 198–235.

Harsanyi, J. C. 1955. Cardinal Welfare, Individualistic Ethics, and Interpersonal Comparisons of Utility, *Journal of Political Economy*, 63, 4: 309–21.

Hirai, T. 2017. *The Creation of the Human Development Approach*, Cham: Palgrave Macmillan.

Kynch, J. and Sen, A. K. 1983. Indian Women: Well-Being and Survival, *Cambridge Journal of Economics*, 7, 3/4: 363–80.

Nozick, R. 1974. *Anarchy, State and Utopia*, Oxford: Blackwell.

Peter, F. 2003. Gender and the Foundations of Social Choice: The Role of Situated Agency, *Feminist Economics* 9, 2: 13–32.

Pressman, S. and Summerfield, G. 2002. Sen and Capabilities, *Review of Political Economy*, 14, 4: 429–33.

Rawls, J. 1971. *A Theory of Justice*, Cambridge, MA: The Belknap Press of Harvard University Press.

Sen, A. K. 1970. *Collective Choice and Social Welfare*, Advanced textbooks in economics. Amsterdam: North-Holland, re-edit 1979.

Sen, A. K. 1972. Technical Choice and Employment in the Non-wage Sector, *World Employment Programme: Economic Research on Technology and Employment*, Geneva: ILO.

Sen, A. K. 1975. *Employment, Technology and Development*, Oxford: Clarendon Press.

Sen, A. K. 1977. On Weights and Measures: Informational Constraints in Social Welfare Analysis, *Econometrica*, 45, 7: 1539–72.

Sen, A. K. 1979. Utilitarianism and Welfarism, *Journal of Philosophy*, 76, 9: 463–89.

Sen, A. K. 1980. Equality of What?, in S. McMurrin, ed., *The Tanner Lectures on Human Values*, Vol. 1, Salt Lake City: University of Utah Press; Cambridge: Cambridge University Press: 197–220.

Sen, A. K. 1981. *Poverty and Famines: An Essay on Entitlement and Deprivation*, Oxford: Clarendon Press.

Sen, A. K. 1983a. Economics and the Family, *Asian Development Review*, 1, 2: 14–26.

Sen, A. K. 1983b. Development: Which Way Now?, *The Economic Journal*, 93, 372: 745–62.

Sen, A. K. 1984. Family and Food: Sex Bias in Poverty, in A. K. Sen, *Resources, Values and Development*, Oxford: Blackwell: 346–68.

Sen, A. K. 1985. *Commodities and Capabilities*, Amsterdam: North-Holland.

Sen, A. K. 1987. *Hunger and Entitlements*, Helsinki: World Institute for Development Economic Research, United Nations University.

Sen, A. K. 1989. Cooperation, Inequality, and the Family, *Population and Development Review*, 15: 61–76.

Sen, A. K. 1990a. Individual Freedom as a Social Commitment, *New York Review of Books*, 37, 10: 49–54.

Sen, A. K. 1990b. Gender and Cooperative Conflicts, in I. Tinker, ed., *Persistent Inequalities*, New York, Oxford University Press: 123–49.

Sen, A. K. 1992. *Inequality Reexamined*, Oxford: Clarendon Press.

Sen, A. K. 1994. Amiya Kumar Dasgupta (1903–1992), *The Economic Journal*, 104, 426: 1147–55.

Sen, A. K. 1997. Development Thinking at the Beginning of the XXI Century, in L. Emmerij, ed., *Economic and Social Development into the XXI Century*, Washington, DC: Inter-American Development Bank.

Sen, A. K. 1999a. Autobiography, *The Nobel Prizes 1998*, Tore Frängsmyr, Nobel Foundation, Stockholm, www.nobel.se/economics/laureates/1998/sen-autobio.html.

Sen, A. K. 1999b. Democracy as a Universal Value, *Journal of Democracy*, July, 10, 3: 3–17.

Sen, A. K. 1999c. *Development as Freedom*, New York: Anchor Books.

Sen, A. K. 2001. Tagore and His India, *The New York Review*, 28 August, www.nobel.se /literature/articles/sen/index.html.

Sen, A. K. 2009. *The Idea of Justice*, Cambridge, MA: The Belknap Press of Harvard University Press.

Sen, A. K. 2012. Values and Justice, *Journal of Economic Methodology*, 19, 2: 101–8.

Sen, A. K. 2013. The Ends and Means of Sustainability, *Journal of Human Development and Capabilities*, 14, 1: 6–20.

Sen, A. K. and Sengupta, S. 1983. Malnutrition of Rural Indian Children and the Sex Bias, *Economic and Political Weekly*, 18: 855–64.

Shaikh, N. 2004. Interview of Amartya Sen, *Asia Society Online*, 6 December.

Swedberg, R. 1990. Amartya Sen, in R. Swedberg, *Economics and Sociology: Redefining Their Boundaries – Conversations with Economists and Sociologists*, Princeton, NJ: Princeton University Press: 249–67.

UNDP 1990. *Human Development Report*. New York; Oxford: Oxford University Press.

UNDP 1995. *Human Development Report*. New York; Oxford: Oxford University Press.

UNDP 2010a. *Human Development Report*. New York; Oxford: Oxford University Press.

UNDP 2010b. A 20th Anniversary Human Development Discussion with Amartya Sen, pre-launch material for the *Human Development Report 2010*.

14

Conclusion

Roger E. Backhouse, Antoinette Baujard and Tamotsu Nishizawa

1 Theory and Practice

In the Introduction to this volume we focused on various definitions of welfarism in order to create a list of ways in which economists might depart from it. Whichever definition we adopt, welfarism implies that the only information relevant to social welfare is the utilities of individuals: that if no one's utility is affected by some change then social welfare cannot be affected. Conversely, non-welfarism occurs when economists start to depart from such informational restrictions. For example, it is possible to remain an individualist, but to take account of information that goes beyond individuals' utilities. It is also possible to question individualism, taking the position that social welfare may have a social dimension, not reducible to the utilities of individuals making up the society. Once the move from welfarism has been made, numerous ethical issues arise, from whether to embrace non-consequentialist ethics to the dangers of paternalism when welfarism is abandoned.

Economists often talk of "the fundamental theorems of welfare economics": that, subject to certain conditions, every competitive equilibrium is Pareto-efficient, and that every Pareto-efficient allocation can be achieved as a competitive equilibrium provided that endowments can be suitably allocated.[1] Such language places Pareto-efficiency at the heart of

---

[1] Blaug (2007) discusses the history of the fundamental theorems. In that he argued that some of the "classic" authors cited, notably Adam Smith, were not thinking in terms of the static equilibrium framework that underlies the fundamental theorems, his conclusions are consistent with ours.

welfare economics, which makes sense if, and only if, a welfarist approach is adopted. Thus, in as far as economists emphasize the concept of Pareto-efficiency, it is natural to conclude that their approach is welfarist. In contrast, as the Introduction tried to make clear, the chapters in this volume show that economists, including some of those most closely associated with the emergence of the mainstream of economics, have repeatedly engaged in non-welfarist analysis.

We also made the claim that these departures from welfarism occurred when economists engaged with practice but in the Introduction we did not explain why this was the case. Why should consideration of practice make it more difficult to sustain a welfarist position than when engaging with pure theory?[2] It is easy to explain the appeal of welfarism when economists remain at the level of theory. Individualism has obvious attractions and when combined with the analytical tractability of the concept of Pareto-efficiency, or utilitarianism, there is a strong incentive to adopt a welfarist perspective. In contrast, when economists turn to practice, they face problems that push them away from welfarism.

2 Reasons for Moving beyond Welfarism

A strict welfarist approach leads naturally to an emphasis on the Pareto criterion: that the only case in which one can be sure that a change is welfare-enhancing is when it makes at least one person better off without making anyone worse off. To go beyond that requires making interpersonal utility comparisons, or the introduction of some additional criterion that goes beyond welfarism. This may be unproblematic for the theorist, who can conclude that equilibria are, or are not, Pareto-efficient. However, in practice, outside the world of abstract, simplified models, the Pareto criterion typically provides insufficient guidance. This may not necessitate going beyond welfarism – for example, it might be possible to adopt a utilitarian approach – but in practice it usually does, for several reasons.

---

[2] In the interests of simplicity and clarity, we write as though there is a clear distinction between theory and practice, but nothing depends on this. We accept that such a distinction is impossible to draw precisely, being analogous to the problem of defining "applied" economics (see Backhouse and Biddle 2000; Backhouse and Cherrier 2017). For example, whether a game-theoretic analysis of a particular type of auction is theory or application is unanswerable outside a specific context. What can be said is that the closer an economist is to practice, the stronger the factors we discuss here become.

2.1 Awareness That Other Values Matter

Economists have argued that, at least in Western, democratic societies, individualism and the Pareto criterion are generally accepted values. Other values are more controversial. However, when deriving normative conclusions about policy and social decisions, economists have frequently introduced other values including:

- a fair distribution of resources (Pigou discussed in Chapter 4, Samuelson in Chapter 8, Musgrave in Chapter 10 and Arrow in Chapter 11);
- freedom, autonomy and liberal values (Hobson discussed in Chapter 2, Hicks in Chapter 7, capabilitarianism in Chapter 12 and Sen in Chapter 13);
- fulfillment and quality of life (Hobson discussed in Chapter 2, Marshall in Chapter 3, capabilitarianism in Chapter 12 and Sen in Chapter 13);
- the formation of human character (Ruskin discussed in Chapter 1, Hobson in Chapter 2 and Marshall in Chapter 3);
- the intrinsic importance of the environment (Ruskin discussed in Chapter 1, and many environmental economists described in Chapter 9);
- the provision to everyone of primary goods or needs (Pigou discussed in Chapter 4 and Rawls in Chapter 7);
- equality of opportunity and non-discrimination (Hobson discussed in Chapter 2 and Arrow in Chapter 11).

It is clear why such issues have been unattractive to theorists preferring to remain neutral over values. These issues are controversial, often hard to define precisely, and they raise questions about how different values are to be weighed against each other. One reason why it is difficult to weigh these aims against each other is that some of them are linked to means rather than ends. Provision of primary goods is arguably a means, whereas utility and quality of life are ends. Other aims, such as equal opportunity, rights and liberal values will be means for some people and ends for others. The multidimensionality of some of these ends also poses problems, as does the requirement, common in a policy context, that decisions should be based on objective information. Problems also arise because of interdependencies in society and the different ways in which this can be conceptualized. For example, where Hobson and Marshall saw society as an organism, Pigou, Musgrave and environmental economists focus more narrowly on interdependence that can be captured through concepts of public goods and externalities.

However, even if these aims pose great theoretical and conceptual problems, they are often inescapable when offering advice on practical problems, in specific political and social contexts. For example, as Medema showed in Chapter 9, environmental economists debating the implications of the Coase Theorem in the 1970s could not avoid confronting the question of whether it was fair to force victims of pollution to bribe polluters to reduce emissions. In late-Victorian England, on the other hand, the evolution of human character was an issue that would often be raised when policies were discussed and it was common for economists to take a paternalist attitude toward the working classes in a way that would be unacceptable today. Ruskin (discussed in Chapters 1 and 2) imposed values closely related to his views on art and was clearly paternalist. Marshall's position was different, but, as Nishizawa's discussion in Chapter 3 shows, when discussing policy, he attached great importance to the elimination of poverty and securing the material means necessary for all people, including the working classes, to have a full life and to develop their human faculties. This dependence on the specific political and social context accounts for the great diversity in case studies in the different chapters. However, beneath this diversity there remain important common features.

2.2 Difficulties with Getting Reliable or Meaningful Information

Pigou (discussed by Yamazaki in Chapter 4) assumed that measurement was possible for what he called economic welfare – that part of welfare that could be measured in terms of money. This implies a neat separation between the realms of economics (economic welfare) and ethics (non-economic welfare). However, as Suzumura (Chapter 7) explains, there are serious operational problems that make it difficult to draw a clear distinction between what belongs to economics and what belongs to ethics – between facts and values. Pigou's monetary test, the idea for which he took from Marshall, sounds attractive but is in practice difficult to apply, raising serious problems for welfare economics. Suzumura (Chapter 7) recalls Putnam's opinion (2002, p. 44): "The worst thing about the fact/value dichotomy is that in practice it functions as a discussion-stopper, and not just a discussion-stopper, but a thought-stopper." A similar claim was made by Samuelson (see Chapter 8) when he argued that utility and welfare were two distinct concepts, each requiring different types of information. For example, the difficulties involved in comparing different individuals' utilities make it difficult to even conclude that trade is better than no trade whenever trade makes one person better off and another worse off.

2.3 Observed Problems with Market Outcomes

The theorist typically works with abstract goods, implying that there is no basis for privileging some goods over others. In contrast, when engaging with specific practical problems, in which goods are identified, it may become clear that certain goods are more important than others. For example, it may become clear that certain goods need to be provided in a society in which there are social interactions and unavoidable externalities – that they should be considered as "merit goods" (Musgrave; see Chapter 10). It may be that people do not realize how valuable these goods are, or that the benefit to society exceeds the benefits individuals derived from purchasing them. Similar issues arise with the provision of public goods, which will typically be underprovided by the market. It is easy for the theorist to ignore such goods, but when tackling specific applied problems it will be harder to avoid them.

Much the same can also be said of income distribution. When operating at an abstract level, the economist may ignore problems of inequality and poverty in order to focus on other things. As Pigou (see Chapter 4) recognized, people have different tastes and this will have consequences for their choices and actions, making it difficult to assess how far inequalities are the result of individual choice and how far they indicate unfair treatment of some people that needs to be put right. However, it may become harder to ignore inequality or poverty when confronted with specific instances of poverty and the consequences of an unequal distribution of income. For example, child poverty often provokes a reaction of indignation. Tackling child poverty is impossible without addressing the situation of the families in which children are located, implying a need to address distributional issues that go beyond welfarism. Among economists discussed here, Samuelson (see Chapter 8) argued repeatedly that the value judgments involved in Pareto-efficiency would need to be supplemented by other ethical criteria.

2.4 Individuals and Society

Objections to using individual preferences or utilities as a measure of welfare is reinforced if individuals are seen as social creatures, whose preferences are influenced by the societies in which they live. In the modern world, it is hard not to take such a view. Besides, as individuals are embedded in a network of multiple interrelations, their welfare is strongly affected by a number of external, agglomeration or spillover effects. This explains a strong departure from, not only ethical individualism but also methodological individualism. As Walras (quoted in Chapter 5) argued, "When human beings ... act in order to consume, produce and survive, they cannot ignore the existence of the division of labor and therefore the interdependence and the solidarity among all human destinies." As Desmarais-Tremblay explains in Chapter 10, Richard Musgrave held strongly to such a view. There is a long tradition, running at least from Thorstein Veblen to John Kenneth Galbraith that illustrates the way in which wants are socially determined. People are interdependent.

2.5 Issues Relating to Paternalism

In the nineteenth century, it was common for economists, generally members of the upper classes, to adopt a paternalist attitude toward the working classes. Marshall's views about how the working classes could improve themselves, discussed in Chapter 3, have already been noted. In a similar manner, Hobson (discussed in Chapter 2) assumed that his ethical values about the relative merits of different activities and types of consumption were generally held. Such views are not surprising in a world in which it was routine to view Western society, run by white, upper-class men, as the apex of civilization. In contrast, for modern economists, paternalist attitudes need to be justified (something Musgrave, discussed in Chapter 10, tried to do).

The situation was very different in the liberal Western societies fighting communism in the postwar period. In those societies, individuals were considered as the best judge of their own interests (see Amadae 2003). This made welfarism very attractive on account of its respect for individuals' subjective preferences and its avoidance of paternalism. Changes in society can therefore go a long way toward explaining the shift from paternalism in the early twentieth century toward non-paternalist views and the emergence of welfarism based on subjective utilities from the 1930s onward.

In contrast, when tackling specific applied problems, it is harder for economists, whatever their philosophical or ideological preferences, to avoid some of the objections to welfarism and that eventually justifies a need for paternalism. As Samuelson (quoted in Chapter 8) asks, "what about the person choosing suicide even though, if he remained alive, he would soon change his mind?" Similar issues arise in the context of addiction (an addict may regret having developed an addiction) and more generally with activities, the consequences of which are unknown at the time choices are made. In other words, subjective preferences, as they exist when individuals take decisions, may not be the appropriate criterion by which to assess the consequences of an action for someone's welfare. Whilst the economic theorist can ignore these issues, using hostility to paternalism as a defense of this strategy, such a defense becomes more difficult when operating at a more concrete, practical level, and this makes it easier to support non-welfarist arguments.

It is however often difficult to justify non-welfarist views without falling into paternalism. For example, within capabilitarian theories, if an economist identifies the list of basic functionings for a person, he is being paternalist toward her as she could not have a voice on what she personally has reasons to value (Chapter 12). Because he values human agency, Sen has supported public deliberation in order to provide legitimacy for the information used in welfare economics (Chapter 13). Conclusions derived from welfare theories, whether they are welfarist or non-welfarist, may be conducive to a richer public debate, but they cannot be a substitute for it.

3 Economics as a Moral Science

As we have explained, welfarism is attractive to many economists. It clearly respects individualism and avoids problems of paternalism. It also fits well with the aim, clearly articulated by Lionel Robbins (1932), to make economics into a science, with positive economics clearly demarcated from ethics. As Robbins contended, people differ fundamentally in their ethical views and it is not the task of the economic scientist to arbitrate between different ethical positions. However, as this volume shows, when economists have turned to practical problems they have frequently turned to non-welfarist arguments for reasons discussed in the previous section. In doing this, many economists have, whether consciously or unconsciously, brought additional ethical judgments, beyond individualism and non-paternalism, to bear on economic problems.

One result of Robbins's injunction was that, from around the 1960s, welfare economics effectively disappeared from much of economics (Atkinson 2001). The background to that was that there was, for many years, great doubt about what welfare economics could achieve. Hicks (1939, p. 697) wrote of "the euthanasia of our science." He believed that compensation tests provided grounds for reversing this, but this optimism did not last long. The work of Tibor Scitovsky, Kenneth Arrow, Ian Little, Paul Samuelson and Jan de V. Graaff seemed to imply that welfare economics was impossible (Mishan 1960, p. 218; see also Chipman and Moore 1978; Mongin 2006; Igersheim 2019). However, what Atkinson meant by "the strange disappearance of welfare economics" was not that economists stopped making normative statements, but that, from around the 1960s, they stopped analyzing the principles underlying normative statements, something that it had been common for earlier generations of economists to do.[3] Where economists did discuss welfare issues from a theoretical point of view, the dominant approach centered on Pareto-efficiency and what came to be called the two fundamental theorems of welfare economics, rigorously proved by Kenneth Arrow (1951) and Gerard Debreu (1951). This terminology, of "fundamental theorems," appears to date from much the same time as the time to which Atkinson dates the disappearance of welfare economics (Blaug 2007).

However, what happened was not that consideration of the principles underlying welfare economics disappeared, but that this became a specialized activity. Taking its cue from the work of Arrow, John Harsanyi, John Rawls and others, a new field of welfare economics emerged, placing the subject on an axiomatic foundation. This field, symbolized by the journal *Social Choice and Welfare*, developed as an interdisciplinary field straddling the boundaries between economics, philosophy and political science (see in this regard Fleurbaey 2000, 2007; Fleurbaey and Mongin 2005). This, of course, is the background to the work discussed in Chapters 7 and 11. In addition, in some other fields, explicit discussion of ethical issues was taken seriously. A major example is the problem of economic development, out of which capability theories emerged (see the discussions of capability theory in Chapter 12 and of Sen's work in Chapter 13). For example, capability theorists and Sen have tackled explicitly methods of dealing with the issue of paternalism, focusing on the

---

[3] Atkinson (2001, p. 194) cited the work of Ian Little, Jan de V. Graaff and Tibor Scitovsky in the 1950s and the – slightly later – work of William Baumol. Hicks's manifesto, discussed in Chapter 7, also dates from this period.

potential role of discussion and deliberation. Much work has also been done on how to conceptualize justice and how to balance the issue of justice against dimensions of welfare with which economists are more comfortable.

This is the context in which we need to think about the claim made in this book that, despite the preference of theorists for welfarist theories, when they have turned to practice, economists have frequently made non-welfarist arguments. This use of non-welfarist arguments strengthens the claim made by economists including Kenneth Boulding (1969), Amartya Sen (2004) and Anthony Atkinson (2009) that economics should become a "moral science."[4] What we mean by this is that economics should embrace discussions of ethics as one of the pillars on which normative economics should rest, abandoning the strict separation of economic science from ethics advocated by Robbins.

An important implication of such a change is that it may require a change in the way economists conceive their subject. At least until recently, economics was dominated by theory, conceived as a process involving the specification of assumptions in such a way as to make it possible to use mathematics to derive precise conclusions of general applicability. Welfarist criteria such as Pareto-efficiency, or other welfarist criteria such as utilitarianism or a modified Rawlsian criterion (maximizing the minimum utility achieved by any member of society) fitted conveniently into this approach, for they provided precise welfare criteria that can produce very general welfare conclusions. Such criteria can be used widely, even in macroeconomic models based on representative (identical) agents, a context in which ethical dilemmas relating to income distribution are absent. Welfare implications can be derived using essentially the same methods as those used to derive comparative statics results from the models. In contrast, if a broader range of ethical criteria were to be used (for example, applying certain notions of justice or fairness), it would often be necessary to think about problems in different ways, for they do not always provide a criterion that can be applied mechanically to a model. As an example, take Rawls's maximin criterion. Rawls applied this to the provision of primary goods, not to overall consumption, which implies that it becomes necessary to distinguish between primary and non-primary goods.

---

[4] The idea of economics as a moral science has, of course, a much longer history. The reason we pick out Boulding and Atkinson, is that in other settings the implications were more complicated. In nineteenth-century Cambridge, for example, the notion of "moral sciences" had institutional as well as intellectual implications.

As a consequence, if economists are to take note of the conclusions reached in modern welfare economics, they may have to be open to arguments that cannot be fully expressed formally, or which rest on ethical judgments (e.g. ethical judgments are involved in deciding which goods count as primary goods). Atkinson (2009) provides several examples. For example, reducing social exclusion, a concept that, however meaningful, is hard to incorporate in an economic model, may be a powerful reason for targeting employment as a policy objective. If our concern is with welfare, it may make sense to focus on indicators such as the Human Development Index rather than the simpler concept of national income, or on some other index based on recent welfare and equity theories (e.g. Fleurbaey 2009; Fleurbaey and Blanchet 2013).

If economists are to be more open to conclusions reached by specialists in welfare economics and social choice theory, it is likely that they will need to be prepared to approach the subject in a different way. Welfarism, with its reliance on utilities, holds out the prospect of a completely general welfare that can be analyzed using the tools traditionally used in economic theory. Broadening the set of welfare criteria to include factors such as justice, which cannot be quantified in such a way that they can be measured against utility, may require going beyond economists' traditional methods. It may be necessary to engage in deliberations over factors that are not quantifiable and have to be articulated verbally. In other words, being open to a broader range of non-welfarist arguments may involve a move away from economic theory as that is commonly understood.

This is potentially a radical change, but it would reflect a change that has already taken place in relation to empirical methods (see Backhouse and Cherrier 2017). When the 2019 Nobel Prize in Economic Sciences was given to Abhijit Banerjee, Esther Duflo and Michael Kremer for their use of experimental methods to alleviate poverty, they explained that their results were different from those traditionally sought by economists.[5] Their work did not produce completely general results but results tailored to specific situations. This was important because the effectiveness of policies typically depended on details of the situation that would not be apparent to a traditional economic theorist. Similarly, as large data sets have become available, economists have developed new econometric techniques in which a major concern, if not the predominant one, is identification. As a result, formal economic theory, of the type that fitted so well with the

---

[5] The three lectures can be found at www.nobelprize.org/prizes/economic-sciences/2019/summary/.

Pareto criterion and other welfarist criteria, has become less central to the field. Considering the numerous social and political practical consequences of any theoretical assertions, perhaps a similar change is required in relation to welfare economics. In the same way that some economists have become more open to psychology, and those parts of economics bordering on psychology, perhaps they should be more open to ethical philosophy and those parts of economics that engage with it, even if this means moving beyond traditional welfare economics. Only if economists move beyond welfarism and consider all relevant ethical values, will it be possible to deal with the full range of practical issues with which normative economics ought to be concerned.

References

Amadae, S. M. 2003. *Rationalizing Capitalist Democracy: The Cold War Origins of Rational Choice Liberalism*. Chicago: University of Chicago Press.

Arrow, K. J. 1951. An Extension of the Basic Theorems of Classical Welfare Economics, in *Proceedings of the Second Berkeley Symposium on Mathematical Statistics and Probability*, J. Neyman (ed.), Berkeley and Los Angeles: University of California Press: 507–532.

Atkinson, A. B. 2001. The Strange Disappearance of Welfare Economics. *Kyklos* 54(2–3), 193–206.

Atkinson, A. B. 2009. Economics as a Moral Science. *Economica* 76(1), 791–804.

Backhouse, R. and Biddle, J. 2000. The Concept of Applied Economics: A History of Ambiguity and Multiple Meanings. *History of Political Economy* 32(5), 1–24.

Backhouse, R. E. and Cherrier, B. 2017. The Age of the Applied Economist. *History of Political Economy* 49(Supplement), 1–33.

Blaug, M. 2007. The Fundamental Theorems of Modern Welfare Economics, Historically Contemplated. *History of Political Economy* 39(2), 185–207.

Boulding, K. 1969. Economics as a Moral Science. *American Economic Review* 59(1), 1–12.

Chipman, J. S. and Moore, J. C. 1978. The New Welfare Economics, 1939–1974. *International Economic Review* 19: 547–584.

Debreu, G. 1951. The Coefficient of Resource Utilization. *Econometrica* 19(3), 273–292.

Fleurbaey, M. 2000. Choix social: une difficulté et de multiples possibilités. *Revue Economique* 51(5), 1215–1232.

Fleurbaey, M. 2007. Social Choice and Just Institutions: New Perspectives. *Economics and Philosophy* 23, 15–43.

Fleurbaey, M. 2009. Beyond GDP: The Quest for a Measure of Social Welfare. *Journal of Economic Literature* 47(4), 1029–1075.

Fleurbaey, M. and Blanchet, D. 2013. *Measuring Welfare and Assessing Sustainability*. Oxford: Oxford University Press.

Fleurbaey, M. and Mongin, P. 2005. The News of the Death of Welfare Economics Is Greatly Exaggerated. *Social Choice and Welfare* 25(2), 381–418.

Hicks, J. R. 1939. The Foundations of Welfare Economics. *Economic Journal* 49 (196), 696–712.

Igersheim, H. 2019. The Death of Welfare Economics: History of a Controversy. *History of Political Economy* 51(5), 827–865.

Mishan, E. J. 1960. A Survey of Welfare Economics, 1939–59. *Economic Journal* 70 (278), 197–265.

Mongin, P. 2006. Value Judgments and Value Neutrality in Economics. *Economica* 72(290), 257–286.

Putnam, H. 2002. *The Collapse of the Fact/Value Dichotomy and Other Essays.* Cambridge: Harvard University Press.

Robbins, L. 1932. *An Essay on the Nature and Significance of Economic Science*, 2nd. ed. 1935, London: Macmillan.

Sen, A. K. 2004. *L'économie est une science morale.* Paris: La Découverte, Poche.

Index

Printed in the United States
by Baker & Taylor Publisher Services